Theories of International Relations

Theories of International Relations

Fourth Edition

Scott Burchill
Andrew Linklater
Richard Devetak
Jack Donnelly
Terry Nardin
Matthew Paterson
Christian Reus-Smit
Jacqui True

palgrave
macmillan

First edition 1996
Second edition 2001
Third edition 2005
Fourth edition 2009

First Published 1996 by
PALGRAVE MACMILLAN
Palgrave Macmillan in the UK is an imprint of Macmillan Publishers Limited, registered in England, company number 785998, of Houndmills, Basingstoke, Hampshire RG21 6XS.

Palgrave Macmillan in the US is a division of St Martin's Press LLC, 175 Fifth Avenue, New York, NY 10010.

Palgrave Macmillan is the global academic imprint of the above companies and has companies and representatives throughout the world.

Palgrave® and Macmillan® are registered trademarks in the United States, the United Kingdom, Europe and other countries

ISBN-13: 978–0–230–21922–9 hardback
ISBN-10: 0–230–21922–5   hardback
ISBN-13: 978–0–230–21923–6 paperback
ISBN-10: 0–230–21923–3   paperback

This book is printed on paper suitable for recycling and made from fully managed and sustained forest sources. Logging, pulping and manufacturing processes are expected to conform to the environmental regulations of the country of origin.

A catalogue record for this book is available from the British Library.

Library of Congress Cataloging-in-Publication Data

Theories of international relations / Scott Burchill ... [et al.]. —
    4th ed.
        p. cm.
Includes bibliographical references and index.
ISBN 978–0–230–21922–9—ISBN 978–0–230–21923–6
1. International relations—Philosophy. I. Burchill, Scott, 1961–
JZ1242.T48 2009
327.101—dc22   2008046674

10   9   8   7   6   5
18 17 16 15 14 13 12 11

Printed and bound in China

Contents

Preface to the Fourth Edition

The fourth edition adds two new chapters on International Political Theory by Terry Nardin and on Historical Sociology by Andrew Linklater. All the other chapters are substantially revised and updated.

The production of this volume would not have occurred as smoothly without the editorial skills of Costas Laoutides and Carla Dunne's mastery of the Internet. We would again like to express our appreciation for the encouragement of Steven Kennedy and Stephen Wenham at Palgrave Macmillan. The hard work and ongoing commitment of our co-authors is the key to the success of a monograph which first appeared in 1996 and remains an important resource for students interested in the theories of International Relations.

SCOTT BURCHILL
ANDREW LINKLATER

List of Abbreviations

APEC	Asia Pacific Economic Cooperation
CND	Campaign for Nuclear Disarmament
FDI	Foreign Direct Investment
GAD	Gender and Development
ICC	International Criminal Court
ICJ	International Court of Justice
ILO	International Criminal Court
IMF	International Monetary Fund
MAI	Multilateral Agreement on Investments
MNC	Multi-National Corporation
NAFTA	North American Free Trade Agreement
NATO	North Atlantic Treaty Organization
NGO	Non-Governmental Organization
NTB	Non-Tariff Barriers
OECD	Organisation for Economic Co-operation and Development
SAP	Structural Adjustment Policy
TNC	Trans-National Corporation
UN	United Nations
UNDP	United Nations Development Programme
UNICEF	United Nations Children's Fund (Formerly: United Nations International Children's Emergency Fund)
UNIFEM	United Nations Development Fund for Women
UNHCR	United Nations High Commissioner for Refugees
WCED	World Commission on Environment and Development
WID	Women in International Development
WMD	Weapons of Mass Destruction
WTO	World Trade Organization

1 | Introduction

SCOTT BURCHILL AND ANDREW LINKLATER

Frameworks of analysis

From its inception as a separate field of study, International Relations has been a theoretical discipline. Two of the foundational texts in the field, E. H. Carr's, *The Twenty Years' Crisis* (first published in 1939) and Hans Morgenthau's *Politics Among Nations* (first published in 1948) were works of theory in three central respects. Each developed a broad framework of analysis which distilled the essence of international politics from disparate events; each sought to provide future analysts with the theoretical tools for understanding general patterns underlying seemingly unique episodes; and each reflected on the forms of political action which were most appropriate in a realm where the struggle for power was preeminent. Both thinkers were motivated by the desire to correct what they saw as deep misunderstandings about the nature of international politics lying at the heart of the liberal project – especially the belief that the struggle for power could be tamed by international law and the idea that the pursuit of self-interest could be replaced by the shared objective of promoting security for all. Not that Morgenthau and Carr thought the international political system was condemned for all time to revolve around the relentless struggle for power and security. Their main claim was that all efforts to reform the international system which ignored the struggle for power would quickly end in failure. More worrying in their view was the danger that attempts to bring about fundamental change would compound the problem of international relations. They believed the liberal internationalist world-view had been largely responsible for the crisis of the inter-war years.

Many scholars, particularly in United States during the 1960s, believed that Morgenthau's theoretical framework was too impressionistic in nature. Historical illustrations had been used to support rather than demonstrate ingenious conjectures about general patterns of international relations. Consequently, the discipline lagged significantly behind the study of economics which used a sophisticated methodology drawn

1

from the natural sciences to test specific hypotheses, develop general laws and predict human behaviour. Proponents of the scientific approach attempted to build a new theory of international politics, some for the sake of better explanation and higher levels of predictive accuracy, others in the belief that science held the key to understanding how to transform international politics for the better.

The scientific turn led to a major disciplinary debate in the 1960s in which scholars such as Hedley Bull (1966b) argued that international politics were not susceptible to scientific enquiry. This is a view widely shared by analysts committed to diverse intellectual projects. The radical scholar Noam Chomsky (1994: 120) has claimed that in international relations 'historical conditions are too varied and complex for anything that might plausibly be called "a theory" to apply uniformly' (1994: 120). What is generally known as 'post-positivism' in International Relations rejects the possibility of a science of international relations which uses standards of proof associated with the physical sciences to develop equivalent levels of explanatory precision and predictive certainty (Smith, Booth and Zalewski 1996). In the 1990s, a major debate occurred around the claims of positivism. The question of whether there is a world of difference between the 'physical' and the 'social' sciences was a crucial issue, but no less important were disputes about the nature and purpose of theory. The debate centred on whether theories – even those that aim for objectivity – are ultimately 'political' because they generate views of the world which favour some political interests and disadvantage others. This dispute has produced very difficult questions about what theory is and what its purposes are. These questions are now central to the discipline – more central than at any other time in its history. What, in consequence, is it to speak of a theory of international politics?

Diversity of theory

One purpose of this volume is to analyse the diversity of conceptions of theory in the study of international relations. Positivist or 'scientific' approaches remain crucial, and are indeed dominant in the United States, as the success of rational choice analysis demonstrates. But this is not the only type of theory available in the field. An increasingly large number of theorists are concerned with a second category of theory in which the way that observers construct their images of international relations, the methods they use to try to understand this realm and the social and political implications of their 'knowledge claims', are leading preoccupations. They believe it is just as important to focus on how we approach the study of world politics as it is to try to explain global phenomena. In other words the very process of theorizing itself becomes a vital object of inquiry.

Steve Smith (1995: 26–7) has argued that there is a fundamental division within the discipline 'between theories which seek to offer *explanatory* (our emphasis) accounts of international relations' and perspectives which regard 'theory as *constitutive* (our emphasis) of that reality'. Analysing these two conceptions of theory informs much of the discussion in this introductory chapter. In addition, theory now also embraces cognate fields such as historical sociology and international political theory, which are leaving their own distinctive marks on the study of international relations.

The first point to make in this context is that constitutive theories have an increasingly prominent role in the study of international relations, but the importance of the themes they address has long been recognized. As early as the 1970s Hedley Bull (1973: 183–4) argued that:

> the reason we must be concerned with the theory as well as the history of the subject is that all discussions of international politics . . . proceed upon theoretical assumptions which we should acknowledge and investigate rather than ignore or leave unchallenged. The enterprise of theoretical investigation is at its minimum one directed towards criticism: towards identifying, formulating, refining, and questioning the general assumptions on which the everyday discussion of international politics proceeds. At its maximum, the enterprise is concerned with theoretical construction: with establishing that certain assumptions are true while others are false, certain arguments valid while others are invalid, and so proceeding to erect a firm structure of knowledge.

This quotation reveals that Bull thought that explanatory and constitutive theory are both necessary in the study of international relations: intellectual enquiry would be incomplete without the effort to increase understanding on both fronts. Although he wrote this in the early 1970s, it was not until later in the decade that constitutive theory began to enjoy a more central place in the discipline, in large part because of the influence of developments in the cognate fields of social and political theory. In the years since, with the growth of interest in international theory, a flourishing literature has been devoted to addressing theoretical concerns, much of it concerned with constitutive theory. This focus on the process of theorizing has not been uncontroversial. Some have argued that the excessive preoccupation with theory represents a withdrawal from an analysis of 'real-world' issues and a sense of responsibility for policy relevance (Wallace 1996). There is a parallel here with a point that Keohane (1988) made against post-modernism which is that the fixation with problems in the philosophy of social science leads to a neglect of important fields of empirical research.

Critics of this argument maintain that it rests on unspoken or undefended theoretical assumptions about the purposes of studying international relations, and specifically on the belief that the discipline should be concerned with issues which are more vital to states than to civil society actors aiming to change the international political system (Booth 1997; Smith 1997). Here it is important to recall that Carr and Morgenthau were interested not only in explaining the world 'out there' but in making a powerful argument about what states could reasonably hope to achieve in the competitive world of international politics. Smith (1996: 113) argues that all theories do this whether intentionally or unintentionally: they 'do not simply explain or predict, they tell us what possibilities exist for human action and intervention; they define not merely our explanatory possibilities, but also our ethical and practical horizons'.

Smith questions what he sees as the false assumption that 'theory' stands in opposition to 'reality' – conversely that 'theory' can be tested against a 'reality' which is already 'out there' (see also George 1994). The issue here is whether what is 'out there' is always theory-dependent and invariably conditioned to some degree by the language and culture of the observer and by general beliefs about society tied to a particular place and time. And as noted earlier, those who wonder about the point of theory cannot avoid the fact that analysis is always theoretically informed and likely to have political implications and consequences (Brown 2002). The growing feminist literature in the field discussed in Chapter 10 has stressed this argument in its claim that many of its dominant traditions are gendered in that they reflect specifically male experiences of society and politics. Critical approaches to the discipline which areas discussed in Chapters 8 and 9 have been equally keen to stress that there is, as Nagel (1986) has argued in a rather different context, 'no view from nowhere'.

To be fair, many exponents of the scientific approach recognized this very problem, but they believed that science made it possible for analysts to rise above the social and political world they were investigating. What the physical sciences had achieved could be emulated in social-scientific forms of enquiry. This is a matter to come back to later. But debates about the possibility of a science of international relations, and disputes about whether there has been an excessive preoccupation with theory in recent years, demonstrate that scholars do not agree about the nature and purposes of theory or concur about its proper place in the wider field.

International Relations is a discipline of theoretical disagreements – a 'divided discipline', as Holsti (1985) called it.

Contested nature

Indeed it has been so ever since those who developed this comparatively new subject in the Western academy in the aftermath of World War I first debated the essential features of international politics. Since then, but more keenly in some periods than in others, almost every aspect of the study of international politics has been contested. What should the discipline aim to study: Relations between states? Growing transnational economic ties, as recommended by early twentieth-century liberals? Increasing international interdependence, as advocated in the 1970s? The global system of dominance and dependence, as claimed by Marxists and neo-Marxists from the 1970s? Globalization, as scholars have argued in more recent times? These are some examples of how the discipline has been divided on the very basic question of its *subject matter*.

How, in addition, should international political phenomena be studied: by using empirical data to identify laws and patterns of international relations? By using historical evidence to understand what is unique (Bull 1966a) or to identify some traditions of thought which have survived for centuries (Wight 1991)? By using Marxist approaches to production, class and material inequalities? By emulating, as Waltz (1979) does, the study of the market behaviour of firms to understand systemic forces which make all states behave in much the same way? By claiming, as Wendt (1999) does in his defence of constructivism, that in the study of international relations it is important to understand that 'it is ideas all the way down?' These are some illustrations of fundamental differences about the appropriate *methodology* or *methodologies* to use in the field.

Finally is it possible for scholars to provide neutral forms of analysis, or are all approaches culture-bound and necessarily biased? Is it possible to have objective knowledge of facts but not of values, as advocates of the scientific approach argued? Or, as some students of global ethics have argued, is it possible to have knowledge of the goals that states and other political actors should aim to realize such as the promotion of global justice (Beitz 1979) or ending world poverty (Pogge 2002) These are some of the *epistemological* debates in the field, debates about what human beings can and cannot know about the social and political world. Many of the 'great debates' and watersheds in the discipline have focused on such questions.

In the remainder of this introductory chapter we will examine these and other issues under the following headings:

- The foundation of the discipline of International Relations
- Theories and disciplines
- Explanatory and constitutive theory
- Inter-disciplinary theory
- What do theories of international relations differ about?
- What criteria exist for evaluating theories?

One of our aims is to explain the proliferation of theories since the 1980s, to analyse their different 'styles' and methods of proceeding and to comment on a recurrent problem in the field which is that theorists often appear to 'talk past' each other rather than engage in productive dialogue. Another aim is to identify ways in which meaningful comparisons between different perspectives of International Relations can be made. It will be useful to bear these points in mind when reading later chapters on several influential theoretical traditions in the field. We begin, however, with a brief introduction to the development of the discipline.

The foundation of the discipline of International Relations

Although historians, international lawyers and political philosophers have written about international politics for many centuries, the formal recognition of a separate discipline of International Relations is usually thought to have occurred at the end of World War I with the establishment of a Chair of International Relations at the University of Wales, Aberystwyth. Other Chairs followed in Britain and the United States. International relations were studied before 1919, but there was no discipline as such. Its subject matter was shared by a number of older disciplines; including law, philosophy, economics, politics and diplomatic history – but before 1919 the subject was not studied with the great sense of urgency which was the product of World War I.

It is impossible to separate the foundation of the discipline of International Relations from the larger public reaction to the horrors of the 'Great War', as it was initially called. For many historians of the time, the intellectual question which eclipsed all others and monopolized their interest was the puzzle of how and why the war began. Gooch in England, Fay and Schmitt in the United States, Renouvin and Camille Bloch in France, Thimme, Brandenburg and von Wegerer in Germany, Pribram in Austria and Pokrovsky in Russia deserve to be mentioned in this regard (Taylor 1961: 30). They had the same moral purpose, which was to discover the causes of World War I so that future generations might be spared a similar catastrophe.

The human cost of the 1914–18 war led many to argue that the old assumptions and prescriptions of power politics were totally discredited. Thinkers such as Sir Alfred Zimmern and Philip Noel-Baker came to prominence in the immediate post-war years. They believed that peace would come about only if the classical balance of power were replaced by a system of collective security (including the idea of the rule of law) in which states transferred domestic concepts and practices to the international sphere. Central here was a commitment to the nineteenth-century belief that humankind could make political progress by using reasoned debate to develop common interests. This was a view shared by many liberal internationalists, later dubbed 'idealists' or 'utopians' by critics who thought their panaceas were simplistic. Carr (1939/1945/1946) maintained that their proposed solution to the scourge of war suffered from the major problem of reflecting, albeit unwittingly, the position of the satisfied powers – 'the haves' as opposed to the 'have-nots' in international relations. It is interesting to note that the first complaint about the ideological and political character of such a way of thinking about international politics was first made by a 'realist' such as Carr who was influenced by Marxism and its critique of the ideological nature of the dominant liberal approaches to politics and economics in the nineteenth century. Carr thought that the same criticism held with respect to the 'utopians', as he called them.

The war shook the confidence of those who had invested their faith in classical diplomacy and who thought the use of force was necessary at times to maintain the balance of power. At the outbreak of World War I few thought it would last more than a few months and fewer still anticipated the scale of the impending catastrophe. Concerns about the human cost of war were linked with the widespread notion that the old international order, with its secret diplomacy and secret treaties, was immoral. The belief in the need for a 'clean break' with the old order encouraged the view that the study of history was an unreliable guide to how states should behave in future. In the aftermath of the war, a new academic discipline was thought essential, one devoted to understanding and preventing international conflict. The first scholars in the field, working within universities in the victorious countries, and particularly in Britain and the United States, were generally agreed that the following three questions should guide their new field of inquiry:

1. What were the main causes of World War I, and what was it about the old order that led national governments into a war which resulted in misery for millions?
2. What were the main lessons that could be learned from World War I? How could the recurrence of a war of this kind be prevented?

3. On what basis could a new international order be created, and how could international institutions, and particularly the League of Nations, ensure that states complied with its defining principles?

In response to these questions, many members of the first 'school' or 'theory' of international relations maintained that war was partly the result of 'international anarchy' and partly the result of misunderstandings, miscalculations and recklessness on the part of politicians who had lost control of events in 1914. The 'idealists' argued that a more peaceful world order could be created by making foreign policy elites accountable to public opinion and by democratizing international relations (Long and Wilson 1995; Chapter 2). According to Bull (quoted in Hollis and Smith 1990: 20):

> the distinctive characteristic of these writers was their belief in progress: the belief, in particular, that the system of international relations that had given rise to the First World War was capable of being transformed into a fundamentally more peaceful and just world order; that under the impact of the awakening of democracy, the growth of the 'international mind', the development of the League of Nations, the good works of men of peace or the enlightenment spread by their own teachings, it was in fact being transformed; and that their responsibility as students of international relations was to assist this march of progress to overcome the ignorance, the prejudices, and the sinister interests that stood in its way.

Bull brings out the extent to which normative vision animated the discipline in its first phase of development when many thought World War I was the 'war to end all wars'. Only the rigorous study of the phenomenon of war could explain how states could create a world order in which the recurrence of such a conflict would be impossible. Crucially, then, the discipline was born in an era when many believed that the reform of international politics was not only essential but clearly achievable. Whether or not the global order can be radically improved has been a central question in the study of international relations ever since.

The critics' reaction to this liberal internationalism dominated the discipline's early years. Carr (1939; 1945; 1946: Chapter 1), who was one of the more scathing of them, maintained that 'utopians' were guilty of 'naivety' and 'exuberance'. Visionary zeal stood in the way of dispassionate analysis. The realist critique of liberal internationalism launched by Carr immediately before World War II, and continued by various scholars including Morgenthau in the United States in the 1940s and 1950s, led to the so-called first 'great debate'. Whether this debate actually occurred has been contested by recent scholars (Wilson 1998); however the myth of a great debate between the realists and the idealists gave the discipline its identity in the years following World War II. Interestingly Carr (1939; 1945; 1946), who criticized the utopians for their 'naivety' also turned his guns on the realists, accusing them of 'sterility' and 'complacency'. Theories acquire dominance in any discipline for different reasons, such as the extent to which they prevail in debates with their adversaries (sometimes more imagined than real). They can also be the beneficiary of widespread beliefs that they are right for the times or more relevant to the dominant events of the day than are other perspectives. The '20 years' crisis' culminating in World War II and followed by the Cold War era led in any case to the dominance of realism.

The purpose of theory in the early years of the discipline was to change the world for the better by removing the blight of war. A close connection existed between theory and practice: theory was not disconnected from the actual world of international politics. This was true of the liberal internationalists who believed 'the world to be profoundly other than it should be' and who had 'faith in the power of human reason and human action' to change it so 'that the inner potential of all human beings [could] be more fully realized' (Howard 1978: 11). It was no less true of the realists who thought that theory had a stake in political practice, most obviously by trying to understand as dispassionately as possible the constraints on realizing the vision which the 'utopians' had been too anxious to embrace. It was the realist position in the dispute about what could and could not be achieved in a world of competing states which gave the discipline its identity in the 1950s and 1960s.

Theories and disciplines

Over 40 years ago, Wight (1966a) posed the question, 'Why is there no International Theory?'. His reason for the absence of traditions of international theory ('speculation about the society of states, or the family of nations, or the international community') which even begin to match the achievements of political theory ('speculation about the state') was as follows. Domestic political systems had witnessed extraordinary developments over the centuries including the establishment of public education and welfare systems. But in terms of its basic properties, the international political system had barely changed at all. Wight called it 'the realm of recurrence and repetition' which was 'incompatible with progressivist theory'. Whereas political theory was rich in its characterizations of 'the good life', international theory was confined to questions of 'survival'. The language of political theory and law which was a language 'appropriate to man's control of his social life' had no obvious use for analysts of international affairs (Wight 1966a: 15, 25–6, 32).

At first glance Wight sided with the realists in their debate with those with a utopian temperament. But in an influential set of lectures given at the London School of Economics in the 1950s and 1960s, Wight (1991) protested against the reduction of thinking about international relations to two traditions of thought. What was lost in the division of the field into 'realism' and 'idealism' was a long tradition of inquiry (the 'rationalist' or 'Grotian' tradition) which regarded the existence of the society of states as its starting point. This perspective which has come to be known as the English School (Chapter 4) has been influential especially in Britain, and also in Australia and Canada. Its distinguishing quality is that international relations are neither as bleak as realists suggest nor as amenable to change as utopians ('revolutionists', in Wight's language) believe. There is, members of the English School argue, a high level of order and cooperation in the relations between states, even though they live in a condition of anarchy – a condition marked by the absence of a power standing above and able to command sovereign states.

Four decades on, we can no longer refer, as Wight did, to the 'paucity' of international theory. As this volume will show, there are now many rich strands of international theory, many of which are not constrained by the problem of state survival or by the apparent absence of a vocabulary with which to theorize global politics. How did this change come about, and where does it leave earlier discussions about the possibility of progress in international relations?

We can begin to answer these questions by noting that the 1960s and 1970s saw the rapid development of the study of International Relations as new academic departments and centres appeared not only in the United States and Britain but in several other places. This period also saw the rapid proliferation of approaches to the field. The preoccupation with war and conflict remained, the nuclear age leading to the rise of a new sub-field of strategic studies in the 1950s and 1960s. However, the boundaries of the discipline expanded, in the period now under discussion, to include foreign policy analysis, itself divided into several divisions, one aiming for a predictive science of foreign policy behaviour which might lead to better 'crisis management' (Hill 2003). The 1970s witnessed the rise of study of international interdependence – or, rather, its re-emergence, because liberal internationalists such as Zimmern had identified the expansion of international trade as a crucial level of analysis. Liberal theories of interdependence and the later 'neo-liberal institutionalist' analysis of international regimes argued that the economic and technological unification of the human race required new forms of international cooperation. To those influenced by the socialist tradition, however, international interdependence was a misnomer. The reality was a system of global dominance and dependence which divided the world between 'core' and 'periphery'. The phrase, 'the inter-paradigm debate' was used in the 1970s and 1980s to show that an early consensus about the nature of the discipline (which was always incomplete) had been replaced by a broad spectrum of contending approaches, a condition that survives to this day (Banks 1985; Hoffman 1987). Only some of these approaches (neo-realism being by far the most important – see Chapter 2) continue to regard the international system as a unique 'anarchic' domain which can be analysed in isolation from social and economic developments within and across societies. The influence of other disciplines and cognate fields is now pronounced in the subject, and many strands of International Relations theory deny that the subject has a distinctive subject matter or can proceed without borrowing heavily from languages of inquiry in other fields of investigation. The import of various ideas from social and political theory is one development which has become increasingly prominent in the 1980s and 1990s.

In the course of this volume we will examine a number of the more influential theories, including liberal internationalism, realism, neo-realism and the English School, as well as less influential approaches such as Marxism and newer perspectives such as constructivism, feminism and green political thought. We will also consider the established field of international political theory, and the emerging interest in linkages between historical sociology and International Relations which advocates (in ways that will be of special interest to students of Marxism, constructivism and the English School) focusing on long-term processes of change in international or world politics.

In this way, we hope to provide a snapshot of contemporary debates about the nature and purposes of International Relations theory. We have chosen to call them 'theories', but in the literature over the years they have also been referred to as 'paradigms', 'perspectives', 'discourses', 'schools of thought', 'images' and 'traditions'. What they are called is less important than what they set out to do, and how they differ from one another. The following descriptions of theory capture some of their diverse purposes:

- Theories explain the laws of international politics or recurrent patterns of national behaviour (Waltz 1979).
- Theories that draw on history and historical sociology, not least in order to suggest that claims about the recurrent nature of international politics should be treated with suspicion and to show that the nature of contemporary events will remain elusive unless they are analysed in conjunction with long-term processes of development.

- Theories attempt either to explain and predict behaviour or to understand the world 'inside the heads' of actors (Hollis and Smith 1990).
- Theories are traditions of speculation about relations between states which focus on the struggle for power, the nature of international society and the possibility of a world community (Wight 1991).
- Theories use empirical data to test hypotheses about the world such as the absence of war between liberal-democratic states (Doyle 1983).
- Theories analyse and try to clarify the use of concepts such as the balance of power (Butterfield and Wight 1966).
- Theories criticize forms of domination and perspectives which make the socially constructed and changeable seem natural and unalterable (critical theory).
- Theories reflect on how the world ought to be organized and analyse ways in which various conceptions of human rights or global social justice are constructed and defended (international political theory or global ethics).
- Theories reflect on the process of theorizing itself; they analyse epistemological claims about how human beings know the world and ontological claims about what the world ultimately consists of – for example, whether it basically consists of sovereign states or individuals with rights against and obligations to the rest of humanity (constitutive theory).

This list shows that practitioners in the field do not agree about what is involved in theorizing international relations. When we compare theories we are comparing different and seemingly incommensurable phenomena. There is no agreement about what counts as the best line of argument in any theory, and no agreement about whether their principal achievements can be combined in a unified grand theory. Post-structuralist theory – or theories, since its advocates would deny there is a single approach to which all faithfully adhere (Chapter 9) – rejects the possibility of one total theory of international relations. More basically, and as already noted, there is a good deal of overlap between different theories but no consensus about what the term, 'international relations', actually signifies. Its most obvious meaning is the analysis of relations between nations – more accurately, states, but this is the approach taken by realists and neo-realists and rejected or substantially qualified by exponents of competing perspectives, some of whom think the term 'global politics' or 'world politics' is a better term for describing what the subject should study in the contemporary age (Baylis and Smith 2005).

Though far from exhaustive, the following list summarizes some disciplinary preoccupations in recent times:

- *Dominant actors* – traditionally this was the sovereign state but the list now includes transnational corporations (TNCs), transnational classes and 'casino capitalists', international organizations such as the World Trade Organization (WTO), international non-governmental organizations (NGOs) such as Amnesty International, new social movements including women's and ecological movements, and international terrorist organizations such as Al-Qaeda.
- *Dominant relationships* – strategic relations between the great powers traditionally, but also in recent years trade relations between the advanced industrial societies, the 'liberal peace', relations of dominance and dependence between the core and periphery in the capitalist world economy and forms of solidarity within 'global civil society'.
- *Empirical issues* – the distribution of military power, arms control and crisis management but also globalization, global inequality, identity politics and national fragmentation, the universal human rights culture, the plight of refugees, gender issues, environmental conservation, transnational crime and the global drugs trade and HIV/AIDS.
- *Ethical issues* – the just war, the rights and wrongs of humanitarian intervention, the case for and against the global redistribution of power and wealth, duties to nature, to future generations and to non-human species, respect for cultural differences and the rights of women and children.
- *Issues in the philosophy of the social sciences* – methodological disputes about the possibility of a science of international politics, competing epistemological and ontological standpoints, the nature of causation and the idea of historical narrative.
- *The prospects for multidisciplinarity* – recasting the discipline by using liberal and radical approaches to develop international political economy was the most significant shift towards interdisciplinarity in the 1980s and 1990s. Building links with social theory, historical sociology, international political theory and 'world history', and dismantling barriers between International Relations, Political Theory and Ethics have been leading developments since the 1990s.

Quite how to deal with such a rich diversity of themes is one of the central questions every theory of international relations must address. Theories have to rely on some principles of selection to narrow their scope of inquiry; they discriminate between actors, relationships, empirical issues and so forth which they judge most important or regard as trivial. Waltz's neo-realist theory is one of the most debated illustrations of this process of selectivity. Waltz (1979) maintained that theory must abstract from the myriad forces at work in international politics while recognizing that in reality 'everything is connected with everything else'. But theory must 'distort' reality – and Waltz offers a complex argument about the philosophy of social sciences and the achievements of economics to explain this – if it is to explain what Waltz regards as the central puzzle of world politics: the 'dismaying persistence' of the international states-system and the recurrence of the struggle for power and security over several millennia. Waltz argued that international economic relations, international law and so forth are undoubtedly interesting phenomena but they must be ignored by a theory with the purposes he sets for it.

It is useful to compare this argument with Cox's (1981; 1983) claim – influenced by Marxism – that a theory of international relations has to deal with social forces (including class relations), states and world order if it is to understand the nature of global hegemony and identify 'counter-hegemonic' movements which are working to promote realizable visions of a better form of world order. In this approach, the question of what is most important in world politics is not answered by providing a list of the most powerful actors and relationships but by inquiring into the causes of inequalities of power and opportunities between human beings and by identifying the political movements which are spearheading the struggle against these asymmetries – movements which are not as powerful as states but, in Cox's analysis, more important than them *because of the values they are trying to realize* (for further discussion, see Chapters 6 and 8).

In Cox's argument – and this is a position common to the various strands of radical scholarship in the field, the question of what is important in international relations is not an empirical problem which can be solved by looking at what is 'out there' in the 'real world'; it is fundamentally a political question, one that begins with the issue of whose interests are protected and whose are disadvantaged or ignored by the dominant political and economic structures. Such matters are not resolved by empirical inquiry – first and foremost they are ethical matters which have crept to the centre of the field over the last 20 or so years (see Chapter 12).

This raises important issues about how theories acquire disciplinary dominance or hegemony. The post-positivist turn has made such matters prominent in the field, but they have a more ancient lineage. Since the 1960s, for example, radical scholars in the United States such as Yergin (1990) and Chomsky (1969) have analysed the close connections which have often existed between the academic study of International Relations and the world of government, especially in the United States (for an appraisal of Chomsky's work, see the Forum on Chomsky, *Review of International Studies* 2003). They have stressed how the dominant political needs of the time, as defined by government, have favoured some theories over others so that one perspective acquires hegemony while others make dissenting claims on the margins of the field. Strategic Studies is a case in point, as many radical scholars stressed its close connections with the 'military-industrial complex' in the 1960s. Realism was the dominant ideology of the US political establishment in the late 1960s and early 1970s when the Nixon Administration broke with the Cold War ideology which had impeded the development of amicable relations with the Soviet Union and China (Henry Kissinger, Nixon's National Security Advisor and later Secretary of State, had been a leading realist academic prior to 1968). Since the 1980s, the dominant ideology has been neo-liberal economics, which has had enormous influence through the 'Washington Consensus' in promoting the deregulation of world markets (see Chapter 3). A fascinating illustration of the changing political fortunes of academic theories is that realism has come to have a dissenting role with respect to recent US foreign policy while remaining one of the dominant traditions in the American academy. The phenomenon of 'realists against the war' (many leading realist scholars published their opposition to the prospect of war against Iraq in *The New York Times* in 2002) is an example of how dominance in one domain may not be converted into dominance in the other.

It is necessary to stress the politicized nature of the discipline because the politics of International Relations can determine how broad the spectrum of 'legitimate theoretical opinion' can actually be. For example, Marxist scholars have highlighted the limits of expressible dissent in the discipline's attempt to uncover the cause of World War I. They have pointed to the conceptual and ideological parameters beyond which the investigators into war causes could not, or would not, proceed. For opinion to be considered legitimate it had to fall between the poles of 'idealism' at one end of the spectrum and 'realism' at the other. According to these Marxists, certain facts were axiomatically excluded as not belonging to the inquiry at all. Tensions within society, such as class struggles and economic competition between colonial powers – during this period a popular Marxist explanation of the origins of war – were not considered seriously within the discipline at this time. One commentator has suggested that the theory of imperialism was deliberately excluded because, by locating the causes of war within the nature of the capitalist system, it posed a direct threat to the social order of capitalist states: 'this false doctrine had to be refuted in the interest of stabilizing bourgeois society . . . the [historians] acted and reflected within the social context of the bourgeois university, which structurally obstructed such revolutionary insights' (Krippendorf 1982: 27). Feminists have made a similar claim about the exclusion of their presence and perspectives from the concerns of international relations, arguing that the organization of the academy was designed in ways that occluded inquiry into masculine power.

Explanatory and constitutive theory

One aim of studying a wide variety of International Relations theories is to make international politics more intelligible – to make better sense of the actors, structures, institutions, processes and particular episodes mainly, but not only, in the contemporary world. At times, theories may be involved in testing hypotheses, in proposing causal explanations with a view to identifying main trends and patterns in international relations – hence the claim that they are *explanatory* theories.

But why study international relations in this way? Is it obvious that the student of international relations needs theory at all? Is it not more centrally important to investigate the facts which are already out there? Halliday's three answers to this last question are instructive:

> First, there needs to be some preconception of which facts are significant and which are not. The facts are myriad and do not speak for themselves. For anyone, academic or not, there needs to be criteria of significance. Secondly, any one set of facts, even if accepted as true and as significant, can yield different interpretations: the debate on the 'lessons of the 1930s' is not about what happened in the 1930s, but about how these events are to be interpreted. The same applies to the end of the Cold War in the 1980s. Thirdly, no human agent, again whether academic or not, can rest content with facts alone: all social activity involves moral questions, of right and wrong, and these can, by definition, not be decided by facts. In the international domain such ethical issues are pervasive: the question of legitimacy and loyalty – should one obey the nation, a broader community (even the world, the cosmopolis), or some smaller sub-national group; the issues of intervention – whether sovereignty is a supreme value or whether states or agents can intervene in the internal affairs of states; the question of human rights and their definition and universality (Halliday 1994: 25).

In this view, theories are not 'optional extras' or interesting 'fashion accessories'. They are a necessary means of bringing order to the subject matter of International Relations. Theories are needed to conceptualize contemporary events. As Doyle (1983) argues in his writings on the liberal peace, an explanation of the absence of war between liberal states for almost two centuries has to begin by discussing what it means to describe a state as 'liberal' and what it means to claim there has been 'no war'. As Suganami (1996) has argued, an explanation of what causes war or what makes peace possible between societies, will be unsatisfactory unless it deals with the question of what it means to say that 'x' causes 'y'. Conceptual analysis – an inherently philosophical activity – is a necessary part of any attempt to explain or understand world politics.

International relations comprise a plethora of events, issues and relationships which are often enormous in scale and bewildering in their complexity. Theories can help the observer to think critically, logically and coherently by sorting these phenomena into manageable categories so that the appropriate units and level of analysis can be chosen and, where possible, significant connections and patterns of behaviour identified.

To the scholar of the 'international', theories are unavoidable. After all, the interpretation of 'reality' is always contingent on theoretical assumptions of one kind or another. To reiterate the point, the events and issues which comprise international relations can be interpreted and understood only by reference to a conceptual framework. The theory of international relations provides us with a choice of such frameworks.

The process we undertake when theorizing is also in dispute and, as Bull insisted, critical, reflective examination is always required. Gellner (1974: 175) asks whether it is possible or meaningful to distinguish 'between a world of fact "out there" and a cognitive realm of theory that *retrospectively* (our emphasis) orders and gives meaning to factual data'. If, as some post-structuralists maintain, there is no Archimedean standpoint which makes objective knowledge about an external reality possible, then the very process of separating 'theory' from 'practice', or the 'subject' from the 'object' it seeks to comprehend, is deeply problematical. Indeed, the very process of using positivist social science to acquire 'objective knowledge' may be deeply ideological. Far, then, from rising above the 'particular' to produce 'universal' truths about the social world, analysis may simply reflect specific cultural locations and sectional interests and reproduce existing forms of power (George and Campbell 1990).

These questions lead to a second category of theory, *constitutive* international theory. Everyone comes to the study of international relations with a specific language, cultural beliefs and preconceptions, as well as specific life-experiences which affect their understanding of the subject. Language, culture, religion, ethnicity, class and gender are a few of the factors which shape world views. Indeed it is possible to understand and interpret the world only within particular cultural and linguistic frameworks: these are the *lenses* through which we perceive the world. One of the main purposes of studying theory is to enable us to examine these lenses to discover just how distorted and distorting any particular world-view may be. This is why it is important to ask why, for example, realists focus on specific images which highlight states, geo-politics and war while remaining blind to other phenomena such as class divisions and material inequalities.

As noted earlier, in the theory of international relations it is important to be as concerned with how we *approach* the study of world politics as we are with events, issues and actors in the global system. It is necessary to examine background assumptions because all forms of social analysis raise important questions about the moral and cultural constitution of the observer. It is important to reflect upon the cognitive interests and normative assumptions which underpin research. The point here is to become acutely aware of hidden assumptions, prejudices and biases about how the social and political world is and what it can be. According to various 'critical' perspectives, it is futile or unrealistic to attempt to dispense with these assumptions. Indeed, post-structuralist approaches have called for the celebration of diverse experiences of the world of international relations while maintaining that all standpoints should be subject to forms of critical analysis which highlight their closures and exclusions (George and Campbell 1990). We can best do this by devel-oping an awareness of the diversity of images of international relations. The task of constitutive international theory is to analyse the different forms of reflection about the nature and character of world politics and to stress that these forms of knowledge do not simply mirror the world, but also help to shape it.

Inter-disciplinary theory

Although at the outset conceived as a separate discipline, International Relations has always been influenced by cognate fields of study. In recent times it has been shaped by inter-disciplinary studies which are not easily categorized as either explanatory or constitutive theoretical approaches. Nor are they obviously normative or empirical. Two of these fields, inter-national political theory and historical sociology, are germane to so many theoretical discussions about global politics today, that they have been given separate chapters in this volume.

Sometimes regarded as empirical theory, international political theory considers a range of philosophical and historical questions raised in domestic settings, for the international environment. Though not norma-tively prescriptive, international political theory seeks to understand the grounds on which a range of ethical and normative choices in international politics are made. Issues such as just-war theory, global justice and humanitarian intervention now occupy a central place in the theory of international relations. What is the basis of a good international society? When do our obligations to people in other political communities – and to humanity generally – supersede our duties to fellow nationals? These subjects and questions contain moral and philosophical assumptions, but they are unavoidably political issues as well. International political theory reflects on the presuppositions and the politics which lie in the foundations of these discussions. It also reminds us that international thought has a history which deserves serious consideration by all scholars who deploy theoretical arguments without always being fully aware of how those theoretical tools were forged.

As its title suggests, historical sociology is concerned with identifying and understanding long-term patterns and processes of change in international relations. These include the changing configurations of power in global politics, the changing shape and functions of political communities, and the effects of economic forces on bounded communities and their societies. Historical sociology is also concerned with how ideas have carved the ethical and cultural contours of international politics over time.

Like international political theory, historical sociology has many different strands and traditions. Some embrace grand historical narratives with an eye to uncovering distinctive patterns and themes, while others can be considered an antidote to 'presentism' – providing historical context to ensure that the analysis of supposedly unique contemporary events takes account of their relationship with processes that may stretch back decades or centuries, and in some cases even millennia. Phenomena such as the globalization of capitalism and its implications, democratization after the Cold War, the history of states-systems and the moral development of the species are just a few of the subjects upon which historical sociologists have reflected and significantly contributed to our knowledge of global politics.

What do theories differ about?

Although this volume identifies major perspectives, the authors do not want to give the impression that schools of thought are monolithic and homogeneous theoretical traditions. Although they may share some basic assumptions, the exponents of any perspective can have widely differing and even conflicting positions on the issues raised earlier. Feminism and Marxism are examples of very broad 'churches' which display great diversity – and can on occasion seem as different from each other as the main perspectives in the field. Realism has its internal variations; so has the English School, the many branches of critical theory and so on. To someone who is new to the field, this diversity can be frustrating but there is nothing abnormal about differences of perspective within the same broad theoretical tradition. Heterogeneity is a strength and an obstacle to ossification.

It is possible to compare and contrast sub-schools of International Relations because they do have much in common. It is possible to focus on what they generally agree are the issues worth disagreeing about, on what they think are the principal stakes involved in understanding the world and in creating more sophisticated modes of analysis. Here is it necessary to proceed with great caution because no account of the main stakes can do justice to the many debates and controversies in the field. There is bound to be some arbitrariness in any attempt to make sense of the discipline as a whole. However, with that caveat, we believe it is useful to consider what the main perspectives have concluded about the following four issues: certainly a brief summary of where these theories stand on these issues may enable newcomers to chart a path through the thicket of major controversies in the field.

Object of analysis and scope of the enquiry

The first is the *object of analysis and the scope of the enquiry*. Debates about the object of analysis have been especially important in the discipline since the 'level of analysis' debate (Singer 1961; Hollis and Smith 1990: 92–118). One of the best illustrations of what is at stake here is Waltz's discussion of the causes of wars. In *Man, the State and War*, Waltz (1959) argued that three different levels of analysis (or three 'images') had been explored in the literature on this subject: (a) human nature; (b) the structure of political systems; and (c) the nature of the international system. Waltz showed how many psychologists have tried to explain war by looking at the innate aggressiveness of the species; many liberals and Marxists maintained that war is the product of how some political systems are organized. Liberals maintained that war was the result of autocratic government; Marxists saw it as a product of capitalism. From each standpoint, war was regarded as a phenomenon which could be abolished – by creating liberal regimes in the first case, and by establishing socialist forms of government in the second. According to students of the third level of analysis, war is a product of the anarchic nature of international politics and the unending competition for power and security. Waltz argued for the primacy of this 'third image of international politics', which stressed that war is inevitable in the context of anarchy (while claiming that the other two levels of analysis also contribute to the study of war origins).

Thinking back to an earlier part of the discussion, we can see that the dominance of realism was in large part a consequence of its argument about the most important level of analysis for students of the field. We can also see that some of the main changes in the discipline have been the result of discontent with the realists' concentration on the problem of anarchy and its virtual exclusion of all other domains of world politics. When feminists argue for bringing women within the parameters of discussion, or the English School argues for focusing on international society, when constructivists urge the importance of understanding the social construction of norms, ideas and so on, they are involved in fundamental disciplinary debates about the correct *object* (or level) of analysis.

Purpose of social and political enquiry

They are also involved in crucial debates about the *purpose of social and political enquiry*. Returning to Waltz, in his account of the causes of war (and later in his classic work, *Theory of International Politics*, 1979), he maintained that the purpose of analysis is to understand the limits on political change, more specifically to show that states are best advised to work with the existing international order rather than to try to change it radically. Above all else, they should ensure as far as they can the preservation of a *balance of power* which deters states from going to war although it cannot always prevent it. Ambitious projects of global reform are, on this analysis, destined to fail. Members of the English School do not deny the importance of the balance of power but they stress the need to attend to all the phenomena that make international order possible including the belief that the society of states is legitimate and, in the aftermath of Western colonialism, willing to be responsive to claims for justice advanced by 'Third World' states. Other perspectives include the liberal argument that the purpose of analysis is to promote economic and social interdependence between individuals across the world and, in the case of many radical approaches to the field, to create new forms of political community and new forms of human solidarity.

For the neo-realist, the purpose of the analysis is defined by the fact that international anarchy makes many of these visions utopian and dangerous. For many opponents of neo-realism, its purpose of inquiry is too quick to resign to what it regards as unchangeable; one of the main purposes of international political inquiry is to resist the perceived fatalism, determinism and conservatism of this position. In this context, the emergence of critical approaches to international relations (whether derived from Marxism and the Frankfurt School or located within developments in French social theory) has been especially important. Their purpose is to criticize neo-realist claims about the 'knowable reality' of international politics. Post-structuralists, for example, maintain that 'reality' is discursively produced (that is, constructed by discourse): it is 'never a complete, entirely coherent "thing", accessible to universalized, essentialist or totalized understandings of it . . . [it] is always characterized by ambiguity, disunity, discrepancy, contradiction and difference' (George 1994: 11). It can never be contained, in other words, within one grand theory or reduced to one set of forces which are judged more important than all others. For the post-modernist, neo-realism is just another construction of the world, one that should be challenged because it does 'violence' to reality and because it has the obvious political consequence of maintaining that efforts to change that world are futile.

Critiques of the neo-realist purpose of inquiry have had huge implications for the scope of inquiry mentioned earlier. One consequence has been to make questions of ontology more central to the field. As Cox (1992b: 132) argued, 'ontology lies at the beginning of any enquiry. We cannot define a problem in global politics without presupposing a certain basic structure consisting of the significant kinds of entities involved and the form of significant relationships among them.' He added that 'ontological presuppositions [are] inherent in . . . terms such as "International Relations", which seems to equate nation with state and to define the field as limited to the interactions among states' (Cox 1992b: 132). Cox displayed a preference for focusing on how domestic and international dominant class forces, states and powerful international institutions combine to form a global hegemonic order. Debates about the 'basic structure of international politics' are not just about what is 'out there' and how we come to know 'reality' (more on this later); they are also inextricably tied up with different views about the purposes of political inquiry. Cox (1981: 128) emphasized this point in the striking claim that 'theory is always *for* someone and *for* some purpose'.

In one of the most influential distinctions in the field, Cox claimed that neo-realism has a 'problem-solving' purpose, its main task being to ensure that existing political arrangements 'function more smoothly' by minimizing the potential for conflict and war. Of course, Cox did not underestimate the importance of this endeavour, but he challenges its sufficiency. The main problem, as he saw it, is that neo-realism assumes that the world is frozen in particular ways and ultimately unchangeable through political action. But the consequence of taking 'the world as it finds it . . . as the given framework for action' is that neo-realism confers legitimacy on that order and the forms of dominance and inequality which are inherent in it. (There is a direct parallel here with one of the central themes in post-structuralist thought – ultimately derived from Foucault's writings – on how forms of knowledge are connected with forms of power (Chapter 9).) On the other hand, critical theory, Cox (1981, 1992b) maintained, had a broader purpose which is to reflect on how that order came into being, how it has changed over time and may change again in ways that improve the life-chances of the vulnerable and excluded. A broadly similar critical purpose runs through all the main radical approaches to the field, including feminism, green political theory and 'critical constructivism'. All are actively libertarian in that they are broadly committed to the normative task of exposing constraints upon human autonomy which can in principle be removed.

Appropriate methodology

Debates about the purpose of international political enquiry lead to a third point of difference between approaches which revolves around the *appropriate methodology* for the discipline. Key questions are best approached by recalling that politically motivated scholarship is deeply controversial and often anathema to many scholars. The main issue is the status of normative claims. Is it possible to provide an objective account of why human beings should value autonomy and rally around a project of promoting universal human emancipation? Exponents of scientific approaches have argued that objective knowledge about the ends of social and political is unobtainable; post-structuralists have argued that the danger is that any doctrine of ideal ends will become the basis for new forms of power and domination. In the 1990s, debates about what constitutes the 'knowable reality' of international relations (ontological questions) were accompanied by increasingly complex discussions about how knowledge is generated (epistemological questions). Of course, the 'great debate' in the 1960s was very much concerned with epistemological issues, with the advocates of science such as Kaplan and Singer supporting quantificationist techniques and hypothesis-testing while 'traditionalists' such as Bull defended the virtues of history, law, philosophy and other classical forms of academic inquiry as the best way to approach international politics. As noted earlier, this was a debate (with its origins in the late eighteenth century) about the extent to which the methods of the natural sciences can be applied the study of society and politics. It was also a debate about the possibility of a neutral or 'value-free' study of international relations.

Such debates are far from being resolved – or, at least, there is no consensus in the field as to how to resolve them. Various forms of critical theory joined the critique of scientific approaches, claiming (as Horkheimer and Adorno had done in the 1940s) that they are inseparable from efforts to create new forms of social and political power. However, scientific approaches continue to have the upper hand in the American study of International Relations. They have been central to studies of the liberal peace (see Doyle 1983), and one analyst has claimed that the observation that there has been no war between liberal states for nearly two centuries is the nearest thing to a law in world politics (Levy 1989). It is also important to note the increasing prominence in the United States of 'rational choice' or 'game-theoretical' approaches as applied to studies of cooperation between 'rational egoists' (see Keohane 1984).

Distinct area of intellectual endeavour

A fourth point of difference between perspectives revolves around the issue of whether the discipline should be conceived as a *relatively distinct area of intellectual endeavour* or considered as a field which can develop only by drawing heavily on other areas of investigation, such as historical sociology and the study of world history (see Buzan and Little 2001, who call for closer ties with the study of world history). The more the analyst sees international politics as a realm of competition and conflict, the stronger the tendency to regard it as radically different from other academic fields. Here, its anarchic character is often seen as separating the study of International Relations from other social sciences, and the relevance of concepts and ideas drawn from outside the discipline is assumed to be limited. We have already encountered this theme in Wight's (1966a) paper, 'Why is there no International Theory?'

Neo-realism is also associated with the view that, like most of the states it studies, International Relations has sharply defined boundaries. Waltz (1979) is explicit on this point, claiming that the international political system should be regarded as a 'domain apart' – although he looks beyond the field to economics and to developments in the philosophy of science to develop his thesis about international anarchy. The more dominant tendency in recent international theory has been to embrace multidisciplinarity as a way of escaping the perceived insularity of the field. Many theorists have looked to developments in European social theory, post-colonial thinking and sociology more generally to explore new areas of investigation; some look to studies of ethics and political theory for insight. Many of the questions which have fascinated feminist scholars – about patriarchy, gender identity, etc. – can be answered only by going outside classical disciplinary boundaries. This is also manifestly true of much recent thinking about green politics which necessarily looks beyond the conventional discipline (Chapter 11). The most recent phase in the history of globalization has led many to deepen this move towards multidisciplinarity (Scholte 2000). The upshot of these developments is that the boundaries of International Relations have been keenly contested and in many sub-fields substantially redrawn. This does not mean the end of International Relations as an academic discipline, although the extent to which it borrows from other fields without having much influence on the wider humanities and social sciences is, for some, a real cause for concern (see Buzan and Little 2001). On the other hand, cross pollination from cognate fields can also enrich the study of international relations. All theories of international relations have to deal with the state and nationalism, with the struggle for power and security, and with the use of force, but they do not deal with these phenomena in the same way. Different conceptions of the scope of the inquiry, its purpose and methodology mean that issues of war and peace which formed the classical core of the subject are conceptualized and analysed in increasingly diverse ways.

Evaluating theories

We probably should not expect too much from any empirical theory. No single theory identifies, explains or understands all the key structures and dynamics of international politics. International historians such as Gaddis (1992–93) stressed that none of the major traditions of international theory predicted the collapse of the Soviet Union and its immediate consequences for Europe and the rest of the world. But many theorists do not believe that their purpose is prediction or concede that theories should be assessed by how well they can predict events. An assessment of different theories cannot begin, then, by comparing their achievements in explaining international political reality 'out there'.

What we have tried to show in this introduction, and the other chapters demonstrate, is that some of the most interesting debates revolve around the question of *what it means to provide a good account* of any dimension of international politics. We do not claim that this volume provides an exhaustive survey of the field at the current time, and we do not deny the claims of other perspectives which lack representation here. But we do believe that a comparison of the nine main theories considered in this volume, and the two interdisciplinary studies, will show why the nature of a good account of international political phenomena is keenly contested and why *debates about this matter are important*. This is why the great proliferation of theoretical approaches should be applauded rather than lamented as evidence that the discipline has lost its way or has collapsed into competing 'tribes'. One can begin to decide if one has a good account of any international political phenomenon only by engaging with different theories. In this way, analysts of international relations become more self-conscious about the different ways of practising their craft and more aware of omissions and exclusions which may reflect personal or cultural biases. This theme is crucially important if those of a critical persuasion are broadly right that all forms of inquiry have political implications and consequences, most obviously by creating narratives which privilege certain standpoints and experiences *to some degree*.

There is one final point to make before commenting briefly on the chapters that follow. Here, it is necessary to return to a comment made at the start of this introduction, namely that the realists and the liberal internationalists have been involved in a major controversy about the forms of political action that are most appropriate in a realm in which the struggle for power and security is pre-eminent. It is also worth recalling Steve Smith's claim that theories 'do not simply explain or predict, they tell us what possibilities exist for human action and intervention; they define not merely our explanatory possibilities, but also our ethical and practical horizons' (1996: 113). Now the analyst of any dimension of international politics may not be concerned with the possibilities for 'human action and intervention'; and many theorists of international relations would deny that this is what theory is essentially about. There is no reason to suggest an agenda that all good theories should follow. But to look at the main perspectives and at the debates between them is to see that the issue of whether or not the international political system can be reformed is *one* recurrent question which concerns all of them. For those who think global reform is possible, other questions immediately follow. How are different visions of international political life to be assessed, and what are the prospects for realizing them? We suggest these questions provide one measure of a good account of world politics. Others will disagree. To decide the merits of different positions on the possibilities for 'human action and intervention' – whether large or small – one needs to be familiar with at least the perspectives which are considered in this volume.

In Chapter 2, Jack Donnelly analyses classical realism which dominated the field for at least the first 50 years of its existence and which remains highly influential in the discipline today. The writings of early realists such as Carr and Morgenthau remain key reference points in contemporary debates more than five decades after their first publication. Interestingly, as explained in Chapter 2, neo-realism which emerged in the late 1970s and which was at the heart of most debates during the following two decades, was one of the main challenges to classical realism. However, neo-realism is largely concerned with the critique of liberal approaches (as well as Marxist and other radical approaches to the field) which it thinks guilty of exaggerating the ability of global economic and social processes to change the basic structure of international politics. In Chapter 3, Scott Burchill discusses the development of the liberal tradition, noting in particular how many contemporary neo-liberal accounts of the world market and the defence of free trade, resonate with ideas promoted by economic liberals in the nineteenth century. However, contemporary liberalism contains much more than a particular conception of how freeing trade and global markets from the hands of the state can promote material prosperity and establish the conditions for lasting peace. Other features of the perspective which have been influential in recent years include the defence of the universal human rights culture and the development of international criminal law, the study of 'cooperation under anarchy' associated with neo-liberal institutionalism and the immensely important discussion of the liberal peace. These features of recent liberal thinking about international relations will also be discussed in Chapter 3.

In Chapters 4 and 5, Andrew Linklater analyses the English School and Marxism. Neither has enjoyed the global influence of realism/neo-realism and liberalism/neo-liberalism, although the English School has been particularly influential in British International Relations. The years since 1998 have seen renewed interest in the English School theory of international society and in its position as a 'third way' between the pessimism of realism and the more idealistic forms of liberalism and various radical perspectives including Marxism. Chapter 4 pays particular attention to the contribution of Wight, Vincent and Bull to the discipline, and notes their special relevance for contemporary discussions about human rights, humanitarian intervention and the use of force in international affairs. Chapter 5 turns to Marxism, which has often been criticized by neo-realists and members of the English School although neither anchored its critique in a careful interpretation of one of its main theoretical adversaries. Whether the rejection of Marxism overlooked its ability to make a significant contribution to the field is a question that Chapter 5 considers in detail. Particular attention will be paid to Marx's writings on globalization, to Marxist analysis of nationalism and internationalism, and to reflections on the importance of forms of production – and specifically the development of modern capitalist forms of production – for global politics. The 'critical' dimensions of Marxism – its interest not only in explaining the world, but in changing it – are also noted in this chapter.

In Chapter 6 Andrew Linklater explains how important trends within historical sociology have started to influence theoretical debates within International Relations. Historical sociology identifies patterns and processes of change in the broader sweep of history – over the long term. The evolution of the states system, the spread of capitalism and the changing nature of political communities are just three key themes examined by historical sociologists which are central to contemporary debates within International Relations. The provision of historical context to the contemporary discussion of global politics makes historical sociology an indispensable tool in the hands of theorists in the field.

Marxism provided the intellectual background for the development of critical theory as developed by members of the Frankfurt School such as Horkheimer and Adorno in the 1930s, and by Habermas, Honneth and others in more recent times. In Chapter 7, Richard Devetak explains the central aims of critical theory and their impact on various theorists such as Ashley in the early 1980s, and on Ken Booth (1991a, b) and Cox who have defended a version of international politics committed to the idea of human emancipation. Although the term 'critical theory' was initially associated with the Frankfurt School which derived many of its ideas from a dialogue with orthodox Marxism, it is also strongly associated with post-structuralism, a perspective which is deeply suspicious of the emancipatory claims of classical Marxism. In Chapter 8, Richard Devetak explains the post-structural turn in the social sciences by considering the writings of Derrida, Foucault and Lyotard, and analyses its influence on International Relations since the 1980s. Its critique of the 'Enlightenment project' of universal human emancipation is an important element of this chapter, as is the stress on the critique of 'totalizing' perspectives which are judged to be a threat to the flourishing of human differences.

Constructivism, which Christian Reus-Smit discusses in Chapter 9, has emerged as a powerful challenge to orthodox perspectives in the field, most crucially to theories which assume that states derive certain interests from their location in an anarchic condition. In a famous challenge to those approaches, Alexander Wendt (1992) argued that 'anarchy is what states make of it'. The claim was that anarchy is socially constructed, that it is shaped by the beliefs and attitudes of states; it is not an unchanging structure which imposes certain constraints on states and compels all to participate in an endless struggle for power and security. Constructivism which has focused particularly on the relationship between interests and identities encompasses several competing approaches. Some are influenced by post-structuralism, others by critical theory in the Frankfurt School tradition; some share the neo-realist focus on analysing relations between states in isolation from other processes (systemic constructivism) whereas others see the states-system in connection with a range of national and global cultural and political phenomena (holistic constructivism).

In Chapter 10, Jacqui True sheds light on a subject which first came onto the International Relations agenda in the mid-1980s, namely feminism. This perspective is not reducible to a study of the position of women in the global order, although many feminists such as Cynthia Enloe did set out to explain how women are affected by war and by developments in the global economy, including structural adjustment policies (SAPs) in the 1980s and 1990s. The invisibility of women in mainstream approaches and in many critical alternatives was one reason for the development of the feminist literature. However, feminist perspectives have been no more homogeneous than other theoretical standpoints. Some feminists, such as Christine Sylvester (1994a, 2002), have used post-structuralist approaches to question 'essentialist' accounts of women, their interests and rights. One concern has been to question claims that the dominant Western conceptions of 'woman' are valid for women everywhere. Other feminists, such as Steans (1995), have been influenced by the Marxist tradition. It is important to repeat that feminism is not simply interested in the place of women in the global political and economic order. It is also preoccupied with constructions of gender including constructions of masculinity, and with how they affect forms of power and inequality and, at the epistemological level, knowledge claims about the world.

Matthew Paterson discusses developments within green political thinking in Chapter 11. Environmental degradation, transnational pollution and climate change have had a significant impact on the study of global politics. These issues have featured in studies of 'international regimes' with responsibility for environmental issues. Questions of global justice have been at the heart of discussions about the fair distribution between rich and poor and about moral responsibilities to reverse environmental harm. Obligations to non-human species and to future generations have been important themes in environmental ethics. Green political thought has criticized the dominant assumptions until the 1960s about infinite economic growth and the faith in the virtues of unbridled capitalism. Questions about the prospects for 'ecologically responsible' states and global environmental citizenship which have been discussed in recent green political thought have special relevance for students of international relations. These are some of the ways in which green political thought and practice have tried to reconfigure the study of international relations so that more attention is devoted to the long-term fate of the planet and the different lifeforms which inhabit it.

Finally in Chapter 12, Terry Nardin considers the recent impact of international political theory on contemporary theoretical debates in the theory of international relations. Drawing on debates within 'domestic' political theory, international political theory examines the political, philosophical and ethical basis of key concerns within international relations, including assumptions which underwrite the discussion of global justice, debates over what constitutes a just war, as well as disputes about the merits of humanitarian intervention. International political theory also reminds us about the history of international thought and the broader intellectual connections between political philosophy and international politics which have not always been properly acknowledged.

Most of the authors in this volume identify with one or other of the perspectives analysed in this book, but none argues that any one theory can solve the many problems which arise for theorists of international relations. We see merit in all the approaches surveyed, and we certainly believe it is essential to engage with all theoretical perspectives from the 'inside', to see the world from different theoretical vantage-points, to learn from them, to test one's own ideas against them and to think carefully about what others would regard as the vulnerabilities of one's perspective, whatever it may be. Those who teach the theory of international relations are sometimes asked 'what is the correct theory?'. We hope our readers will conclude there is no obviously correct theory which solves all the problems listed in this introduction and considered in more detail in the pages below. Some may concur with Martin Wight (1991) that the truth about international relations will not be found in any one of the traditions but in the continuing *dialogue and debate* between them. This is almost certainly the right attitude to adopt when approaching the study of international theory for the first time, and it may still be the best conclusion to draw from one's analysis.

# Realism

JACK DONNELLY

Political realism, *Realpolitik*, 'power politics', is the oldest and most frequently adopted theory of international relations.* Every serious student must not only acquire a deep appreciation of political realism but also understand how her own views relate to the realist tradition. Therefore, let me lay my cards on the table at the outset. Normatively, I rebel against the world depicted in realist theory and I reject realism as a prescriptive theory of foreign policy. Analytically, however, I am no more an anti-realist than I am a realist. Realism, I will argue, is a limited yet powerful and important approach to and set of insights about international relations.

Like most of the other theories or approaches considered in this volume, realism has two faces. On the one hand, it is a general orientation rooted in a central substantive focus – in this case, power. On the other hand, it is a body of explanatory theories, models, or propositions – in the case of realism, emphasizing anarchy and the balance of power. This chapter begins and concludes by looking at the general character of the realist approach. In between, the focus is on particular realist explanations.

Defining realism

Although definitions of realism differ in detail (see Donnelly 2000: 6–9; Cusack and Stoll 1990: Chapter 2), they share a clear family resemblance, 'a quite distinctive and recognizable flavour' (Garnett 1984: 110). Realists emphasize the constraints on politics imposed by human selfishness ('egoism') and the absence of international government

---

* Smith (1986) and Donnelly (2000) provide book-length introductions. Doyle (1997) and Wight (1992) consider realism in relation to two alternative traditions. Donnelly (1992), Forde (1992), Grieco (1997), Jervis (1998) and Wohlforth (2008) are representative single-chapter introductions. On the place of realism in the academic discipline of international studies see Donnelly (1995); Kahler (1997), Guzzini (1998), Schmidt (1998) and Vasquez (1998).

('anarchy'), which require 'the primacy in all political life of power and security' (Gilpin 1986: 305). Emblematic twentieth century figures include Reinhold Niebuhr, Hans Morgenthau, George Kennan, Kenneth Waltz, and John Mearsheimer in the United States and E. H. Carr in Britain. In the history of Western political thought, Niccolò Machiavelli and Thomas Hobbes are usually considered realists.

Rationality and state-centrism are frequently identified as core realist premises (e.g. Keohane 1986: 164–5; Lynn-Jones and Miller 1995: ix). But no (reasonably broad) theory of international relations presumes irrationality. And if we think of 'states' as a shorthand for polities or political 'units,' state-centrism is widely shared across international theories. The core or realism lies in the conjunction of anarchy and egoism and the resulting imperatives of power politics.

Realists recognize that human desires range widely and are remarkably variable. They emphasize, however, 'the limitations which the sordid and selfish aspects of human nature place on the conduct of diplomacy' (Thompson 1985: 20). 'It is above all important not to make greater demands on human nature than its frailty can satisfy' (Treitschke 1916: 590). As Machiavelli put it (1970: Book I, Chapter 3), in politics we must act as if 'all men are wicked and that they will always give vent to the malignity that is in their minds when opportunity offers'.

A few theorists (e.g. Niebuhr 1932; Tellis 1995/96: 89–94) adopt realism as a general theory of politics. Most, however, treat realism as a theory of *international* politics. This shifts our attention from human nature to political structure.

'The difference between civilization and barbarism is a revelation of what is essentially the same human nature when it works under different conditions' (Butterfield 1949: 31). Within states, egoism usually is substantially restrained by hierarchical political rule. In international relations, anarchy – the absence of government – allows, even encourages, the worst aspects of human nature to be expressed. As John Herz put it (1976: 10), anarchy assures the centrality of the struggle for power 'even in the absence of aggressivity or similar factors' (cf. Waltz 1979: 62–3). 'Structural realism' is the standard label for such realist accounts that give predominant emphasis to international anarchy. 'Neo-realism' is the other standard term, pointing towards an earlier generation of more complicated and eclectic realists.

These earlier 'classical realists,' without denying the centrality of anarchy, also emphasized human nature. For example, Morgenthau (1962: 7) argued that 'the social world [is] but a projection of human nature onto the collective plane' (cf. Niebuhr 1932: 23). Classical realists 'see that conflict is in part situationally explained, but . . . believe that even were it not so, pride, lust, and the quest for glory would cause the war of all against all to continue indefinitely. Ultimately, conflict and war are rooted in human nature' (Waltz 1991b: 35 . Classical realists also often emphasized the role of statesmanship and the analysis of the attributes of state power.

More recently, a new group of realists has staked out a third, somewhat intermediate approach, the combines analyses of structures and the internal attributes of states. These 'neo-classical realists' (Rose 1998; Schweller 2003) focus on the ways in which characteristic patterns of domestic political systems interact with international structural forces to produce state behaviour.

Realists can be further distinguished by the intensity and exclusivity of their commitment to core realist premises. Here we can think of a continuum of positions. 'Radical' realists exclude almost everything except power and self-interest from (international) politics. The Athenian envoys to Melos in Thucydides' *The Peloponnesian War* (Bk. V, ch. 85–113) express such a view, but it is held by few if any international theorists. 'Strong' realists stress the predominance of power, self-interest, and conflict but allow modest space for politically salient 'non-realist' forces and concerns. Niebuhr, Carr, Morgenthau, Waltz, and Mearsheimer, the leading realists of their generations, all lie in this range of the continuum. As Carr put it, 'we cannot ultimately find a resting place in pure realism' (1946: 89). 'Weak' or 'hedged' realists accept the realist analysis of the 'problems' of international politics but are open to a wider range of political possibilities and see more important elements of international relations lying outside the explanatory range of realism.

Weak realism gradually shades into something else. At some point (non-realist) 'hedges' outweigh the (realist) 'core.' Conversely, analysts operating from other perspectives may appeal to characteristically realist forces and explanations that 'hedge' their own theories.

Hobbes and classical realism

Chapter 13 of Thomas Hobbes' *Leviathan*, originally published in 1651, imagines politics in a pre-social state of nature. The result is an unusually clear theory that gives roughly equal weight to human nature and international anarchy.

The Hobbesian state of nature

Hobbes makes three simple assumptions:

1. Men are equal. (The language not only reflects standard seventeenth century usage but a deeply gendered, masculinist perspective, see Tickner 1988; Chapter 9.)
2. They interact in anarchy.
3. They are motivated by competition, diffidence, and glory.

The conjunction of these conditions leads to a war of all against all.

Men are equal in the elemental sense that 'the weakest has strength enough to kill the strongest, either by secret machination or by confederacy with others' (para. 1). 'From this equality of ability ariseth equality of hope in the attaining of our ends' (para. 3). I am as good as you are and thus ought to have (at least) as much as you. But scarcity prevents each from having as much as he desires – which makes men enemies.

Enmity is exacerbated by the passions of competition, diffidence, and glory. 'The first maketh men invade for gain; the second, for safety; and the third, for reputation' (para. 7). Even where one is not seeking gain, fear leads to defensive war, for 'there is no way for any man to secure himself so reasonable as anticipation' (para. 4). And every man's desire 'that his companion should value him at the same rate he sets upon himself' (para. 5) leads to conflict over reputation.

Add the absence of government and the mixture becomes volatile and vicious. 'During the time men live without a common power to keep them all in awe, they are in that condition which is called war; and such a war as is of every man against every man' (para. 8). Although fighting is not constant, any dispute may quickly degenerate into violence. As a result, human industry has little scope for operation 'and the life of man [is] solitary, poor, nasty, brutish, and short' (para. 10).

It is important to see that this state of war is a necessary logical consequence of the model. The Hobbesian logic of conflict can be evaded only if one or more of the model's assumptions either does not hold or is counter-balanced by other forces. For example, fundamental power inequalities may lead to imposed hierarchical order, which substantially mitigates conflict and violence. Even in anarchy, containing the pursuit of gain and glory would reduce the frequency or intensity of conflict, because diffidence leads to war primarily through fear of predation. Among countervailing forces, Hobbes identifies 'the passions that incline men to peace' and reason, which 'suggesteth convenient articles of peace upon which men may be drawn to agreement' (para. 14). He has little confidence, however, in their power to overcome the more egoistic passions, especially in the absence of government to enforce rules of cooperation.

Assessing Hobbesian realism

Hobbes acknowledges (para. 12) that such a savage state never existed across the entire globe. I would suggest that we go further and abandon any pretence at history or comparative anthropology. Hobbes, in this reading, identifies a logic of interaction, an ideal type model of pressures and tendencies. When equal actors interact in anarchy, driven by competition, diffidence, and glory, generalized violent conflict can be predicted.

Theory is artful abstraction. It directs our attention away from the welter of 'confusing details' towards what is 'most important.' Theories are beacons, lenses, filters that direct us to what, according to the theory, is essential for understanding (some part of) the world. Much as a good caricature selects, exaggerates and wilfully distorts in order to capture the defining features of its subject, a good theory intentionally oversimplifies in order to highlight forces that are typically central to behaviour.

The proper question, then, to pose of Hobbes' theory, or any theory, is not whether it accurately describes the world. Of course it doesn't; much, even most, of politics lies outside the scope of the theory. We should ask instead whether Hobbes' theoretical assumptions help us to understand important elements of international politics.

Hobbes' belief that human nature is naturally given and largely unalterable certainly is contentious. Most analysts, however, would agree that the prevalence of competition, diffidence, and glory is sufficiently frequent and central to make it an often fruitful simplifying assumption.

As for anarchy, the fact that it has been largely overcome by hierarchical political rule within most states actually increases the likelihood that it will persist internationally. Even vicious and inefficient governments usually provide considerable security for the lives and property of their citizens. This dramatically reduces the pressures to replace the international state of nature with international government. Because neither states nor their subjects face a life that is solitary, poor, nasty, brutish, and short, international anarchy is much more tolerable than its domestic counterpart. It also reflects the strong desire of states and their citizens for autonomy, expressed in contemporary practices of state sovereignty.

The assumption of equality is in some ways the most problematic aspect of the Hobbes model. Material inequality regularly leads to hierarchy and inequality in forms such as bilateral relations of domination, spheres of influence, hegemony, and empire. But among 'great powers' – states with the capacity to inflict punishing damage, even the threat of death, on any other power in the system – the Hobbesian assumption of equality holds. (Note that this suggests that (Hobbesian) realism is a theory of great power politics, rather than a general theory of international relations. Relations between fundamentally unequal powers would be governed by another logic of interaction.)

Each of Hobbes' assumptions thus would seem to be applicable to important parts of international relations. The crucial question is the extent to which other factors and forces push in different directions. How much of international relations, in what circumstances, is governed by the Hobbesian conjunction of anarchy, egoism, and equality? To use social scientific jargon, what are the relative impacts of 'endogenous variables' (factors included within the theory) and 'exogenous variables' (those not included)? We will return, recurrently, to this question as we proceed.

Waltz and structural realism

Hobbes' 'classical' realism gives roughly equal emphasis to anarchy and egoism. Most realist work in the past three decades, by contrast, has been more or less rigorously structural, largely as a result of the influence of Kenneth Waltz.

Waltzian structuralism

Structural realism aims to set aside those features of international relations that depend on the character of the actors or the nature of their interactions in order to highlight the constraining impact of the structure of the international system in which they are embedded. Political structures, Waltz argues, are defined by their ordering principle (How are units related to one another?), differentiation of functions (How are political functions allocated?), and distribution of capabilities (How is power distributed?).

Hierarchy and anarchy, which Waltz associates with domestic and international politics respectively, are the two principal political ordering principles. Units either stand in relationships of authority and subordination (hierarchy) or they do not (anarchy). Striking qualitative differences exist 'between politics conducted in a condition of settled rules and politics conducted in a condition of anarchy' (Waltz 1979: 61). Some of those differences are the focus of the following sub-sections.

Anarchy, Waltz contends, largely eliminates functional differentiation between the units. In anarchic/international orders, every unit must 'put itself in a position to be able to take care of itself since no one else can be counted on to do so' (1979: 107). Differences between states 'are of capability, not function' (1979: 96). 'National politics consists of differentiated units performing specified functions. International politics consists of like units duplicating one another's activities' (1979: 97).

If all international orders are anarchic, and if this implies minimal functional differentiation, then international political structures differ only in their distributions of capabilities. They are defined by the changing fates of great powers. More abstractly, international orders vary according to the number of great powers; that is, the polarity (number of poles of power) of the system.

Balancing

The central theoretical conclusion of structural realism is that in anarchy states 'balance' rather than 'bandwagon' (Waltz 1979: 126). In hierarchic political orders, actors tend to 'jump on the bandwagon' of a leading candidate or recent victor, because 'losing does not place their security in jeopardy' (Waltz 1979: 126). 'Bandwagoners' attempt to increase their gains (or reduce their losses) by siding with the stronger party. In anarchy, however, bandwagoning courts disaster by strengthening someone who later may turn on you. The power of others – especially great power – is always a threat when there is no government to turn to for protection. 'Balancers' attempt to reduce their risk by opposing a stronger or rising power.

Weak states have little choice but to guess right and hope that early alignment with the victor will bring favourable treatment. Only foolish great powers, however, would accept such a risk. Instead, they will balance, both internally, by reallocating resources to national security, and externally, through alliances and other (formal and informal) agreements.

Structural pressures to balance explain important yet otherwise puzzling features of international relations. Consider Soviet-American relations. The United States opposed the Russian Revolution and for two decades remained implacably hostile to the Soviet Union. Nonetheless, the rise of Hitler's Germany propelled the US and the USSR into alliance in World War II. Notwithstanding their intense internal differences and history of animosity, they balanced against a common threat. After the war, the US and the Soviet Union again became adversaries. In this version of the story, though, internal and ideological differences did not cause renewed rivalry (although they may have increased its virulence and influenced its form). Enmity was structurally induced. In a bipolar world, each superpower is the only serious threat to the security of the other. Each, whatever its preferences or inclinations, must balance against the other.

The Cold War, in this account, was not 'caused' by anyone but was the 'natural' result of bipolarity. Soviet expansion into Central and Eastern Europe arose from neither vicious rulers in the Kremlin nor rabid anti-communists in Washington. It was the normal behaviour of a

country that had been invaded from the west, with devastating consequences, twice in 25 years, in addition to the invasion a century earlier.
Cold War conflicts in Southeast Asia, Central America, and Southern
Africa likewise were not part of a global communist conspiracy but
rather ordinary efforts by a great power to increase its international
influence.

This example suggests a very important interpretative point. Realism
provides a theoretical account of how the world works. It can be used for
peaceful purposes – there are a number of Quaker realists – as well as for
war. For example, hundreds of thousands of lives might have been saved,
and millions of injuries avoided, had the United States pursued a realist
bipolar rivalry with the Soviet Union rather than an ideological Cold
War. Leading realists such as Niebuhr and Morgenthau were early and
vocal critics of the war in Vietnam. Robert Tucker (1985) opposed the
Reagan administration's support of armed counter-revolution in
Nicaragua. And not a single prominent realist supported the American
invasion of Iraq in 2003.

Prisoners' Dilemma, relative gains, and cooperation

Anarchy and egoism greatly impede cooperation. Prisoners' Dilemma
offers a standard formal representation of this logic. Imagine two criminal colleagues taken in separately by the police for questioning. Each
is offered a favourable plea bargain in return for testimony against the
other. Without a confession, though, they can only be convicted of a
lesser crime. Each must choose between cooperating (remaining silent)
and defecting (testifying against the other). Imagine also that both have
the following preference ordering: (1) confess while the other remains
silent; (2) both remain silent; (3) both confess; and (4) remain silent
while the other confesses. Assume finally that their aversion to risk
takes a particular form: they want to minimize their maximum possible
loss.

If both cooperate (remain silent) both receive their second choice
payoff (conviction on the lesser charge). But cooperation leaves each
vulnerable to the worst possible outcome (serving a long prison term –
and knowing that your partner put you there). Each can assure against
disaster by confessing (defecting). The rational choice thus is to defect
(confess) *even though both know that they both could be better off by
cooperating*. Both end up with their third choice, because this is the only
way to assure that each avoids the worst possible outcome.

Conflict here does not arise from any special defect in the actors. They
are mildly selfish but not particularly evil or vicious. Far from desiring
conflict, both prefer cooperation. They are neither ignorant nor ill

informed. In an environment of anarchy, even those capable of mastering their own desires for gain and glory may be pushed by fear towards treating everyone else as an enemy.

Anarchy, in other words, can defeat even our best intentions – which realists see as rare enough to begin with. Without insurance schemes that reduce the risk of cooperating, and without procedures to determine how to divide the gains, even those who want to cooperate may remain locked in a vicious cycle of mutually destructive competition. For example, states may engage in not merely costly but counter-productive arms races because arms control agreements cannot be independently verified.

Herbert Butterfield calls this 'Hobbesian fear.' 'If you imagine yourself locked in a room with another person with whom you have often been on the most bitterly hostile terms in the past, and suppose that each of you has a pistol, you may find yourself in a predicament in which both of you would like to throw the pistols out of the window, yet it defeats the intelligence to find a way of doing it' (1949: 89–90). The 'security dilemma' (see esp. Glaser 1997) has a similar logic. 'Given the irreducible uncertainty about the intentions of others, security measures taken by one actor are perceived by others as threatening; the others take steps to protect themselves; these steps are then interpreted by the first actor as confirming its initial hypothesis that the others are dangerous; and so on in a spiral of illusory fears and "unnecessary" defences' (Snyder 1997: 17).

Anarchic pressures towards balancing and against cooperation are reinforced by the relativity of power. Power is control over outcomes, 'the ability to do or effect something' (*Oxford English Dictionary*). It is less a matter of absolute resources – how much 'stuff' one has – than of relative capabilities. Facing an unarmed man, a tank is pretty powerful. The same tank facing a squadron of carrier-based attack jets is not very powerful at all.

The relativity of power requires states to 'be more concerned with relative strength than with absolute advantage' (Waltz 1979: 106). Bandwagoning seeks absolute gains, aligning early with a rising power to gain a share of the profits of victory. Balancing pursues relative gains.

Actors who focus on relative gains, however, will find it much more difficult to cooperate. One must consider not only whether one gains but, more importantly, whether one's gains outweigh those of others (who, in anarchy, must be seen as potential adversaries). Even predatory cooperation is problematic unless it maintains the relative capabilities of the cooperating parties. In fact, states may be satisfied with conflicts that leave them absolutely worse off – so long as their adversaries are left even worse off.

Polarity

The preceding two sub-sections have considered some of the theoretical implications of anarchy, the ordering principle of international relations. If, following Waltz, we see minimal functional differentiation in anarchic orders, then the other principal contribution of structural realism should lie in its analysis of the impact of the distribution of capabilities. How does polarity, the number of great powers in a system, influence international relations?

Unipolarity has become a hot topic since the end of the Cold War. Waltzian balancing logic (Layne 1993; Mastanduno 1997) suggests that unipolarity is unstable. Balancing will facilitate the rise of new great powers, much as a rising hegemon (e.g. Napoleonic France) provokes a 'grand coalition' that unites the other great powers. Other theorists, however, argue that this expectation is overly simplistic (Wohlforth 1999). And recent comparative empirical work suggests that failures to balance against a rising hegemon are at least as common as balancing (Hui 2005; Kaufman, Little and Wohlforth 2007; Wohlforth *et al.* 2007). But whatever its frequency or resilience, unipolarity (and resistance to it) gives international relations a very different character from systems with two or more great powers.

Recent talk of American hegemony has also led to greater attention to an alternative stream of realist analysis that was overshadowed by the turn to structuralism. Robert Gilpin in *War and Change in World Politics* (1981) developed a model of hegemonic rise and fall. 'Power Transition Theory,' associated particularly with A. F. K. Organski and Jacek Kugler (e.g. Organski and Kugler 1980) has also stressed hegemonic rise and fall and the central dynamic in international relations. (For a survey of the development of the power transition literature, see DiCicco and Levy 1999.)

Schweller (1998) has shown that tripolar systems have a distinctive structural logic. And systems with very many or no great powers – the two are effectively equivalent – have a different structural logic than multipolar systems with a few (four, five, or a couple more) great powers. Whereas systems with a one, two, three, or a few great powers are monopolistic or oligopolistic, those with many or no great powers are more like competitive markets.

Most of the attention, however, has focused on the differences between bipolar and multipolar orders. For example, conflicts in the periphery pose little threat to the general bipolar balance. In multipolar systems, where power is divided among more actors, a change in the periphery of the same absolute magnitude may have a noticeable impact on the general balance. The significance of such a difference, however, is obscure. Should peripheral conflicts be more frequent in bipolar systems because they are less destabilizing and thus 'safer' (for the great powers)? Or should they be less frequent because there are no compelling reasons to become involved?

There is thus considerable disagreement over the relative stability of bipolar and multipolar systems. The classic mid-1960s accounts of Waltz (1964), Deutsch and Singer (1964), and Rosecrance (1966) argue, respectively, for bipolarity, multipolarity, and 'bi-multipolarity' (both/neither). More recent and more sophisticated accounts try to incorporate, for example, the impact of different forms of alignment (Christensen and Snyder 1990) and changes across time in the distribution of capabilities (Copeland 1996). Unfortunately, empirical tests are constrained by the fact that in 2,500 years of Western history there have been as few as four bipolar systems (Athens-Sparta in the fifth century BCE, Carthage-Rome in the third century BCE, the Hapsburg-Bourbon rivalry in the sixteenth century, and the US–USSR).

The nature of structural predictions

Part of the problem with the debate on the relative stability of bipolar and multipolar orders is that posing the question in structural terms is probably misguided. For example, a rising 'revisionist' or 'revolutionary' power with a high propensity for risk poses very different problems than a risk-averse, satisfied, 'status quo' power. Such considerations fall outside the scope of structural theory. If their effects characteristically are as great or greater than those of polarity, there can be no answer to the (structural) question of the relative stability of bipolar and multipolar orders.

Structures push states in certain directions. They do not mechanically determine outcomes. States are also subject to numerous other pressures and influences – which often are decisive in determining outcomes. This does not make polarity or anarchy unimportant. It just happens that other forces sometimes are more powerful – and, as a result, structural expectations are likely to be misleading, or simply wrong.

The predictions of structural realism are, as Waltz repeatedly notes, 'indeterminate' (1979: 124, 122, 71; 1986: 343). They identify forces that press in particular directions. It is the job of the analyst, not the theorist, to determine where a particular theoretical logic applies in the world. Whether a 'good theory,' in the sense of a rigorous logic of interaction, is a 'good' theory to apply in any particular case depends not on the theory but on contingent facts about the world.

We can thus identify three types of theoretical failures. If a predicted outcome does not occur because the assumptions of the theory are not satisfied in the case under consideration, the 'failure' is entirely attribut-able to the analyst. If the underlying assumptions are satisfied but the predicted results do not occur, the failure is attributable to the theory. The most interesting situation, however, is when the theoretically predicted pressures operate but are overwhelmed by other forces.

The significance of this third type of theoretical 'failure' depends on which exogenous variables prevail, how often, and in what kinds of cases. We will also want to know how powerful those exogenous forces must be to overcome the effects of the endogenous variables. If endoge-nous variables almost always hold up against all but the strongest expres-sions of a few exogenous variables, the theory is relatively powerful. If a wide range of relatively weak exogenous variables regularly swamp the endogenous variables, the theory is not exactly 'wrong' – the predicted pressures do still operate – but it is not very useful.

Every theory must make simplifying assumptions. Fruitful assump-tions abstract from factors that are typically less important to determin-ing outcomes than those highlighted by the theory. Many of the disagreements between realists and their critics can be seen as, in effect, disputes about the frequency and significance of realism's failures, and what type of failures they are.

Motives matter

How far we can go with purely structural theories; that is, with anarchy, the distribution of capabilities, and nothing else? Not very far.

Abstracting from versus assuming motives

Waltz claims to 'abstract from every attribute of states except their capa-bilities' (1979: 99) and talks of 'units,' abstract, characterless concentra-tions of capabilities. In fact, however, his theory, by his own admission, 'is based on assumptions about states,' 'built up from the assumed moti-vations of states' (1996: 54; 1979: 118). There is a huge difference between abstracting from all particulars and assuming certain ones. And the substance of realist assumptions about states accounts for much of the distinctive character of the theory.

Hobbes' war of all against all arises not from anarchy alone but also from equal individuals driven by competition, diffidence, and glory. Homeric heroes seeking fame through great deeds, Nietzschean indi-viduals driven by a will to power, and *homo economicus* may behave very differently in the same anarchic structure. As Butterfield puts it, 'wars would hardly be likely to occur if all men were Christian saints, competing with one another in nothing, perhaps, save self-renunciation' (Butterfield 1979: 73).

Even Waltz, despite repeated claims to the contrary, admits this. 'Structurally we can describe and understand the pressures states are subject to. We cannot predict how they will react to the pressures without knowledge of their internal dispositions' (1979: 71). To abstract from all attributes of states (other than capabilities) leaves the theory no predictive power. Thus in practice Waltz, like other realists, relies heavily on knowledge of or assumptions about the interests and intentions of states.

This would not be seriously problematic if Waltz had a clear and coherent account of state motivation. He does claim that states 'are unitary actors with a single motive – the wish to survive' (1996: 54). Unfortunately, though, Waltz also allows that 'some states may persistently seek goals that they value more highly than survival' (1979: 92). He then goes on to argue that states seek wealth, advantage, and flourishing (1979: 112; 1986: 337; 1993: 54), peaceful coexistence (1979: 144), peace and prosperity (1979: 144, 175), and sovereignty, autonomy, and independence (1979: 204, 107, 104), as well as acting out of pride and feeling put upon (1993: 66, 79). And, as if this were not enough, he claims that states 'at minimum, seek their own preservation and, at maximum, drive for universal domination' (1979: 118) – which rules out little beyond charity and beneficence.

(Re-)Incorporating the State

Over the past two decades, realists have adopted three principal strategies to incorporate motives in ways that make their predictions more determinate yet rigorous. The first major move was made by Stephen Walt (1987) who, empirically examining alliance behaviour, concluded that states balance not against power but against threat. Consider, for example, the very different American behaviour towards British, French, and Chinese (or Israeli, Indian, and North Korean) nuclear arsenals, which weigh about equally in the global distribution of capabilities. Unfortunately, realism has had very little to say about threats. And structural realism in principle has nothing to say about threat (as opposed to capabilities), leaving the crucial explanatory variable outside the scope of the theory.

A second strategy has been to make consistent, precise, and determinate motivational assumptions. Survival and domination can be seen as extreme statements of defensive and expansive orientations. Modelling states as driven by one or the other leads to what are typically called defensive and offensive realism (e.g. Lynn-Jones 1995; Labs 1997: 7–17;

Zakaria 1998: 25–42; Taliaferro 2000, 2001; Snyder 2002). In effect, the distinction drawn by many classical realists between status quo or satisfied and revolutionary or revisionist powers has been revived and given a largely structural twist.

On the defensive realist side, Michael Mastanduno argues that 'realists expect nation-states to avoid gaps that favour their partners, but not necessarily to maximize gaps in their own favour. Nation-states are not 'gap maximizers.' They are, in Joseph Grieco's terms, 'defensive positionalists' (Mastanduno 1991: 79 n. 13). John Mearsheimer, the leading exponent of offensive realism, however, argues that 'states seek to survive under anarchy by maximizing their power relative to other states' (1990: 12). His states are 'short-term power maximizers' (1995: 82); that is, *offensive* positionalists. As Fareed Zakaria puts it, 'the best solution to the perennial problem of the uncertainty of international life is for a state to increase its control over that environment through the persistent expansion of its political interests abroad' (1998: 20).

Note, however, that it is an empirical, not a theoretical, question whether states are defensive or offensive positionalists. And the historical record clearly shows examples of both. Therefore, it would be foolish to simply 'be' an offensive realist or a defensive realist. There may be good reasons to reach first for one model or the other, either in general or in particular types of circumstances. For example, Mearsheimer's *The Tragedy of Great Power Politics* (2001) might be read as an effort to explain, through the logic of anarchy, how and why offensive motivations characteristically take priority in the behaviour of great powers. But both have some potential value and need to be available to analysts as potentially useful tools.

The third strategy, which has generated some of the most innovative and interesting recent work within the realist tradition, has been to supplement rather than refine structural realism. Neo-classical realists have in effect argued that purely structural theory, no matter how sophisticated, rarely produces sufficiently determinate predictions to offer adequate understanding. 'States often react differently to similar systemic pressures and opportunities, and their responses may be less motivated by systemic-level factors than domestic ones' (Schweller 2006: 6). Realists, therefore, must 'open up' the state, which in structural theories is treated as a 'black box'.

The neo-classical project is to investigate patterns in state behaviour that interact with structural forces. For example, Jack Snyder (1991) has examined the domestic political forces and processes that lead states not to rational balancing but reckless imperial over-reach. Randall Schweller (2006: Chapter 2), by looking at variables such as elite cohesion and regime stability, has developed five 'causal schemes' that seek to predict when states will balance in Waltzian (or Waltian) ways and when they are likely to 'underbalance.'

Waltz is content to say a 'small number of big and important things' (1986: 329; cf. 1979: 70) about (all) international systems. Neo-classical realists want to be able to say more things. And they are interested in patterns that apply only in particular types of systems or circumstances. Neo-classical realists thus are willing to give up the simplicity and generality of structural theories in return not just for greater depth and detail but a much wider range of coverage.

System and structure

Making assumptions about the motives of states does not necessarily remove a theory from the set of systems theories. To appreciate this, we need to distinguish between units and levels of analysis: that is, between the thing (unit) to be explained and the (analytical level of the) thing that explains. The state, for example, is the standard unit of analysis in realist theories, which characteristically seek to explain state behaviour. State behaviour, however, may be explained at the level of the state (e.g. national history or ideology), at the system level (e.g. anarchy induces a balancing pursuit of relative gains), or the individual level (e.g. the impact of a particular national leader).

Neo-classical realism self-consciously combines system-level and state-level explanatory variables. Most versions of offensive and defensive realism, by contrast, are largely or exclusively structural. There is another type of structural option, however, that has been ignored or rejected by realists: rather than treat all state motives as determined at the unit level, universal, or simply matters of assumption, we could look for system-level forces that *variably* shape the behaviour of the unit.

The most striking example is Alexander Wendt's (1999: Chapter 6) demonstration that anarchic orders function very differently when actors see each other as 'enemies' out to destroy each other, 'rivals' who compete but do not threaten each others' survival, and 'friends' who have renounced force in their relations. Realism in effect becomes a special case; what Wendt calls the 'Hobbesian' anarchy of enemies. Sovereignty, understood as rights to territorial integrity and political independence, transforms relations into those among 'Lockean' rivals, with the rivalry having been substantially moderated by the abolition of aggressive war.

There are at least two ways to read such a move. We might want to expand the conception of structure to include unit type (e.g. Kaufman 1997: 181–5; Reus-Smit 1999). Alternatively, we might want to keep a narrow definition of structure but refuse to follow Waltz in collapsing system theory into structural theory. Both options, but especially the second, suggest additional directions for expanding the range of realist thinking.

A system is a bounded space defined by: (a) units that interact differently, and usually much more intensively, with each other than with those outside the system; (b) the structure within which they interact; and (c) the characteristic interactions of the units within that structure. System-level patterns in the processes of state interaction have the promise for providing much richer and more determinate realist theories.

Process formations

Glenn Snyder has suggested greater attention to what he calls 'process variables,' patterns of interaction that are neither structural nor at the level of the unit; that is, are systemic but not structural. Operating largely (although not entirely) outside the realist framework, Barry Buzan and Richard Little talk similarly about 'process formations' (Buzan and Little 2000: 79, 379; cf. Buzan, Jones and Little 1993: 48–50) a slightly more felicitous term.

Snyder (1997) has developed this idea particularly in relation to alliance politics. Consider alignment. As a rough first approximation, states can be seen to stand in relations of amity or enmity, seeing themselves as allies or adversaries. This has systematic consequences. For example, states are more likely to balance against adversaries than allies. Conversely, relative gains considerations may be substantially muted among allies, as illustrated by U.S. support for European integration in the 1950s and 1960s.

Both allies and adversaries may have common or competing interests, which also help to make predictions more determinate. Common interests facilitate cooperation – although anarchy and relative gains always cut against successful cooperation. Conversely, competing interests may impede or prevent balancing against a common enemy.

Waltzian structural realism allows us only to predict *that* balances will form. Taking alignment, interests, and other process variables into account allows us to predict which particular balances are likely or unlikely to develop. 'If, as Waltz says, system structures only 'shape and shove,' [process variables] give a more decided push' (Snyder 1997: 32).

The cost, however, as with neo-classical realism, is greater complexity and less generality. Structure influences all states. Particular process variables influence only some parts of the system.

Parsimony and scope are great theoretical virtues; to explain everything with a single variable is the theorist's utopia. It is important that we appreciate the attractions of Waltz' ability to say some important things about international relations, more or less anywhere and any time, based only on anarchy and the distribution of capabilities. Such a theory, within the domain of its operation, has considerable power. Snyder, however, argues – correctly in my view – that Waltz is guilty of 'excessive parsimony, in the sense that the explanatory gain from some further elaboration would exceed the costs in reduced generality' (1996: 167).

This does not, however, sacrifice system-level theorizing. Alignment, for example, is about the *distribution* of amity and enmity and thus no less systemic than the distribution of capabilities. The system level of theorizing is not restricted to structure (which is only one of the defining elements of a system).

Norms, institutions, and identities

Snyder (1996: 169) also identifies what he calls structural modifiers, 'system-wide influences that are structural in their inherent nature but not potent enough internationally to warrant that description'. He looks at military technology and norms and institutions. On the role of military technology, consider, for example, the special character of nuclear weapons, which Waltz (however inconsistently) uses to explain the Cold War peace between the superpowers (1990), or the impact of the relative advantage of offensive or defensive forces on conflict and the propensity to war (e.g. Glaser and Kaufmann 1998; Van Evera 1998). Here I will briefly consider norms and institutions.

Norms and institutions are clearly structural in domestic society. 'They create the hierarchy of power and differentiation of function that are the hallmarks of a well-ordered domestic polity, but that are present only rudimentarily in international society. In principle, they are also structural internationally' (Snyder 1996: 169).

As both this quote and the earlier reference to potency make clear, the actual impact of international norms and institutions is an empirical, not a theoretical, question. Shared values and institutions may in particular cases shape and shove actors even more strongly than (Waltzian) structure. Consider not only the European Union but also the Nordic countries and the US–Canadian relationship. The literature on pluralistic security communities (e.g. Adler and Barnett 1998) emphasizes the potential impact of institutions, values, and identities even in the high politics of international security.

Even at the global level, norms and institutions can have considerable influence. Sovereignty and other rights of states are a matter of mutual recognition, not capabilities. Power alone will not even tell us which of their rights states actually enjoy. It simply is untrue that, as the Athenians at Melos put it, 'the strong do what they can, the weak suffer what they must' (Thucydides: V.89). The strong often are constrained by the rights of even weak states. They may, of course, violate the rules of sovereignty. But predictions based on, say, the norm of non-intervention are no more 'indeterminate' than those based on anarchy or polarity. It is an empirical not a theoretical question whether the logic of rights or the logic of power more frequently accounts for international behaviour. And, whatever the general pattern, if a logic of rights matters more in any particular instance, that is the essential point. Our analytical framework should not hide this fact from us.

Consider also the principle of self-determination, which played a central role in creating scores of new, usually weak, states. Most post-colonial states have survived not through their own power or the power of allies but because of international recognition. Their survival – which offensive realists in particular must find inexplicable – has been further enhanced by the effective abolition of 'aggressive' war in the second half of the twentieth century.

Pursuing this line of analysis leads us well into the weak or hedged range of the realist spectrum – or off the scale altogether. Snyder clearly is a realist: he emphasizes anarchy and the struggle for power and is generally sceptical of the power of norms and institutions. But his approach is unusually open.

The typical realist approach is much more sceptical of norms and institutions, as suggested by titles like *The False Promise of International Institutions* (Mearsheimer 1994/95) and *Sovereignty: Organized Hypocrisy* (Krasner 1999). Institutions and norms are treated as largely reducible to the material interests of the powerful. They are at best 'intervening variables' that can be expected to have independent effects only in minor issue areas far removed from the struggle for power. (An interesting, but little explored, alternative is represented by the effort of Randall Schweller and David Priess (1997) to theorize institutions from within a realist framework.)

Realists are a bit less reluctant to talk about identities – although usually this seems to be done unwittingly. This is most evident in the classical realist distinction between status quo and revisionist powers or the parallel split between offensive and defensive structural realists. But there are many other examples. 'Great power' signifies not merely unparalleled material capabilities but also a managerial role in international society (Simpson 2004; Waltz 1979: Chapter 9; Bull 1977: Chapter 9) and an identity type. Balance of power is also a complex set of institutions (Gulick 1967; Bull 1977: Chapter 4; Cronin 1999: Chapter 1) The sovereign territorial state is a particular system-wide construction of 'unit' identity (Cronin 1999; Reus-Smit 1999).

Structural realists, however, have no theoretical basis for incorporating identity. Like Waltz on state motivation, identity conceptions are implicitly, and illicitly, incorporated into an analysis that presents itself in different terms. (Neo-) classical realists do have theoretical space for identity and institutional roles, but few have pursued the issue systematically. One notable exception is Schweller's work on revisionist powers (1994; 1999: 18–23), which aims to meld structural, motivational, and identity elements into a coherent and rigorous realist account.

Constancy and change

Identities, institutions, and norms are important for our purposes here not so much because they are central concerns of most realists but because they represent the principal points of substantive divergence between realist and other approaches in contemporary international theory. They also indirectly raise the issue of change. A standard complaint about realism is its inability to comprehend fundamental change in international relations. The implications of this charge, however, are less damning than critics often imagine.

Realism is a theory 'tuned' to explaining constancy. Realists are more impressed by the repeated occurrence of certain patterns across time than by the undeniable historical and cultural diversity of actors and interactions in international relations. They emphasize constancy not accidentally but by self-conscious theoretical choice. Although others may not share this judgement, it is one about which reasonable people may reasonably disagree.

The failure of realism to account for the end of the Cold War is a large part of the explanation of its declining popularity over the past 15 years. Ironically, though, realists can fairly claim that they never attempted to explain change. They can even note that no other theory of international relations did a better job. Everyone was caught by surprise. It is understandable that dramatic change is held up against a theory that emphasizes constancy. But whatever kind of failure it represents is shared by all other prominent theories of international relations.

Morality and foreign policy

In popular and foreign policy discussions, 'realist' most frequently refers to arguments against pursuing international moral objectives. Although in principle simply a special case of the broader issue of norms and institutions, the place of morality in foreign policy has been a central concern of the classical realist tradition. It is also an issue of vital substantive importance. Therefore, it is well worth discussion here, even though it has been a peripheral concern of academic realists over the past three decades, whose concerns have been more scientific and scholarly.

Do states pursue moral objectives?

The subordination of morality to power often is presented as a descriptive statement of the facts of international political life. 'The actions of states are determined not by moral principles and legal commitments but by considerations of interest and power' (Morgenthau 1970: 382). 'States in anarchy cannot afford to be moral. The possibility of moral behaviour rests upon the existence of an effective government that can deter and punish illegal actions' (Art and Waltz 1983: 6).

Such claims are obviously false. Just as individuals may behave morally in the absence of government enforcement of moral rules, states often can and do act out of moral concerns. Consider, for example, the outpouring of international aid in the wake of the Indian Ocean tsunami and other natural and political disasters.

It simply is not true, of either men or states, that they 'never do good unless necessity drives them to it,' that 'all do wrong to the same extent when there is nothing to prevent them doing wrong' (Machiavelli 1970: Book I, ch. 2, 58). States sometimes, even frequently, value compliance with ethical and humanitarian norms for reasons that have little or nothing to do with the threat of coercive enforcement. And even when states do violate norms because of the absence of enforcement, the independent ethical force of an infringed norm frequently is a significant part of the normative calculus of both the state acting and those who judge it.

The costs of compliance and violation

Even in anarchy, coercive enforcement is possible at times, most obviously through self-help. Furthermore, mechanisms exist to induce, even when they cannot compel, compliance. Public opinion, both national and international, can be a powerful force – as can be the persuasion of friends, allies, and interested parties. In some cases, the power and authority of intergovernmental institutions may be significant. More generally, international law, which includes some obligations that are also moral obligations, is no more frequently violated than domestic law. In any case, violations typically do have costs for states (although not always sufficiently high costs to compel compliance).

Realists rightly emphasize that a powerful state bent on violating a moral or legal norm usually can get away with it – and that when it can't, that usually is because of the power of other states. Nonetheless, states do sometimes comply with moral norms both for their own sake and out of consideration of the costs of noncompliance. As a matter of fact, states regularly conclude that in some instances they *can* afford to be moral, despite international anarchy.

For example, humanitarian interventions in Kosovo, East Timor, and Darfur, however tardy and limited, simply cannot be understood without the independent normative force of the anti-genocide norm and humanitarian principles. Such normative concerns rarely are the sole motive behind foreign policy action. Often, though, they are an important element of the calculus. And few significant foreign policy actions reflect just a single self-interested motive. Foreign policy is driven by the intersection of multiple motives, some of which are ethical in a large number of countries.

Pursuing moral objectives such as spreading democracy or combating preventable childhood diseases certainly may be costly. But no political goals can be achieved without cost. Just as the cost of pursuing economic objectives is no basis for excluding economic interests from foreign policy, the costs of pursuing moral objectives do not justify categorically excluding them from foreign policy agendas. The proper course is to weigh the costs and benefits of pursuing any and all relevant interests, moral and non-moral interests alike. Moral values are indeed values and therefore must be taken into account in any truly reasonable and realistic political calculus. Thus even Mearsheimer allows that 'there are good reasons to applaud the 1978 Vietnamese invasion of Cambodia, since it drove the murderous Pol Pot from power' (1994/95: 31).

Realists often suggest that ordinary citizens and even politicians, especially in democracies, tend to underestimate the costs of – and thus overestimate the space available for – the pursuit of moral interests. But to the extent this is true, most non-realists would offer the same criticisms. There is nothing distinctively realist about insisting that foreign policy should be based on a rational calculation of costs and benefits.

Realism as a prescriptive theory

Perhaps the strongest realist arguments appeal to the nature of states and statesmanship. The doctrine of *raison d'état* (reason(s) of state) holds that 'where international relations are concerned, the interests of the state predominate over all other interests and values' (Haslam 2002: 12). Because the 'primary obligation' of any government 'is to the *interests* of the national society it represents,' 'the same moral concepts are no longer relevant to it' (Kennan 1954: 48; 1985/86: 206). Morgenthau thus talks about 'the autonomy of politics' (1948/1954/1973: 12; 1962: 3).

Such arguments, however, are ethical arguments. They concern *which* values are appropriate in international relations, not whether foreign policy is appropriately subject to normative evaluation. 'Power politics may be defined as a system of international relations in which groups consider themselves to be ultimate ends' (Schwarzenberger 1951: 13). Thus Morgenthau talks of 'the moral dignity of the national interest' (1951: 33). Joel Rosenthal's social history of post-war American realists is nicely titled *Righteous Realists* (1991).

There is also a central ethical dimension to realist arguments that different standards apply to the public actions of national leaders and the actions of private individuals (e.g. Carr 1939/1945/1946: 151; Thompson 1985: 8; Kennan 1954: 48). 'Unlike the solitary individual who may claim the right to judge political action by universal ethical guidelines, the statesman will always make his decision on the basis of the state's interest' (Russell 1990: 51). Like other professionals, statesmen have a professional obligation to give priority to the interests of their 'clients.' Much as a defence lawyer is ethically bound to (within certain limits) give an aggressive defence to a guilty client, and a doctor (within certain limits) is required to do what is best for her patient rather than society as a whole, so a statesman is, by the nature of her office, required to do what is best for her state and its interests. The resulting foreign policy, however, although 'amoral' in the sense that it is not shaped or directly judged by the principles of ordinary morality, is neither 'value free' nor beyond ethical or other normative limits.

It may be true that when national survival is at stake, responsible national leaders have no choice but to abandon all other considerations, including morality. Even most moralists would agree with Machiavelli that 'when the safety of one's country wholly depends on the decision to be taken, no attention should be paid either to justice or injustice' (1970: Book 1, ch. 41). But such an argument applies no less against non-moral objectives, such as pursuing economic interests and supporting an ally. And survival rarely is at stake in international relations.

It simply is not true that 'the struggle for power is identical with the struggle for survival' (Spykman 1942: 18). Neither is it true that 'the system forces states to behave according to the dictates of realism, or risk destruction' (Mearsheimer 1995: 91). Many moral foreign policy objectives pose no risk to national survival. And other national interests simply do not have the ethical priority of survival. Much as a lawyer who learns that her client is planning to commit a murder ordinarily is required to breach client confidentiality, the ethical obligations of the statesman to the national interest sometimes must be balanced against other norms and values.

There is no compelling theoretical reason why a state should not place a high value on, for example, fighting communism, Islamo-fascism, or world poverty. Appeals to *raison d'état* and statesmanship cannot determine what interests the state has or ought to have. 'The national interest' is what the term manifestly indicates, namely, those interests/values that are held by the nation. The insistence of some realists (e.g. Morgenthau 1948/1954/1973: 5, 10) that states define their interest in terms of power reflects a deeply contentious, and descriptively inaccurate, prescriptive theory of foreign policy.

Morality and moralism

Realists certainly are correct to criticize 'moralism', the belief that international relations can appropriately be judged *solely* by conventional moral norms. But few if any serious theorists or activists have actually believed that. Even the inter-war peace activists that realists pejoratively dismiss as idealists in fact usually held far more sophisticated views (Lynch 1999).

To the extent that there is a tendency toward moralism in foreign policy, especially in the United States, realists may offer a healthy corrective. It might have been scandalous, 500 years ago, for Machiavelli to argue that a good statesman must 'learn to be able not to be good, and to use this and not use it according to necessity' (1985: Chapter 15). Today, however, almost all students of international relations agree that sometimes the good statesman ought to act in ways inconsistent with the principles of private morality – for example, to give greater consideration to preserving the lives of her own soldiers than the soldiers of her adversary.

Controversy arises over when, where, and how frequently violating moral norms is truly necessary. Realists suggest that anarchy and egoism so severely constrain the space for the pursuit of moral concerns that it is only a small exaggeration to say that states in anarchy cannot afford to be moral. This, however, is (at most) a contingent empirical fact. It provides no grounds for categorically excluding morality from foreign policy. Even if the primary obligation of the statesman is to the national interest, that is not her exclusive obligation. States not only are free to, but in fact often do, include certain moral objectives in their definition of the national interest.

Realists rightly remind us of the dangers of ignoring 'realities' rooted in anarchy and egoism. A narrow vision of 'the national interest defined in terms of power' (Morgenthau 1948/1954/1973: 4, 10) certainly deserves consideration in debates over a state's international objectives. But arguments that 'no ethical standards are applicable to relations between states' (Carr 1946: 153) and that 'universal moral principles cannot be applied to the actions of states' (Morgenthau 1948/1954/1973: 9) not only cannot bear critical scrutiny but prove not even to reflect the considered views of most leading self-identified realists – despite their unfortunate tendency to repeat and emphasize such indefensibly exaggerated claims.

As John Herz notes, 'the mitigation, channelling, balancing, or control of power has prevailed perhaps more often than the inevitability of power politics would lead one to believe' (1976: 11). In fact, on careful examination we find that most leading realists acknowledge that moral and ethical principles are 'operative but not controlling' (Thompson 1985: 22). Carr argues that 'it is an unreal kind of realism which ignores the element of morality in any world order' (1946: 235). Morgenthau talks of 'the curious dialectic of ethics and politics, which prevents the latter, in spite of itself, from escaping the former's judgement and normative direction' and allows that 'nations recognize a moral obligation to refrain from the infliction of death and suffering under certain conditions despite the possibility of justifying such conduct in the light of . . . the national interest' (1946: 177; 1948: 177). Niebuhr not only insists that 'an adequate political morality must do justice to the insights of both moralists and political realists' but argues that the 'ultimate purpose' of realist analysis 'is to find political methods which will offer the most promise of achieving an ethical social goal for society' (1932: 233, xxiv).

How to think about realism (and its critics)

We have identified an unfortunate tendency among realists to push an important insight well beyond the breaking point. Not only are realists prone to rhetorical exaggerations – consider, for example, Nicholas Spykman's claim that 'the search for power is not made for the achievement of moral values; moral values are used to facilitate the attainment of power' (1942: 18) – but even more moderate statements regularly lack the necessary qualifications. Note the absence of an adverb like often, frequently, or even usually in Kennan's claim, quote above, that nonmoral considerations 'must be allowed to prevail.' Likewise, Mearsheimer, although allowing that institutions matter 'on the margins,' on the same page asserts the obviously false claim that institutions that 'have no independent effect on state behavior' (1994/95: 7).

Strong adherents of a theory often unthinkingly slide from (justifiable) theoretical simplifications to (unjustifiable) descriptive claims. As I have noted repeatedly, theories must abstract, simplify, and thus exaggerate. The danger arises when these simplified theoretical models are presented as categorical empirical claims. That realists are no less prone to this confusion than adherents of other theories is ironic but not particularly surprising.

Waltz nicely captures the contribution of realism: it identifies a few 'big, important, and enduring patterns' (1979: 70). Were realists, and Waltz himself, always this modest, the discipline, especially in the United States, would be much better off – particularly if realists took to heart the negative implication that realism does not comprehend most big and important things. Realism simply cannot explain the vast majority of what happens in international relations.

The realist response that they explain 'the most important things' is a contentious normative judgement. Furthermore, given the 'indeterminacy' of most realist predictions, it is by no means clear that realism offers deep or satisfying explanations of even the things to which it applies (compare Wendt 1999: 18, 251–9). But even if realism does adequately explain the few most important things, there is no reason to restrict the discipline to those. Certainly we do not want medicine to restrict itself to studying and treating only the leading causes of death.

That realism cannot account for substantial swathes of international relations is no reason to denigrate or marginalize it. Realists, though, must allow the same for other theories. Realism must be an important, even essential, part of a pluralistic discipline of international studies. No less. But no more.

The familiar question 'Are you a realist?' may be appropriate if we understand realism as a moral theory or worldview. A few realists, particularly Augustinian Christians such as Niebuhr (1941; 1943) and Butterfield (1953), have treated realism in such terms. Among contemporary academic realists, Robert Gilpin (1986; 1996) perhaps borders on holding such a view. But worldviews – natural law, Islam, Kantianism, Christianity, Aristotleanism, humanism – are not usually what we have in mind by 'theories of international relations.' If we are talking about analytical or explanatory theory, 'being' (or 'not being') a realist makes little sense.

Unless realist predictions or explanations are almost always correct across something like the full range of international relations – and neither realism nor any other theory of international relations even approximates this – no serious student or practitioner of international relations would want to 'be' a realist in the sense of always applying or acting upon realist theory. But unless realism never provided valuable insights or explanations – and even its strongest critics do not suggest this – no reasonable person would want to 'be' an anti-realist in the sense of never using realist theories.

The proper questions are how regularly, in what domains, and for what purposes does realism – or any other theory – help us to understand or act in the world. My general answer is 'a lot less often than most realists claim, but a lot more frequently than many critics would like to allow'. More important than this general answer, though, is the fact that, depending on one's political interests and substantive concerns, one might appropriately use realism regularly, occasionally, or almost never in one's analyses or actions.

Realism *must* be a part of the analytical toolkit of every serious student of international relations. But if it is our only tool – or even our primary tool – we will be woefully under-equipped for our analytical tasks, our vision of international relations will be sadly impoverished, and, to the extent that theory has an impact on practice, the projects we undertake in the world are liable to be mangled and misshapen.

3 | **Liberalism**

SCOTT BURCHILL

Liberalism is the most enduring and influential philosophical tradition to have emerged from the European Enlightenment. It is a theory which champions scientific rationality, freedom and the inevitability of human progress. It is an approach to government which emphasizes individual rights, constitutionalism, democracy and limitations on the powers of the state. It is also a model of economic organization which argues that market capitalism best promotes the welfare of all by most efficiently allocating scarce resources within society.

Despite its ancient lineage, liberalism's influence today can be measured by its authorship of the two most profound trends in contemporary international politics – the spread of democracy after the Cold War and the globalization of the world economy.

There are many strands of liberal thought which influence the study of international relations. The chapter will begin by analysing the revival of liberal thought after the Cold War. It will then explain how liberal attitudes to war, the spread of democracy and human rights continue to inform political thinking and government behaviour. The influence of economic liberalism, in particular interdependency theory and liberal institutionalism, will then be assessed before liberal arguments for globalization and the impact of non-state terrorism on liberal thought are measured. The conclusion will judge the contribution of liberalism to the theory of international relations.

After the Cold War

The demise of Soviet Communism at the beginning of the 1990s enhanced the influence of liberal theories of international relations within the academy, a theoretical tradition thought to have been discredited by perspectives such as realism, which emphasize the recurrent features of international relations. In a reassertion of the teleology of liberalism, Fukuyama claimed in the early 1990s that the collapse of the

Soviet Union proved that liberal democracy had no serious ideological competitor: it was 'the end point of mankind's ideological evolution' and the 'final form of human government' (Fukuyama 1992: xi–xii). It is an argument that has been strengthened by transitions to democracy in Africa, East Asia, East Europe and Latin America.

For Fukuyama, the end of the Cold War saw the triumph of the 'ideal state' and a particular mode of political economy, 'liberal capitalism', which 'cannot be improved upon': there can be 'no further progress in the development of underlying principles and institutions' (Fukuyama 1992, xi–xii). According to Fukuyama, the end of the East-West conflict confirmed that liberal capitalism was unchallenged as a model of, and endpoint for, humankind's political and economic development. There 'is a fundamental process at work that dictates a common evolutionary pattern for *all* human societies – in short, something like a Universal History of mankind in the direction of liberal democracy' (Fukuyama 1992: xi–xii, 48).

Fukuyama's belief that Western forms of government and political economy are the ultimate destination for the entire species poses a number of challenges for the study of international relations. First, his claim that political and economic development terminates at liberal-capitalist democracy assumes that the Western path to modernity will not face a future rival, and will eventually command global consent. Second, Fukuyama's argument assumes that national, religious and cultural distinctions are no barrier to the triumph of liberal democracy and capitalism. Third, Fukuyama's thesis raises vital, unanswered questions about governance and political community. For example, what are the implications of globalization for nation-states and their sovereign powers? What about societies which reject market capitalism and parliamentary democracy?

The post-Cold War optimism of many liberals has been tempered by a series of unexpected events which, at the very least, suggest the path to modernity remains a rocky one. The rise of Islamist terrorism, democratic reversals in states such as Thailand, and resistance to the coercive spread of democracy in Afghanistan and Iraq, suggest Fukuyama's celebration of the end of history may have been premature.

Liberals believe that progress in human history can be measured by the elimination of global conflict and the adoption of principles of legitimacy that have evolved in domestic political orders. This constitutes an *inside-out* approach to international relations, where the behaviour of states can be explained by their endogenous arrangements. It also leads to Doyle's important claim that 'liberal democracies are uniquely willing to eschew the use of force in their relations with one another', a view which rejects the realist contention that the anarchical nature of the international system means states are trapped in a struggle for power and security (Linklater 1993: 29).

The liberal view: 'inside looking out'

In the 1990s Fukuyama revived a long-held view among liberals that the spread of legitimate domestic political orders would eventually bring an end to international conflict. This neo-Kantian position assumes that particular states, with liberal-democratic polities, constitute an ideal which the rest of the world will emulate. Fukuyama is struck by the extent to which liberal democracies have transcended their violent instincts and institutionalized norms which pacify relations between them. He is particularly impressed by the emergence of shared principles of legitimacy among the great powers. The projection of liberal-democratic principles to the international realm provides the best prospect for a peaceful world order because 'a world made up of liberal democracies . . . should have much less incentive for war, since all nations would reciprocally recognize one another's legitimacy' (Fukuyama 1992: xx).

This approach is rejected by neo-realists who claim that the moral aspirations of states are thwarted by the absence of an overarching authority which regulates their behaviour towards each other. The anarchical nature of the international system tends to homogenize foreign policy behaviour by socializing states into the system of power politics. Requirements for strategic power and security are paramount in an insecure world, and override the ethical pursuits of states, regardless of their domestic political complexions.

In stressing the importance of legitimate domestic orders in explaining foreign policy behaviour, realists such as Waltz believe that liberals are guilty of 'reductionism' when they should be highlighting the 'systemic' features of international relations. The differences between 'inside-out' and 'outside-in' approaches to international relations is an important line of demarcation in modern international theory (Waltz 1991a: 667). The extent to which the neo-realist critique of liberal internationalism can be sustained will be a major consideration of this chapter.

Fukuyama's argument is more than a celebration of the fact that liberal capitalism has survived the threat posed by Marxism. It also implies that neo-realism has overlooked 'the foremost macropolitical trend in contemporary world politics: the expansion of the liberal zone of peace' (Linklater 1993: 29). Challenging the view that anarchy conditions international behaviour is Doyle's argument that there is a growing core of pacific states which have learned to resolve their differences without resorting to violence. The expansion of this pacific realm is the most significant feature of the contemporary world. If this claim can be upheld it will constitute a significant comeback for an international theory widely thought to have been terminally damaged by Carr in his critique of liberal utopianism in the late 1930s. It also poses a serious challenge to theoretical assumptions that war is an endemic feature of international life (Doyle 1986: 1151–69).

War, democracy and free trade

The foundations of contemporary liberal internationalism were laid in the eighteenth and nineteenth centuries by liberals proposing preconditions for a peaceful world order. In broad summary they concluded that the prospects for the elimination of war lay with a preference for democracy over aristocracy and free trade over autarky. In this section we will examine these arguments in turn, and the extent to which they inform contemporary liberal thought.

Prospects for peace

For liberals, peace is the normal state of affairs: in Kant's words, peace can be perpetual. The laws of nature dictated harmony and cooperation between peoples. War is therefore both unnatural and irrational, an artificial contrivance and not a product of some peculiarity of human nature. Liberals believe in progress and the perfectibility of the human condition. With faith in the power of human reason and the capacity of human beings to realize their inner potential, they remain confident that the stain of war can be removed from human experience (Gardner 1990: 23–39; Hoffmann 1995: 159–77; Zacher and Matthew 1995: 107–50).

A common thread, from Rousseau, Kant and Cobden, to Schumpeter and Doyle, is that wars were created by militaristic and undemocratic governments for their own vested interests. Wars were engineered by a 'warrior class' bent on extending their power and wealth through territorial conquest. According to Paine in *The Rights of Man* (1791), the 'war system' was contrived to preserve the power and the employment of princes, statesmen, soldiers, diplomats and armaments manufacturers, and to bind their tyranny ever more firmly upon the necks of the people' (Howard 1978: 31). Wars provide governments with excuses to raise taxes, expand their bureaucratic apparatus and increase their control over their citizens. The people, on the other hand, were peace-loving by nature, and only plunged into conflict by the whims of their unrepresentative rulers.

War was a cancer on the body politic. But it was an ailment that human beings, themselves, had the capacity to cure. The treatment which liberals began prescribing in the eighteenth century has not changed: the 'disease' of war could be successfully treated with the twin medicines of *democracy* and *free trade*. Democratic processes and institutions would break the power of the ruling elites and curb their propensity for violence. Free trade and commerce would overcome the artificial barriers between individuals and unite them everywhere into one community.

For liberals such as Schumpeter, war was the product of the aggressive instincts of unrepresentative elites. The warlike disposition of these rulers drove the reluctant masses into violent conflicts which, while profitable for the arms industries and the military aristocrats, were disastrous for those who did the fighting. For Kant, the establishment of republican forms of government in which rulers were accountable and individual rights were respected would lead to peaceful international relations because the ultimate consent for war would rest with the citizens of the state (Kant 1970: 100). For both Kant and Schumpeter, war was the outcome of minority rule, though Kant was no champion of democratic government (MacMillan 1995). Liberal states, founded on individual rights such as equality before the law, free speech and civil liberty, respect for private property and representative government, would not have the same appetite for conflict and war. Peace was fundamentally a question of establishing legitimate domestic orders throughout the world – 'When the citizens who bear the burdens of war elect their governments, wars become impossible' (Doyle 1986: 1151).

The dual themes of domestic legitimacy and the extent to which liberal-democratic states exercise restraint and peaceful intentions in their foreign policy have been taken up more recently by Doyle, Russett and others. In a restatement of Kant's argument that a 'pacific federation' (*foedus pacificum*) can be built by expanding the number of states with republican constitutions, Doyle claims that liberal democracies are unique in their ability and willingness to establish peaceful relations among themselves. This pacification of foreign relations between liberal states is said to be a direct product of their shared legitimate political orders based on democratic principles and institutions. The reciprocal recognition of these common principles – a commitment to the rule of law, individual rights and equality before the law, *and* representative government based on popular consent – means that liberal democracies evince little interest in conflict with each other and have no grounds on which to contest each other's legitimacy: they have constructed a 'separate peace' (Doyle 1986: 1161; Fukuyama 1992: xx). This does not mean that they are less inclined to make war with non-democratic states, and Doyle is correct to point out that democracies maintain a healthy appetite for conflicts with authoritarian states, as recent conflicts in the

Middle East and Central Asia attest. But it does suggest that the best prospect for bringing an end to war between states lies with the spread of liberal-democratic governments across the globe. The expansion of the zone of peace from the core to the periphery is also the basis of Fukuyama's optimism about the post-Communist era (Doyle 1986, 1995, 1997; Russett 1993).

There are both structural and normative aspects to what has been termed 'democratic peace theory'. Some liberals emphasize the institutional constraints on liberal-democratic states, such as public opinion, the rule of law and representative government. The checks and balances provided by elections, divisions of power and other legal-political restrictions make wars more difficult for liberal states to contrive. Others stress the normative preference for compromise and conflict resolution which can be found in many liberal democracies.

A combination of both explanations strengthens the argument that liberal-democratic states do not resolve their differences violently, although realist critics point to definitional problems with the idea of liberal democracy, the question of covert action, and ask why the constraints on war-making don't apply in relations with authoritarian states. Realists argue that at best democratic peace theory identifies a correlation in international politics rather than an 'iron law' or theory (Maoz and Russett 1993; Owen 1994).

The argument is also extended by Rawls, who claims that liberal societies are also 'less likely to engage in war with non-liberal outlaw states, except on grounds of legitimate self-defence (or in the defence of their legitimate allies), or intervention in severe cases to protect human rights' (Rawls 1999: 49). Recent US-led wars in Afghanistan and Iraq pose significant challenges to the claim that only self-defence and humanitarianism incline liberal-democratic states to war.

A related argument by Mueller (1989) claims that we are already witnessing the obsolescence of war between the major powers. Reviving the liberal faith in the capacity of people to improve the moral and material conditions of their lives, Mueller argues that, just as duelling and slavery were eventually seen as morally unacceptable, war is increasingly viewed in the developed world as repulsive, immoral and uncivilized. That violence is more widely seen as an anachronistic form of social intercourse is not due to any change in human nature or the structure of the international system. According to Mueller, the obsolescence of major war in the late twentieth century was the product of moral learning, a shift in ethical consciousness away from coercive forms of social behaviour. Because war brings more costs than gains and is no longer seen as a romantic or noble pursuit, it has become 'rationally unthinkable' (Mueller 1989).

The long peace between states of the industrialized world is a cause of profound optimism for liberals such as Fukuyama and Mueller, who are confident that we have already entered a period in which war as an instrument of international diplomacy is becoming obsolete. But if war has been an important factor in nation-building, as Giddens, Mann and Tilly have argued, the fact that states are learning to curb their propensity for violence will also have important consequences for forms of political community which are likely to emerge in the industrial centres of the world. The end of war between the great powers may have the effect of weakening the rigidity of their political boundaries and inspiring a wave of sub-national revolts, although the new wave of anti-Western terror has complicated matters in this regard by encouraging states to solidify their boundaries and make greater demands on the loyalty of citizens.

Far from sharing the post-Cold War optimism of liberals, realists such as Waltz and Mearsheimer argue that the collapse of bipolarity in the early 1990s was a cause for grave concern. Mutual nuclear deterrence maintained a stabilizing balance of power in the world, whereas unipolarity would not last, eventually leading to volatility and war. As Waltz argues, 'in international politics, unbalanced power constitutes a danger even when it is American power that is out of balance' (Waltz 1991a: 670). Accordingly, the expansion of a zone of peace is no antidote to the calculations of raw power in an anarchical world.

Recent conflicts in the Balkans, Central Asia and the Persian Gulf – all involving major industrial powers – are a reminder that the post-Cold War period remains volatile and suggest that war may not yet have lost its efficacy in international diplomacy. None of these constitutes conflicts between democratic states but they are no less important to the maintenance of world order. These and other struggles in so-called 'failed states' such as Afghanistan, Somalia and other African states, are a reminder that the fragmentation of nation-states and civil wars arising from secessionist movements have not been given the same attention by liberals as more conventional inter-state wars.

Democratic peace theory provides few guidelines for how liberal states should conduct themselves with non-liberal states. Rawls, however, is concerned with the extent to which liberal and non-liberal peoples can be equal participants in a 'Society of Peoples'. He argues that principles and norms of international law and practice – the 'Law of Peoples' – can be developed and shared by both liberal and non-liberal or decent hierarchical societies, without an expectation that liberal democracy is the terminus for all. The guidelines and principal basis for establishing harmonious relations between liberal and non-liberal peoples under a common Law of Peoples, takes liberal international theory in a more sophisticated direction because it explicitly acknowledges the need for utopian thought to be realistic (Rawls 1999: 11–23).

As the number of East Asian and Islamic societies which reject the normative superiority of liberal democracy grows, doubt is cast on the belief that the non-European world is seeking to imitate the Western route to political modernization. This has also been graphically illustrated in the wave of anti-Western Islamist terror since 2001. Linklater suggests that it is not so much the spread of liberal democracy *per se* which has universal appeal, 'but the idea of limited power which is present within, but not entirely synonymous with, liberal democracy' (Linklater 1993: 33–6; Rawls 1999). The notion of limited power and respect for the rule of law contained within the idea of 'constitutionalism' may be one means of solving the exclusionary character of the liberal zone of peace. It is a less ambitious project and potentially more sensitive to the cultural and political differences among states in the current international system. It may avoid the danger of the system bifurcating into a privileged inner circle and a disadvantaged and disaffected outer circle (Linklater 1993: 33). The greatest barrier to the expansion of the zone of peace from the core is the perception within the periphery that this constitutes little more than the domination of one culture by another.

The spirit of commerce

Eighteenth and nineteenth-century liberals felt that the spirits of war and commerce were mutually incompatible. Many wars were fought by states to achieve their mercantilist goals. According to Carr, 'the aim of mercantilism . . . was not to promote the welfare of the community and its members, but to augment the power of the state, of which the sovereign was the embodiment . . . wealth was the source of power, or more specifically of fitness for war'. Until the Napoleonic wars, 'wealth, conceived in its simplest form as bullion, was brought in by exports; and since, in the static conception of society prevailing at this period, export markets were a fixed quantity not susceptible of increase as a whole, the only way for a nation to expand its markets and therefore its wealth was to capture them from some other nation, if necessary by waging a trade war' (Carr 1945: 5–6).

Free trade, however, was a more peaceful means of achieving national wealth because, according to the theory of comparative advantage, each economy would be materially better off than if it had been pursuing nationalism and self-sufficiency (autarky). Free trade would also break down the divisions between states and unite individuals everywhere in one community. Artificial barriers to commerce distorted relations between individuals, thereby causing international tension. Free trade would expand the range of contacts and levels of understanding between the peoples of the world and encourage international friendship and understanding. According to Kant, unhindered commerce between the peoples of the world would unite them in a common, peaceful enterprise. 'Trade ... would increase the wealth and power of the peace-loving, productive sections of the population at the expense of the war-orientated aristocracy, and ... would bring men of different nations into constant contact with one another; contact which would make clear to all of them their fundamental community of interests' (Howard 1978: 20; Walter 1996). Similarly Ricardo believed that free trade 'binds together, by one common tie of interest and intercourse, the universal society of nations throughout the civilized world' (Ricardo 1911: 114).

Conflicts were often caused by states erecting barriers which distorted the natural harmony of interests commonly shared by individuals across the world. The solution to the problem, argued Adam Smith and Tom Paine, was the free movement of commodities, capital and labour. 'If commerce were permitted to act to the universal extent it is capable, it would extirpate the system of war and produce a revolution in the uncivilized state of governments' (Howard 1978: 29). Writing in 1848, John Stuart Mill also claimed that free trade was the means to bring about the end of war: 'it is commerce which is rapidly rendering war obsolete, by strengthening and multiplying the personal interests which act in natural opposition to it' (Howard 1978: 37). The spread of markets would place societies on an entirely new foundation. Instead of conflicts over limited resources such as land, the industrial revolution raised the prospect of unlimited prosperity for all: material production, so long as it was freely exchanged, would bring human progress. Trade would create relations of mutual dependence which would foster understanding between peoples and reduce conflict. Economic self-interest would then be a powerful disincentive for war.

Liberals believe unfettered commercial exchanges would encourage links across frontiers and shift loyalties away from the nation-state. Leaders would eventually come to recognize that the benefits of free trade outweighed the costs of territorial conquest and colonial expansion. The attraction of going to war to promote mercantilist interests would be weakened as societies learn that war can only disrupt trade and therefore the prospects for economic prosperity. Interdependence would replace national competition and defuse unilateral acts of aggression and reciprocal retaliation.

Interdependence and liberal institutionalism

Free trade and the removal of barriers to commerce is at the heart of modern interdependency theory. The rise of regional economic integration in Europe, for example, was inspired by the belief that conflict between states would be reduced by creating a common interest in trade and economic collaboration among members of the same geographical region. This would encourage states, such as France and Germany, which traditionally resolved their differences militarily, to cooperate within a commonly agreed economic and political framework for their mutual benefit. States would have a joint stake in each other's peace and prosperity. The European Union is a good example of economic integration engendering closer economic and political cooperation in a region historically bedevilled by national conflicts.

As Mitrany argued, initial cooperation between states would be achieved in technical areas where it was mutually convenient, but once successful it could 'spill over' into other functional areas where states found that mutual advantages could be gained (Mitrany 1948: 350–63). In a development of this argument, Keohane and Nye have explained how, via membership of international institutions, states can significantly broaden their conceptions of self-interest in order to widen the scope for cooperation. Compliance with the rules of these organizations not only discourages the narrow pursuit of national interests, it also weakens the meaning and appeal of state sovereignty (Keohane and Nye 1977). This suggests that the international system is more normatively regulated than realists believe, a position further developed by English School theorists such as Wight and Bull, as discussed in Chapter 4.

A development of this argument can be found in liberal institutionalism which shares with neo-realism an acceptance of the importance of the state and the anarchical condition of the international system, though liberal institutionalists argue that the prospects for cooperation, even in an anarchical world, are greater than neo-realists allow (Young 1982; Nye 1988; Powell 1994). Liberal institutionalists claim that cooperation between states can be organized and formalized in institutions. 'Institutions' in this sense means sets of rules which govern state behaviour in specific policy areas, such as the Law of the Sea.

Accepting the broad structures of neo-realism, but employing rational choice and game theory to anticipate the behaviour of states, liberal institutionalists demonstrate that cooperation between states can be enhanced even without the presence of a hegemonic player which can enforce compliance with agreements. For them, anarchy is mitigated by regimes and institutional cooperation which brings higher levels of regularity and predictability to international relations. Regimes – sets of principles, norms, rules and decision-making procedures – constrain state behaviour by formalizing the expectations of each party to an agreement where there is, for example, a pandemic, drug trafficking or organized crime. They reflect the inability of individual states to solve global issues without broader cooperation. They enhance trust, continuity and stability in a world of otherwise ungoverned anarchy.

Neo-realists and neo-liberals disagree about how states conceive of their own interests. Whereas neo-realists, such as Waltz, argue that states are concerned with 'relative gains' – meaning gains assessed in comparative terms (who will gain more?), neo-liberals claim that states are concerned with maximizing their 'absolute gains' – an assessment of their own welfare independent of their shared interests (what will gain me the most?). Institutions then assume the role of encouraging cooperative habits, monitoring compliance, enforcement where possible, and sanctioning cheaters and defectors.

Today, regimes are said to exist in a growing range of policy areas, including environmental regulation (e.g. climate change), global finance and trade, and counter-terrorism.

Neo-realists argue that states will baulk at cooperation if they expect to gain less than their rivals. Liberal institutionalists, on the other hand, believe international relations need not be a zero-sum game, as many states feel secure enough to maximize their own gains regardless of what accrues to others. Mutual benefits arising out of cooperation are possible because states are not always preoccupied with relative gains – hence the opportunities for constructing regimes around issues and areas of common concern.

Liberal institutionalists acknowledge that cooperation between states is likely to be tenuous and limited, particularly where enforcement procedures are weak and cheating brings gains. However, in an environment of growing regional and global integration, states can often discover – with or without the encouragement of a hegemon – a coincidence of strategic and economic interests which can be turned into a formalized agreement determining the rules of conduct. In areas such as environmental degradation and the threat of terrorism, the argument for formalized cooperation between states is compelling.

According to Rosecrance (1986), the growth of economic interdependency has been matched by a corresponding decline in the value of territorial conquest for states. In the contemporary world the benefits of trade and cooperation among states greatly exceed those of military competition and territorial control. In their mercantilist phase, nation-states regarded the acquisition of territory as the principal means of increasing national wealth. More recently it has become apparent that additional territory does not necessarily help states to compete in an international system where the 'trading state' rather than the 'military state' is becoming dominant. In the 1970s state elites began to realize that wealth is determined by their share of the world market in value-added goods and services. This understanding had two significant effects. First, the age of the independent, self-sufficient state is over. Complex layers of economic interdependency ensure that states cannot act aggressively without risking economic penalties imposed by other members of the international community, a fate even for great powers. It also makes little sense for a state to threaten its commercial partners, whose markets and capital investment are essential for its own economic growth. Second, territorial conquest in the nuclear age is both dangerous and costly for rogue states. The alternative – economic development through trade and foreign investment – is a much more attractive and potentially beneficial strategy (Rosecrance 1986; Strange 1991).

Neo-realists have two responses to the liberal claim that economic interdependency is pacifying international relations (Grieco 1988). First, they argue that in any struggle between competing disciplines, the anarchic environment and the insecurity it engenders will always take priority over the quest for economic prosperity. Economic interdependency will never take precedence over strategic security because states must be primarily concerned with their survival. Their capacity to explore avenues of economic cooperation will be limited by how secure they feel, and the extent to which they are required to engage in military competition with others. Second, the idea of economic interdependence implies a misleading degree of equality and shared vulnerability to economic forces in the global economy. Interdependence does not eliminate hegemony and dependency in inter-state relations because power is very unevenly distributed throughout the world's trade and financial markets. Dominant players such as the United States have usually framed the rules under which interdependency has flourished. Conflict and cooperation is therefore unlikely to disappear, though it may be channelled into more peaceful forms.

Human rights

The advocacy of democracy and free trade foreshadows another idea which liberal internationalism introduced to international theory. Liberals believe the legitimacy of domestic political orders is largely contingent upon upholding the rule of law and the state's respect for the human rights of its citizens. If it is wrong for an individual to engage in socially unacceptable or criminal behaviour, it is also wrong for states.

References to essential human needs are implicit in some of the earliest written legal codes from ancient Babylon, as well as early Buddhist, Confucian and Hindu texts, though the first explicit mention of universal principles governing common standards of human behaviour can be found in the Western canon.

The idea of universal human rights has its origins in the Natural Law tradition, debates in the West during the Enlightenment over the 'rights of man' and in the experience of individuals struggling against the arbitrary rule of the state (Donnelly 2003). The Magna Carta in 1215, the development of English Common Law and the Bill of Rights in 1689 were significant, if evolutionary steps along the path to enshrining basic human rights in law, as were intellectual contributions from Grotius (the law of nations), Rousseau (the social contract) and Locke (popular consent, limits of sovereignty). An early legal articulation of human rights can be found in the American Declaration of Independence in 1776 ('we take these truths to be self-evident, that all men are created equal, and that they are endowed by their Creator with certain unalienable Rights, that amongst these are Life, Liberty and the pursuit of Happiness') and in France's Declaration of the Rights of Man and the Citizen in 1789 ('all men are born free and equal in their rights').

The development of human rights occurred as cultural and legal practices in the Western world changed. These included the expansion of moral communities as empathy for human suffering spread beyond the confines of particularist locales, the rejection of torture as an instrument for establishing the truth in legal processes, and the redefinition of human relationships, including greater respect for the autonomy of the body, found in literature and art from the late eighteenth century (Hunt 2007).

Human beings are said to be endowed – purely by reason of their humanity – with certain fundamental rights, benefits and protections. These rights are regarded as inherent in the sense they are the birthright of all, inalienable because they cannot be given up or taken away and universal since they apply to all regardless of nationality, status, gender or race. Liberals have a normative commitment to human rights, believing certain values and standards should be universally applied.

The extension of these rights to all peoples has a particularly important place in liberal thinking about foreign policy and international relations for two reasons. First, these rights provide a legal foundation to emancipation, justice and human freedom. Their denial by state authorities is an affront to the dignity of all and a stain on the human condition. Second, states which treat their own citizens ethically and allow them meaningful participation in the political process are thought to be less likely to behave aggressively internationally. The task for liberals has been to develop and promote moral standards which would command universal consent, knowing that in doing so states may be required to jeopardize the pursuit of their own national interests. This has proven to be a difficult task, despite evident progress on labour rights, the abolition of slavery, the political emancipation of women in the West, the treatment of indigenous peoples and the end of white supremacy in South Africa (Dunne and Wheeler 1999; Donnelly 2003).

The creation of important legal codes, instruments and institutions in the post-World War II period is a measure of achievement in the area. The most important instruments are the Universal Declaration of Human Rights (1948), the International Covenant on Civil and Political Rights (1966) and the International Covenant on Economic, Social and Cultural Rights (1966), while the International Labour Organization (ILO) and the International Court of Justice (ICJ) play a significant institutional and symbolic role in the protection of human rights. A greater concern about genocidal crimes, the outlawing of cruel and inhuman punishment and the rights of detainees apprehended on the battlefield are a reflection of progress in the area.

In his seminal account, Vincent (1986) identified the right of the individual to be free from starvation as the only human right which is likely to become a global consensus. The world community, regardless of religious or ideological differences, agrees that a right to subsistence was essential to the dignity of humankind. Beyond this right, nation-states struggle to find agreement, not least because the developing world is suspicious that human rights advocacy from metropolitan centres is little more than a pretext for unwarranted interference in their domestic affairs. Most states are reluctant to give outsiders the power to compel them to improve their ethical performance, although there is a growing belief that the principle of territorial sovereignty should no longer be used by governments as a credible excuse for avoiding legitimate international scrutiny – hence the growing concern with international humanitarian intervention (Wheeler 2000).

Marxists have dismissed liberal human rights as mere bourgeois freedoms which fail to address the class-based nature of exploitation contained within capitalist relations of production. Realists would add that 'conditions of profound insecurity for states do not permit ethical and humane considerations to override their primary national considerations' (Linklater 1992b: 27). After all, it is interests which determine political action and in the global arena, politics is the amoral struggle for power to advance these interests. Other critics claim that the implementation of these rights, for example the abolition of child labour on the sub continent – would consign millions to greater levels of poverty.

Liberals struggle to avoid the charge that their conceptions of democracy and human rights are culturally specific, ethnocentric and therefore irrelevant to societies which are not Western in cultural orientation. To many societies, appeals to universality merely conceal the means by which one dominant society imposes its culture upon another, while infringing on its sovereign independence. The promotion of human rights from the core to the periphery assumes a degree of moral superiority – that the West not only possesses moral truths which others are bound to observe, but that it can sit in judgement on other societies.

The issue is further complicated by the argument that economic, social and cultural rights should precede civil and political rights – one made earlier by Communist states and more recently by a number of East Asian governments. Sometimes this is characterized as a struggle between first and second generation rights. This claim is a direct challenge to the idea that human rights are indivisible and universal, and may constitute a revolt against the West. It implies that the alleviation of poverty and economic development in some societies depends on the initial denial of political freedoms and human rights to the citizen. However, the claim that rights can be prioritized in this way – that procedural and substantive freedoms are incompatible – is problematic and widely seen, with some justification, as a rationalization by governments for authoritarian rule.

An increasing number of conservative political leaders in East Asia have also argued that there is a superior Asian model of political and social organization comprising the principles of harmony, hierarchy and consensus (Confucianism) in contrast to what they regard as the confrontation, individualism and moral decay which characterizes Western liberalism. Regardless of how self-serving this argument is – and it is rarely offered by democratically elected rulers – it poses a fundamental challenge to Fukuyama's suggestion that in the post-Cold War period liberal democracy faces no serious universal challenges. It is clear that a number of states, including those self-consciously Islamic societies, are not striving to imitate the Western route to political modernization. Some reject it outright.

Recent years have also seen considerable slippage in the Western world's commitment to universal human rights. The 'war on terror' led by the United States provided a more permissive attitude to the use of torture, the incarceration without trial of enemy combatants and the rendition of enemy suspects to third countries for more coercive interrogation than would be permitted in the West. The exposure of these practices weakened any moral force the West may have invoked for the universal spread of human rights.

Even if universal rules and instruments could be agreed upon, how could compliance with universal standards be enforced? Liberals are divided over this issue, between non-interventionists who defend state sovereignty, and those who feel that the promotion of ethical principles can justify intervention in the internal affairs of other states (see Bull 1984a; Wheeler 2000).

Recent examples of so-called humanitarian intervention in Cambodia,

Rwanda, Serbia, Somalia and East Timor pose a growing challenge to the protection from outside interference traditionally afforded by sovereignty claims. This also applies to the prosecution of those suspected of committing war crimes and crimes against humanity by international tribunals such as the ICJ (Forbes and Hoffman 1993). The embryonic International Criminal Court established in 2002 (ICC) may be seen as a further expression of liberal sentiments which oppose the arbitrary cruelty of political leaders and the use of agencies of the state to inflict harm on minorities and opponents. However, its very structure and functions limit the sovereign right of a government to administer the internal affairs of their state free from outside interference. States like the United States and Russia, which refuse to ratify the ICC for reasons of sovereignty, will therefore come under increasing pressure in the years ahead to conform with what appears to be a growing global consensus.

Celebrated trials (Milosevic, Saddam) and attention given to non-trials (Pinochet, Suharto) indicate a significant shift away from the traditional provision of sovereign immunity to heads of state and others guilty of war crimes and crimes against humanity. Whereas in the past, justice, if dispensed at all, would come from within the state, the establishment of international legal fora and the further development of international law in this area are largely due to the influence of liberal internationalism and its emphasis on the importance of global benchmarks and the rule of law. It is true that cases like these never truly escape the political atmosphere of the day, in particular the domestic political climate in each country directly involved, however the fact that they arise at all within international legal jurisdictions indicates significant progress towards a system of global justice.

Modern forms of humanitarian intervention follow a pattern established in the middle of the eighteenth century when the British and Dutch successfully interceded on behalf of Prague's Jewish community, which was threatened with deportation by authorities in Bohemia. The protection of Christian minorities at risk in Europe and in the Orient in the eighteenth and nineteenth centuries by the Treaty of Kucuk-Kainardji (1774) and the Treaty of Berlin (1878) are also part of the same legal precedent, as is the advocacy of British Prime Minister Gladstone in the second half of the nineteenth century and US President Wilson early in the twentieth century. Vietnam's invasion of Cambodia in 1978, when refracted through the ideological prism of the Cold War, highlighted the politically contingent nature of humanitarian intervention in the modern period. Liberals who support both the sovereign rights of independent states and the right of external intervention in cases where there is an acute humanitarian crisis, find it difficult to reconcile both international norms (Chomsky 1999a).

Globalization and terrorism

Fukuyama's post-Cold War optimism is on firmer ground if we consider the extent to which economic liberalism has become the dominant ideology of the contemporary period. The move towards a global political economy organized along neo-liberal lines is a trend as significant as the likely expansion of the zone of peace. Early in the twenty-first century, the world economy more closely resembles the prescriptions of Smith and Ricardo than at any previous time. As MacPherson forecast, this development is also a measure of 'how deeply the market assumptions about the nature of man and society have penetrated liberal-democratic theory' (MacPherson 1977: 21). The dark cloud on the horizon, however, is as serious as it was unexpected. The contemporary wave of anti-Western Islamist terror represents a significant blockage on the path to globalization and confronts liberals with a range of intellectual dilemmas and policy reversals for which they were unprepared.

Before examining the extent to which liberalism has shaped the contours of the world economy today and the impact of Islamist terror, it is important to recognize that the experience of laissez faire capitalism in the nineteenth century challenged many liberal assumptions about human beings, the market and the role of the state.

Critics such as Polanyi highlighted the extent to which material self-gain in a market society was necessary for survival in an unregulated market economy, rather than a reflection of the human condition in its natural state. It is unwise for liberals to generalize from the specific case of market capitalism – to believe that behaviour enforced as a result of a new and presumably transient form of political economy was a true reflection of a human being's inner self (Polanyi 1944; Block and Somers 1984).

State intervention in the economic life of a society was in fact an act of community self-defence against the destructive power of unfettered markets which, according to Polanyi, if left unregulated, threatened to annihilate society. However, state intervention in the economy was also necessary for markets to function – free trade, commercial exchanges and liberal markets have always been policies of the state and have not emerged organically or independently of it.

As List and many since have explained, the state plays a crucial role in the economic development of industrial societies, protecting embryonic industries from external competition until they are ready to win global market shares on an equal footing. There are few, if any examples of states emerging as industrial powerhouses by initially adopting a policy of free trade. Protectionism and state coordinated economic development have been key early ingredients of economic success in the modern world, as the post-war experience of East Asia suggests.

Liberalism and globalization

To a significant extent, the globalization of the world economy coincided with a renaissance of neo-liberal thinking in the Western world. The political triumph of the 'New Right' in Britain and the United States in particular during the late 1970s and 1980s was achieved at the expense of Keynesianism, the first coherent philosophy of state intervention in economic life. According to the Keynesian formula, the state intervened in the economy to smooth out the business cycle, provide a degree of social equity and security, and maintain full employment. Neo-liberals, who favoured the free play of 'market forces' and a minimal role for the state in economic life, wanted to 'roll back' the welfare state, in the process challenging the social-democratic consensus established in most Western states during the post-war period.

Just as the ideological predilection of Western governments became more concerned with efficiency and productivity and less concerned with welfare and social justice, the power of the state to regulate the market was eroded by the forces of globalization, in particular the de-regulation of finance and currency markets. The means by which domestic societies could be managed to reduce inequalities produced by inherited social structures and accentuated by the natural workings of the market, declined significantly. In addition, the disappearance of many traditional industries in Western economies, the effects of technological change, increased competition for investment and production and the mobility of capital, undermined the bargaining power of labour. The sovereignty of capital began to reign over both the interventionary behaviour of the state and the collective power of organized working people.

There is a considerable debate over globalization, between liberals who believe it constitutes a fundamentally new phase of capitalism and statists who are sceptical of such claims (Held *et al.* 1999; Held and McGrew 2000). Liberals point to the increasing irrelevance of national borders to the conduct and organization of economic activity. They focus on the growth of free trade, the capacity of transnational corporations (TNCs) to escape political regulation and national legal jurisdictions, and the liberation of capital from national and territorial constraints (Ohmae 1995; Friedman 2000; Micklewait and Wooldridge 2000). Sceptics, on the other hand, claim that the world was less open and globalized at the end of the twentieth century than it was in the nineteenth. They suggest that the volume of world trade relative to the size of the world economy is much the same as it was in 1914, though they concede that the enormous explosion of short-term speculative capital transfers since the collapse of the Bretton Woods system in the early 1970s has restricted the planning options for national governments. Significantly,

sceptics want to distinguish between the idea of an international economy with growing links between separate national economies, which
they concede, and a single global political economy without meaningful
national borders or divisions, which they deny (Weiss 1998; Chomsky
1999b; Hirst and Thompson 1996; Hobsbawm 2000).

The next section will examine the extent to which liberal ideas have
shaped the current economic order. It will focus on the contemporary
nature of world trade, the questions of sovereignty and foreign investment and the challenges to liberal ideas recently posed by Islamic
terrorism.

The nature of 'free trade'

For neo-liberals, the principles of free trade first enunciated by Smith and
Ricardo continue to have contemporary relevance. Commercial traders
should be allowed to exchange money and goods without concern for
national barriers. There should be few legal constraints on international
commerce, and no artificial protection or subsidies constraining the freedom to exchange. An open global market, where goods and services can
pass freely across national boundaries, should be the objective of policy
makers in all nation-states. Only free trade will maximize economic
growth and generate the competition that will promote the most efficient
use of resources, people and capital.

Conversely, protectionism is seen as a pernicious influence on the body
politic. Policies which protect uncompetitive industries from market
principles corrupt international trade, distort market demand, artificially
lower prices and encourage inefficiency, while penalizing fair traders.
Protection is the cry of 'special' or 'vested' interests in society and should
be resisted by government in 'the national interest'. It penalizes developing nations by excluding them from entry into the global marketplace
where they can exploit their domestic advantage in cheap labour.

The cornerstone of the free trade argument is the theory of comparative advantage, which discourages national self-sufficiency by advising
states to specialize in goods and services they can produce most cheaply
– their 'factor endowments'. They can then exchange their goods for
what is produced more cheaply elsewhere. As everything is then
produced most efficiently by the discipline of the price mechanism, the
production of wealth is maximized and everyone is better off. For Smith,
the 'invisible hand' of market forces directs every member of society in
every state to the most advantageous position in the global economy. The
self-interest of one becomes the general interest of all.

The relevance of the theory of comparative advantage in the era of
globalization has come under question (Strange 1985; Bairoch 1993;

Daly and Cobb 1994 ; Clairmont 1996). The first difficulty is that it was devised at a time when there were national controls on capital movements. Ricardo and Smith assumed that capital was immobile and available only for national investment. They also assumed that the capitalist was first and foremost a member of a national political community, which was the context in which he established his commercial identity: Smith's 'invisible hand' presupposed the internal bondings of community, so that the capitalist felt a 'natural disinclination' to invest abroad. Smith and Ricardo could not have foreseen 'a world of cosmopolitan money managers and TNCs which, in addition to having limited liability and immorality conferred on them by national governments, have now transcended those very governments and no longer see the national community as their context' (Daly and Cobb 1994: 215). The emergence of capitalists who freed themselves from community obligations and loyalties, and who had no 'natural disinclination' to invest abroad, would have appeared absurd. Highly mobile and volatile capital markets are a major challenge for the theory of comparative advantage.

The second problem is that the forms of international trade have changed dramatically over recent decades. The idea of national, sovereign states trading with each other as discrete economic units is becoming an anachronism. Intra-industry or intra-firm trade dominates the manufacturing sector of the world economy. Over 40 per cent of all trade now comprises intra-firm transactions, which are centrally managed interchanges within TNCs (that cross international borders) guided by a highly 'visible hand'. Intra-firm trade runs counter to the theory of comparative advantage which advises nations to specialize in products where factor endowments provide a comparative cost advantage. The mobility of capital and technology, and the extent to which firms trade with each other, means that 'governments in virtually all industrial societies now take an active interest in trying to facilitate links between their own domestic firms – including offshoots of multinationals – and the global networks' in strategic industries. They can no longer remain at arm's length from business as neo-liberal economic theory demands (Emy 1993: 173).

Similarly, the globalization of the world economy has seen the spread of manufacturing industries to many developing countries and the relocation of transnational manufacturing centres to what are often low-wage, high-repression areas – regions with low health and safety standards where organized labour is frequently suppressed or illegal. TNCs are becoming increasingly adept at circumventing national borders in their search for cheap labour and access to raw materials, and few states can refuse to play host to them. The creation of new centres of production occurs wherever profit opportunities can be maximized because investment decisions are governed by absolute profitability rather than comparative advantage. For liberals, this is the best way of encouraging much-needed foreign investment in the developing world and establishing a trade profile for countries which might otherwise be excluded from world trade altogether.

Modern trading conditions have diverged significantly from the assumptions which underpin the neo-liberal analysis of how markets and trade actually work. The internationalization of production, the mobility of capital and the dominance of transnational corporations are just three developments which render theories of comparative advantage some-what anachronistic. The idea of national sovereign states trading with each other as discrete economic units is steadily becoming the exception rather than the rule. Neo-mercantilist theory, which stresses the maxi-mization of national wealth, also fails to explain contemporary trade realities. A more accurate description is 'corporate mercantilism', with 'managed commercial interactions within and among huge corporate groupings, and regular state intervention in the three major Northern blocs to subsidize and protect domestically-based international corpora-tions and financial institutions' (Chomsky 1994: 95). If there is such a thing as a nation's comparative advantage it is clearly a human achieve-ment and certainly not a gift of nature, though this view remains unorthodox within powerful economic circles.

The third challenge to the relevance of the theory of comparative advantage is the steady erosion of the rules which have underpinned multilateral trade in the post-war era. While there has been a reduction in barriers to trade *within* blocs such as the European Union and the North American Free Trade Agreement (NAFTA), they have been raised *between* blocs. Tariffs have come down but they have been replaced by a wide assortment of non-tariff barriers (NTBs), including import quotas and voluntary restraint agreements. This is a concern to small, 'fair' traders which are incapable of matching the subsidies provided by Europeans and North Americans. States which unilaterally adopt free market doctrines while leading industrial societies head in the opposite direction place themselves in a vulnerable position in the world economy. But regardless of whether tariff barriers and NTBs are dismantled, the world market would not be 'free' in any meaningful sense, because of the power of the TNCs to control and distort markets through transfer pric-ing and other devices.

The proliferation of free trade agreements and organizations such as NAFTA, Asia Pacific Economic Cooperation (APEC) and the WTO and the growing importance of international organizations such as the G8, the International Monetary Fund (IMF) and World Bank is indicative of the influence of neo-liberalism in the post-Cold War period. These are powerful transnational bodies which embody free trade as their govern-ing ideology. To their supporters, they provide developing societies with the only opportunity to overcome financial hardship and modernize their economies. To their critics, however, they impose free market strictures on developing societies. They are organizations which institutionalize market relationships between states. By locking the developing world into agreements which force them to lower their protective barriers, NAFTA and the WTO, for example, prevent the South from developing trade profiles which diverge from the model dictated by their supposed 'comparative advantage'. The IMF and the World Bank, on the other hand, make the provision of finance (or, more accurately, 'debt') to devel-oping societies conditional on their unilateral acceptance of free market rules for their economies – the 'conditionality' of the so-called 'structural adjustment policies' or SAPs.

Critics attack these institutions for legitimizing only one kind of global order, based on unequal market relations. Specifically, the institutions are criticized for imposing identical prescriptions for economic development on all countries, regardless of what conditions prevail locally. Developing societies are expected to adopt the free market blueprint (sometimes called the 'Washington Consensus') – opening their economies up to foreign investment, financial de-regulation, reductions in government expenditure and budgetary deficits, the privatization of government-owned enterprises, the abolition of protection and subsidies, developing export orientated economies – or risk the withholding of much needed aid and finance. And because they are required to remove national con-trols on capital movements – which make it possible for states to reach their own conclusions about investment and spending priorities – the direction of their economic development is increasingly set by amor-phous financial markets which act on profit opportunities rather than out of any consideration of national or community interest.

Arguments for free trade are powerfully made on the grounds of economic efficiency and as the only way of integrating the developing world into the wider global economy. Protectionism within the North disadvantages the South by pricing their economies out of markets in the industrialized world, thus denying them the opportunity to modernize their economies. For economic liberals, free trade is a battle which must be fought within and outside the industrialized world.

Sovereignty and foreign investment

The enormous volumes of unregulated capital liberated by the collapse of the Bretton Woods system in the early 1970s, have transformed the relationships between states and markets. Credit (bonds and loans), investment (Foreign Direct Investment, or FDI) and money (foreign exchange) now flow more freely across the world than commodities. The resulting increase in the power of transnational capital and the diminution of national economic sovereignty is perhaps the most impressive realization of liberal economic ideas (Strange 1996, 1998).

The relationship between a nation's economic prosperity and the world's money markets is decisive. Because most states are incapable of generating sufficient endogenous wealth to finance their economic development, governments need to provide domestic economic conditions which will attract foreign investment into their countries. In a world where capital markets are globally linked and money can be electronically transferred around the world in microseconds, states are judged in terms of their comparative 'hospitality' to foreign capital: that is, they must offer the most attractive investment climates to relatively scarce supplies of money. This gives the foreign investment community significant leverage over policy settings and the course of a nation's economic development generally, and constitutes a diminution in the country's economic sovereignty.

The power of transnational finance capital in the modern period can scarcely be overestimated. The volume of foreign exchange trading in the major financial centres of the world, estimated at over $US1.5 trillion per day, has come to dwarf international trade by at least 60 times. UN statistics suggest that the world's 100 largest TNCs, with assets of over $US5 trillion, account for a third of the total FDI of their home states, giving them increasing influence over the economies of host countries.

The brokers on Wall Street and in Tokyo, the clients of the 'screen jockeys' in the foreign exchange rooms, and the auditors from credit ratings agencies such as Moody's and Standard & Poor's, pass daily judgements on the management of individual economies, and signal to the world's financial community the comparative profit opportunities to be found in a particular country. Inappropriate interventionary policies by government can be quickly deterred or penalized with a (threatened) reduction in the nation's credit rating, a 'run' (sell off) on its currency or an investment 'strike'. The requirements of the international markets can be ignored only at a nation's economic peril. Not only have nation-states lost direct control over the value of their currencies and the movements of capital around the world, they can no longer determine the institutional settings in which capital markets operate. Neo-liberals regard this development as a positive change, believing that on the question of allocating resources, markets rather than the governments know what is in peoples' best interests.

Finance markets, dominated by large banks and financial institutions, insurance companies, brokers and speculators, exist only to maximize their own wealth. There is no compelling reason for them to act in the interests of the poor, the homeless, the infirm or those who are deprived of their basic human rights by their own governments. States which cede economic sovereignty to these global players in the name of free trade and commerce therefore run the risk of elevating private commercial gain to the primary foreign policy objective of the state.

When the foreign investment community is freed from state barriers and controls, and able to choose the most profitable location for its capital, it has the effect of homogenizing the economic development of nation-states across the globe. In what is effectively a bidding war for much-needed infusions of capital, states are driven by the lowest common denominator effect to reduce their regulations, standards, wages and conditions, in order to appear attractive to the investor community. Priority is given to the drive for efficiency and profits. The threat of disinvestment becomes the stick for markets to wield over the heads of government. For liberals, this is a pleasing reversal of modern history which they see as a struggle for liberation from the clutches of arbitrary state power. Ironically, in many instances the key to attracting overseas investment is for the host government to provide the transnational investor with subsidies and protection from market forces. In some cases, this is the only way states can win and maintain the confidence of global markets.

The ill-fated 1995–8 Multilateral Agreement on Investments (MAI) was a vivid illustration of just how far governments in the developed world have been prepared to follow liberal advice and surrender their discretionary economic power to the markets. In this case Organisation for Economic Co-operation and Development (OECD) members were offering voluntarily to restrict their own ability to discriminate against foreign capital. The MAI is a reminder that, as with the establishment of national markets in the nineteenth century, globalization is not the result of the gradual and spontaneous emancipation of the economic sphere from government control. On the contrary, it has been the outcome of conscious and sometimes violent state intervention by advanced capitalist states. Just as domestically the labour market can be 'freed' only by legislative restrictions placed on trades unions, the creation of the post-war liberal trading regime and the de-regulation of the world's capital markets in the 1970s required deliberate acts by interventionary states.

During the current phase of globalization, national economic sovereignty has not so much been lost but either enthusiastically given away or begrudgingly surrendered. The state's capacity to direct the national economy has been deliberately and significantly undercut by the globalization of relations of production and exchange. Significant sovereign power has been ceded to bond holders, fund managers, currency traders, speculators, transnational banks and insurance companies – groups that by definition are democratically unaccountable in any national jurisdiction. In effect, the world economy has come to resemble the global strategic environment. It has become anarchic in character and, as a consequence, the competition for economic security is as intense as the search for strategic security.

Unsurprisingly, concern about a growing 'democratic deficit' has arisen within and outside liberal political philosophy. According to Eric Hobsbawm, economic globalization is undermining liberal democracy as participation in the market replaces participation in politics: the voter in elections is being displaced by the consumer in the market.

Hobsbawm identifies three areas where the power and authority of the state has been undermined by globalization. The first sees the state's monopoly of coercive force being eroded by non-state actors, such as terrorists, who seek weapons of mass destruction. Second, the commitment and loyalty of citizens to the state is weakening. The capacity for states to conscript citizens for military service, to administer colonial rule, and to compel people to abide by the law (e.g. speed cameras, computer hacking and viruses, music downloading), has significantly reduced. It is becoming more difficult for democratic governments to mobilize their populations for war, regardless of their ruling ideology. Finally, the ability of governments to provide public goods – arbitration, law and order, personal security, etc. – has been damaged by the liberation of market forces, such as the privatization of state services and the de-regulation of capital markets. The state as an essential unit of liberal democracy is weakening while public antipathy to globalization grows (Hobsbawm 2007).

David Held's (1995) advocacy of cosmopolitan democracy is seen as utopian by hard-nosed, realists, however it is a serious attempt to bring some of the forces of globalization under a degree of popular control. Proposals such as regional parliaments and the devolution of sovereign power to regional bodies, universal human rights benchmarks entrenched in domestic jurisdictions and monitored by international courts, radical reform of the United Nations (UN) and the promotion of a global civil society are serious suggestions for extending and modernizing democratic politics. The work of Held and his colleagues is an important reminder that as well as rendering significant economic change, globalization has important political challenges and implications which liberals cannot ignore (Archibugi and Held 1995; Held 1995; Archibugi 1998).

Non-state terrorism

Whether or not the current wave of Islamic militancy is the latest chapter in a long-standing revolt against the West, there can be little doubt that it represents a direct challenge to both the claim that liberal democracy is the universal destination for the species and the assumption that globalization is inexorable. However incoherent and unlikely it is as a political programme, Islamic terrorism is profoundly anti-secular and an opponent of liberal modernity (Gray 2004).

It seems premature and misleading for liberals to claim that the emergence of Al-Qaeda and affiliated groups which perpetrate transnational terrorism constitutes a victory for the deterritorialization of world politics (Buzan 2003: 297, 303). Rather as David Harvey notes, 'the war on terror, swiftly followed by the prospect of war with Iraq . . . [has] allowed the state to accumulate more power,' a claim difficult to refute and one that poses an unexpected challenge to liberals who believed that globalization was finally eroding the sovereign significance of the state (Harvey 2003: 17). The national security state has been revived.

The resuscitation of state power across the industrialized world after the 9/11 attacks has taken numerous forms, including new restrictions on civil liberties, greater powers of surveillance and detention, increased military spending and the expansion of intelligence services. The threats posed by Islamic terror and the dangers of Weapons of Mass Destruction (WMD) have also been matched by an increase in state intervention around the world, in particular by US-led coalitions acting in Afghanistan and Iraq. With each subsequent terrorist assault, states which consider themselves innocent victims have been emboldened to interfere in each others' internal affairs – even pre-emptively.

Pre-emption, the disarmament of states alleged to possess WMD, regime change, humanitarianism and the spread of democracy have all been invoked as public justifications for these interventions, although critics have pointed to traditional geo-strategic rationales beneath the surface. Many states, such as China, Israel and Russia, have also used the cover provided by the 'war against terror' to settle domestic scores with secessionists, dissidents and those resisting their territorial occupations. Others seem to be victims of 'blowback', reaping disastrous and unintended consequences from earlier foreign policy actions. Regardless of what the true motives of these interventions are, the irony of socially conservative, economically neo-liberal governments expanding the reach and size of government should not be lost on anyone (Johnson 2002).

The return of the overarching state is perhaps an unsurprising response to community calls for protection from non-state terrorism. When citizens of a state require emergency medical relief, as many victims of the Bali bombings did in October 2002, there is little point appealing to market forces for help. Nor can those responsible for attacks such as the Beslan school atrocity in September 2004 be hunted down, disarmed and prosecuted by privately owned TNCs. Even if the state is no longer prepared to insulate its citizens from the vicissitudes of the world economy, it is still expected to secure them from the threat of terrorism. Only the state can meet these and many other challenges such as 'border protection' and transnational crime. There are no market-based solutions to the dangers posed by what seems to be the latest chapter in the revolt against the West.

Since the end of the Cold War, realists such as Kenneth Waltz have argued that in the absence of effective countervailing pressures, the United States is likely to become increasingly unilateral in seeking to secure its foreign policy interests, and in so doing rely on military power to realize its vision of a new world order. The 'war against terror' has seemingly changed little in this regard. If anything, these events have enhanced a trend which some liberals had either believed or hoped had passed into history.

Historian Eric Hobsbawm has observed that 'the basic element to understanding the present situation is that 9/11 did not threaten the US. It was a terrible human tragedy which humiliated the US, but in no sense was it any weaker after those attacks. Three, four or five attacks will not change the position of the US or its relative power in the world' (Hobsbawm 2002).

This view is similar to Waltz's claim that the problem of terrorism does not challenge the continuities of international politics. 'Although terrorists can be terribly bothersome', says Waltz, 'they hardly pose threats to the fabric of a society or the security of the state . . . Terrorism does not change the first basic fact of international politics – the gross imbalance of world power' in favour of the United States. 'Instead, the effect of September 11 has been to enhance American power and extend its military presence in the world' (Waltz 2002: 348–53).

Realists in the United States also led the intellectual opposition to Washington's attack on Iraq in March 2003, arguing that Saddam Hussein had been successfully contained, that he was prevented from using his WMD against the West because of the likely consequences to him and that for similar reasons he couldn't risk passing these weapons – if he in fact possessed them – to groups such as Al-Qaeda. As during the Second Cold War in the Reagan era, realists found themselves in the unusual position of being at the limits of respectable dissent in debates over the Iraq war as a consequence of the influence of the misnamed neo-conservatives, whose muscular liberalism underwrote the administration of George W. Bush (Mearsheimer and Walt 2002; Hobsbawm 2007).

Conclusion

At the beginning of this chapter, it was argued that liberalism was an 'inside-out' approach to international relations, because liberals favour a world in which the endogenous determines the exogenous. Their challenge is to extend the legitimacy of domestic political arrangements found within democratic states to the relationships between all nation-states. To put it another way, liberals believe that democratic society, in which civil liberties are protected and market relations prevail, can have an international analogue in the form of a peaceful global order. The domestic free market has its counterpart in the open, globalized world economy. Parliamentary debate and accountability is reproduced in international fora such as the United Nations. And the legal protection of civil rights within liberal democracies is extended to the promotion of human rights across the world. With the collapse of Communism as an alternative political and economic order, the potential for continuity between the domestic and the international became greater than in any previous period.

Fukuyama had reason to be optimistic. The spread of liberal democracies and the zone of peace was an encouraging development, as is the realization by states that trade and commerce is more closely correlated with economic success than territorial conquest. The number of governments enjoying civilian rather than military rule has increased, and ethical considerations and ideas of human justice have a permanent place on the diplomatic agenda. There can be little doubt that the great powers are now much less inclined to use force to resolve their political differences with each other and it appears that liberal democracies are in the process of constructing a separate peace.

The globalization of the world economy means that there are few obstacles to international trade. Liberals want to remove the influence of the state in commercial relations between businesses and individuals, and the decline of national economic sovereignty is an indication that the influence of the state is diminishing. TNCs and capital markets wield significant influence over the shape of the world economy, in the process homogenizing the political economies of every member state of the international community.

Globalization has undermined the nation-state in other ways that have pleased liberals. The capacity of each state to direct the political loyalties of its citizens has been weakened by an increasing popular awareness of the problems faced by the entire human species. The state cannot prevent its citizens turning to a range of sub-national and transnational agents to secure their political identities and promote their political objectives. Sovereignty is no longer an automatic protection against external interference called 'humanitarian intervention'. And decision making on a range of environmental, economic and security questions has become internationalized, rendering national administration less important than transnational political cooperation.

Despite these important changes, there are also counter-trends which can be identified. Realists would argue that liberals such as Ohmae are premature in announcing the demise of the nation-state. They would remind the enthusiasts for globalization that as a preferred form of political community, the nation-state still has no serious rival. There are currently around 200 nation-states in the world asserting their political independence, and figure grows each year.

Realists cite a number of important powers retained by the state despite globalization, including monopoly control of the weapons of war and their legitimate use, and the sole right to tax its citizens. They would argue that only the nation-state can still command the political allegiances of its citizens or adjudicate in disputes between them. And it is still only the nation-state which has the exclusive authority to bind the whole community to international law.

They would question the extent to which globalization today is an unprecedented phenomenon, citing the nineteenth century as period when similar levels of economic interdependence existed. They would also point to the growing number of states which reject the argument that Western modernity is universally valid or that political development always terminates at liberal-capitalist democracy. More recently realists have highlighted the expanding reach of the state as a result of the latest wave of anti-Western Islamic militancy – a significant reversal for liberals who anticipated the imminent demise of the nation-state. Islamism is a direct challenge to liberal assumptions about economics and politics terminating at a liberal capitalist consensus.

Unpredictable challenges have left liberalism on the back foot, questioning whether the linear path to improving the human condition is as straight and as inexorable as they thought only a few short years ago.

4 | The English School

ANDREW LINKLATER

The 'English School' is a term that was coined in the 1970s to describe a group of predominantly British, or British-inspired, writers for whom international society is the primary object of analysis (Jones 1981; Linklater and Suganami 2006). Its most influential members include Hedley Bull, Martin Wight, John Vincent and Adam Watson whose main publications appeared between the mid-1960s and the late 1980s (see Bull 1977; Wight 1977; 1991; Watson 1982; Bull and Watson 1984; Vincent 1986). Robert Jackson, Tim Dunne and Nicholas Wheeler have been among the most influential members of the English School in more recent years (Dunne 1998; Jackson 2000; Wheeler 2000). Since the late 1990s, the English School has enjoyed a renaissance in large part because of the efforts of Barry Buzan, Richard Little, Andrew Hurrell and several other scholars (Little 2000; Buzan 2001; 2003; Hurrell 2007). The English School remains one of the most important approaches to international politics although its influence is probably greater in Britain than in most other societies where International Relations is taught.

The foundational claim of the English School is that sovereign states form a society, but an anarchic one since they do not have to submit to a higher power. The fact that states have succeeded in creating a society of sovereign equals is regarded as one of the most fascinating dimensions of international relations. There is, it is argued, a remarkably high level of order, and surprisingly little inter-state violence, given the absence of a world-wide monopoly of power. Readers are invited to reflect on the probable level of violence, fear, insecurity and distrust in even the most stable of domestic societies should sovereign authority collapse. A condition of chaos would most likely ensue, but this is not the central characteristic of world politics.

That is not to suggest that the English School underestimates the importance of force in relations between states. Its members regard violence as an endemic feature of the 'anarchical society' (the title of Hedley Bull's most famous work, 1977) but they add that international

86

law and morality control it to a significant extent. Confusion about the main purpose of the School can result from the evidence that some members seem unreservedly realist at times. This is most apparent in Wight's essay, 'Why is there no International Theory?' (1966a, which maintained that domestic politics is the sphere of the good life whereas international politics is the realm of security and survival (Wight 1966a: 33). Realism is also evident in his argument that international relations are 'incompatible with progressivist theory'. In a statement that seems to place him squarely in the realist camp, Wight (1996a: 26) maintained that Sir Thomas More would recognize the basic features of international politics in the 1960s since nothing fundamental has changed over the last few centuries. Some have argued that the English School is essentially a British variant on realism that exaggerates the importance of the veneer of society and pays insufficient attention to its role in safeguarding the privileges of leading powers and their dominant interests (for a critical discussion, see Wheeler and Dunne 1996).

Members of the English School are attracted by elements of realism and idealism, yet gravitate towards the middle ground, never wholly reconciling themselves to either point of view. This is precisely how Wight (1991) described 'rationalism' or the 'Grotian tradition', from which the English School is descended, in an influential series of lectures that were delivered at the London School of Economics in the 1950s. He argued that 'rationalism' was the 'via media' between realism and what he called 'revolutionism' – that medley of perspectives which he associated with the belief that global peace and justice are imminent (see also Wight 1966a: 91). Reference was made to Grotius' comment in his great work, *De Jure Belli ac Pacis* first published in 1625, that those who believe that anything goes in war are as deluded as those who believe that the use of force can never be justified. Grotius envisaged an international society in which violence between Catholic and Protestant states would give way to a condition of relatively peaceful coexistence. In his lectures, Wight lamented the way in which debates between realism and utopianism in the inter-war years had neglected the *via media* with its distinctive focus on international society.

In short, members of the English School (and this is a loose collection of scholars with open borders) maintain that the international system is more orderly and civil than realists and neo-realists suggest. But since violence is probably ineradicable in their view, they are at odds with utopians who believe in the possibility of perpetual peace. There is no expectation that the international political system will come to enjoy levels of close cooperation and security that exist in stable national societies. There is, then, more to international politics than realists suggest but there will always be less than the cosmopolitan desires. That is why it makes sense to argue that English School analysts think there has been limited progress in international politics.

The nature of the *'via media'* can be explored further by noting the contrasts with realism and 'revolutionism'. Also important is exploring the claim that the English School offers a limited progressivist account of world politics. As Chapter 2 has shown, realism emphasizes the unending competition for power and security in the world of states. Sovereignty, anarchy and the security dilemma are crucial terms in its lexicon. The idea of progress is largely absent from its vocabulary. Moral principles and social progress are seen as relevant to domestic politics where trust prevails and where security is provided by the state, but cosmopolitan projects are thought to have marginal relevance for international relations where states must provide for their own security and distrust is pervasive. In the latter domain, moral principles serve to legitimate national interests and to stigmatize principal competitors: they are not the basis for some experiment in world political organization that will supersede the nation-state.

The existence of a more or less unbridgeable gulf between domestic and international politics is a central theme in realist and neo-realist thought. By contrast, cosmopolitan thinkers envisage a world order – but not necessarily a world government – in which universal moral principles are taken seriously, and the gulf between domestic and international politics is reduced. From that approach, global political reform is not only possible but of vital importance to end the struggle for power and security. The tension between those two approaches has been crucial to the history of international thought and was especially evident in the so-called 'first debate' between realists and idealists.

The characteristics of that debate need not detain us. Suffice it to note that it was mainly focused on whether the development of a strong sense of moral obligation to human beings everywhere is the key to building peaceful international relations. Liberal internationalists thought that realism was unjustifiably pessimistic about the feasibility of radical change and lacking in political imagination. Realists countered by maintaining that liberal internationalists were naively optimistic about the prospects for a new world order based on the rule of law, open diplomacy and collective security, and they added that such ideas were dangerous because they distracted attention from the main purpose of foreign policy which is to ensure the immediate security and survival of the state. The violence of 'the inter-war years' and the tensions peculiar to the bipolar era secured the victory of realism.

Bull argued that realists focus on struggles for power and security in an international system while liberal or 'utopian' thinkers reflect on the possibility of a world community. The English School recognizes that their respective positions contain valuable insights. Realist observations about how adversaries try to out manoeuvre, control and overpower one another in the condition of anarchy are undeniably important, but they capture only part of the substance of world politics. Despite the fact that each state possesses a monopoly of control of the instruments of violence, the international system is far from a state of war. Common interests in restraining the use of force have led states to develop the art of accommodation and compromise that has made international society possible.

Watson (1987) later argued that a 'strong case can be made out, on the evidence of past systems as well as the present one, that the regulatory rules and institutions of a system usually, and perhaps inexorably, develop to the point where the members become conscious of common values and the system becomes an international society'. That might seem to give the utopian thinker hope that more radical developments are achievable, but it was not the conclusion to which English School thinkers are generally drawn. The latter argue that the advocates of utopian visions of a universal human community can point to evidence that concerns about human rights, peace and justice have influenced the development of world politics. Like realists, members of the English School begin with the condition of anarchy but they are more inclined to take arguments for global reform seriously rather than allocate them peripheral status or to describe them as arenas in which states compete for influence and power. But English School works invariably stress that visionaries are wrong in thinking that the current international order is a stepping stone to a world community. The crucial point is not that states are locked in a struggle for power but that they have different conceptions of human rights and global justice along with conflicting beliefs about how such ideals can be implemented. Recent debates about whether this is an appropriate moment to support humanitarian intervention in response to regimes that are guilty of gross violations of human rights illustrate the kind of moral disagreement which the English School regards as typical of international society (Jackson 2000; Wheeler 2000). Indeed, members of the English School stress that noble efforts to improve international politics have the potential to produce major moral disagreements that can sour relations between states and damage international order. Most have been sceptical of proposals for large-scale global change, and most have doubted that any such vision will ever appeal to the majority of nation-states or persuade the great powers to sacrifice vital political and economic interests.

The crucial point then is that realism and revolutionism have failed to recognize the significance of efforts to build and maintain international society. The English School insists, however, that the survival of that society can never be taken for granted. It can easily be undermined by anti-status quo or expansionist powers. There is no guarantee that the modern society of states will survive indefinitely, or that it will succeed in keeping crude self-interest at bay, but as long as international society survives it will be important to understand its foundations and to ask how it can be strengthened. Observing that demands for morality and justice have always influenced international relations, Wight (1977: 192) maintained that 'the fundamental political task at all times [is] to provide order, or security, from which law, justice and prosperity may afterwards develop'. During the Cold War years, English School writers were inclined to stress the importance of order rather than justice or prosperity, but since the mid-1980s many have taken a more explicitly normative stance on issues of poverty and human rights. In the more optimistic world of the early 1990s, members of the 'critical international society' approach were especially interested in the possibility that states could be 'good international citizens' that cooperated to promote cosmopolitan values (Dunne 1998; Wheeler and Dunne 1998).

English School writings have long maintained that the great powers can be 'great responsibles' that do not always place self-interest ahead of preserving international order. However, the great powers usually pose the most serious threat to international society (Wight 1991: 130). In the current phase of American hegemony, a principal theme in English School theory has become especially central, namely whether international society is ultimately dependent on the existence of a balance of military power. Dunne (2003) foregrounds this question in his discussion of the emergence since 9/11 of the doctrine of 'preventive war' in response to US fears that hostile regimes will share weapons of mass destruction with terrorist groups. Such discussions reveal how great powers rewrite the rules of international society to suit their interests – or, as in the case of the US position on the International Criminal Court, ignore any that they regard as inconvenient (Ralph 2007). Other English School writers continue to examine the ways in which international society can be improved. Two examples are Wheeler's reflections on the case for introducing a limited principle of humanitarian intervention into international society and Keal's argument for changes to improve the position of the world's indigenous peoples (Wheeler 2000; Keal 2003). Indeed, one would expect proponents of an approach that is positioned between the poles of realism and utopianism to maintain this focus on the prospects for improving international society and on the obstacles that stand in the way. No member of the English School is naive about the possibility of radical global change, but differences between more 'radical' and more 'conservative' proponents have appeared in recent years, and not least over the issue of humanitarian intervention.

The remainder of this chapter is in four sections. The first focuses on the idea of order and society in core English School texts. The second considers English School analyses of the relative importance of order and justice in the traditional European society of states. That is followed by a discussion of the 'revolt against the West' and the emergence of the first universal society of states in which demands for justice are frequently heard. The fourth section returns to the question of English School reflections on the limited progress that has occurred in international relations, and it offers some final observations about the idea that its position as the *via media* gives it an advantage over other positions in the field.

From power to order: international society

We have seen that the English School analyses the surprisingly high level of order that exists between independent political communities in the condition of anarchy. Some such as Wight (1977: 43) were fascinated by the small number of international societies that have existed in human history and by their relatively short life-spans, all previous examples having been destroyed by empire after a few centuries. Wight (1977: 35–9) also noted the propensity for internal schism in the form of international revolutions that have brought transnational forces and ideologies rather than sovereign communities into conflict. He posed the interesting question of whether commerce first brought different societies into contact, thereby creating the context in which a society of states could develop (1977: 33). In his remarks about the three international societies about which most is known (the Ancient Chinese, the Graeco-Roman and the modern society of states) he maintained (1977: 33–5) each emerged in a region that possessed a high level of linguistic and cultural unity. Independent political communities felt they belonged to the 'civilized' world and were superior to their neighbours. A sense of their 'cultural differentiation' from allegedly semi-civilized and barbaric peoples facilitated communication between them, making it easier to define the rights and duties that bound them together in an exclusive international society.

Writing on the evolution of modern international society, Wight's protégé, Hedley Bull (1977: 82) observed that in 'the form of the doctrine of natural law, ideas of human justice historically preceded the development of ideas of interstate or international justice and provided perhaps the principal intellectual foundations upon which these latter ideas at first rested'. Those words seem to echo Wight's position that some sense of cultural unity is essential before an international society can develop. But that was not Bull's position. He stressed that international society can exist in the absence of linguistic, cultural or religious agreement.

Clarifying the point, Bull introduced a distinction between an international system and an international society which does not exist in Wight's own work. A 'system of states (or international system)', he argued, 'is formed when two or more states have sufficient contact between them, and have sufficient impact on one another's decisions to cause them to behave – at least in some measure – as parts of a whole' (1977: 9–10). A society of states exists 'when a group of states, conscious of certain common interests and common values, form a society in the sense that they conceive themselves to be bound by a common set of rules in their relations with one another, and share in the working of common institutions' (1977: 13). This important distinction underpinned Bull's efforts to develop a more precise account of how international societies develop.

As we have seen, Bull maintained that order can exist between states that do not feel they belong to a common civilization. A pragmatic need to coexist will suffice to produce what Bull (1977: 316) called a 'diplomatic culture' – those conventions and institutions that preserve order between states that are divided by culture and ideology. He added that a diplomatic culture is likely to be stronger if it is anchored in an 'international political culture' – that is, if states share the same general way of life. Illustrating the point, Bull and Watson argued that, in the nineteenth century, the European society of states did rest on an international political culture, but with the expansion of that society to include all parts of the world, the sense of belonging to a common civilization has declined. Even so, the basic rules of the international society that first developed in Europe have been accepted by a large majority of its former colonies, now equal sovereign members of the first universal society of states. No international political culture currently underpins the diplomatic culture; however Bull (1977: 316–17) thought that condition might change if different elites across the world come to share a 'cosmopolitan culture' of modernity.

Bull (1977: 53–5) provides the most detailed analysis of the foundations of international order. He argues that all societies – domestic and international – have arrangements for protecting the three 'primary goals' of placing constraints on violence, upholding property rights and ensuring that agreements are kept. The fact that those primary goals are common to domestic and international society explains Bull's rejection of 'the domestic analogy' which is the idea that international order will not develop until states surrender their powers to centralized institutions of the kind that exist at the national level (Suganami 1989). As we have seen, English School writers break with realism because they believe that states can enjoy the benefits of society without transferring sovereign powers to a higher authority. Bull's approach argues that states are usually committed to limiting the use of force, ensuring respect for property and preserving trust in their relations with one another as independent political communities. Those shared interests – rather than any common culture or way of life – are the ultimate foundation of international society.

Nation-states and international society are both concerned with protecting primary goals but the inter-state order is distinctive because of its 'anarchical' nature. The citizens of a state are governed by 'primary rules' that specify how they should behave, and also by 'secondary rules' that determine how such primary rules are created, interpreted and enforced (Bull 1977: 133). Central institutions have the authority to make primary and secondary rules in viable nation-states. But in international society, states create their own primary rules as well as the secondary rules that govern their creation, interpretation and enforcement. In addition, international society has a set of unique primary goals (Bull 1977: 16–20). The idea that only sovereign states can be members of international society (and not individuals or business corporations) is one such distinguishing feature – so is the conviction that the society of states is the only legitimate form of global political organization, and the belief that states should respect one another's sovereignty. Those goals may conflict with one another, as Bull observed in his writings on order and justice which will be considered later in this chapter.

Societies of states exist because most political communities want to constrain the use of force and to bring civility to their external relations. An interesting question is whether some states are more likely than others to attach special value to international society and to protect its institutions that include diplomacy, international law and the practice of balancing the power of those states that aspire to impose their will on others. English School writers argue that international society can be multidenominational and include states that have radically different cultures and philosophies of government. Indeed, in their view a central task of diplomacy is to promote understanding and discover common ground between societies that are wedded to very different cultures and prone to misunderstand each other's aspirations and intentions. English School thinkers are unconvinced by those who think that the members of the society of states must have the same ideology (Wight 1991: 41–2). However, writers such as Wight also argued that European societies that had a strong commitment to constitutional politics played a vital role in the formation of international society (Linklater 1993). It is important to consider that theme in the light of neo-realist and liberal discussions of the relationship between the states-system and its constituent parts.

Kenneth Waltz (1979) has maintained that the international system compels states to take part in the struggle for power and security irrespective of regime-type and ideological persuasion. Criticizing neo-realism,

Michael Doyle (1986) has argued that liberal states have a strong predisposition towards establishing peace with each other, though not with non-liberal states to the same extent. The crucial issue here is how far the 'inside' affects the 'outside' – that is, how far domestic national preferences can shape international order and how far they are overridden by the constraints of anarchy. For English School writers, it is important to understand how the 'inside' influences the 'outside' and vice versa. Wight's essay (1977) on how principles of international legitimacy have changed over the centuries illustrates the point. In that period, dynastic principles of government were replaced by the idea that the people or the nation is the rightful owner of sovereign power; the rules governing membership of international society altered in the process (see also Clark 2005). In an important comment, Wight (1977: 153) added that 'these principles of legitimacy mark the region of approximation *between* international and domestic politics. They are principles that prevail (or are at least proclaimed) *within* a majority of the states that form international society, as well as in the relations between them' (emphasis in the original). Exactly the same point is relevant to recent US claims that legitimate members of international society should respect human rights or be committed to democracy.

English School writers are critical of neo-realism because it neglects the ways in which struggles over domestic and international legitimacy affect world politics. That emphasis makes the English School a natural ally of constructivist approaches to the importance of principles of legitimacy and global norms in international affairs (Edelman 1990; Clark and Reus-Smit 2007; see Chapter 8). At the same time, the former persuasion is critical of contentions that international society depends on a consensus about the regimes that are the rightful members; it is committed to analysing the principles that make it possible for very different social systems to live together amicably. A focus on the 'normative' and 'institutional' factors that give international society its own 'logic' has long been a distinguishing feature of English analysis (Bull and Watson 1984: 9). The increasingly multi-cultural and multi-religious character of contemporary international society only serves to underline the importance of its approach to international order and mutual understanding.

Order and justice in international relations

English School writers have been interested in the processes that transform systems of states into societies of states and in the norms and institutions that prevent the collapse of civility and the emergence of unbridled power. They have been concerned with whether societies of states can develop means of promoting justice for individuals and their immediate associations. We have seen that Bull distinguished between international societies and international systems, but he also distinguished between different types of international society in order to understand the relationship between order and justice in world affairs.

Bull (1966a) introduced an influential distinction between the 'pluralist' and 'solidarist' (or 'Grotian') conceptions of international society. He stressed that the 'central Grotian assumption is that of the solidarity, or potential solidarity, of the states comprising international society, with respect to the enforcement of the law' (Bull 1966a: 52). Solidarism is apparent in the Grotian conviction that there is a clear distinction between just and unjust wars, and in the assumption 'from which [the] right of humanitarian intervention is derived . . . that individual human beings are subjects of international law and members of international society in their own right' (1966a: 64; see Jeffery 2006 on the complexities involved in locating the English School within 'a Grotian tradition'). As expounded by the eighteenth-century international lawyer, Vattel, pluralism rejected that approach. Its central thesis is that 'states do not exhibit solidarity of this kind, but are capable of agreeing only for certain minimum purposes which fall short of that of the enforcement of the law' (1966a: 52). Related arguments are that states – not individuals – are the basic members of international society which has no legitimate interest in matters that fall within their respective national jurisdictions (1966a: 68). Having made this distinction, Bull asked whether the evidence suggested that world politics since the end of World War II were moving gradually from a pluralist to a solidarist international society. The answer provided in Bull (1977: 73) was that expectations of greater solidarity were 'premature'.

To understand his reasoning and its continuing influence, it is necessary to turn to Bull's discussion of primary goals in international society (1977: 16–18, Chapter 4). Bull argued that the goal of preserving the sovereignty of each state has often clashed with the common interest in preserving the balance of power. On three occasions in the eighteenth century, Polish independence was sacrificed for the sake of international equilibrium. The League of Nations decided against defending Abyssinia from Italian aggression because Britain and France needed Italy to balance the might of Nazi Germany. In such cases, order took priority over justice that insists that all sovereign states should be treated equally. Contemporary international society contains other examples of the tension between order and justice. Order and stability require efforts to prevent nuclear proliferation, but justice suggests that all states – and not just the great powers – have the right to acquire weaponry that they regard as central to their defence (1977: 227–8). In this context, it is worth noting that US hegemony and the idea of preventive warfare have created fears that more states will strive to acquire nuclear weapons for reasons of prestige and self-defence, and will appeal to principles of justice to justify their ambitions.

It is also significant that states have different and often conflicting ideas about justice, and that international society can suffer if states try to impose their views on others. Efforts to apply principles of justice to international relations are often highly selective in any event, as various war crimes tribunals since the end of World War II have revealed (1977: 89). What some regard as legitimate international punishment is tantamount to 'Victor's justice' to others. That point has arisen in conjunction with the trials of Milosevic and Saddam Hussein in recent times. Different responses to NATO's military action against Serbia in 1999 further illustrate the point. What leaders such as Blair regarded as essential to rid the world of murderous regimes is the 'new imperialism' for others. Significantly, Bull was keen to stress that Western liberals had to recognize that their views about fundamental human rights do not appeal to many groups and societies in non-Western regions. Advocates of universal human rights had to appreciate that tensions over the meaning of such rights were unavoidable in a multicultural society of states; they had to try to understand those deep moral and cultural differences rather than conclude that other peoples were simply less rational or unenlightened (1977: 126; see also Bull 1979a).

Bull maintained that states often disagree about the meaning of justice but they can concur about how best to maintain international order. Most agree that each state should respect the sovereignty of the others and that they should observe the principle of non-intervention. Each society can then promote its notion of the good life within its own territory, secure that it is recognized as an equal by all others. Bull repeatedly emphasized the difficulties of resolving tensions between order and justice, but he also argued that the purpose of international society is to promote 'order in human society as a whole'. It is 'order among all mankind', he maintained, that has 'primary value, not order within the society of states' (1977: 22). It was incumbent on 'intelligent and sensitive persons' to take visions of 'a world society or community' seriously (1977: 289). That apparent cosmopolitanism sits awkwardly alongside his conviction that there is little evidence that societies are converging on what it would mean to build a world community. But the key point was that states should try to promote world order when circumstances allow, using diplomacy to promote mutual understanding and respect, and recognizing that progress in this domain is likely to be slow and precarious (see Buzan 2004 for a discussion of the relationship between world and international society).

Wight's claim that 'rationalism' is the *via media* between realism and revolutionism is worth recalling at this point. Considered alongside Bull's writings on order and justice, that point can be taken to mean that the English School believes that the existence of a society of states is evidence of progress in agreeing on basic principles of coexistence. The tension between order and justice is a reminder that progress has not advanced very far. Revolutionists are accused of failing to recognize the difficulty that states face in progressing together in the same normative direction. It follows that the English School must always be interested in how naked power or a lack of prudent diplomacy can undo the limited progress that has occurred in creating an international society; but it must also be interested in whether there are any signs that states are making progress (or could make more progress) towards a more just world order.

The development of English School thinking about human rights is fascinating in this regard. Bull (1977: 83) argued that pluralism has triumphed over solidarism in the history of modern international society. Prior to the twentieth century, the solidarist belief in the primacy of individual human rights had survived but 'underground', prompting the reaction that states seemed to have entered into 'a conspiracy of silence . . . about the rights and duties of their respective citizens' (1977: 83). Many states – and especially those that have thrown off imperial rule in recent decades – have feared that human rights law will be used as a pretext for great power interference in their internal affairs. Western self-assurance about the rights that should be respected across the world as a whole has often been counter-productive. However, the long-term trend over recent decades has favoured the introduction of solidarist measures to promote the international protection of human rights (Bull 1984a).

That is the starting-point for the argument of Vincent (1986) which contended that the right of the individual to be free from starvation and malnutrition is one human entitlement on which all states can agree despite deep ideological and other differences. He argued that the lack of the basic means of subsistence should shock the conscience of humankind and stimulate global action. Consensus on that matter would represent a significant advance in relations between the Western world (which has traditionally been concerned with order rather than justice) and the non-Western world (which has stressed the need for global justice). This shift towards solidarism is deeply significant given that Vincent (1974) had previously been a strong advocate of non-intervention as a basic principle of international order. But in his later work, he observed that states are increasingly under pressure to comply with the international law of human rights (Vincent and Wilson 1994). Some human rights violations might be so shocking that states have to consider setting aside the usual convention that they should not intervene in each other's internal affairs. Whether and how they should do so are questions that became central to international relations with the fall of Yugoslavia and genocide in Rwanda, and earlier in Kampuchea (Dunne and Wheeler 1999). International action to try those suspected of war crimes and gross human rights violations has progressed but, as the debate over NATO's military action against Serbia in 1999 demonstrated, there is no global consensus about when sovereignty can be overridden for the sake of human rights.

Indeed, two very different tendencies appeared in English School writings in the mid to late 1990s. Dunne and Wheeler (1999) argued that the end of bipolarity made it possible for states to agree that new principles of humanitarian intervention should be embedded in the constitution of international society. They added that the aspiring 'good international citizen' should intervene in societies where there is a 'supreme humanitarian emergency', even though such action might breach existing international law. That standpoint was rejected by Jackson (2000: 291ff.) who stressed the risk that humanitarian intervention might create rivalry and suspicion between the great powers. Jackson (2000) stressed that many of the most serious violations of human rights occur during military conflicts. In consequence, preserving constraints on violence between states and stability between the great powers should take priority over 'humanitarian war', if there is a need to choose between them.

The 'revolt against the West' is a subject for the next section, but one of its dimensions, namely the demand for racial equality, is pertinent to this discussion. Bull (in Bull and Watson 1984) and Vincent (1984b) argued that the rejection of white supremacism has been a central theme in the transition from a European to a universal society of states. The demand for racial equality demonstrated that international order would not endure unless Third World peoples realized basic aspirations for justice. Order was an issue here – political instability in Southern Africa was possible as long as white supremacist regimes endured – but the immorality of apartheid was a sufficient reason for international action. That aspect of the revolt against the West adds force to Wight's point that modern international society is unusual in making the legitimacy or illegitimacy of systems of government a matter of great moral importance for the whole international community (Wight 1977: 41). US concerns about tyrannical regimes in the Middle Eastern societies have sought to extend such considerations, but clearly without the consensus that existed about the immorality of apartheid (Bull 1982: 266).

The revolt against white supremacism reveals how progress towards solidarism can occur, but also how limited it is likely to be. As Bull (1977: 95) maintained, such advances depend on a general consensus that change is needed to promote justice, and that it will strengthen international society and contribute to order. Crucially, they depend on the backing of the great powers which have the capacity to obstruct global action (as the US position on action to deal with climate change has revealed). Despite the obstacles, Watson (1987: 152) stated that Bull and he 'inclined [towards the] optimistic view' that states in the contemporary system are 'consciously working out, for the first time, a set of transcultural values and ethical standards'. The growth of the human rights culture and recent developments in international criminal law lend support to that view. We have to remember that societies are still in an early phase of dealing with the economic, environmental and military issues that have arisen as a result of unprecedented levels of global interconnectedness (see Chapter 6). Whether they can make further progress in such domains depends in part on the extent to which the great powers can demonstrate appropriate levels of 'moral vision' (see Bull 1983: 127–31). But crucially with the rise of world society, much will also depend on how far non-governmental organizations can influence public opinion and government action, not least by altering the dominant principles of international legitimacy so that more attention is given to freeing humanity from unnecessary harm (Heins 2008; see also Buzan 2004 and Clark 2007 on the relationship between world and international society).

It is hard to tell whether Bull and Watson believed that the expansion of international society to include the West's former colonies would lead to greater solidarism or demonstrate that hopes for progress in that direction are still 'premature' (see Mayall 1996; Wheeler 2000). Pursuing the theme, Jackson (2000: 181) has argued that the diverse nature of international society in the post-colonial era makes the pluralist conception of international society all the more essential. He has contended that pluralism is the best arrangement that societies have devised thus far for reconciling the desire for order with the demand for independence. Bull was perhaps equivocal on this point. The gradual emergence of an elite 'cosmopolitan culture of modernity' was encouraging (Bull 1977: 317). However, that culture was still heavily 'weighted in favour of the dominant cultures of the West' (Bull 1977: 317). More seriously, and here the increased importance of religion in world politics immediately comes to mind, there was evidence that various groups in the West and non-West were drifting ever further apart. It was important to remember, Bull (1984a: 6) argued, that when Third World groups first issued demands for justice, they did so as 'supplicants' in a world dominated by the Western powers, where it was vital to use Western terms in order to elicit a sympathetic response. But the revival of indigenous cultures and the emergence of new elites in non-Western societies set new processes in motion. Many groups placed 'new interpretations' on 'Western values', and some dispensed with them entirely, raising large questions about whether many of the demands issuing from non-Western groups were 'compatible with the moral ideas of the West' (Bull 1984a).

Those comments invite some remarks about the alleged coming 'clash of civilizations' that have been debated since the early to mid 1990s, and especially following the attacks on the US, Spain, Britain, Bali and so forth by Islamic terrorists (Huntington 1993). As we shall see in the next section, Bull believed in the 1980s that the great majority of new states had accepted Western international society with its principles of sovereignty and non-intervention. There is no obvious reason to depart from that conclusion. On the other hand, cultural and religious differences between many Western and non-Western groups have increased further over the last 25 years, and the gulf may well deepen in the future. (One must also remember that Islamic fundamentalism is not the sole challenge to 'Western modernity', and that Christian fundamentalism is no less at odds with what are perceived to be pernicious trends in modern secular social systems). English School inquiry emphasizes the need to understand the political, economic and other grievances that may find expression in anti-Western values, and it looks to diplomacy to deal with widespread dissatisfaction with regional and global order. Nothing in English School analysis suggests that such efforts are destined to succeed or indeed that they are bound to fail. Some may think that the rise of religion in world politics poses problems for the English School analysis of international society which has mainly dealt with the rise and spread of secular political arrangements. However, the approach that has long had an interest in religion and world politics (see Thomas 2001; Hall 2006; Jackson 2008) advises against two temptations: exaggerating the novelty of the current era or discounting the fact that new challenges have appeared that may require great practical wisdom in combining the use, or threat, of force with compromise and accommodation.

The revolt against the West and the expansion of international society

The impact of the revolt against the West upon the modern society of states was a central theme in Bull and Watson's writings in the 1980s. Their key question was whether the diverse civilizations that had been brought together by Europe's expansion have a common desire to belong to an international society as opposed to an international system. To answer that question it was necessary to recall the world of the late eighteenth century. Four dominant regional international orders (the Chinese, European, Indian and Islamic) existed in that era. Most 'governments in each group had a sense of being part of a common civilization' that was superior to all others (Bull and Watson 1984: 87). European states were committed to the principle of sovereign equality within their continent, but they denied that non-Europeans had such rights. Exactly how Europe should behave towards its colonies was always a matter of dispute. Some claimed the right to enslave or annihilate conquered peoples while others defended their equal membership of the society of humankind and their entitlement to be treated humanely. The dominant theories of empire in the twentieth century, as expressed in the League of Nations' mandates system and in the trusteeship system of the United Nations, maintained that colonial powers had a duty to prepare non-European peoples for their eventual admission into the society of states on equal terms with the founding Western members (Bain 2003).

The Europeans believed that this transition would take decades if not centuries, in part because other civilizations had to divest themselves of the hegemonial conception of international society in which they positioned themselves at the centre of the world. Traditional China, for example, defined itself as the 'Middle Kingdom' which deserved tribute from other societies that were thought to be at a lower stage of development. Traditional Islamic views of international relations distinguished between the House of Islam (Dar al Islam) and the House of War (Dar al Harb) – between believers and infidels – though the possibility of a temporary truce (Dar al Suhl) with non-Islamic powers was acknowledged. No less committed to a hegemonial view of international order, the European powers believed that societies that had yet to reach their 'standard of civilization' should be barred from international society (Gong 1984).

What that meant was that different civilizations belonged to an international system in the eighteenth century. With the expansion of Europe, other peoples were forced to comply with its conception of world politics. Gradually, most of those societies came to accept European principles of international society. But they only came to enjoy equal membership of that society after a long battle to weaken Europe's confidence in its moral and political superiority and belief in its right to determine their fate.

Bull (in Bull and Watson 1984: 220–4) called this struggle 'the revolt against the West' and divided it into five main phases. The first was 'the struggle for equal sovereignty' undertaken by societies such as China and Japan that had 'retained their formal independence' in the age of imperialism but were considered 'inferior' by the Western powers. Those societies were governed by unequal treaties that were 'concluded under duress'. Because of the principle of 'extra-territoriality', they were denied the right to settle disputes involving foreigners according to domestic law. Following the legal revolt against the West, Japan joined the society of states in 1900, Turkey in 1923, Egypt in 1936 and China in 1943. The political revolt against the West was a second phase in this process in which the colonies demanded freedom from imperial domination. The racial revolt which included the struggle to abolish slavery and the slave trade as well as all forms of white supremacism was the third part of the quest for freedom and dignity. A fourth was the economic revolt against the forms of inequality and exploitation that are inherent in a Western-dominated global commercial and financial system. The fifth revolt, the cultural revolt, was a protest against Western cultural imperialism, including the West's assumption that it was entitled to decide how other peoples should live, not least by universalizing liberal-individualistic conceptions of human rights.

Bull maintained that the first four dimensions of the revolt of the Third World attempted to persuade the colonial powers to take their own moral principles seriously in relations with non-European parts of the world. Together, they appeared to signify a desire to emulate the Western path of development. But, as noted earlier, the cultural revolt was different because it was often 'a revolt against Western values as such' (Bull and Watson 1984: 223). The inevitable question was whether the expansion of international society which occurred because of the revolt against the West would lead to new forms of conflict and disharmony. The importance of that question has been underlined by the religious revolt, and specifically by certain Islamic reactions against the West, embodied in Al-Qaeda, that vigorously oppose American support for Israel, its policy of supporting what are held to be corrupt pro-Western elites in the Middle East, as well as the spread of Western secular values. Significantly, the 'September 11' terrorist attacks on the United States were not accompanied by diplomatic demands that are invariably compromised during the usual 'give and take' of politics. That might seem to be a new form of revolt against the West in which the use of force did not conform with Clausewitz's famous dictum that war is the continuation of politics by other means, although terrorist attacks are clearly designed to compel the US and others to withdraw from the Islamic world.

Where that revolt against the West will lead, and what it will mean for the future of international society, will be central questions for years to come. For some, there is no sharper reminder of the value of Samuel Huntington's controversial thesis that new fault-lines are emerging around ancient divisions between civilizations – contrary to Francis Fukuyama's belief in the global triumph of liberal democracy that stimulated much debate in the aftermath of the collapse of the Soviet Union

(Fukuyama 1992; Huntington 1993). Some who find Huntington's view of civilizations too simplistic stress the need to understand what the larger cultural revolt means for international society. Chris Brown (1988) has argued that many non-Western societies and groups have challenged 'the modern requirement', which is the assumption that developed during the Spanish conquest of the Americas that the West has the right to make other societies conform to its values. This raises the interesting question of whether an agreement about pluralist principles of world political organization is all that very different societies can accomplish, and possibly all they should aim for.

The position that Bull and Watson took in the 1980s was that cultural conflicts and an emerging cosmopolitan culture of modernity were developing in tandem. That was to suggest that support for both the 'pluralist' and 'solidarist' images of international society might increase (but in different regions) in the coming phase of world politics. Arguably, support for the universal culture of human rights and for international criminal law has grown in recent years, as has the commitment to national sovereignty in the wake of the fear of the 'new imperialism'. Bull and Watson believed that, by the 1980s, an order that reflected the interests of non-Western states had largely been constructed. They were adamant that international society would not command the support of many non-Western peoples unless still more radical changes took place (Bull and Watson 1984: 429). A radical redistribution of power and wealth from North to South was essential (Bull 1977: 316–17). Although Bull (1984a: 18) continued to argue that 'justice is best realized in the context of order', he was more inclined in his last writings to argue that greater justice was imperative to protect international order and society.

Bull did not live to witness the further expansion of international society through the fragmentation of the Soviet bloc and the disintegration of several Third World societies. New challenges for international society have been posed by national-secessionist movements that argue that sometimes justice can only be realized 'at the price of order' (Keal 1983: 210). New problems have been created by the appearance of 'failed states' (Helman and Ratner 1992–93), by gross violations of human rights in civil conflicts, by regimes that are in a state of war with sections of their own population, by governments that might provide a safe haven for terrorist organizations such as Al-Qaeda, and by fears that the possible disintegration of nuclear powers (Pakistan is often mentioned in this context) could result in weapons of mass destruction falling into the hands of terrorist groups with no compunction in causing the maximum level of suffering to civilian populations. But, as we shall see, such developments tend to reinforce Bull and Watson's claim

that modern international society is increasingly divided between pluralist and solidarist principles of world political organization (Hurrell
2002).

Robert Jackson's *Quasi-States* (1990) offered a new approach to the
expansion of international society by focusing on what has become a
core issue of world politics, namely the problem of the 'failed state'.
Jackson's starting-point was that Third World states were admitted into
the society of states as sovereign equals without any guarantees that they
could govern themselves effectively. Indeed, in 1960 the UN General
Assembly departed from the long-standing principle that a people first
had to demonstrate a capacity for good government before self-govern-
ment could be granted. Many new states acquired 'negative sovereignty'
– the right of freedom from external interference – but lacked 'positive
sovereignty' – or the ability to satisfy the basic needs of their populations.
One consequence was that ruling elites were legally free to do as they
pleased within their respective territories. Violators of human rights
could appeal to Article 2 (paragraph 7) of the United Nations Charter
which states that the international community has no right 'to intervene
in matters which are essentially within the domestic jurisdiction of any
state'.

Jackson (1990) raised the issue of whether a more effective system of
global trusteeship would have prepared the colonies for political independence, and some have argued that the international community has to
take responsibility for governing states which are no longer viable (see
also Helman and Ratner 1992–93). A related question has been whether
the consent of the government of a failing or failed state is essential
before the international community can act to protect vulnerable peoples
(Helman and Ratner 1992–93).

Genocide in Rwanda, violence against the people of East Timor, the
humanitarian crisis in Sudan, and ethnic cleansing in the Balkans
reopened the debate about the rights and wrongs of humanitarian intervention. As noted earlier, the debate over NATO's involvement in
Kosovo in 1999 revealed there is no consensus on whether the right of
sovereignty can be overridden by an allegedly higher principle of protecting human rights. Some observers supported NATO's actions on the
grounds that states have duties to the whole of humanity and not just to
conationals (Havel 1999: 6). Others condemned NATO for what they
saw as a breach of the UN Charter and for a highly selective approach to
dealing with human rights violations which often added to the misery of
the local population (Chomsky 1999a; Wheeler 2004). The debate over
the recent war in Iraq has deepened these divisions. Some defended military action to remove a tyrannical regime. Others accused the American
and British governments of placing their interests above international

society by acting without the consent of the United Nations Security Council, of failing to act prudently, and overlooking that the logic of intervention is the long-term commitment to social reconstruction that domestic publics may quickly tire of and which the 'target' society may come to resent. Echoes of older tensions between the 'pluralist' and 'solidarist' conceptions of international society can be heard in those different reactions to how to deal with human rights violators and with regimes that are deemed to be 'outlaws' in international society. It remains to be seen whether the society of states can agree on the need for intervention in specific humanitarian emergences without weakening general support for sovereignty which remains one of the main constraints on the use of force (Roberts 1993; see also Vincent and Wilson 1994). In examining such issues, the English School comes into its own.

Progress in international relations

Quite how far progress is possible is one of the most intriguing questions in International Relations. Wight (1966b: 26) maintained that the international system is 'the realm of recurrence and repetition', a formulation that can also be found in Waltz's classic statement of neo-realism (Waltz 1979: 66). The argument of this chapter is that the English School points to limited progress in the shape of agreements about how to maintain order and, to a lesser degree, about how to promote global justice. Bull's writings often suggested that order is prior to justice, the point being that international order is a fragile achievement and that states simply cannot agree on the meaning of global justice. On those occasions, Bull seems to be aligned with what Wight described as the 'realist' wing of rationalism but, elsewhere, he is closer to its 'idealist' wing (Wight 1991: 59). Towards the end of his life, Bull seemed more sympathetic to the 'solidarist' point of view that has stimulated further reflections on the prospects for internationalism and the significance of world society (see Dunne 1998: Chapter 7; Buzan 2004).

That apparent change of heart is most pronounced in the Hagey Lectures delivered at the University of Waterloo in Canada in 1983 (Bull 1984b). It is illustrated by the comment that 'the idea of sovereign rights existing apart from the rules laid down by international society itself and enjoyed without qualification has to be rejected in principle', not least because 'the idea of the rights and duties of the individual person has come to have a place, albeit an insecure one' within the society of states 'and it is our responsibility to seek to extend it' (Bull 1984b: 11–12). The 'moral concern with welfare on a world scale' was evidence of a 'growth of . . . cosmopolitan moral awareness' which amounted to 'a major change in our sensibilities' (1984b: 13). The changing global agenda made it necessary for states to become the 'local agents of a world common good' (1984b: 14). Such ideas have lost none of their importance in a period in which international society struggles to find diplomatic approaches to global environmental politics, a dimension of international affairs that the English School has largely neglected with the notable exception of Hurrell (1994; 2006; 2007: Chapter 9).

It would be a mistake to suggest that Bull had come to think that solutions to global problems would be any easier to find, or that the point would soon be reached where 'terrible choices' would no longer need to be made (1984b: 14). Scepticism invariably blunted the visionary impulse. This is evident from his observation that new, post-sovereign political communities might yet develop in Western Europe. An intriguing passage in Bull's *The Anarchical Society* (1977: 267) states that the time may be ripe for new principles of regional political organization which recognize the need for sub-national, national and supranational tiers of government but reject the notion that any of them should enjoy exclusive sovereignty. However, such a world would not be free from dangers. Medieval international society, with its complex structure of overlapping jurisdictions and multiple loyalties, had been more violent than the modern states-system (Bull 1977: 255). Bull (1979b) therefore advanced a qualified defence of the society of states which argued, against those of a more utopian disposition, that most states still play a 'positive role in world affairs'. Despite its numerous defects, international society was unlikely to be bettered by any other form of world political organization in the foreseeable future.

We have considered how the English School differs from realism and neo-realism; it is now necessary to turn to its assessment of 'revolutionism' and the critiques of international society that have been advanced by advocates of that perspective. Bull (1977: 22) argued that the essence of revolutionism can be found in the Kantian belief in 'a horizontal conflict of ideology that cuts across the boundaries of states and divides human society into two camps – the trustees of the immanent community of mankind and those who stand in its way, those who are of the true faith and the heretics, the liberators and the oppressed'. Bull believed that the Kantian interpretation of international society believed that diplomatic conventions should be set aside in the quest for the unification of humankind. 'Good faith with heretics' had no intrinsic value; it had no more than 'tactical convenience' because 'between the elect and the damned, the liberators and the oppressed, the question of mutual acceptance of rights to sovereignty or independence does not arise' (1977: 24).

Many writers, including Stanley Hoffmann (1990: 23–4), have argued that Kant was 'less cosmopolitan and universalist in his writings on international affairs than Bull suggests'. Indeed, for all his cosmopolitanism (which ranges from his belief in a duty of hospitality to strangers to his conviction that human groups should cooperate to promote international law and world peace), Kant defended a society of sovereign states based on the principle of non-intervention. But what most troubled English School thinkers such as Bull and Wight was the 'revolutionist' belief that peace or order cannot exist until all societies have the same universal ideology – a belief that Wight (1991: 421–2) wrongly imputed to Kant (see MacMillan 1995). That concern is also evident in the earlier realist critique of the dangers of the crusading mentality in world politics (Chapter 3). What they share is the fear of ideologues who are intolerant of different views, who are impatient to remove the imperfections of international society, by violence if necessary, and who lack practical wisdom by failing to appreciate how the use of force – as events in post-war Iraq have demonstrated – can have wholly unexpected and disastrous consequences (Mayall 2000).

Wight stressed that 'rationalism' overlapped with realism and revolutionism. We have seen one point of convergence between realism and the English School. A degree of overlap between the English School and revolutionism can be found in Wight's lectures where he compared Kant to the rationalist who is first and foremost 'a reformist, the practitioner of piecemeal social engineering' (Wight 1991: 29). The principal works of the English School shied away from visions of how humanity should be organized. The discussion of world society in Buzan (2004) supports a structuralist form of explanation that departs from their traditional interest in normative issues in world politics while building on the preliminary observations that Bull and Vincent advanced on the important question of how international and world society are inter-related. It is clear that Bull spoke for many in the English School when he maintained that there was no reason to think that political thinkers will succeed where diplomats have repeatedly failed, namely in identifying moral principles which all or most societies can regard as the key to a radically improved international order. On the other hand, a basic humanism informed Bull's argument that international order must ultimately be judged by what it contributes to world order, Wight's claim that the function of politics is to promote order and security 'from which law, justice and prosperity may afterwards develop', and also Jackson's and Bain's thesis that, despite noble intentions, the advocates of humanitarian intervention may increase suffering that could have been avoided by the prudent reliance on the tried and tested conventions in international relations, however disappointing that may seem from a 'utopian' point of view (Bain 2003; Jackson 2000). One might add that a concern with what Dunne and Wheeler (1999) have called 'suffering humanity' runs through the leading English School approaches whether pluralist or solidarist, whether supportive of humanitarian intervention or opposed to it, whether keen to defend human rights or quick to stress the tendency for realist dynamics to assert themselves in the course of 'humanitarian' projects.

Before drawing this chapter to a close it is useful to consider how the English School stands in relation to some other branches of international relations theory. There is a parallel between the English School analysis of international society and neo-liberal institutionalist arguments about how cooperation is possible even in the context of anarchy. Members of the English School have not followed neo-liberal institutionalists by using game theory to explain how cooperation can exist between rational egoists (Keohane 1989a). Unlike many North American scholars, including constructivists, they have paid scant attention to issues of epistemology and methodology, and that has been described as explaining a certain confusion in the US about the nature of its research programme (Finnemore 2001). English School writers are in the main close to the constructivist argument that the interests of states must always be considered in conjunction with the moral and legal principles of international society, even though they have been less reflective about the significance of the philosophy of the social sciences for their mode of analysis (Linklater and Suganami 2006: part one, Chapter 8). Similarly, members of the English School agree with constructivism that anarchy is to use Wendt's famous phrase, 'what states make of it' (Wendt 1992). They share the belief that sovereignty is not an unchanging reality but alters its meaning in accordance with shifting ideas about, for example, the place of human rights in international society. As Bull argued, states can create an international system or an international society out of anarchy, and to some degree they may be able to make that society conform with basic principles of human justice (see also Wight 1977 and Reus-Smit 1999). Nothing is pre-ordained here; everything depends on how states think of themselves as separate political communities and what they take to be their rights against, and duties to, the rest of humankind, and how far they are prepared to use diplomacy, patiently and prudently, to establish common moral and political ground. That is why members of the English School have been especially interested in the legal and moral dimensions of world politics and in the relationship between order and justice, and why constructivist discussions of global norms and legitimacy have special relevance for traditional English School concerns (Edelman 1990; Clark and Reus-Smit 2007; Raymond 1997).

The idea of 'critical international society', as defended by Dunne and Wheeler, has made connections between critical social theory and the

English School (see also Heins 2008: Introduction). In the main, it should be stressed, English School writers are sceptical of what they see as partisan social inquiry. For their part, critical theorists of different persuasions have drawn extensively on English School writing (see Der Derian 1987; Linklater 1998). Certainly, Wight's lectures contain a wealth of insight on the question of cultural diversity in international politics which has been central to post-structuralist inquiry (Wight 1991). The analysis of the expansion of international society raises large questions about the relationship between moral and legal universals and support for respect for cultural differences which remain central to critical approaches and indeed to the whole sub-field of international political theory or global ethics. But with some exceptions, members of the English School have not been especially active in that area (Williams 2006; Dunne 2008).

The English School has devoted most attention to the 'diplomatic dialogue' between states (Watson 1982), noting in particular its importance for restraining force, promoting understanding between different cultures, resolving political differences and exploring the prospects for cooperation. Questions about how international society should be organized have been less important than questions about how this diplomatic community has developed, what it has achieved, and the problems that it most frequently encounters – namely the difficulties in taming the competition for power and security, in overcoming ideological differences and in dealing with the demands of the 'have-nots' in international society. In dealing with such questions the English School has made a unique contribution to the study of world politics.

Conclusion

In *The Twenty Years' Crisis 1919–1939*, E. H. Carr (1939/1945/1946: 12) argued that international theory should avoid the 'sterility' of realism and the 'naivety' of idealism. The English School can claim to have passed this test of a good international theory. Its members have analysed elements of society and civility which have been of little interest to realists. Although they have been principally concerned with understanding international order, the English School has also considered the prospects for global justice and some have made the moral case for creating a more just world order. Few of its members are persuaded by utopian or revolutionist arguments which maintain that states can settle their most basic differences about morality and justice. This is the key to the claim that the English School is the *via media* between realism and revolutionism.

The English School argues that international society is a precarious achievement whose survival is far from guaranteed, and it stresses that, without it, more radical political developments are unlikely to take place. It is to be expected that there will always be two sides to the English School: the realist side that is quick to detect threats to international society and the more cosmopolitan side that identifies possibilities for making that society more responsive to the needs of the weak and vulnerable. The relationship between those different orientations will continue to change in response to historical circumstances. The Cold War years did little to encourage forward-looking interpretations of world order; the passing of bipolarity was more conducive to the development of solidarism; developments since 9/11 have shown how the resurgence of national security politics can quickly weaken conventions on force – witness the development of the doctrine of 'preventive war', the US decision to set aside the Geneva conventions in dealing with terrorist suspects or 'unlawful combatants', and the weakening of the global norm that prohibits torture. Fears about the proliferation of weapons of mass destruction have raised the question of whether a new phase of geo-political rivalry is emerging. Whatever the future holds, the ideas of 'system', 'society' and 'community' which are central to the study of the diplomatic dialogue will provide analysts with important conceptual tools for understanding the course of events. For those reasons, the English School analysis of international society will remain central to attempts to comprehend the shifting sands of world politics.

5 | Marx and Marxism

ANDREW LINKLATER

In the mid-1840s Marx and Engels wrote that capitalist globalization was transforming the international states-system. They believed that conflict and competition between nation-states had yet to come to an end, but the main fault-line in the future would revolve around the divisions between the two main social classes: the national bourgeoisie that controlled different systems of government and an increasingly cosmopolitan proletariat. The outline of a new social experiment was already contained within the most advanced political movements of the industrial working classes. Through revolutionary action, the international proletariat would embed the Enlightenment ideals of liberty, equality and fraternity in a system of universal cooperation that would free all human beings from exploitation and oppression (Marx and Engels 1977).

Many traditional theorists of international relations have pointed to the failings of Marxism or the 'materialist interpretation of history'. Marxism has been the foil for arguments that international politics have long revolved around competition and conflict between independent political communities, and will do so long into the future. Realists such as Kenneth Waltz claimed that Marxism was a 'second-image' account of international relations which believed that the rise of socialist *regimes* would suffice to eliminate conflict between states. Its utopian aspirations were bound to be dashed by the struggle for power and security which is inherent in international anarchy, and the subject of what Waltz (1959; 1979) called 'third-image' analysis. English School thinkers such as Martin Wight maintained that Lenin's *Imperialism: The Highest Stage of Capitalism* (1916) might appear to be a study of international politics, but it was too preoccupied with the economic aspects of human affairs to be regarded as a serious contribution to the field (Wight 1966a). Marxists had underestimated the crucial importance of nationalism, the state and war, and the significance of the balance of power, international law and diplomacy for the structure of world politics.

New interpretations of Marxism have appeared since the 1980s: the perspective has been an important weapon in the critique of realism, and there have been many innovative attempts to harness its ideas in developing a more complex approach to international relations (Cox 1981; 1983; Gill 1993a; 2003; Halliday 1994; Rosenberg 1994; Teschke 2003). Mediated by the Frankfurt School, its impact on critical international theory has also been immense (see Chapter 6). Crucially, it has been an important resource in the area of international political economy where scholars have analysed the interplay between states and markets, the states-system and the capitalist world economy, the spheres of power and production. For some, the collapse of the Soviet Union and the triumph of capitalism marked the death of Marxism as political theory and practice. In the 1990s, some argued that the relevance of Marxism had increased with the passing of the age of bipolarity and accelerating economic globalization (Gamble 1999). A biography of Marx in the late 1990s argued that his analysis of how capitalism had broken down Chinese Walls and unified the human race had finally come of age with the collapse of the Soviet Union (Wheen 1999). For others, the resurgence of national security politics since '9/11', coupled with the increasing importance of religion in international affairs, provides a reminder that Marxism has little grip on the most basic realities of international politics. In American IR – matters are different in Europe where the 'Left Academy' has always been stronger – the mood has shifted from the 'mild' resistance to Marxism of the Cold War years to the present condition in which it 'has virtually disappeared as a serious strand of academic inquiry' (Falk 1999: 37).

Since Marx's writings in the 1840s, the main strength of historical materialism has been its analysis of how capitalism has become the dominant system of production world-wide. Many Marxists conceded in the 1970s and 1980s that the approach had a weak grasp of the importance of the nation-state and violence in the modern world. Since then, few have kept faith with Marx's belief that the triumph of capitalism would be short-lived, or preserved the belief that inexorable laws would result in its destruction and replacement by Communism. Interesting questions are raised by the fact that modern forms of globalization have been accompanied by renewed ethnic violence and national fragmentation. Insightful though they were about the advance of capitalist globalization and growing economic inequalities, Marx and Engels did not foresee the role that nationalism would continue to play in world politics. Marxists such as Lenin stressed that globalization and national fragmentation are two sides of the global diffusion of capitalist production. Perspectives such as dependency theory and world-systems theory which will be considered later in this chapter have offered complex accounts of the transformative role of the spread of capitalism to all parts of the globe over the last few centuries. Furthermore, particular Marxist writers such as Gramsci have been major influences on attempts over the past 25 years to understand the nature of global hegemony.

Leaving aside for the moment the question of how far Marxism casts light on geo-politics, it is important to ask whether Marxist analyses of capitalist globalization and fragmentation invite reconsideration of the tendency on the part of many IR authors to ignore or dismiss Marxism. It is also important to ask whether its project of constructing a critical theory of global politics is one respect in which Marxism advanced beyond the dominant Anglo-American approaches to international relations. It is interesting to recall that, in the 1930s, members of the Frankfurt School maintained that the intellectual challenge was to preserve the 'spirit' but not the 'letter' of classical Marxism (Friedman 1981: 35–6). Although his work over the past 20 years has little connection with Marxism, Habermas famously called for the 'reconstruction of historical materialism', for preserving the strengths and cancelling the weakness of Marxist scholarship (Linklater 1990b; see also Chapter 6). Those working within the Marxist tradition continue to explore ways of reconstructing its approach to politics and history in order to cast light on structures and processes that are neglected by mainstream approaches to the field.

It is impossible to discuss the varieties of Marxism in a short chapter which has the task of considering the significance of historical materialism for International Relations (see Joseph 2006 for a broad-ranging survey of Marxist perspectives). The approach taken here begins by describing the main features of historical materialism and by explaining how international relations were considered within that framework. Section two summarizes key themes in the Marxist analysis of nationalism and imperialism. There follows a brief overview of the orthodox critique of Marxism within international relations and its rehabilitation since the 1980s as political economy and critical theory became central to debates. The final section evaluates the Marxist tradition in the light of recent developments in international relations theory.

Class, production and international relations in Marx's writings

One of Marx's main ambitions was to provide an overview of the history of human development from the earliest phases of social existence to the contemporary era. Human history, he argued, had been a laborious struggle to satisfy basic material needs, to understand and tame nature, to resist class domination and exploitation, and to overcome fear and distrust of other communities. Societies had succeeded in mastering hostile natural forces that had once been beyond their control and understanding. They had transformed their relationship with the physical environment with the result that it had become possible to imagine a world that abolished material scarcity. But Marx's view was that human history, and specifically since the rise of capitalism, had unfolded in a tragic manner. Power over nature had increased to unprecedented levels, but individuals were trapped within an international social division of labour, exposed to unfettered market forces and exploited by new forms of factory production that turned workers into 'appendages to the machine' (Marx 1977a: 477). Marx maintained that capitalism had produced levels of global interconnectedness that had reduced fear and estrangement between societies. Nationalism, he observed, had no place in the political imagination of the advanced sections of the proletariat which supported a cosmopolitan project. But capitalism was a system of largely unchecked human exploitation in which the bourgeoisie controlled and profited from the labour-power of subordinate classes. It was the root cause of an alienating condition in which the human race – the bourgeoisie as well as the proletariat – was at the mercy of global structures and forces which it had created. Crucially, the point was not only to describe these conditions from a position of intellectual detachment. Marx (1977b: 158) wrote that philosophers had only interpreted the world; the point was to change it. An end to alienation, exploitation and estrangement was the ideal that drove the attempt to understand the laws of capitalism and the broader sweep of human history. This concern with human emancipation is a major part of the Marxist legacy that recent critical approaches to international political economy have developed.

Marx believed that the historical role of the forces of production (technology) and the relations of production (class relations) had been neglected by the Hegelian movement with which he was closely associated in his formative intellectual years. Hegel had focused on the evolution of various forms of self-consciousness (political, historical, religious and so forth) that the human race had experienced in the course of coming to understand more about itself. After his death, and as part of the struggle over Hegel's legacy, the Left Hegelians attacked religion, believing it was a form of 'false consciousness' that prevented human beings from comprehending what they are and can become. For Marx, religious belief was not an intellectual mistake which had to be corrected by philosophical analysis but an expression of the frustrations and aspirations of people that had to struggle with the material conditions of everyday life. Religion was 'the opium of the masses' and the 'sigh of an oppressed creature' (Marx 1977c: 64). Revolutionaries had to understand and challenge the social conditions that gave rise to the solace of religious beliefs. The 'critique of heaven', as Marx put it, had to become 'the critique of earth' (1977c).

Here it might be added that Marx was wedded to the belief that the long-term trend in human history was towards the secularization of society, a conviction that has come to be regarded as obsolete given the religious revival in recent times. Perhaps the failings of Marxism as a secular theory should be added to those listed earlier – although questions always arise about how far religious beliefs can be understood as a response to economic and political frustrations, as Marx had emphasized. Those who believe that the religious revival amounts to a return to the ignorance and sympathy that the Enlightenment looked certain to overcome need look no further than Marx's writings for support. Those who think that religion is a mode of experience that satisfies spiritual needs that may be quintessentially human will find the Marxist belief in the ideal of secularization entirely alien to their beliefs. Those who think that religion should be more central to (or at the centre of) political life will find no support for their cause in Marx's thought which was unreservedly hostile to religion. That is not to imply that all forms of Marxism are necessarily antagonistic to religion. Liberation theology in Latin America, for example, sought to link Marxism and Christianity in the struggle against oppression.

The pivotal theme in the materialist conception of history is that individuals must satisfy their most basic physical needs before they can do anything else. In short, humans have bodies that can only be preserved through labour, or through profiting from the labour of others. The main practical consequence is that for millennia the mass of humanity has had to surrender control of its labour-power simply to survive. Those who owned the means of production – feudal lords, slave-owners, factory owners and so on – have exploited subordinate classes but that has invariably led to class conflict in the form of slave revolts, peasant rebellions and the struggles of the industrial proletariat in more recent times. Class struggle for Marx had been the principal form of conflict in human history. Political revolution had been the main agent of historical development, and technological innovation had been the driving-force behind social change.

Marx (1977d: 105) wrote that history was the continuous transformation of human nature. Put differently, human beings have not only modified the natural world by working on it; they have also changed themselves, acquiring new needs and aspirations in the process. From that perspective, the history of the human species could be understood by tracing the development of the modes of production which, in the West, included primitive communism, slave societies, feudalism and capitalism, soon to be replaced – it was thought – by socialism on a world-wide scale. The fact that Marx believed that socialism would be a global phenomenon deserves further comment. Traditionally, war, imperialism and commerce had destroyed the isolation of earlier societies; capitalism however brought all social systems within a single stream of universal history and made them conscious of their global interdependence. Few mainstream students of international relations have recognized the importance of this interest in the economic and technological unification of the human species which has been central to recent accounts of globalization (see Halliday 1988a; Gill 1993a; Rosenberg 2000). One might also note how Marxist concerns with such long-term processes that have affected humanity as a whole have parallels in approaches to world history and international relations (see Chapter 7).

In his reflections on capitalism, Marx argued that universal history came into being when the social relations of production and exchange became global and when more cosmopolitan tastes emerged, as illustrated by the desire to consume the products of distant societies and to enjoy an increasingly 'world literature'. However, the forces that unified humanity also prevented the growth of universal solidarity by pitting members of the bourgeoisie against the proletariat, and by forcing members of the working class to compete with each other for scarce employment. Marx's belief was that new forms of solidarity between the exploited classes were emerging as a result of widening inequalities, and specifically because of the disjuncture between the extraordinary wealth that capitalism generated and the poverty of individual life. International working class solidarity was triggered by the remarkable way in which capitalist societies used the language of freedom and equality to justify their existence, while systematically denying real freedom and equality to subordinate classes.

Large normative claims are raised by the question of what it means to be truly free and equal. In general, Marx and his collaborator, Engels, were dismissive of the study of ethics, but they were not dispassionate in their analysis of industrial capitalism (Lukes 1985; Brown 1992b). Indeed, Marx's own purpose was made clear in *The Eighteenth Brumaire of Louis Bonaparte* where he wrote that human beings make their history but not under conditions of their own choosing (Marx 1977e: 300). His point was that humans create their history because they possess the power of self-determination which other species either do not have or cannot exercise to the same degree. And yet humans cannot make history just as they please because class structures exploit them and constrain their freedom of action. A distinctive political project is contained within that observation, namely building the conditions in which human beings can make more of their history – global history in the modern era – under conditions they have chosen for themselves.

Although Marx rejected Hegel's study of history and politics, he kept faith with one of Hegel's most central themes which is that in the course of their history human beings acquire a deeper appreciation of what it means to be free and a better understanding of how society must be altered if freedom is to be realized. In line with his belief that history revolves around the labour process, Marx observed that freedom and equality under capitalism meant that bourgeois and proletarian entered into a labour contract as legal equals, but massive social inequalities placed workers at the mercy of the bourgeoisie, and exposed them to the effects of growing inequalities and the disastrous effects of periodic and inevitable capitalist crises. He took the view that proletarian organizations understood that socialist planning was necessary to truly realize the ideals of freedom and equality that capitalist societies defended. Marx's condemnation of capitalism has to be seen in that light. The critique of the capitalist order rests on a distinctive methodology, which was derived from Hegel's writings, and focused on the tensions and contradictions within any society that may lead to its destruction and to the emergence of higher forms of life.

The society in question was no longer national but global. Marx shared Kant's conviction that efforts to realize freedom within the sovereign state were ultimately futile since they could be destroyed by the sudden impact of external events. For Kant, war was the dominant threat to the creation of the perfect society; hence his belief in the priority of working for perpetual peace. For Marx, global capitalist crisis was the recurrent danger, and the reason for rejecting what would later be known as 'socialism in one country'. Human freedom could be only achieved through forms of universal cooperation to remake world society as a whole. The fascination with globalization and its political effects is one reason why Marx had little to say about relations between states. Marx and Engels (the latter had a keen interest in strategy and war) were perfectly aware of the role of geo-politics in human history, if too inclined to stress the economic sources of statecraft. They knew that war and conquest had forced humans into ever larger political associations, but their main goal was to understand the role that capitalism had played in creating global social and political relations, the assumption being that capitalism would not last forever but would be destroyed by internal crises and contradictions.

Some of the most striking passages in Marx and Engels' writings reveal that they were forerunner of the 'hyper-globalization' thesis. The essence of capitalism is to 'strive to tear down every barrier to intercourse', to 'conquer the whole earth for its market' and to annihilate the tyranny of distance by reducing 'to a minimum the time spent in motion from one place to another' (Marx 1973: 539). In a famous passage in *The Communist Manifesto*, Marx and Engels (1977) claimed that:

The bourgeoisie has through its exploitation of the world-market given a cosmopolitan character to production and consumption in every country . . . All old-fashioned national industries have been destroyed or are daily being destroyed . . . In place of the old wants, satisfied by the productions of the country, we find new wants, requiring for their satisfaction the products of different lands and climes. In place of the old local and national seclusion and self-sufficiency, we have [the] universal interdependence of nations . . . The bourgeoisie, by the rapid improvement of all instruments of production, by the immensely facilitated means of communication, draws all, even the most barbarian nations, into civilisation. The cheap prices of its commodities are the heavy artillery with which it batters down all Chinese walls, with which it forces the barbarians' intensely obstinate hatred of foreigners to capitulate. It compels all nations, on pain of extinction, to adopt the bourgeois mode of production . . . i.e. to become bourgeois themselves. In one word, it creates a world after its own image. (Marx and Engels 1977: 224–5)

As noted earlier, that remarkable statement had clear implications for revolutionary strategy. The sense of 'nationality' might already be 'dead' among the enlightened proletariat, but the national bourgeoisies still controlled state structures, and used nationalism to dampen down class conflict. Marx and Engels believed that each proletariat would first have to settle scores with its own national bourgeoisie, but revolutionary struggle would be national only in form. The capture of state power was a stepping-stone to the larger task of realizing cosmopolitan ideals (1977: 230, 235).

Realists such as Waltz have argued that at the outbreak of the World War I national proletariats realized that they had more in common with their bourgeoisies than with each other. The realist argument was that no-one with an understanding of nationalism, the state and war should have been surprised by that turn of events, yet many socialists were dismayed by divisions within the European proletariat. For realists, the failure to anticipate that outcome demonstrates the central flaw in Marxism – its economic reductionism, as manifested in the belief that capitalism is the key to understanding the nature and possibilities of the modern world (Waltz 1959). That is one of the most influential interpretations of Marxism in International Relations. There are three points to make about it.

First, although Marx and Engels were among the first to reflect on the new era of rapid economic and social globalization, they believed that class conflict within particular nation-states would trigger the decisive revolutions of the time (Giddens 1981). They assumed that revolution would quickly spread from the region in which it first erupted to other capitalist societies. It has been pointed out that the relatively peaceful international system of the mid-nineteenth century encouraged such beliefs; theories of the state were replaced by theories of society and the economy in that era (Gallie 1978). Reflecting that shift in social and political thought, Marx (1973: 109) argued that relations between states were important but of 'secondary' or 'tertiary' importance when compared with systems of production. In a letter to Annenkov, Marx (1966: 159) asked whether 'the whole organisation of nations, and all their international relations [is] anything else than the expression of a particular division of labour. And must not these change when the division of labour changes?'. That is a question rather than an answer, but a rhetorical one perhaps. It might be regarded as evidence that Waltz and others have been right to stress the failings of economic reductionism. But on another level, Marx's point is instructive. Relations between states may often have their own autonomy, or relative autonomy, but one cannot understand them in long-term perspective without taking account of larger structural changes in social and political organization that stem from economic development and technological innovation.

Second, as a result of the growing importance of nationalism as of the 1848 revolutions, Marx and Engels were forced to reconsider their ideas about the impending demise of the nation. They wrote that the Irish and the Poles were the victims of national rather than class domination, adding that freedom from national oppression was essential if a worldwide proletarian organization was to develop (Marx and Engels 1971; Benner 1995). They took account of the persistence of national animosities while remaining convinced that national differences would decline and possibly disappear in the coming decades and centuries (Halliday 1999: 79). The decline of the long peace which appeared after the Napoleonic wars led to other adjustments in their position. Stressing the role of force throughout human history, Engels envisaged unprecedented levels of violence and suffering in the next major European conflict, suggesting that military competition rather than capitalist crisis might be the spark that finally ignited the proletarian revolution. Interestingly, Engels recognized that the possibility of major war meant that the socialist movement had to be seen to take matters of national security and the defence of the homeland more seriously (Gallie 1978; see also Carr 1953).

Third, as Gallie (1978) has noted, those intriguing comments about nationalism, the state and war did not lead Marx and Engels to rework their early statements about the explanatory power of historical materialism. An unhelpful distinction between the economic base of society and the legal, political and ideological superstructure remained central to the main summaries of the perspective. Too often, the state was regarded as an instrument of the ruling class, although it was recognized that, in some circumstances, it could acquire significant autonomy from dominant class forces. However, Marx and Engels' political writings revealed greater subtlety than did their summations of historical materialism. The latter continued to regard class and production as central, to claim that economic power is the dominant form of power in society, and to consider the emancipatory project as fundamentally about promoting the transition from capitalism to socialism (Cummins 1980).

Marx's analysis of capitalism remains a key reference-point for anyone interested in critical theories of world politics. However, a preoccupation with class exploitation obscured other forms of domination and suffering that critical social theory should address, including racial and gender based-oppression. Others were left with the challenge of re-orientating critical social analysis. Something of the kind is evident in the work of the Austro-Marxists who provided a richer discussion of the relationship between nationalism and globalization. Writing in the early part of the twentieth century, Karl Renner and Otto Bauer argued that Marx and Engels had underestimated the impact of cultural differences on human history, the enduring appeal of national loyalties, and the need to satisfy demands for cultural autonomy in the future socialist world (Bottomore and Goode 1978). Marx and Engels had been vague at best about whether or not national differences would survive in post-capitalist society. The Austro-Marxists were clear that cultural differences should survive and indeed flourish under socialism. They offered a broader conception of human emancipation that was anchored in a more complex sociology of the relationship between class loyalties and national identities.

Those were controversial ideas that clashed with the socialist vision that was developing in Soviet Russia under Lenin and Stalin; however, they indicated one way of reworking the spirit of Marxism that continues to this day. The rise of Soviet Marxism-Leninism meant that what Gouldner (1980) described as the anomalies, contradictions and latent possibilities within the Marxist tradition were suppressed in a closed, system of supposed scientific truths. As Anderson (1983) noted, many encrustations formed around Marxism in that period, but writings on nationalism and imperialism early in the twentieth century moved the discussion of globalization and fragmentation forward in innovative ways.

Nationalism and imperialism

We have seen that Marx and Engels' writings raised key questions about the tension between centrifugal and centripetal forces in the modern world, and that they began to grapple with the peculiar paradox that human societies were becoming more closely interconnected, and indeed internationalist in some ways, and yet national loyalties seemed somehow oblivious to those changes. Assumptions about how capitalist globalization would be replaced by socialist internationalism had to be rethought as a result of the increased importance of nationalism and geopolitical rivalries in the late nineteenth century. The theory of capitalist imperialism should be seen in that context.

Lenin (1968) and Bukharin (1972) developed a distinctive approach to explain the causes of World War I. They argued that the conflict was the result of a desperate need for new outlets for the surplus capital that had been accumulated by the dominant capitalist societies. The approach has been largely discredited on familiar grounds – for assuming the primacy of economic forces. But, despite its flaws, it was concerned with understanding how political communities became more nationalistic in this period, an inescapable preoccupation given earlier assumptions that the historical trend was towards closer cooperation between different national proletariats (Linklater 1990b: Chapter 4).

The theory of capitalist imperialism remains interesting as an attempt to equip critical social theory with a more complex understanding of globalization and nationalism, capitalism and warfare. A central aim was to criticize the liberal proposition that industrial capitalism was committed to free trade internationalism which would eventually lead to peace between nations. Marx's claim that capitalism was destined to experience frequent crises was central to the approach. Lenin and Bukharin maintained that the dominant tendency of the era was the rise of new mercantilist states that were willing to use force to achieve their economic and political objectives. National accumulations of surplus capital were regarded as the main reason for the demise of a relatively peaceful international system but Lenin did at least recognize that the decline of British hegemony and the changing balance of military power contributed to the gradual relaxation of constraints on the use of force in relations between national societies.

Lenin and Bukharin maintained that nationalist and militarist ideologies blurred class loyalties and stymied class conflict in that evolving global environment. In *Imperialism: The Highest Stage of Capitalism*, Lenin (1968: 102) claimed that no 'Chinese wall separates the [working class] from the other classes'. Indeed, a labour aristocracy bribed by colonial profits and closely aligned with the bourgeoisie had developed in monopoly capitalist societies. With the outbreak of World War I, the working classes, which had become 'chained to the chariot of . . . bourgeois state power', had responded to nationalist pleas to defend the homeland (Bukharin 1972: 166). It was assumed, however, that the shift of the 'centre of gravity' from class conflict to inter-state rivalry would not last indefinitely. The horrors of war would reveal to the working classes that their 'share in the imperialist policy [was] nothing compared with the wounds inflicted' by it (1972: 167). Instead of 'clinging to the narrowness of the national state', and succumbing to the patriotic ideal of 'defending or extending the boundaries of the bourgeois state', the proletariat would finally resume its mission of 'abolishing state boundaries and merging all the peoples into one Socialist family' (1972: 167).

Whatever one's position on the details of the theory of capitalist imperialism, it had the virtue of focusing critical inquiry on the ways in which the tensions between globalization and nationalism are played out at the level of political communities. This theme (which has been important in the social sciences over recent decades) was central to Lenin's thought:

> Developing capitalism knows two historical tendencies in the national question. The first is the awakening of national life and national movements, the struggle against all national oppression, and the creation of national states. The second is the development and growing frequency of international intercourse in every form, the breakdown of national barriers, the creation of the international unity of capital, of economic life in general, of politics, science etc. (Lenin 1964: 27)

Globalization and fragmentation were inter-related in Lenin's account of how capitalism spreads unevenly across the world, a theme that was more central to Trotsky's analysis of the 'combined and uneven development' of capitalism and to the later phenomenon of Third World Marxism (Knei-Paz 1978). It remains a key conceptual tool in contemporary Marxism (Rosenberg 2007). Moreover, the idea of the 'labour aristocracy' introduced a theme that would be taken further in the neo-Marxist schools of dependency theory and world-systems analysis. One had to understand that the proletariat in capitalist societies was as implicated as the bourgeosie in exploiting peripheral peoples in the world capitalist system. The latter sought to escape exploitation through national independence rather than through alliances with an alien industrial proletariat. The troubling question for Marxists was how far, and whether, Marxism should regard nationalist movements as a key ally of class organizations in the struggle for universal emancipation.

Lenin recognized that particular groups such as the Jews were oppressed because of their religion or ethnicity, and that demands for national self-determination were hardly surprising. Although he argued that socialists should support progressive national movements, Lenin rejected the Austro-Marxists' proposed solution to the 'national question'. They had advocated a federal approach that would grant national cultures significant autonomy within existing states. Lenin's view was that national movements had to choose between complete secession and continued membership of the state with exactly the same rights as all other citizens. (It is worth comparing that position with the defence of group rights in more recent reflections on cultural dominance – see, for example, Kymlicka 1989). Lenin's mistaken speculation was that most national movements would decide against secession, realizing that they would sacrifice levels of economic growth that could only be achieved in larger social systems. Movements that did opt for secession would gain freedom from the forms of domination that had bred national enmity or distrust and that, Lenin thought, would prepare the way for closer links between different national proletariats. The point was to avoid the kind of socialist compromise with nationalism favoured by the Austro-Marxists. Proletarian internationalism was more important than creating multicultural political communities.

The approaches that have just been surveyed shared Marx's belief that capitalism was progressive in that it would bring industrial development and material prosperity to the rest of the world (along with liberation from what Marx regarded as slavish superstition). It was assumed that non-Western societies would emulate European patterns of capitalist, followed by socialist, development. Trotsky identified rather different possibilities, namely new social formations that combined elements of capitalist and pre-capitalist societies (Knei-Paz 1978; Rosenberg 2006). As mentioned earlier, post-World War II theories of development and underdevelopment built on such ideas. Dependency theorists argued that exploitative alliances between the dominant class interests in core and peripheral societies prevented the latter's industrialization (Frank 1967). On that argument, secession from the capitalist world economy was essential if the periphery was to industrialize. Building on dependency theory, but avoiding too crude a division between core and peripheral nations, world-systems theory, as developed by Wallerstein in the 1970s and 1980s, challenged the classical Marxist view that capitalism tends to promote economic development everywhere. Wallerstein (1979) maintained that some societies in what he called the 'semi-periphery' move up the hierarchy of power, while others lose position.

Frank and Wallerstein's positions have been described as neo-Marxist because they shift the emphasis from relations of production to relations of exchange or trade in a world market (see also Emmanuel 1972). The intricacies of those debates need not concern us here. The term, neo-Marxist, also serves to highlight the emphasis on economic forces in world history and the tendency to underestimate the autonomy or relative autonomy of the state and the sphere of geo-politics (see also

Chapter 7). But one should not lose sight of crucial dimensions of their approach that include an emphasis on the extent to which capitalist wealth was based on the exploitation of peripheral societies. Rather than thinking in terms of how capitalism developed in the West and began to transform the rest of the world especially with the rise of the industrial era (as Marx had done in the *Communist Manifesto*), Frank and Wallerstein argued that Western economic and political development occurred as part of the evolution of an exploitative capitalist world-system over many centuries. Placing the rise of the capitalist West in global perspective was an important step beyond the Eurocentrism of so much classical Marxism. No less significant was the invitation to think from the standpoint of those on the periphery and to be more sympathetic to non-Western political movements including Third World nationalism.

Some further comments on the relationship between Marxism and nationalism conclude this section. Western Marxists disagreed profoundly about whether or not to support Third World national liberation movements, and many feared that the compromise with nationalism would sacrifice the internationalism of classical Marxism (Warren 1980; Nairn 1981). Large questions arise about how far any doctrine of internationalism can escape particular cultural biases and about how far it serves, despite noble intentions, specific political interests and forms of power. Marxism was an outgrowth of the European Enlightenment. It developed during a phase of European dominance, often coupled with a strong sense of superiority over the rest of the world whose destiny was to 'catch up' with advanced societies. Its emancipatory project was formed in a particular historical moment in which the export of Western practices was regarded as the key to liberating non-Western peoples not only from endemic poverty but also from 'outmoded' belief-systems. Those assumptions were rejected by dependency theory and world-systems theory, and by Third World Marxism in the 1960s and 1970s. Those movements can be located in the longer-term struggle to build on the foundations of Marxist critical theory, to find modes of explanation that are not trapped in attempts by nineteenth century Western thinkers to understand *their* world, and to think about domination in ways which address the diverse forms of violence, discrimination and exclusion that exist in the global economic and political system.

The changing fortunes of Marxism in international relations

We have seen that Marxist approaches have analysed the long-term trend towards the economic and technological unification of the human race and the specific role that industrial capitalism has played in that process. Its more structuralist variations have attempted to explain those developments without giving at least explicit support to any particular ethical ideas. Its more humanistic perspectives have kept faith with the early Marx's vision of a system of global cooperation to end poverty and suffering, alienation and exploitation. Debates have been centred on the 'historical subject' that is best placed to secure the transition to universal freedom – if not the proletariat then what would liberate human beings from assorted forms of misery? The following discussion, and Chapters 8 and 9, consider how the main strands of critical theory abandoned 'the paradigm of production' and the belief that the industrial working class could provide freedom for all (without, it should be stressed, identifying an equivalent social force within the structure of modern societies). A prior task is to consider the reception of Marxism in the field of International Relations.

The point has been made that the mainstream consensus in IR was that Marxism had little if anything to offer – apart from a catalogue of errors that serious analysts avoided. Realists maintained that Marxism was largely concerned with how humans acted on nature and only secondarily interested in how societies interacted with each other. The importance of the state, geo-politics and war was obscured by a conceptual framework that invested all resources in analysing systems of production, class structures and class conflict. One consequence was an imperfect understanding of one phenomenon which has long been central to Marxism, namely economic globalization which is, for realists, subordinate to the rivalries between the most powerful states.

The failures of Marxism in practice have often been stressed in order to highlight more basic shortcomings. Waltz (1959) argued that Marxists were unprepared for the realities of promoting socialism in a world of nation-states – and especially for the consequences of having to protect socialism at the national level. Trotsky's remark that he would issue a few revolutionary proclamations as Russia's Commissar for Foreign Affairs before closing shop has often been cited as evidence of dismaying naivety. Extending the point, the speed with which the Soviet regime resorted to traditional methods of diplomacy to promote its survival and security appeared to confirm the realist point of view. Lenin stressed in 1919 that 'we are living not merely in a state, but in a system of states' (quoted in Halliday 1999: 312) – yet far from transforming the international system, Marxism was transformed by it. The Soviet domination of Eastern Europe provoked demands for nationalist self-determination that swept socialist internationalism aside. Conflicts between socialist states demonstrated that regime change might make little impression on the 'logic of anarchy' (Kubalkova and Cruickshank 1980).

The failure to anticipate such developments has often been regarded as evidence of a flawed theory of the state. Many Marxists conceded as much in the 1970s and 1980s in the course of moving away from Marx's thesis that the capitalist state is nothing other than 'the executive committee of the bourgeoisie' (Marx and Engels 1977: 223). Many argued that the state had to have some autonomy from ruling class forces in order to ensure the survival of capitalism. For example, it had to protect capitalists from themselves by ensuring that the labour force had access to basic welfare provision. Following the Italian Marxist, Antonio Gramsci, many argued that the state has the crucial role of pacifying subordinate class forces, not least by incorporating some of their aspirations in national ideologies that effectively protect ruling class hegemony but through the consent of subordinate forces rather than through coercion. Other Marxists took a more radical path, by recognizing the importance of Max Weber's claim that the state derives immense power from its monopoly control of the instruments of violence as well as domestic legitimacy from protecting 'society' from internal and external threats. A large literature in the 1970s and 1980s sought to reorient Marxism so that it took account of the extent to which states often possess considerable autonomy by virtue of their responsibilities for conducting foreign relations (Anderson 1974; Skocpol 1979; Block 1980).

Just as Marxism was absorbing ideas that are usually associated with realism, the field of international relations became more open to Marxist and neo-Marxist interpretations of world politics. One cannot overestimate the importance of dependency theory in persuading large numbers of IR scholars to recognize that the analysis of anarchy seemed oblivious to the existence of a global capitalist system with its attendant and growing inequalities. The fault-line between 'North' and 'South' in the 1960s and 1970s was propitious since it forced academic recognition of the problem of global justice that was now on the diplomatic agenda. As noted earlier, something more than better explanation was involved in the quest for understanding what Wallerstein called 'the modern world-system'. That was the context in which the field became more open to 'critical' persuasions that echoed Marx's belief that humans might yet make their history under conditions of their own choosing.

Influenced by Gramsci in particular, Robert Cox's analysis of social forces, states and world order remains one of the most ambitious attempts to use historical materialism to move beyond conventional international relations theory. Cox analysed the relationship between those three levels, stressing that states and the international institutions that preserve world order do not simply reflect the will of the dominant social classes. Systems of production could be as much a cause as an effect of developments at those other levels. But the point was that one had to understand how their inter-relations found expression in what Gramsci called the 'historic blocs' that govern national societies. Echoing Gramsci's interest in how hegemony operates through a mixture of coercion and consent, Cox argued for analysing world hegemony not in conventional terms, as the domination of one military power over others, but as a constellation of class forces, state structures and international organizations that preserve the domination of capitalism not by force alone but by coopting and placating states and social movements that oppose the current global distribution of political and economic power (Cox 1983).

The neo-Gramscian school has actively developed the study of the origins, development and possible transformation of global hegemony (Gill 1993b). It has analysed how hegemony is maintained through forms of close cooperation between powerful elites inside and outside the core regions of the world system, and also through the large web of international economic and political institutions that have responsibility for what has come to be known as global governance (Gill 1993b; see also Cox 1983). The idea of 'disciplinary neo-liberalism' has extended this mode of investigation by analysing the 'new constitutionalism' – the global institutions that have pressed national governments to accept the dictates of neo-liberal conceptions of the state, society and markets (Gill 1995; 2003). Also important are pressures on national governments to deregulate major sectors of the economy, to allow a greater role for the market and increased access to transnational business corporations (see Morton 2007). Chapter 2 has shown that neo-realism emphasizes how states are forced to conform with the logic of anarchy. The neo-Gramscian approach detects similar socializing mechanisms within the architecture of global capitalism. Mindful no doubt of Marx's claim that societies contain the seeds of their own destruction, the approach has also focused on 'the resistances these engender' (Rupert 2003: 181; also Rupert 2000, and Rupert and Solomon 2005). Reflecting the broader movement within Marxism in the twentieth century, the emphasis falls on what Cox, following Gramsci, called the 'counter-hegemonic' elements in the global system that challenge dominant power structures and transnational political alliances along with their legitimating belief-systems. But no claims are made about privileged movements that are poised to change the world-system in its entirety, and almost no-one now seriously suggests that political resistance demonstrates that a global transition from capitalism to socialism is under way.

Marxists or historical materialists in IR have succeeding in re-characterizing the modern world-system. Halliday (1994: 61) captures this well by arguing that 'the modern inter-state system emerged in the context of the spread of capitalism across the globe, and the subjugation of pre-capitalist societies. This socio-economic system has underpinned both the character of individual states and . . . their relations with each other: no analysis of international relations is possible without reference to capitalism, the social formations it generated and the world system they comprise' (see also Rosenberg 1994). This claim is compatible with the realist thesis that states often act independently of dominant class forces, although it is a clear invitation not to concentrate on that domain without understanding the ways in which, depending on the power at their disposal, states have shaped, and been shaped by, the process of capitalist globalization. It is necessary to add that Marxists have stressed not only capital flows and other indices of advances in globalization but also the structural accompaniments of that process. Crucially important is the rise of a transnational capitalist class that seeks to shape the world economic and political system, and not least by promoting its hegemonic vision of the alleged efficiencies of open markets (Robinson and Harris 2000; van der Pijl 1998). Such arguments overturn Marx's belief that capitalist globalization would lead to the political unity of the industrial proletariat while the bourgeoise remained largely national in orientation. They stress that the dominant free market ideologies serve to insulate the 'economic' domain from 'democratic deliberation', while capitalist social relations leave individuals, who have been torn from their traditional communities, powerless in the face of advancing global forces (Robinson and Harris 2000). Those revisions of Marx's argument stress how the vision of humans steering their course of development under conditions they have freely chosen continues to be thwarted.

It is fair to say that recent Marxist scholarship – and particularly what might be described as the 'Sussex School' – has been at the forefront of efforts to bring 'economic' and 'political' forces within a single conceptual framework, although it must immediately be stressed that a central aim of recent historical materialism is to explain how they came to appear to be separate in modern times (Rosenberg 1994). Rosenberg's thesis is that they were not separate in pre-capitalist societies and pre-modern international systems, and only appear to be so in the modern capitalist era. Analysing the different ways in which 'economic' and 'political' forces have been related to each other then becomes central to a mode of investigation that is sensitive to the diverse historical contexts in which relations between states take place. On that argument, it is important to note the close link between state power and the appropriation of the wealth of other humans over the millennia. Only with modern capitalism, has wealth been accumulated through the operation of markets rather than through the use of physical force – although writers such as Wallerstein (1979: Chapter 1) have maintained that the hegemonic power has usually imposed free market arrangements on others in order to promote its own interests. From such perspectives, it is not Marxism but neo-realism which is guilty of reductionism by stating that international relations in all times and places can be explained in terms of an unchanging 'logic of anarchy'. The rejection of the simplifying notion of the 'Westphalian Era', and the analysis of complex developments within the modern international system since its alleged beginning in 1648, is another example of the synthesizing power of historical materialism (Teschke 2003). One might add that the approach comes into its own when it analyses the long-term relationship between the states-system and capitalism, and when it analyses how their interplay has shaped the current form of global hegemony and the instruments of global governance (Bromley 1999; Gamble 1999; Hay 1999).

As noted earlier, some forms of Marxism are largely structuralist in orientation and analyse large-scale change without engaging in any explicit moral theorizing. But much of the influence of Marxism in IR is the result of its commitment to a critical or emancipatory project. Its normative engagement has been a further hindrance to engagement with Marxism in the field. Many scholars have long been opposed to 'political' scholarship, although a large literature has questioned protestations of neutrality and objectivity (see Chapters 6 and 7). The influence of Cox's distinction between 'problem-solving' theory and 'critical' theory on international relations since the early 1980s cannot be overestimated (Cox 1981: 128). A more detailed discussion will be found in Chapter 6, but some comments are necessary here to consider one theme that was developed in the discussion of nationalism, namely whether efforts to free Marxism from its earlier restrictions have come at a very high price. The issue is whether greater openness to diverse influences on, and different progressive movements in, world politics reveals that it has lost its traditional central place in the development of critical social theory.

Cox's protest against neo-realism was that it has a problem-solving focus, and is centrally interested in how the existing international order can be made to 'function more smoothly' (Cox 1981). Critical theory has a different purpose – it could just as easily be said that it endeavours to solve different problems – which is analysing the evolution of structures of power and inequality that constrain human freedom unnecessarily or unfairly. Large questions immediately arise about what counts as an indefensible restriction of freedom and what might be deemed necessary for the functioning of society, but Marxism has not been in the forefront of important attempts to develop global ethics or international political theory (Chapter 12). But what needs to be stressed is that a critical orientation shapes the nature of the empirical engagement with the social world. A comparison with neo-realism may be instructive. That approach has focused on what it believes are the permanent features of international anarchy. It has not been interested in explaining change (see however Gilpin 1981). Critical perspectives are concerned with the possibilities of less constraining, or freer, social relations that are latent in existing societies. The empirical focus therefore falls on the points of resistance noted earlier, on struggles over the dominant structures and the ideologies that legitimate them. From a neo-realist position, those tensions may be interesting but they are not the most important dimensions of world politics. From a critical Marxist perspective, the zones of resistance have special significance, not because they dictate the course of events (that is rarely the case) but because they are indications of political discontent that could, in principle at any rate, lead to the transformation and improvement of social relations. Whether they will have that effect will be decided by political action. Its scope for altering the course of social development will depend on the many factors that Marx and Marxism have analysed – on whether structures are stable or in crisis, whether levels of legitimacy are high or low, on how historic blocs deal with the forces of resistance, and on the political and organizational skills of counter-hegemonic movements.

Whether Marxism is best placed to comprehend those forces is a moot point. The very proliferation of approaches to critical theory tends to suggest that it is not. Feminist, post-structuralist and post-colonialism approaches have stepped into deal with significant lacunae in Marxist explanation – the traditional neglect of patriarchy, or constructions of identity and difference, and the importance of race in imperial and post-imperial power structures. The development of Cox's writings in the 1990s is instructive because it took greater account of what is called 'identity politics' (struggles for recognition on the part of minority nations, indigenous peoples and so forth). Those writings displayed a keen interest in civilizational identities, and specifically in how they might shape the development of a post-Western international system. A normative vision runs through those writings, and it has less to do with reducing material inequalities than with envisaging 'a post-hegemonic order . . . in which different traditions of civilization . . . coexist' through advances in 'mutual recognition and mutual understanding' (Cox 1992b, 1993: 265). It is worth adding that there are affinities between this approach and the English School's emphasis on the need for greater understanding in today's multi-cultural or multi-civilizational international society of states (Chapter 4).

It is useful to turn to Habermas's notion of the 'reconstruction of historical materialism' to consider the impact of related arguments on the relationship between Marxism and critical social theory. In the 1970s, Habermas argued that Marxism overestimated the influence of 'labour' on the organization of societies and on the course of human history. Too little account was taken of 'interaction' – the forms of communication that have made it possible for human beings to live together in viable societies. That was not to claim that the 'paradigm of production' was worthless or to suggest that social theory could ignore the relationship between society and nature. Rather it was to argue that a more comprehensive approach to society and politics had to focus on human achievements in the area of morality and culture. Extending the point, Habermas maintained that Marxism had been right to draw attention to social learning processes that had led to increased mastery over nature. But learning in that sphere did not guarantee that humans could live together in viable societies. To understand how that was possible, it was essential to analyse learning in the moral sphere, and specifically the development of the ethical ideal that societies are answerable to all persons whose interests are affected by their actions. That approach, which is known as the discourse theory of morality, did not only criticize Marxism for failing to deal with moral and cultural evolution; it is also took issue with its lack of a systematic position on ethics. On that argument, the project of emancipation must not only challenge material inequalities but support the democratization of institutions at all levels – local, national and international – so that all human beings can be represented in decision-making processes that may affect them (Habermas 1979; Roderick 1986).

Habermas's ethical stance is clearly linked with Marx's vision of a world in which humans make their history without the burden of unnecessary constraints and confinements. The question is what if anything is distinctively Marxist about it. In his later work, Habermas owes more to liberal-democratic political theory than to classical Marxism. But the point arises in different ways. Whenever historical materialism moves significantly away from the thesis that class and production are central to social organization and human development, one must ask if there is much that is uniquely Marxist in the revised account. Likewise, the shift from the position that critical theory is principally concerned with class domination to the belief that it must address oppression in all its manifestations – embracing race, ethnicity, gender and so forth – immediately raises the question of whether the evolving position marks the transition to 'post-Marxist' critical theory. That is not to suggest that class, race, ethnicity and so forth follow separate paths of development. One cannot explain ethnicity or gender domination without taking account of class divisions in society. But nor can class inequalities be grasped without understanding intersections with gender and other forms of domination. One of the tasks of post-Marxist critical theory is to explain the diverse relationships between those social divisions and differences.

Some theorists have maintained that this argument does not go far enough. The main point is that, notwithstanding his criticisms of Marxism, Habermas remains committed to the Enlightenment ideal of a cosmopolitan world community in which every human being is free from unnecessary social constraints, an ideal that may well contain the potential of new forms of domination. That concern is often a response to the forms of oppression that were committed, in the name of Marxism, in state-socialist societies. It can be deepened by recalling that Marx and Engels were often condescending towards, or contemptuous, of non-Western societies, and certain that Western colonialism and the expansion of capitalism were essential for the liberation of the 'peoples without history'. The argument was expressed in many different ways in twentieth century social and political theory. The founders of Frankfurt School critical theory, Horkheimer and Adorno (1972), argued in the 1940s that Marxism shared the Enlightenment belief that greater scientific and technological knowledge would prepare the way for greater human freedom. However, its main effect was to create the foundations for new forms of bureaucratic domination. In addition, post-structuralist thinkers have stressed the danger that visions of universal emancipation will simply reconstitute relations of power and domination (Chapter 9). The more specific concern is that notions of universal emancipation will erase human differences in the quest for community and consensus. (It is worth adding that it is unclear whether or not Marx thought that the socialist state should eliminate religion. However, his approach to society and politics was secular through and through, and there is no obvious place for religious differences in Marx's vision of universal freedom).

It is not possible in this chapter to ask whether Marxist critical theory has an effective reply to fears that its vision of universal emancipation contains the seeds of political domination. What must be stressed is that Marx's writings received support from what might seem to be an unlikely source – from the founder of deconstructionist theory, Jacques Derrida (see Chapter 7). In a discussion of the contemporary relevance of Marx and Engels' *Communist Manifesto*, Derrida (1994a; 1994b) argued for a 'new International' on the grounds that 'violence, inequality, exclusion, famine, and thus economic oppression [have never] affected as many human beings in the history of the Earth and of humanity'. Defending the 'spirit of Marxism', he proceeded to call for the revision of Marx's vision of the 'withering away of the state' (Derrida 1994a: 56). That ideal had to be freed from its connections with notions of socialist internationalism and from the dictatorship of the proletariat. The 'new International' would protest against 'the state of international law, the concepts of state and nation', and break with inherited assumptions about exclusionary sovereign states and national conceptions of citizenship. Derrida (1994a: 58) envisages a form of political community in which the state no longer possesses 'a space which it . . . dominates' and which 'it never dominated without division'. The argument is that radical theorists should devote more attention to the state, citizenship, political community and international law than historical materialists have done in the past (see Mievelle 2005 for a Marxist approach to the development and political purposes of international law). Such an inquiry should be undertaken, Derrida added, in the 'spirit of Marxism'. The point is that critical theory should include the traditional problems of inequality and economic oppression in an approach that operates on a much broader front. Systems of production are important for critical social analysis but they form one element of a larger whole. The implication is that the initiative often lies with other varieties of critical theory but that they should nevertheless continue to recognize the lasting achievements and continuing vitality of the Marxist tradition.

Marxism and international relations theory today

Marxism was the dominant version of Western critical theory until recently: it combined a powerful analysis of human history as a whole with a detailed political economy of the evolution of industrial capitalism and a conception of universal emancipation that could be realized through class struggle. No other approach to politics and history has operated on this scale. For this reason alone, historical materialism contains what has been called 'indispensable' ideas (Elias 1994: 119); it has advanced a vision of a comprehensive historical social science that has yet to be equalled.

Such points have had little effect on how mainstream approaches to international relations have understood Marxism. As noted earlier, the dominant view has been that Marxism privileges the realm of class and production, and has little of substance to add to mainstream accounts of the state, nationalism and war, or diplomacy, the balance of power and international law. There is little doubt that the evidence of Marxism in power often contributed to the belief that it had no real understanding of geo-political forces. Neo-realists such as Waltz (1979) defined their position in relation to the failings of classical Marxism, specifically by describing Lenin's account of imperialism as the opposite of what a theory of international politics should be. Those are some of the reasons why Marxism is virtually absent from mainstream interpretations of international relations, especially in the United States.

The neo-realist position failed to deal with Marxism on its terms – as a mode of critical social analysis that did not just describe dominant power structures but sought to understand the zones of resistance and

the possibility of social arrangements that would enhance human freedom. Those who recognize the distinctive nature of Marxism as critical
theory have found reason to dispute its account of society and politics
and vision of universal emancipation. Central here is its failure to address
racial, ethnic and gender inequalities, or its inability to incorporate them
within its conceptual framework without surrendering much that is
distinctively Marxist. It may therefore be the fate of Marxists to be
attacked from both sides – that is, by exponents of both mainstream and,
with exceptions, critical approaches.

And yet Marxism remains an important tradition of thought and a
vital source of ideas for many analysts of international relations. As
explained in this chapter it is most apparent in the writings of scholars
who reject what they see as simplistic accounts of world politics that
reduce everything to the logic of anarchy. Crucially important is the
belief that the modern international system should be understood in
conjunction with the development of capitalism over the last few
centuries, and alongside the emergence of a modern world-system with
distinctive structures of hegemony, patterns of inequality and zones of
resistance. The continuing relevance of Marxism for the study of globalization must also be underlined. Much of the literature on globalization
gives the impression that this is a novel development in world politics
that requires new forms of political theory and practice. But, as this chapter, has attempted to show, Marx in the 1840s was centrally concerned
with the analysis of globalization – and neo-Marxists such as Frank and
Wallerstein regard the contemporary phase of globalization as the most
recent stage in a process that stretches back many centuries – and over
many millennia in Frank's later writings (Frank and Gills 1993). The
historical impact of capitalism is central to those approaches that follow
Marx in thinking that it has been made been the main agent of globalization in human history (see Rosenberg 2000).

The last point indicates that Marxism has not given up its interest in
providing an account of human history as a whole. Indeed, Marx's own
comments about early societies have provided the stimulus for precisely
such an endeavour. Marx argued that warfare was one of the 'conditions
of production' of the first human societies (van der Pijl 2007). Their
members had to work on nature to satisfy their basic material needs but
they also had to use force to protect their resources from marauders or
invaders. Those were not unrelated activities in early societies – nor have
they been entirely separate in the development of the human race,
although rare is the perspective that analyses their interaction over long-
term horizons. The examination of the relationship between 'modes of
production' and 'modes of foreign relations' in van der Pijl (2007) is
especially noteworthy for that reason – and is evidence of the continuing

significance of the Marxist tradition for studies of world history and for historical sociology.

Conclusion

Despite the criticisms that have been made of it, Marxism has contributed to the theory of international relations in at least these three respects. First, historical materialism with its emphasis on production, property relations and class is an important counter-weight to realist and neo-realist arguments that claim that the struggle for military power and national security has determined world politics for millennia. Second, Marxists and neo-Marxists have developed accounts of the modern world-system that aim to show how relations between communities have been shaped by, and also shape, the globalization of the capitalist system of production. A third theme, which first appeared in Marx's critique of liberal political economy, is that explanations of the social world are rarely as objective and innocent as they may appear. They may perform the role, however unintentionally, of enabling imperfect social arrangements to 'function more smoothly'. That is the basis for its conception of a critical social theory which aims to produce knowledge of how human beings – all human beings – might yet live without the forms of domination that have appeared over and over again in the history of the species. Distinctive forms of critical international theory have been established on such foundations. One must doubt that critical theory can be simply Marxist, but reasons have been offered for thinking that it can continue to derive important insights from the Marxist tradition. Perhaps there is still much to be said for the claim that all critical theory proceeds, and should proceed, in the 'spirit of Marxism'.

6 | Historical Sociology

ANDREW LINKLATER

Chapter 5 explained that Marx's analysis of industrial capitalism was part of a larger inquiry into the evolution of human society from the earliest times to the modern era. Marx highlighted the increased power of the human species over the natural world and the globalization of all aspects of social life. By analysing the impact of large-scale structural change on everyday life and collective action, Marx was a pioneer of historical sociology which has been defined as that 'tradition of research devoted to understanding the character and effects of large-scale structures and fundamental processes of change' (Kelly 2003; Skocpol, quoted in Hobden 1998: 3). Several overviews of historical sociology have maintained that it also investigates the relationship between grand structures and everyday life (Abrams 1982: Chapter 1; Skocpol 1984: Chapter 1; Smith 1990: 3).

Before turning to recent efforts to build links between historical sociology and International Relations it is important to stress that the focus on long-term processes of change distinguishes the former area of inquiry from most sociological approaches which have concentrated on immediate or short-term horizons. That focus also marks it off from historical writings that aim to cast light on particular eras, episodes or events that may be regarded as exceptional or unique. Historical sociologists focus on what has been called 'la longue durée', a term that was coined by the French historian, Braudel, to refer to the slow-moving and often barely perceptible developments that are often ignored by analyses of 'high profile' contemporary problems (Burke 2003). Many scholars of international relations have been attracted by historical sociology precisely because it offers relief from what has been described as 'presentism', namely the concentration on short-term horizons and current affairs (Buzan and Little 2000; Elias 1998b). Invariably, the interest in promoting long-term time perspectives is motivated by the belief that the distinctive and possibly unique features of the modern world will remain opaque unless they are placed in the broadest historical context. A separate goal is to synthesize knowledge from various disciplines in order to understand the extraordinary development of the human species from the small, isolated societies with populations of no more than a few dozen that were the norm for most of human history to the large territorial states and complex forms of global interconnectedness that exist today. A central objective, which was also central to Marx's thought, is to understand 'the long-term trend towards the globalization of human society' as a whole (Mennell 1990; see also Buzan and Little 2000). It is intriguing to consider how relations between states have influenced, and been influenced by, that long-term process.

The plain desire to understand social and political change is often the primary motivation for pursuing historical-sociological inquiry. But some have claimed that comprehending long-term processes can provide knowledge that may be used one day to bring unregulated change under human control (Elias 1998a). As the last chapter explained, in Marx's thought, the interest in understanding the development of human society from the earliest times was linked with the political aspiration of not only interpreting but also changing the course of human history.

Whatever its form, historical sociology has been entangled in various methodological controversies about its capacity to contribute significantly to knowledge of the social and political world (see Kiser and Hechter 1991, 1998). Some scholars are suspicious of large-scale narratives that are dependent on detailed works of scholarship that rely on archival work, interviews and other source material for historical evidence. It is certainly the case that approaches to historical sociology are only as good as the specialized scholarly works on which they depend. There is no doubt that any grand synthesis of historical material cannot dwell on detailed controversies in specialized areas of inquiry. More seriously, the synthesis is bound to be selective, raising suspicions that pre-conceived ideas about directions in history lead to over-simplifications of the human past and distorted images of particular phases and episodes. The main response to those concerns is that academic specialization brings its own liabilities such as the loss of overviews of the development of human societies in long-term perspective (see the exchange between Goldthorpe 1991 and Mann 1994). On that approach, historical sociology synthesizes major interpretations of specific eras and episodes in order to trace the development of human society over centuries or millennia. However dependent on primary historical research, historical sociologists bring a distinctive interest in uncovering patterns and directions to history that specialists may not detect. Such grand overviews may act as a stimulus for more specialist work that considers its large themes in specific contexts. The dialectic between general and specific narratives can bring enormous benefits to the social sciences and humanities in general, and to the study of international relations in particular.

It is possible to distinguish between three approaches to historical sociology, although elements from each approach are often combined in individual studies. The first compares historical eras or political systems. Examples include Eisenstadt's study of empires and Wight's conception of a sociology of states-systems. A second approach is concerned with the development of the modern world over the last few centuries. Examples are Braudel and Wallerstein's studies of the capitalist world-system, Tilly's analysis of the rise of the modern state, and Teschke's explanation of the development of the 'Westphalia' era. A third approach extends the inquiry to the entire course of recorded human history. Examples include Mann's analysis of the development of social power over the last five and a half millennia and, in international relations, studies of relations between political communities over many centuries or millennia that include Ferguson and Mansbach (1996), Watson (1993), Buzan and Little (2000) and van der Pijl (2007).

One final point needs to be made before proceeding further. As part of the academic division of labour that emerged in the nineteenth century, sociology focused on changes within societies. Relations between states were usually placed to one side and would fall under the purview of IR in the following century. However, and especially over the last 25 years, sociologists have made international relations more central to their inquiry. It should be stressed that it is lower case rather than upper case 'international relations' that has commanded their attention. That broadening of sociological inquiry has not gone unnoticed in International Relations. Scholars in that field have had a particular interest in how historical sociology can contribute to the attempt to supersede the belief, which neo-realism has championed, that international relations have barely changed in fundamental respects over the millennia (Chapter 2). It is important to add that few IR scholars have attempted to contribute to historical sociology as a field of investigation, just as few historical sociologists have been concerned with advancing IR. Indeed the fact that many are prepared to write about international relations without consulting the IR literature has been described as evidence of 'the failure of IR as an academic project' – its peculiar lack of influence on the humanities and the social sciences more generally (Buzan and Little 2001). Since historical sociology aims at high levels of intellectual synthesis, the question must arise of how specific aspects of the study of international relations can be incorporated in the quest for a more synoptic perspective on society and politics (see Lawson 2007).

The rest of this chapter provides an overview of some leading approaches to historical sociology. Section one explains the rise of historical sociology in the nineteenth century. Sections two and three analyse influential approaches in twentieth century thought, noting how relations between states have moved to the foreground of the discussion. Most of those perspectives have stressed the primacy of material forces such as struggles for coercive power or competitions for economic resources. Sections four and five consider a different set of approaches that focus on the part that moral and cultural forces and collective emotions have played in human history. The sixth section considers recent efforts in IR to develop closer links with historical sociology.

Origins of historical sociology

European Sociology arose in response to fundamental social changes that began in the late eighteenth and early nineteenth centuries – industrialization, democratization, urbanization, bureaucratization, individualization which have been described as core features of the 'the great transformation' of modernity (Nisbet 1966; Mazlish 1989; Dean 1994; Skocpol 1984). Many social thinkers concentrated on the transition from 'community' to 'association' (Ferdinand Toennies), from 'status' to 'contract' (Henry Maine), from feudalism to capitalism (Karl Marx), from 'mechanical' to 'organic' solidarity (Émile Durkheim) and from traditional to legal forms of domination (Max Weber). Analyses of those phenomena attempted to understand how traditional social bonds were being dissolved by the advance of what Marx, following Thomas Carlyle, called the 'cash nexus' between human beings in capitalist society (Mazlish 1989).

Two of the dominant sources of historical sociology illustrate that last point. Marx's analysis of the transition from feudalism to capitalism emphasized that the ties between lord and self had been replaced by contractual relationships that exposed individuals to market forces that were transforming the world as a whole, compressing time and space in the process. Weber attempted to explain how traditional social relations were being replaced by more abstract legal-rational ties under conditions of advancing bureaucratization. Consciously reacting against Marxist reductionism, he stressed the need to understand the influence of religious ideas on social and political change. His analysis of the Calvinist ethic maintained there were 'elective affinities' between its religious outlook and capitalist dispositions that led to the unique patterns of economic and political development in the modern West. Whereas Marx believed that the dominant trends pointed towards the triumph of socialism, Weber argued that socialist societies would not escape the tendency towards increasing levels of bureaucratic domination, or the slide into the 'iron cage' of modernity.

Unlike most nineteenth century sociologists, who were committed to what Giddens (1985: 22–31) has called 'endogenous models of social development', Weber was acutely aware of the influence of nationalism and power politics on modern societies. There is a simple reason for the neglect of those phenomena in sociological thought in the preceding century. Sociology emerged in a period of relative international stability when many leading thinkers believed that the spread of industry and commerce would lead to perpetual peace. Their emphasis was on what has come to be known as globalization. As with more optimistic interpretations of the globalization of society in recent times, many thinkers have argued that it will lead to increasing wealth and prosperity as well as internationalism. Saint-Simon, for example, expressed the widely shared view that history was a journey from the tribe to the state and to a coming association that would embrace the whole of humankind. War and conquest were therefore not central to the dominant sociological voices of the nineteenth century. Adorno's idea that history is a journey from 'the slingshot to the a-bomb' is the product of a later era that witnessed the horrors of industrialized warfare.

In the nineteenth century, sociologists such as Comte linked the discipline with normative claims about how the growth of knowledge could lead to improved social arrangements. That is not an important theme in the dominant strands of historical sociology today, nor is it influential in recent efforts in IR to build links with those approaches. With rare exceptions, the main purpose is explanatory. It is important to add that many nineteenth century studies of the great transformation believed that the triumph of the West was evidence of historical progress. Such views were largely discredited in the twentieth century because of the unprecedented violence of modern warfare and totalitarianism in the USSR and Nazi Germany. Some have maintained that the critique of theories of human progress 'threw the baby out with the bathwater' by turning away from investigations of long-term patterns of change (van Krieken 1998: 66). Several strands of historical sociology have therefore attempted to rehabilitate the focus on long-term change without perpetuating the Eurocentrism and progressivism of many nineteenth century philosophies of history.

Power and production in historical sociology

It is unsurprising that much twentieth century historical sociology focused on the development of material power and systems of production. The spread of industrial capitalism and the expansion of state power which includes its capacity to wage ever more destructive forms of warfare explain that development. It is no less astonishing that historical sociology now emphasizes the influence of geo-politics and war on social and political development over centuries or millennia. It was a short step from sociological accounts of the state's monopoly control of the instruments of violence, as stressed by Weber, to the analysis of how the state is located in an anarchic international system, and how war and geo-political rivalry have shaped social and political structures. As Hobden (1998) and others have argued, that focus on the state, geo-politics and war has encouraged students of international relations to build new connections with historical sociology.

To explain how those two fields of investigation have begun to come together in recent years, it is useful to consider the ways in which Wallerstein and Anderson developed key themes in Marxist and neo-Marxist writings. Marx's principal level of analysis was the rise of industrial capitalism and its spread to other continents in the nineteenth century. During the 1970s, Wallerstein building on Braudel's earlier study of the development of capitalism sought to show that a capitalist world economy comprizing global trading relations had first emerged in the sixteenth century. Wallerstein criticized mainstream sociological accounts of social change that regarded societies as self-contained entities that had developed independently of each other to a significant extent. Building on the writings of dependency theorists such Gunder Frank, Wallerstein replaced those assumptions, which had informed his own earlier work on African societies and politics, with an analysis of how societies had developed according to their position in the capitalist world economy. Wallerstein distinguished between core, peripheral and semi-peripheral positions, and traced the rise and fall of social systems including hegemonic powers over the five centuries in which the capitalist world economy has existed.

Wallerstein argued that the capitalist world economy differs from empires by virtue of being divided into separate states. Early accounts of the world-system described state structures as instruments that were designed to influence how the global economy operated. Great powers, for example, had imposed free trade arrangements on less competitive societies and on possible rivals. As with dependency theory before it, the approach commanded attention in IR because it was an important corrective to what many regarded as its singular preoccupation with geo-politics and its neglect of global economic and social forces. But in IR, critics pointed out that Wallerstein tended to ignore the relatively autonomous sphere of geo-politics and warfare. Similar criticisms were advanced in sociology. In a critique of the tendency to regard states as instruments for manipulating global economic arrangements, Zolberg (1981) argued that the capitalist world economy might not have survived at all but for the alliance that France formed with the Ottoman Empire in the sixteenth century to check Spain's imperial ambitions.

Accusations of economic reductionism do not apply to Anderson's analysis of the transition from feudalism to capitalism which criticized the classical Marxist contention that class struggle was the driving-force behind that epochal change. An appreciation of the decisive role of the absolutist state was missing, he argued, from orthodox accounts. Beginning with the claim that states in early modern Europe were basically feudal – and not capitalist as classical Marxism had suggested – Anderson argued that geo-political rivalries forced the ruling strata to ally with the emerging bourgeoisie to finance the preparation and conduct of war. In short, geo-political rivalries between feudal states had been critical to the move from feudalism to capitalism (Anderson 1974).

Earlier comments about Marx and Weber have shown that the relationship between the 'political' and the 'economic' has long been a bone of contention in historical sociology. Debates about the relative importance of those forces continue, but disputes about causal primacy have largely been settled by widespread support for multi-causal explanation. Marxist approaches to the economic and the political domains remain important, however, for understanding how the modern states-system differs from its predecessors. A recurrent theme in Marxist historical sociology is that states were centrally involved in exploiting labour in pre-capitalist systems of production. The importance of state-organized slavery throughout human history illustrates the point. The capitalist state differs from its predecessors, it is argued, because it does not own or control labour in that way but remains largely behind the scenes, ensuring that contracts are honoured and that criminals are punished, and confining internal violence to moments when force is deemed necessary to deal with rebellion or unrest. The fact that workers enter into free contracts with employers distinguishes capitalist societies from their predecessors. Only in capitalist societies does labour exploitation occur principally in the sphere of market relations.

Such themes are echoed in Anderson's comment that the 'typical medium of inter-feudal rivalry' was 'military' whereas with the rise of 'inter-capitalist competition' it is primarily 'economic' (1974: 33). To put that another way, force was regarded as a legitimate way of seizing wealth in the feudal era, but it is not so regarded in the capitalist world where force and geo-politics are thought to be separate from the economic domain. But a point that is often stressed is that the economic and the political domains only seem to be distinct from each other in capitalist systems given that labour-power is bought and sold freely in the capitalist market (Rosenberg 1994; Teschke 2003). At a deeper level, the argument is, the economic and the political are more deeply connected than dominant approaches to international relations recognize.* The upshot is that it is impossible to understand the evolution of the modern states-system, and its geo-political rivalries and tensions, without analysing one of the major revolutions of the last few centuries – the rise and spread of industrial capitalism (Halliday 1994; Teschke 2003).

Recent approaches to those long-term trends have placed particular emphasis on what Trotsky called the law of 'uneven and combined development' of capitalism – on the different rates of capitalist development across the world, on the complex social and political arrangements and developments that have resulted in the Middle East and elsewhere from the fusion or coexistence of pre-capitalist and capitalist social relations, and on how uneven development has influenced, and is influenced by, processes of change that occur at the level of the state, geo-politics and war (Chapter 5; Rosenberg 1994; 2006).

Virtually all sociological perspectives on the modern world recognize the decisive influence of the interplay between modern industrial capitalism, geo-politics and war, although that is not to imply that they offer the same explanation of the relationship between class dominance and state power or between capitalism and international politics. Influential approaches have shown how the interaction between the growth of coercive capabilities and increasing capital accumulation allowed the territorial state to eclipse other forms of political association such as the small city-states and aspiring empires that competed for power in early modern Europe (Tilly 1992). Some have argued that the modern world should be regarded as the product of relations between four 'logics' – state-building, warfare, capitalism and industrialization (Giddens 1985). A study of revolutions in France in 1789, Russia in 1917 and China in 1949 argued that geo-political rivalries led states to extract wealth from the dominant class which then exploited subordinate classes with greater severity, triggering social and political revolution. The result was not only a change in

---

* Debates about international relations in the Middle Ages are worth noting in this context. In an influential critique of neo-realism, Ruggie (1983) stressed its inability to explain the transition from the medieval to modern international order, a transition which he regarded as a consequence of new conceptions of territoriality and new 'principles of separability' regarding political units. Defending neo-realism, Fischer (1992) argued that the anarchic nature of the medieval and modern international systems compelled political entities to behave in similar ways. From a Marxist perspective, Teschke (1998) has maintained that the nobles' assumed right to use force to appropriate wealth and to settle disputes was an intrinsic feature of ruling class orientations that shaped political behaviour in this era. The neo-realist argument about the effects of anarchy on state action in different eras failed then to comprehend the deeper relations between 'economic' and 'political' phenomena, not that those were separate in the medieval world. Rosenberg (1994) provides a similar critique of the ahistorical nature of neo-realist approaches to earlier international systems.

the balance of power within society, but stronger state structures that were better equipped to deal with geo-political rivalries (Skocpol 1979).

Some of the most influential multi-causal approaches provide a broader focus that encompasses the whole sweep of human history. Especially notable is Mann's account of the development of social power over approximately five millennia (Mann 1986, 1994). Using what he called the 'IEMP model', Mann (1994) traces the impact of relations between *ideological, economic, military and political* power on the evolution of the first states and empires. It is impossible to summarize that ambitious work here, but two features deserve the attention of students of international relations. The first is the focus on the long-term trend towards societies with greater 'intensive' and 'extensive' capabilities – that is with an increased ability to shape the social world within their borders and to project their power well beyond them (Mann 1994: 7). The second is Mann's rejection of the tendency in much sociology to assume that societies can be understood as self-contained, bounded entities. Throughout his analysis of social power, Mann stresses the impact of transnational influences such as universal religions and international phenomena such as war on the configuration of human societies. As noted earlier, recent works such as Buzan and Little (2000) have also analysed the impact of 'economic' and 'political' phenomena on international systems in world history. Notable within the Marxist tradition is the first of three volumes that trace the connections between modes of production and modes of conducting foreign relations from nomadic societies through successions of empires and states to the world of today (van der Pijl 2007).

Power and interdependence in international relations

The emphasis on how state-building and warfare have interacted is central to 'realist' historical sociology as defended by Hintze (1975: 159) almost a century ago in an important critique of Marxist reductionism. To realists and neo-realists, that development in sociology may signify the belated recognition of themes that have been central to state-centric approaches for decades.

But it is far from clear that those movements within sociology signify a victory for neo-realism. Many IR scholars are attracted to historical sociology because of its focus on long-term processes of change. They have been critical of 'presentism' in the field, and of what has been described as 'anarchocentrism' – the belief that anarchy has ensured that the similarities between different eras of international history are always more substantial than the differences. They have opposed the way in which neo-realism derives bold claims about long-term trends in world politics from distinctions between anarchic and hierarchic systems without pausing to consider the detailed history of international relations. In the course of making that argument, they have objected to a tendency to project the characteristics of the modern 'Westphalian' international system onto all past systems (Buzan, Jones and Little 1993; Buzan and Little 2000).

A leading example of an alternative approach supports a 'historical and multicultural perspective' on the interaction between different types of polity (including tribes, states and empires) over the millennia (Ferguson and Mansbach 1996: introduction). That perspective highlights a phenomenon that is missing from the dominant positions in international relations, namely how the capabilities of any political association at any given moment are limited by cross-cutting identities and competing objects of human loyalty (Ferguson and Mansbach 1996: 23). The approach emphasizes how multiple identities and loyalties facilitated the development of new polities with distinctive patterns of external relations, and adds that similar processes may unfold in the future. Similar sensitivities to historical change are also evident in some works of realist accounts of power and interdependence.

Of particular importance is the stress on how successive great power hegemonies over the millennia have entangled human beings in ever wider structures and processes, an emphasis that echoes sociological writings on the role that the state has played in promoting the long-term towards 'the globalization of human society' (Mennell 1990). One aim of the analysis is to explain how that peculiar, recent European invention, the sovereign state, became the dominant form of political organization across the world, an outcome that could not have been predicted in what is now regarded as the late medieval or early modern period. The encroachment of Western influences forced many peripheral societies to create similar state structures in the hope of resisting external influences (Modelski 1978; Gilpin 1981: Chapter 3). Some realists have argued that any belief in the permanence of the modern state must be countered by placing trends over the last few centuries in a broader historical perspective. On that argument, the 'succession of hegemonies' that has dominated world politics in recent times may be replaced by a return to the norm in human history – the rise and fall of empires (Gilpin 1981: 144ff).

That approach largely concurs with Waltz's claim that international politics have not changed fundamentally over the millennia, but it aims for realist 'generalizations' that are more obviously 'based on observations of historical experience' (Gilpin 1981; see also Kaufman, Little and Wohlforth 2007 on analysing the balance of power in world history). The analysis ranges over such diverse phenomena such as technological innovation, the relationship between the 'scale' of political organization and the 'loyalty' that political institutions can command, and levels of economic efficiency or competitiveness in order to explain international political change. In an explicit contrast with the Marxist notion of the uneven development of capitalism, the analysis draws on Thucydides' account of the Peloponnesian War to highlight the importance of the 'uneven growth' of state power for the realist account of international political change (Gilpin 1981: 98).

The structural realist approach to international systems in world history is a second approach which generally concurs with Waltz's analysis of global politics while also grounding broad generalizations in 'observations of historical experience'. That analysis highlights changes in 'interaction capacities' over long-term intervals – that is, changes in how political units are related to each other and in the intensity of the connections between them (Buzan and Little 2000; 2002: 104–5.) In a challenge to Waltz's stress on the primacy of geo-political forces, the perspective highlights developments in 'sector integration', noting in particular how economic ties have acquired unprecedented influence on world politics in recent times, initially as a result of a permissive international environment (see also Gilpin 1981: Chapter 2). Related changes have occurred in levels of collective organization in international systems. The modern states-system surpasses its predecessors in the extent of its institutional refinement, as exemplified by joint efforts to preserve the balance of power and to maintain respect for the other underpinnings of international society such as diplomacy, international organizations and international law (Linklater and Suganami 2006).

A final comment is that the structural realist approach has drawn attention to the impact of a 'wholly new departure in human history' which is 'the widespread acceptance of a universal norm of human equality' (Buzan and Little 2000: 340; see also Crawford 2000: 393). Such changes in the normative domain have found expression in the peculiarly modern phenomena of the universal human rights culture and international criminal law. They have also been regarded as the key to understanding other distinctive episodes in modern world politics such as the delegitimation of colonialism and slavery, two phenomena which have been prevalent in the history of international relations (Crawford 2002). Changes in principles of international legitimacy deserve pride of place in efforts to link historical sociology and International Relations, but they have not been central to approaches that have concentrated on the influence of material production and/or coercive power (see Watson 1992: 208–9; Buzan and Little 2002: 29; Clark 2005).

System and society

To summarize the discussion thus far, various historical sociologists have attempted to explain phenomena that neo-realists have been accused of failing to examine: how sovereign, territorial states that dominate modern world politics replaced the complex webs of local and transnational authorities and loyalties that existed in the medieval era; how such associations acquired their prominence first in Europe and then across the whole world; how such developments are connected with the growth of industrial capitalism and a global capitalist economy; and not least how developments in the realms of power and production are linked with changing ideas about legitimacy in domestic and international politics.

The English School of international relations and constructivism have been especially concerned with counteracting the realist stress on material forces by stressing the importance of the ideational sphere, and specifically changes in morality and culture. Bull's distinction between international systems and societies which was discussed in Chapter 4 clarifies the English School's approach. Whereas systems are constituted by geo-political competition and the frequent outbreak of war, international societies are constituted by common values, interests and institutions. Efforts in IR to build bridges with historical sociology have often ignored 'home grown' historical sociology which has analysed such forms of world political organization, a neglect that can be explained by the fact that members of the British Committee for the Study of International Politics did not complete the investigation of the comparative sociology of states-systems that they initiated in the 1960s (Dunne 1998: 124ff). Wight (1977) provides the best summation of that ambitious enterprise. It described a project that would compare not only the struggle for power, but conceptions of international order and visions of world community in different states-systems – particularly in the ancient Greek, ancient Chinese and modern examples. It speculated that such an inquiry might reveal similar long-term patterns of development, namely the trend towards the oligopolization of physical power in the hands of a few states and finally in one state that transformed the states-system into a universal empire. Without underestimating the importance of war and geo-politics in every historical era, the approach also emphasized the crucial role of moral and cultural forces in international societies (Chapter 4).

Watson (1992) is the main legacy of the British Committee's proposed sociology of states-systems. The analysis provides a panoramic overview of international relations from the rise of the first city-state system in Mesopotamia around five and a half millennia ago to the current global economic and political order. The 'pendulum effect' which is central to that approach to international history notes the alternation between monopolizing tendencies in systems of states and disintegrative forces in world empires (Watson 1992: 252ff). The theme is linked with the idea that the neo-realist distinction between anarchic and hierarchic systems obscures central features of global configurations of power. Those have ranged from the unusual condition in which the world is divided between *separate states* that respect one another's equality, to *hegemony* where one state or group of states determines the external conduct of all others, and *dominion*, where one state or group of states shapes the internal as well as the external affairs of other societies. Empires complete the spectrum (Watson 1992: 13ff). Having introduced this taxonomy, Watson argues that for most of international history the principal configurations of power have fallen between the extremes of empire and a condition of approximate equality.

The emphasis on configurations of power represents the move towards a more structuralist version of the English School that downplays traditional concerns with moral and cultural forces in world politics (see also Buzan 2004). Earlier questions about the evolution of principles of legitimacy have been revived by other approaches to the interpenetration of international and world society, and in constructivist writings (Chapter 4; Clark 2005, 2007; Clark and Reus-Smit 2007). Two traditional themes have been central to those developments – the rules that establish what it means to count as a legitimate member of international society and the norms that establish what counts as 'rightful' and 'wrongful' conduct (Reus-Smit 1999: 30). The focus on the 'moral purpose of the state' in different international systems, and the analysis of how modern conceptions of sovereignty have changed in response to changing principles of legitimacy, are important applications of Wendt's thesis that 'anarchy is what states make of it' (Reus-Smit, 1999; Philpott 2001; Wendt 1992). Such analyses take issue with any focus on structural constraints that neglects the role of ideational forces and the role of global norms.

Morality, culture and the emotions

Reference has been made to changes in large structures that historical sociologists analyse. The idea of structure suggests the brute realities of economic power and coercive capabilities that form major external constraints on human action. However, morality and culture are also important in several accounts of the structured condition in which humans live – indeed from their perspective, it is not possible to understand structures without considering their interdependence with values, norms and identities. The critique of Weber's belief that ideas are like 'switchmen' that determine the tracks along which interests travel makes this point clear (Reus-Smit 2002b). The objection to Weber's thesis is that interests and norms cannot be separated in the manner that the 'switchmen' metaphor suggests. Interests are not formed in isolation from the normative structures; rather norms enter into their very constitution. In International Relations, this conception of the relationship between norms, identities and interests informs the challenge to the neo-realist assumption that anarchy dictates the interests that rational actors must pursue if they are to survive. Such ahistorical generalizations about essential interests overlook the normative frameworks within which interactions between political communities take place.

European sociologists have long recognized the importance of developing a sociology of morals. Durkheim (1993: 32) called for 'a science of ethics' that placed 'moral facts' on the same level as all other social facts, adding that it is possible to 'observe them, describe them, classify them, and look for the laws explaining them'. Parallel themes ran through Weber's sociology of religion which, following the belief that Calvinism had been influential in the rise of Western capitalism, investigated the forms of economic life that Hinduism, Confucianism and other world religions had encouraged. The continuing importance of Weber's approach is evident in Mann's reflections on how the major world religions have often been the 'tracklayer of history' (1986: 342, 363). No less important are Weber's comments on the relationship between world religions and a phenomenon that is central to understanding international relations, namely 'the dualism of in-group and out-group morality'. Across human history, Weber argued, the maxim, 'as you do unto me, I shall do unto you', has usually been confined to relations within bounded communities. The right to depart from that ethic has usually been assumed in relations with other communities although, as Weber (1948: 329ff) noted, world religions such as Christianity and Islam envisaged 'a universal brotherhood' which held that the 'do unto others' principle should apply to all humans including enemies. Those dimensions of his sociology of religious imperatives are important for understanding the tensions between secularizing tendencies and the religious revival in many societies today (Turner 2003).

Weber's ideas have been regarded as laying the basis for a sociology of civilizations (Nelson 1973). Claims about the importance of civilizations became central to International Relations as a result of Huntington's controversial thesis about a possible future 'clash of civilizations'. The approach has been criticized for depicting civilizations as monolithic entities, for underestimating political and other divisions within civilizations, and for neglecting points of convergence such as the commitment to 'universal brotherhood' that have been defended by many world religions. Such debates have rekindled interest in the sub-field of civilizational analysis that appeared in the United States in the 1970s (Mandalios 2003). The main approaches built on Weber's perspective, not least by paying more attention than Weber had done to relations between civilizations including the influence of Islamic theology and science on the European Middle Ages and on the West's eventual rise to power (Nelson 1973). The importance of understanding what Europe borrowed or learned from China and civilizations in its rise to world dominance has become a central theme in historical sociology and world history in recent years (Hobson 2004) and McNeill (1995).

A related theme is what different civilizations have achieved in contributing to universal brotherhood in Weber's language, or to creating 'wider universalities of discourse' that promote sensitivity to the needs of other communities and greater accountability in the conduct of international politics (Nelson 1973: 96). There is a significant link here with Habermas' early work on 'the reconstruction of historical materialism' which considered the structure and evolution of moral codes from early kinship groups to the first states and empires and large-scale social systems and high levels of global interconnectedness that now exist. A central theme in that approach that is especially important for the study of international relations is the extent to which societies developed commitments to the moral idea that they are accountable to everyone who is affected by their actions, including the members of other communities as well as conationals (Habermas 1984a). That focus points towards a sociological analysis of the moral dispositions that influence everyday images of how one's own society should behave towards outsiders.

At this point, large issues arise about the two features of historical sociology that were considered in the opening paragraph of this chapter – namely the interest not only in explaining long-term processes of change but in understanding the relationship between social and political structures and everyday conduct. Approaches to power and production are often better at analysing long-term structural change than at describing its relationship with daily existence. The stress on morality fills a major lacuna here, particularly when attention turns to the role that moral emotions play in binding agents to structures. The observation that social norms are literally embodied in individual's emotional life, and are often observed almost instinctively, captures the essential point that emotions such as shame, guilt, indignation and compassion are not residual phenomena that are 'filled in' once structures are in place

(Barbalet 2000). Emotions such as anger, indignation, compassion and so forth are as much a cause as an effect of the great structural changes that take place at the level of power and production.

Innovative strands of historical sociology have cast light on different aspects of the emotional life. Prominent among them is the study of mentalities that was advanced by the French *Annales* historians, and particularly by Lucien Febvre. In the 1920s, Febvre made the case for a new field of inquiry called historical psychology that was tasked with investigating 'the emotional life of the past'. The aim was to ask how far such basic emotions as fear and pity, cruelty and compassion, altered over time (Burke 1973). The recent sub-field of 'emotionology' has furthered that project by analysing 'the attitudes or standards that society, or a definable group within a society, maintains towards basic emotions and their appropriate expression' (Stearns and Stearns 1985).

Little attention has been paid to the emotions in IR, as Crawford (2000) explains in an important article that stresses the dominant preference for interest-based explanation in the field (also Bleiker and Hutchison 2008). Attention has been drawn to the extent to which emotions such as guilt, shame and compassion have influenced state conduct within international society (Edelman 1990; Raymond 1997). Those approaches have discussed what Sznaider (2001) has called 'campaigns of compassion'. They include studies of how changing attitudes to cruelty contributed to ending the Atlantic slave trade and colonialism, and to promoting support for the international protection of the rights of minority peoples and indigenous peoples (Edelman 1990; Crawford 2002; Rae 2002; Keal 2003). Analyses of global norms have emphasized the causal importance not only of material interests but also of moral ideas and emotions; and they have maintained that the challenge is to bring the study of those phenomena within a single theoretical framework (Raymond 1997). Attention has been drawn to the role of 'transnational moral entrepreneurs' in spearheading efforts to alleviate human suffering, and to the extent to which their success has depended on the support of powerful states (Edelman 1990). Such discussions underline the importance of understanding the relationship between world society and international society (Buzan 2004; Clark 2007).

Analyses of collective moral emotions provide an essential counterweight to the neo-realist view that norms exercise little influence on world politics. The former are significant for studies of 'we-images' that are intrinsic to international security communities, that underpin the 'democratic peace', and facilitate or block the development of trust between states that are locked in seemingly intractable security dilemmas (Adler and Barnett 1998; MacMillan 1998; Booth and Wheeler 2007). By stressing the importance of ideas and agency in world politics, those approaches do more than criticize what they regard as the one-sided focus on structural constraints which has been promoted by analyses of material power; they are also opposed to the general pessimism that runs through those approaches and more interested in exploring opportunities for embedding humanitarian norms in international society.

A higher synthesis?

The last two sections lead to the question of whether a higher level of theoretical synthesis is possible that integrates insights about the impact of material power, systems of production, culture and identity, morality and the emotions on relations between human societies. With that issue in mind, the following turns to Elias's conception of 'process sociology' which is one of the few approaches that suggests how such a synthesis might be constructed.

The nature of 'process sociology' is evident in the investigation of developments in European societies from the fifteenth to the twentieth centuries. Elias was principally concerned with explaining the 'civilizing process' in which Europeans came to think of themselves as superior first to their medieval forebears and, as the centuries passed, to non-European peoples. It is important to add that Elias did not use the term, the civilizing process, to support the view that European civilization was superior to all others; the aim was to understand the long-term processes of change that led to the widespread adoption of that collective self-image.

Elias portrayed medieval Europe as a zone of conflict because of the absence of a monopoly of force. 'Elimination contests' between rivals led to territorial concentrations of power. The monopolization process led to levels of internal pacification that allowed urbanization and new levels of trade and commerce to develop. As a result, more and more people became interconnected in a complex social division of labour. Less reliant on external force for their security, they began to exercise higher levels of self-control over their behaviour. Constraints on violence were embedded in dominant personality types in modern societies, first among the 'the secular upper classes' and then across other social strata (Elias 1983: 55–6).

Changes in the emotional life were as central to the civilizing process as the emergence of stable monopolies of power and lengthening chains of interdependence. The coercive underpinnings of society did not lose their importance, but they were increasingly hidden from view as those with control of the instruments of violence 'retreated to the barracks'. In highly pacified social systems, different social groups came to think that cruel and violent acts were incompatible with their 'civilization'. The result was that public execution and violent punishment were eliminated in many societies, and cruelty to animals and children were outlawed. Compared with the medieval world where superiors thought nothing of injuring and exploiting inferiors, modern societies witnessed the widening of the scope of emotional identification between domestic groups – and even between all human beings to a small, but not insignificant, extent.

The analysis of the civilizing process operated at a high level of synthesis which brought the struggle for power and security, changes in economic life, shifting moral sensibilities and broad movements at the level of human emotions within a single explanatory framework. Not that the synthesis was complete. In his published work, Elias paid little explicit attention to gender (a draft manuscript on that topic was lost), but it might be added that works in historical sociology are generally silent on the gender dimensions of long-term patterns of social and political change (Miller 2003). However, Elias was unusual among sociologists of his generation in integrating domestic and international politics within the one theoretical system. A recurrent theme in his writings is that human beings have repeatedly identified with particular 'survival units' (kinship groups, city-states, nation-states and so forth) that have offered some measure of protection from internal and external threats. Echoing Weber's emphasis on insider/outsider distinctions, he argued that most societies have possessed a double standard of morality, developing strict taboos against killing members of the in-group while tolerating, and at times actively encouraging, violence against outsider communities. As a result, there is little in the way of a counterpart to the civilizing process in the relations between independent political communities – that is, only limited success in pacifying world society and in widening the scope of emotional identification to include all human beings. What had changed over time was the size of the dominant 'survival units'. Elimination contests had led to ever larger territorial monopolies of power that might result in the eventual establishment of a world state.

The last point applied a central element in explaining the development of modern European societies to investigating human history as a whole. However, there was more to human history than the evolution of larger territorial monopolies of power or changes in the organization of violence and in the structure of economic life. Long-term trends had led to higher levels of human interconnectedness not only within but also between the societies involved. Elimination contests and territorial expansions of power, longer chains of economic and social interdependence and the rise of international institutions, were evidence of the long-term trend towards the globalization of human society as a whole

(Mennell 1990). Within pacified social systems, increased interconnectedness created the need for national institutions that were designed to steer the future course of development (Mennell 2007). The scope of emotional identification widened between the members of society, particularly where dominant groups were significantly dependent on less powerful social strata (De Swaan 1995, 1997). A central question for process sociology is whether similar developments are likely in world politics given the absence of a single monopoly of power.

Elias maintained that an 'immense process of integration' has forced societies into global webs of interdependence, introducing pressures to exercise greater self-restraint (not least with respect to the most destructive instruments of violence) and to become more attuned to one another 'over wider areas' and 'over longer chains of action'. The sense of moral responsibility for the suffering of distant strangers had grown to some extent, but there were no guarantees that humanity would become more cosmopolitan. Social groups often resented the encroachment of alien values and the loss of power and influence that resulted from global interdependence. Nationalist or xenophobic 'counter-thrusts' to globalization could not be discounted. The struggle for power and security had not come to an end, nor had the tendency to set aside 'civilized' constraints on violence when communities fear for their security and survival. Those comments about long-term processes in human history do not display much optimism about the prospects for a global civilizing process. However Elias added that current levels of interconnectedness have developed in what might be regarded as 'humanity's prehistory'. Major advances in learning how to coexist amicably might occur over the thousands or millions of years that lie ahead, assuming that the human race does not destroy itself.

On grand narratives

We have seen that process sociology has analysed long-term processes as a whole, both in the modern European context and with respect to developments that have affected the evolution of humanity as a whole. As such, it is the heir to the nineteenth century theories of history, shorn of the belief in the inevitability of social and political progress that Lyotard criticized in his influential critique of the grand meta-narratives (Chapter 8). Elias (2007) maintained those narratives were premature because they relied on what is now known to be unreliable evidence and depended on false assumptions about the superiority of the West. They were perhaps best regarded as preliminary efforts to understand long-term trends towards the globalization of social and economic life that can now be analysed with greater detachment.

Such approaches to historical sociology overlap with the expanding areas of world history and 'new global history' that also focus on changes that have affected humanity as a whole. In International Relations, the latter include works by Buzan and Little (2000), Ferguson and Mansbach (1994), van der Pijl (2007) and Watson (1993). Related perspectives can be found in Mann (1986; 2004), McNeill (1979) and in McNeill and McNeill (2003). Also noteworthy is the emerging sub-field of 'new global history' that analyses the history of globalization (Mazlish and Irigye 2005; Mazlish 2006; see also Denemark *et al.* 2000 and Gills and Thompson 2006). In the main, those writings have developed independently of each other, and it is unclear whether they add up to a coherent narrative. But there is merit in the idea that they have a common interest in understanding the development of human interconnectedness over the last few millennia and centuries (Manning 2003). Such approaches are valuable for students of international relations because they place processes that affect humanity as a whole at the centre of the analysis. They share the interest in interdependence or globalization and the rise of transnational actors and global civil society that has been central to much research in IR over the last 30 to 40 years. They establish the importance of placing relations between communities in a broader study of world history. They are part of a growing recognition of the need for a broad historical analysis of how encounters between strangers (in the form of trade, cultural exchange, migration, war and geo-politics) have led to the current global condition (McNeill 1995).

The attractions of analyses of the development of humanity from the earliest times to the present era are hardly surprising when it is recalled that small-scale societies with a few dozen members dominated human history until relatively recently – until the period between 3500 and 1500BC when hunting and gathering groups shrank to around 1% of the estimated total world population. From that perspective, the trends that have led to the formation of larger social systems, to destructive forms of warfare to high levels of human interconnectedness and to the widening of the scope of emotional identification so that humans can identify with one another over greater distances are quite recent phenomena: they occurred as a result of the agricultural revolution that followed the end of the last Ice Age around 12,000 years ago. Various approaches have stressed the enormous social and political revolutions that were set in motion by the rise of cities and states first in Mesopotamia around 3500BC, and then in other regions of the world (see Scarre 2005). They have placed great emphasis on the great transformations of the modern era that include successive waves of European expansion and the more recent industrial and post-industrial revolutions. Accounts of those phenomena recognize that those processes were not inevitable; they stress that there were periods of reversal and stagnation, and they appreciate that the trend towards higher levels of human integration may not last forever. But they emphasize that the long-term processes of change that were set in motion between 12,000 and 5,000 years ago set the human species on a course that survives to this day and seems likely to continue well into the future (Diamond 1997).

By placing the contemporary era in the broadest possible historical setting, such grand narratives explain more about its remarkable character. They make the case for higher theoretical syntheses to which the study of international relations can contribute for the reasons that were advanced earlier. Many of them have a latent normative agenda, believing that an understanding of 'the trials and tribulations of humanity as a whole' can foster identification with all human beings, possibly 'diminish the lethality of group encounters', and promote more successful political responses to the interlocked economic, ecological, political, military and other challenges that define the present phase of global integration (McNeill 1986: 16).

The belief that the study of world history may have a beneficial political purpose leads to some final observations about the dangers of grand narratives that owe a considerable debt to the writings of Foucault. In *Discipline and Punish*, Foucault took issue with interpretations of European modernity that maintain that the growth of humanitarian sensibilities has had a dramatic effect on social and political institutions over the last two centuries. His writings stressed the way in which modern forms of power operate not through the state's coercive capabilities but through subtle, normalizing practices that find expression in individual self-regulation. Foucault's argument that the rise of the modern prison owed less to public revulsion against violent punishment than to the invention of more effective punitive measures is the best-known expression of his belief that history is a movement from one system of domination to another. The larger point was to warn against linear accounts of the past that may have the effect – unwittingly if not intentionally – of providing modern humans with flattering self-images that stress the advances they have made over earlier, and indeed over contemporaneous, social systems.

Post-colonial analyses that have been inspired by the discussion of Orientalism (see Said 1979) have emphasized the pernicious effects that such progressivist narratives have had in the relations between 'advanced' and 'backward' societies. Distinctions between the 'rationality' of the West and the 'irrationality' of non-Western societies were integral to ideologies of imperial conquest. Similar contrasts have influenced Western images of 'atavistic' ethnic conflict in Africa and elsewhere that have been used to justify the conclusion that intervention is futile. The larger study of such insider-outsider dualisms (or 'self' and 'other' distinctions) in the history of European empire is highly relevant to historical sociology. For the most part, however, 'post-colonial' writings, 'subaltern studies', and mainstream historical sociology have exhibited mutual neglect (see however Chakrabarty 2003).

The main point on which to end is that Foucault's social theory and the post-colonial literature provide a useful reminder of the political dangers of grand narratives, particularly those that are modelled on the nineteenth century accounts of Western progress (see also Patomaki 2007). Accounts of long-term processes of change are less susceptible to such dangers when they concentrate on the development of larger territorial monopolies of violence, on the powerful role of insider-outsider dualisms, and on relatively low levels of emotional identification between the members of different societies that leave vulnerable groups susceptible to violence, economic exploitation, and to indifference or neglect. Historical sociologists are in the main concerned with understanding changing configurations of domestic and international power; most are not committed to the Marxian idea that the point is not only to interpret the world but to change it (Chapter 8). But they raise some of the most important questions in the humanities and social sciences – not the least of them being whether human societies are trapped in global structures and processes that they are powerless to control and whether they may yet discover ways of influencing future developments for the benefit of all human beings.

Conclusion

Efforts to build new bridges between historical sociology and International Relations have grown in recent years. Various scholars in IR have turned to historical sociology to cast light on the varieties of international political life which are obscured by neo-realist analysis. However, historical sociology is a 'post-disciplinary' network of perspectives with different objects of analysis and methodological commitments (Delanty and Isin 2003). Some attach more importance to power and or production than to ideational forces; some place developments at the level of morality and culture at the centre of their orientation; some seek to unite, albeit in different ways, those 'levels' within a single explanatory framework. Objects of analysis also differ. Some perspectives focus on the rise of the modern world; others compare international systems in different eras, some are concerned with long-term historical trends that have come to affect humanity as a whole. The common denominator is that all focus on long-term processes of change that have integrated human societies in complex global structures.

The question of what students of international relations can gain from engaging with those approaches is easily answered. They can develop a deeper understanding of the reasons for the rise and spread of the modern territorial state, of the relationship between capitalism and the state-system, of the influence of changing conceptions of morality and legitimacy at both the domestic and international levels. They can acquire insights into the respects in which the modern system of states is similar to, and also different from, earlier forms of world political organization. That is where the study of international relations can most obviously contribute to, as well as learn from, historical sociology, and how it can explain how relations between independent communities have shaped the development of 'the human web' over centuries and millennia. Current levels of global interconnectedness make it all the more important to understand how societies responded to the challenges of interdependence in the past. Comprehending past achievements and failures in developing solidarities between different communities has its own intrinsic academic value, but it may also be essential if the human race is to solve the problems that have resulted from the early steps towards global economic and social integration.

7 | **Critical Theory**

RICHARD DEVETAK

In the last few years, there has been a significant growth in international relations theories aligned to critical theory with an 'emancipatory intent' (Linklater 2007a: Chapter 11). This growth reflects, in part, the greater interest taken in international relations by the leading critical theorist of the twentieth century, Jürgen Habermas. In his recent writings he has intervened in the debate on NATO's humanitarian war over Kosovo (1999), articulated a forthright critique of the Iraq War (2003a), reflected on the terrorist attacks of September 11 (2003b), continued his support for Europe as a constitutional 'counter-power' (Habermas and Derrida 2003), and comprehensively outlined an alternative vision of cosmopolitan world order (2006: Chapter 8). In addition to Habermas' forays into the study of international relations, there has been growing interest in critical theory within the disciplinary boundaries of International Relations. Andrew Linklater (2007a), the foremost proponent of this approach in international relations, has continued to employ critical theory as a means of pursuing a cosmopolitan and emancipatory politics, and others have emerged to advance the arguments of a critical theory of international relations in general (Anievas 2005, Haacke 2005, Weber, 2002, 2005, 2007), or to apply its insights to particular questions of security (Fierke 2007), the war on terror (Burke 2004, 2005), humanitarian intervention (Bjola 2005; Devetak 2007) and the global trade regime (Kapoor 2004), just to name a few. Leading international relations journals have also published forums and special issues on critical international theory. (See the 'Forum on Habermas' in *Review of International Studies*, 31(1) 2005, and the special issue on 'Critical International Theory After 25 years', *Review of International Studies*, 33 (2007).) Critical theory has finally stamped its presence on international relations.

This chapter will show how critical theories of international relations have come to achieve this position in the discipline. The first part sketches the origins of critical theory; the second offers an examination of the political nature of knowledge claims in international relations; and the third details critical international theory's attempt to place questions of community at the centre of the study of international relations. Differences will emerge among critical theorists, but if there is one thing that holds together the disparate group of scholars who subscribe to 'critical theory', it is the idea that the study of international relations should be oriented by an emancipatory politics.

Origins of critical theory

Critical theory has its roots in a strand of thought which is often traced back to the Enlightenment and connected to the writings of Kant, Hegel and Marx. While this is an important lineage in the birth of critical theory it is not the only possible one that can be traced, as there is also the imprint of classical Greek thought on autonomy and democracy to be considered, as well as the thinking of Nietzsche and Weber. However, in the twentieth century critical theory became most closely associated with a distinct body of thought known as the Frankfurt School (Jay 1973). It is in the work of Max Horkheimer, Theodor Adorno, Walter Benjamin, Herbert Marcuse, Erich Fromm, Leo Lowenthal and, more recently, Jürgen Habermas and Axel Honneth that critical theory acquired a renewed potency and in which the term *critical theory* came to be used as the emblem of a philosophy which questions modern social and political life through a method of immanent critique. It was largely an attempt to recover a critical and emancipatory potential that had been overrun by recent intellectual, social, cultural, political, economic and technological trends.

Essential to the Frankfurt School's critical theory was a concern to comprehend the central features of contemporary society by understanding its historical and social development, and tracing contradictions in the present which may open up the possibility of transcending contemporary society and its built-in pathologies and forms of domination. Critical theory intended 'not simply to eliminate one or other abuse', but to analyse the underlying social structures which result in these abuses with the intention of overcoming them (Horkheimer 1972: 206). It is not difficult to notice the presence here of the theme advanced by Marx in his eleventh thesis on Feuerbach: 'philosophers have only interpreted the world in various ways; the point is to change it' (Marx 1977a: 158). This normative interest in identifying immanent possibilities for social transformation is a defining characteristic of a line of thought which extends, at least, from Kant, through Marx, to contemporary critical theorists such as Habermas and Honneth. This intention to analyse the possibilities of realizing emancipation in the modern world entailed critical analyses of both obstructions to, and immanent tendencies towards, 'the rational organization of human activity' (Horkheimer 1972: 223). Indeed, this concern extends the line of thought back beyond Kant to the classical Greek conviction that the rational constitution of the *polis* finds its expression in individual autonomy and the establishment of justice and democracy. Politics, on this understanding, is the realm concerned with realizing the just life.

There is, however, an important difference between critical theorists and the Greeks which relates to the conditions under which knowledge claims can be made regarding social and political life. There are two points worth recalling in this regard: first, the Kantian point that reflection on the limits of what we can know is a fundamental part of theorizing and, second, a Hegelian and Marxian point that knowledge is always, and irreducibly, conditioned by historical and material contexts; in Mark Rupert's words (2003: 186), it is always 'situated knowledge'. Since critical theory takes society itself as its object of analysis, and since theories and acts of theorizing are never independent of society, critical theory's scope of analysis must necessarily include reflection on theory. In short, critical theory must be *self-reflective*; it must include an account of its own genesis and application in society. By drawing attention to the relationship between knowledge and society, which is so frequently excluded from mainstream theoretical analysis, critical theory recognizes the political nature of knowledge claims.

It was on the basis of this recognition that Horkheimer distinguished between two conceptions of theory, which he referred to as 'traditional' and 'critical' theories. Traditional conceptions of theory picture the theorist at a remove from the object of analysis. By analogy with the natural sciences, they insist that subject and object must be strictly separated in order to theorize properly. Traditional conceptions of theory assume there is an external world 'out there' to study, and that an inquiring subject can study this world in a balanced and objective manner by withdrawing from the world it investigates, and leaving behind any ideological beliefs, values, or opinions which would invalidate the inquiry. To qualify as theory it must at least be value-free. On this view, theory is possible only on condition that an inquiring subject can withdraw from the world it studies (and in which it exists) and rid itself of all biases. This contrasts with critical conceptions that deny the possibility of value-free social analysis.

By recognizing that theories are always embedded in social and political life, critical conceptions of theory allow for an examination of the purposes and functions served by particular theories. However, while such conceptions of theory recognize the unavoidability of taking their orientation from the social context in which they are situated, their guiding interest is one of emancipation from, rather than legitimation and consolidation of, existing social forms. The purpose underlying critical, as opposed to traditional, conceptions of theory is to improve human existence by abolishing injustice (Horkheimer 1972). As articulated by Horkheimer (1972: 215), this conception of theory does not simply present an expression of the 'concrete historical situation', it also acts as 'a force within [that situation] to stimulate change'. It allows for the intervention of humans in the making of their history.

It should be noted that while critical theory has not directly addressed the international level, this in no way implies that international relations is beyond the limits of its concern. The writings of Kant and Marx, in particular, have demonstrated that what happens at the international level is of immense significance to the achievement of universal emancipation. It is the continuation of this project in which critical international theory is engaged. The Frankfurt School, however, never addressed international relations in its critiques of the modern world, and Habermas has made only scant reference to it until recently (see Habermas 1998, 2003, 2006; Habermas and Derrida 2003). The main tendency of critical theory is to take individual society as the focus and to neglect the dimension of relations between and across societies. For critical international theory, however, the task is to extend the trajectory of Frankfurt School critical theory beyond the domestic realm to the international – or, more accurately, global – realm. It makes a case for a theory of world politics which is 'committed to the emancipation of the species' (Linklater 1990a: 8). Such a theory would no longer be confined to an individual state or society, but would examine relations between and across them, and reflect on the possibility of extending the rational, just and democratic organization of political society across the globe (Neufeld 1995: Chapter 1; Shapcott 2001).

To summarize, critical theory draws upon various strands of Western social, political and philosophical thought in order to erect a theoretical framework capable of reflecting on the nature and purposes of theory and revealing both obvious and subtle forms of injustice and domination in society. Critical theory not only challenges and dismantles traditional forms of theorizing, it also problematizes and seeks to dismantle entrenched forms of social life that constrain human freedom. Critical international theory is an extension of this critique to the international domain. The next part of the chapter focuses on the attempt by critical international theorists to dismantle traditional forms of theorizing by promoting more self-reflective theory.

The politics of knowledge in international relations theory

It was not until the 1980s, and the onset of the so-called 'third debate', that questions relating to the politics of knowledge were taken seriously in the study of international relations. Epistemological questions regarding the justification and verification of knowledge claims, the methodology applied and the scope and purpose of inquiry, and ontological questions regarding the nature of the social actors and other historical formations and structures in international relations, all carry normative implications that had been inadequately addressed. One of the important contributions of critical international theory has been to widen the object domain of International Relations, not just to include epistemological and ontological assumptions, but to explicate their connection to prior political commitments.

This section outlines the way in which critical theory brings knowledge claims in international relations under critical scrutiny. First, it considers the question of epistemology by describing how Horkheimer's distinction between traditional and critical conceptions of theory has been taken up in international relations; and second, it elaborates the connection between critical theory and emancipatory theory. The result of this scrutinizing is to reveal the role of political interests in knowledge formation. As Robert Cox (1981) succinctly and famously said, 'theory is always *for* someone and *for* some purpose'. As a consequence, critical international theorists reject the idea that theoretical knowledge is neutral or non-political. Whereas traditional theories would tend to see power and interests as *a posteriori* factors affecting outcomes in interactions between political actors in the sphere of international relations, critical international theorists insist that they are by no means absent in the formation and verification of knowledge claims. Indeed, they are *a priori* factors affecting the production of knowledge, hence Kimberly Hutchings' (1999: 69) assertion that 'international relations theory is not only about politics, it also is itself political'.

Problem-solving and critical theories

In his pioneering 1981 article, Robert Cox followed Horkheimer by distinguishing critical theory from traditional theory – or, as Cox prefers to call it, problem-solving theory. Problem-solving theories are marked by two main characteristics: by a positivist methodology, and by a tendency to legitimize prevailing social and political structures.

Heavily influenced by the methodologies of the natural sciences, problem-solving theories suppose that positivism provides the only legitimate basis of knowledge. Positivism is seen, as Steve Smith (1996: 13) remarks, as the 'gold standard' against which other theories are evaluated. There are many different characteristics that can be identified with positivism, but two are particularly relevant to our discussion. First, positivists assume that facts and values can be separated; second, that it is possible to separate subject and object. This results in the view not only that an objective world exists independently of human consciousness, but that objective knowledge of social reality is possible insofar as values are expunged from analysis.

Problem-solving theory, as Cox (1981: 128) defines it, 'takes the world as it finds it, with the prevailing social and power relationships and the institutions into which they are organized, as the given framework for action. It does not question the present order, but has the effect of legitimizing and reifying it'. Its general aim, says Cox (1981: 129), is to make the existing order 'work smoothly by dealing effectively with particular sources of trouble'. Neo-realism, *qua* problem-solving theory, takes seriously the realist dictum to work with, rather than against, prevailing international forces. By working within the given system it has a stabilizing effect, tending to preserve the existing global structure of social and political relations. Cox points out that neo-liberal institutionalism also partakes of problem-solving. Its objective, as explained by its foremost exponent, is to 'facilitate the smooth operation of decentralized international political systems' (Keohane 1984: 63). Situating itself between the states-system and the liberal capitalist global economy, neo-liberalism's main concern is to ensure that the two systems function smoothly in their coexistence. It seeks to render the two global systems compatible and stable by diffusing any conflicts, tensions, or crises that might arise between them (Cox 1992b: 173). As critical theorist James Bohman (2002: 506) says, such an approach 'models the social scientist on the engineer, who masterfully chooses the optimal solution to a problem of design'. In summary, traditional conceptions of theory tend to work in favour of stabilizing prevailing structures of world order and their accompanying inequalities of power and wealth.

The main point that Cox wishes to make about problem-solving theory is that its failure to reflect on the prior framework within which it theorizes means that it tends to operate in favour of prevailing ideological priorities. Its claims to value-neutrality notwithstanding, problem-solving theory is plainly 'value-bound by virtue of the fact that it implicitly accepts the prevailing order as its own framework' (Cox 1981: 130). As a consequence, it remains oblivious to the way power and interests precede and shape knowledge claims.

By contrast, critical international theory starts from the conviction that because cognitive processes themselves are contextually situated and therefore subject to political interests, they ought to be critically evaluated. Theories of international relations, like any knowledge, necessarily are conditioned by social, cultural and ideological influence, and one of the main tasks of critical theory is to reveal the effect of this conditioning. As Richard Ashley (1981: 207) asserts, 'knowledge is always constituted in reflection of interests', so critical theory must bring to consciousness latent interests, commitments, or values that give rise to, and orient, any theory. We must concede therefore that the study of international relations 'is, and always has been, unavoidably normative' (Neufeld 1995: 108), despite claims to the contrary. Because critical international theory sees an intimate connection between social life and cognitive processes, it rejects the positivist distinctions between fact and value, object and subject. By ruling out the possibility of objective knowledge, critical international theory seeks to promote greater 'theoretical reflexivity' (1995: Chapter 3). Cox (1992a: 59) expresses this reflexivity in terms of a double process: the first is 'self-consciousness of one's own historical time and place which determines the questions that claim attention'; the second is 'the effort to understand the historical dynamics that brought about the conditions in which these questions arose'. Similarly, Bohman (2002: 503) advocates a form of theoretical reflexivity based on the 'perspective of a critical-reflective participant'. By adopting these reflexive attitudes critical theory is more like a meta-theoretical attempt to examine how theories are situated in prevailing social and political orders, how this situatedness impacts on theorizing, and, most importantly, the possibilities for theorizing in a manner that challenges the injustices and inequalities built into the prevailing world order.

Critical theory's relation to the prevailing order needs to be explained with some care. For although it refuses to take the prevailing order as it finds it, critical theory does not simply ignore it. It accepts that humans do not make history under conditions of their own choosing, as Marx observed in *The Eighteenth Brumaire of Louis Bonaparte* (1977e), and so a detailed examination of present conditions must necessarily be undertaken. Nevertheless, the order which has been 'given' to us is by no means natural, necessary or historically invariable. Critical international theory takes the global configuration of power relations as its object and asks how that configuration came about, what costs it brings with it and what alternative possibilities remain immanent in history.

Critical theory is essentially a critique of the dogmatism it finds in traditional modes of theorizing. This critique reveals the unexamined assumptions that guide traditional modes of thought, and exposes the complicity of traditional modes of thought in prevailing political and social conditions. To break with dogmatic modes of thought is to 'denaturalize' the present, as Karin Fierke (1998: 13) puts it, to make us 'look again, in a fresh way, at that which we assume about the world because it has become overly familiar'. Denaturalizing '[allegedly] objective realities opens the door to alternative forms of social and political life'. Implicitly therefore critical theory *qua* denaturalizing critique serves 'as an instrument for the delegitimisation of established power and privilege' (Neufeld 1995: 14). The knowledge critical international theory generates is not neutral; it is ethically charged by an interest in social and political transformation. It criticizes and debunks theories that legitimize the prevailing order and affirms progressive alternatives that promote emancipation.

This immediately raises the question of how ethical judgements about the prevailing world order can be formed. Since there are no objective theoretical frameworks there can be no Archimedean standpoint outside history or society from which to engage in ethical criticism or judgement. It is not a matter of drafting a set of moral ideals and using them as a transcendent benchmark to judge forms of political organization. There is no utopia to compare to facts. This means that critical international theory must employ the method of immanent critique rather than abstract ethics to criticize the present order of things (Linklater 1990b: 22–3; Fierke 2007: Chapter 8).

The task, therefore, is to 'start from where we are', in Rorty's words (quoted in Linklater 1998: 77), and excavate the principles and values that structure our political society, exposing the contradictions or inconsistencies in the way our society is organized to pursue its espoused values. This point is endorsed by several other critical international theorists, including Karin Fierke and Kimberly Hutchings. Immanent critique is undertaken in the absence of 'an independently articulated method' or 'an ahistorical point of reference' (Hutchings 1999: 99; Fierke 2007: 167). Following Hegel's advice, critical international theory must acknowledge that the resources for criticizing and judging can be found only 'immanently', that is, in the already existing political societies from where the critique is launched. The critical resources brought to bear do not fall from the sky, they issue from the historical development of concrete legal and political institutions and social movements. The task of the political theorist is therefore to explain and criticize the present political order in terms of the principles presupposed by and embedded in its own legal, political and cultural practices and institutions (Fierke 1998: 114; Hutchings 1999: 102).

Fiona Robinson (1999) similarly argues that ethics should not be conceived as separate from the theories and practices of international relations, but should instead be seen as embedded in them. In agreement with Hutchings she argues for a 'phenomenology of ethical life' rather than an 'abstract ethics about the application of rules' (Robinson 1999: 31). On her account of a 'global ethics of care', however, it is necessary also to submit the background assumptions of already existing moral and political discourses to critical scrutiny. Fierke, Hutchings and Robinson agree with Linklater that any critical international theory must employ a mode of immanent critique. This means that the theorist must engage critically with the background normative assumptions that structure our ethical judgements in an effort to generate a more coherent fit between modes of thought and forms of political organization, and without relying on a set of abstract ethical principles.

Critical theory's task as an emancipatory theory

If problem-solving theories adopt a positivist methodology and end up reaffirming the prevailing system, critical theories are informed by the traditions of hermeneutics and *Ideologiekritik* (ideology critique). Critical international theory is concerned not only with understanding and explaining the existing realities of world politics, it also intends to criticize and transform them. It is an attempt to comprehend essential social processes for the purpose of inaugurating change, or at least knowing whether change is possible. In Hoffman's words (1987: 233), it is 'not merely an expression of the concrete realities of the historical situation, but also a force for change within those conditions'. Neufeld (1995: Chapter 5) also affirms this view of critical theory. It offers, he says, a form of social criticism that supports practical political activity aimed at societal transformation.

Critical theory's emancipatory interest is concerned with 'securing freedom from unacknowledged constraints, relations of domination, and conditions of distorted communication and understanding that deny humans the capacity to make their future through full will and consciousness' (Ashley 1981: 227). This plainly contrasts with problem-solving theories which tend to accept what Linklater (1997) calls the 'immutability thesis'. Critical theory is committed to extending the rational, just and democratic organization of political life beyond the level of the state to the whole of humanity.

The conception of emancipation promoted by critical international theory is largely derived from a strand of thought which finds its origin in the Enlightenment project. This was generally concerned to break with past forms of injustice to foster the conditions necessary for universal freedom (Devetak 1995b). To begin with, emancipation, as understood by Enlightenment thinkers and critical international theorists, generally expresses a negative conception of freedom which consists in the removal of unnecessary, socially created constraints. This understanding is manifest in Booth's (1991b: 539) definition of emancipation as 'freeing people from those constraints that stop them carrying out what freely they would choose to do'. The emphasis in this understanding is on dislodging those impediments or impositions which unnecessarily curtail individual and collective freedom. Emancipation is a quest for autonomy, for self-determination (Linklater 1990b: 10, 135), but one that 'cannot be gained at the expense of others' (Fierke 2007: 188). It is also an open-ended 'process rather than an end-point, a direction rather than a destination' (Fierke 2007: 190).

In Linklater's account of critical international theory two thinkers are integral: Immanuel Kant and Karl Marx. Kant's approach is instructive because it seeks to incorporate the themes of power, order *and* emancipation (Linklater 1990b: 21–2). As expressed by Linklater (1992b: 36), Kant 'considered the possibility that state power would be tamed by principles of international order and that, in time, international order would be modified until it conformed with principles of cosmopolitan justice'. Kant's theory of international relations is an early attempt to map out a critical international theory by absorbing the insights and criticizing the weaknesses in realist thought under an interest in universal freedom and justice. While Linklater believes Marx's approach to be too narrow in its focus on class-based exclusion, he thinks it nevertheless provides the basis of a social theory on which critical international theory must build. As Linklater observed (1990a: 159), both Marx and Kant share 'the desire for a universal society of free individuals, a universal kingdom of ends'. Both held strong attachments to the Enlightenment themes of freedom and universalism, and both launched strong critiques of particularistic life-forms with the intention of expanding moral and political community.

To conclude this part of the chapter, critical international theory makes a strong case for paying closer attention to the relations between knowledge and interests. One of critical international theory's main contributions in this regard is to expose the political nature of knowledge-formation. Underlying all this is an explicit interest in challenging and removing socially produced constraints on human freedom, thereby contributing to the possible transformation of international relations (Linklater 1990b: 1, 1998).

Rethinking political community

Informing critical international theory is the spirit, if not the letter, of Marx's critique of capitalism. Like Marx, critical international theorists seek to develop a social theory with emancipatory intent (Haacke 2005; Linklater 2007a: Chapter 11). Since the mid-1990s one of the core themes that has grown out of critical international theory is the need to develop more sophisticated understandings of community as a means of identifying and eliminating global constraints on humanity's potential for freedom, equality and self-determination (Linklater 1990b: 7). Linklater's approach to this task, which has set the agenda, is first to analyse the way in which inequality and domination flow from modes of political community tied to the sovereign state, second, to develop a social theory of the states-system, and third, to consider alternative forms of political community which promote human emancipation.

This section elaborates the three dimensions on which critical international theory rethinks political community (see Linklater 1992a: 92–7). The first dimension is normative, and pertains to the philosophical critique of the state as an exclusionary form of political organization. The second is sociological, and relates to the need to develop an account of the origins and evolution of the modern state and states-system and their accompanying harms. The third is the praxeological dimension concerning practical possibilities for reconstructing international relations along more emancipatory and cosmopolitan lines. The overall effect of critical international theory, and its major contribution to international relations, is to focus on the normative foundations of political life.

The normative dimension: the critique of ethical particularism and social exclusion

One of the key philosophical assumptions that has structured political and ethical thought and practice about international relations is the idea that the modern state is the natural form of political community. The sovereign state has been 'fetishized', to use Marx's term, as the normal mode of organizing political life. Critical international theorists, however, wish to problematize this fetishization and draw attention to the 'moral deficits' that are created by the state's interaction with the capitalist world economy. In this section, I outline critical international theory's philosophical inquiry into the normative bases of political life and its critique of ethical particularism and the social exclusion it generates.

The philosophical critique of particularism was first, and most systematically, set out in Andrew Linklater's *Men and Citizens* (1990a). His main concern there was to trace how modern political thought had constantly differentiated ethical obligations due to co-citizens from those due to the rest of humanity. In practice, this tension between 'men' and 'citizens' has always been resolved in favour of citizens. Even if it was acknowledged, as it was by most early modern thinkers, that certain universal rights were thought to extend to all members of the human community, they were always residual and secondary to particularistic ones. Indeed, as Linklater (2007a: 182) observes, this tension has often been exploited for the purposes of devaluing the 'suffering of distant strangers' and sometimes even celebrating their suffering.

Men and Citizens is, among other things, a work of recovery. It seeks to recover a political philosophy based on universal ethical reasoning which has been progressively marginalized in the twentieth century, especially with the onset of the Cold War and the hegemony of realism. That is, it seeks to recover and reformulate the Stoic-Christian ideal of human community. While elements of this ideal can be found in the natural law tradition, it is to the Enlightenment tradition that Linklater turns to find a fuller expression of this ideal. Linklater here is strongly influenced by the thought of Kant, for whom war was undeniably related to the separation of humankind into separate, self-regarding political units, Rousseau, who caustically remarked that in joining a particular community individual citizens necessarily made themselves enemies of the rest of humanity, and Marx who saw in the modern state a contradiction between general and private interests.

The point being made here is that particularistic political associations lead to inter-societal estrangement, the perpetual possibility of war and social exclusion. This type of argument underlies the thought of several Enlightenment thinkers of the eighteenth century, including Montesquieu, Rousseau, Paine and Kant among others, for whom war was simply an expression of *ancien régime* politics and a tool of state. Marx extended the critique of the modern state by arguing that, in upholding the rule of law, private property and money, it masks capitalism's alienation and exploitation behind bourgeois ideals of freedom and equality. Marx, of course, viewed the separation of politics and economics as a liberal illusion created to mask capitalism's power relations. In Rupert's words (2003: 182), one of Marx's enduring insights is 'that the seemingly apolitical economic spaces generated by capitalism – within and across juridical states – are permeated by structured relations of social power deeply consequential for political life'. From this Marxian perspective, modern international relations, insofar as they combine the political system of sovereign states and the economic system of market capitalism, are a form of exclusion where particular class interests parade themselves as universal. The problem with the sovereign state therefore is that as a 'limited moral community' it promotes exclusion, generating estrangement, injustice, insecurity and violent conflict between self-regarding states by imposing rigid boundaries between 'us' and 'them' (Cox 1981: 137, Linklater 1990a: 28).

Such arguments have led in recent times, and especially after a century which saw genocides and unprecedented flows of stateless peoples and refugees, to more general and profound questions about the foundations on which humanity is politically divided and organized. In particular, as Hutchings (1999: 125) notes, it has led critical international theory to a 'questioning of the nation-state as a normatively desirable mode of political organisation'. Consistent with other critical international theorists Hutchings (1999: 122, 135) problematizes the 'idealised fixed ontologies' of nation and state. Hutchings goes further than Linklater, however, by also problematizing the individual 'self' of liberalism. Her intention is to examine the status of all normative claims to self-determination, whether the 'self' is understood as the individual, nation, or state. But insofar as her critique is aimed at placing the 'self' in question as a self-contained entity, Hutchings' analysis complements and extends the philosophical critique of particularism undertaken by Linklater.

Richard Shapcott (2000b, 2001) also continues this critique by inquiring into the way different conceptions of the 'self' shape relations to 'others' in international relations. Shapcott's main concern is with the possibility of achieving justice in a culturally diverse world. Although more influenced by Hans-Georg Gadamer and Tzvetan Todorov than Habermas, Shapcott's critique of the self is consistent with Linklater's and Hutchings'. He rejects both liberal and communitarian conceptions of the self for foreclosing genuine communication and justice in the relationship between self and other. Liberal conceptions of the self, he says, involve a 'significant moment of assimilation' because they are incapable of properly recognizing difference (2000b: 216). Communitarians, on the other hand, tend to take the limits of political community as given and, as a consequence, refuse to grant outsiders or non-citizens an equal voice in moral conversations. In other words, 'liberals underestimate the moral significance of national differences, while communitarians overestimate them. Both, in short, fail to do justice to difference' (Shapcott 2001: Chapter 1).

The common project of Hutchings, Linklater and Shapcott here is to question the boundedness of identity. A less dogmatic attitude towards national boundaries is called for by these critical international theorists, as national boundaries are recognized as 'neither morally decisive nor morally insignificant' (Linklater 1998: 61). They are probably unavoidable in some form. The point, however, is to ensure that national boundaries do not obstruct principles of openness, recognition and justice in relations with the 'other' (Linklater 1998: Chapter 2; Hutchings 1999: 138; Shapcott 2000a: 111).

Critical international theory has highlighted the dangers of unchecked particularism which can too readily deprive 'outsiders' of certain rights. This philosophical critique of particularism has led critical international theory to criticize the sovereign state as one of the foremost modern forms of social exclusion and therefore as a considerable barrier to universal justice and emancipation. In the following section we outline critical international theory's sociological account of how the modern state came to structure political community.

The sociological dimension: states, social forces and changing world orders

Rejecting realist claims that the condition of anarchy and the self-regarding actions of states are either natural or immutable, critical international theory has always been a form of small-'c' constructivism. One of its essential tasks is therefore to account for the social and historical production of both the agents and structures taken for granted by traditional theories.

Against the positivism and empiricism of various forms of realism, critical international theory adopts a more hermeneutic approach, which conceives of social structures as having an intersubjective existence. 'Structures are socially constructed' – that is, says Cox (1992a: 138), 'they become a part of the objective world by virtue of their existence in the intersubjectivity of relevant groups of people'. Allowing for the active role of human minds in the constitution of the social world does not lead to a denial of material reality, it simply gives it a different ontological status. Although structures, as intersubjective products, do not have a physical existence like tables or chairs, they nevertheless have real, concrete effects (1992b: 133). Structures produce concrete effects because humans act *as if* they were real (Cox 1986: 242). It is this view of ontology which underlies Cox's and critical international theory's attempts to comprehend the present order.

In contrast to individualist ontologies which conceive of states as atomistic, rational and possessive, and as if their identities existed prior to or independently of social interaction (Reus-Smit 1996: 100), critical international theory is more interested in explaining how both individual actors and social structures emerge in, and are conditioned by, history. For example, against the Westphalian dogma that the state is a state is a state (Cox 1981: 127), critical international theory views the modern state as a distinctive form of political community, bringing with it particular functions, roles, and responsibilities that are socially and historically determined. Whereas the state is taken for granted by realism, critical international theory seeks to provide a social theory of the state.

Crucial to critical international theory's argument is that we must account for the development of the modern state as the dominant form of political community in modernity. What is therefore required is an account of how states construct their moral and legal duties and how

these reflect certain assumptions about the structure and logic of international relations. Using the work of Michael Mann and Anthony
Giddens in particular, Linklater (1998: Chapters 4–5) undertakes what
he calls an historical sociology of 'bounded communities'.

Linklater's *Beyond Realism and Marxism* (1990b) had already begun
to analyse the interplay of different logics or rationalization processes in
the making of modern world politics. But in *Transformation of Political
Community* (1998), he carried this analysis further by providing a more
detailed account of these processes and by linking them more closely to
systems of inclusion and exclusion in the development of the modern
state. His argument is that the boundaries of political community are
shaped by the interplay of four rationalization processes: state-building,
geo-political rivalry, capitalist industrialization and moral-practical
learning (Linklater 1998: 147–57). Five monopoly powers are acquired
by the modern state through these rationalization processes. These
powers, which are claimed by the sovereign state as indivisible, inalienable and exclusive rights, are: the right to monopolize the legitimate
means of violence over the claimed territory, the exclusive right to tax
within this territorial jurisdiction, the right to demand undivided political allegiance, the sole authority to adjudicate disputes between citizens
and the sole subject of rights and representation in international law
(1998: 28–9).

The combining of these monopoly powers initiated what Linklater
refers to as the 'totalizing project' of the modern, Westphalian state. The
upshot was to produce a conception of politics governed by the assumption that the boundaries of sovereignty, territory, nationality and citizenship must be coterminous (1998: 29, 44). The modern state concentrated
these social, economic, legal and political functions around a single, sovereign site of governance that became the primary subject of international relations by gradually removing alternatives. Of crucial concern to
Linklater is how this totalizing project of the modern state modifies the
social bond and consequently changes the boundaries of moral and political community. Though the state has been a central theme in the study of
international relations there has been little attempt to account for the
changing ways that states determine principles which, by binding citizens
into a community, separate them from the rest of the world.

Linklater's focus on the changing nature of social bonds has much in
common with Cox's (1999) focus on the changing relationship between
state and civil society. The key to rethinking international relations,
according to Cox, lies in examining the relationship between state and
civil society, and thereby recognizing that the state takes different forms,
not only in different historical periods, but also within the same period.

Lest it be thought that critical international theory is simply interested in producing a theory of the state alone, it should be remembered that the state is but one force which shapes the present world order. Cox (1981: 137–8) argues that a comprehensive understanding of the present order and its structural characteristics must account for the interaction between social forces, states and world orders. Within Cox's approach the state plays an 'intermediate though autonomous role' between, on the one hand, social forces shaped by production, and on the other, a world order which embodies a particular configuration of power determined by the states-system and the world economy (1981: 141). It is for this reason that Cox's neo-Gramscian approach has firmly implanted itself in International Political Economy (Rengger and Thirkell-White 2007: 8).

There are two fundamental and intertwined presuppositions upon which Cox founds his theory of the state. The first reflects the Marxist-Gramscian axiom that 'World orders . . . are grounded in social relations' (Cox 1983: 173). This means that observable changes in military and geo-political balances can be traced to fundamental changes in the relationship between capital and labour. The second presupposition stems from Vico's argument that institutions such as the state are historical products. The state cannot be abstracted from history as if its essence could be defined or understood as *prior to* history (Cox 1981: 133). The end result is that the definition of the state is enlarged to encompass 'the underpinnings of the political structure in civil society' (Cox 1983: 164). The influence of the church, press, education system, culture and so on, has to be incorporated into analysis of the state, as these 'institutions' help to produce the attitudes, dispositions and behaviours consistent with, and conducive to, the state's arrangement of power relations in society. Thus the state, which comprises the machinery of government, plus civil society, constitutes and reflects the 'hegemonic social order' (1983).

This hegemonic social order must also be understood as a dominant configuration of 'material power, ideology and institutions' that shapes and bears forms of world order (Cox 1981: 141). The key issue for Cox therefore is how to account for the transition from one world order to another. He devotes much of his attention to explaining 'how structural transformations have come about in the past' (Cox 1986: 244). For example, he has analysed in some detail the structural transformation that took place in the late nineteenth century from a period characterized by craft manufacture, the liberal state and *Pax Britannica,* to a period characterized by mass production, the emerging welfare-nationalist state and imperial rivalry (Cox 1987). In much of his recent writing, Cox has been preoccupied with the restructuring of world order brought about by globalization. In brief Cox, and his colleague Stephen Gill, have offered extensive examinations of how the growing global organization of production and finance is transforming Westphalian conceptions of society and polity. At the heart of this current transformation is what Cox calls the 'internationalization of the state', whereby the state becomes little more than an instrument for restructuring national economies so that they are more responsive to the demands and disciplines of the capitalist global economy. This has allowed the power of capital to grow – 'relative to labour and in the way it reconstitutes certain ideas, interests, and forms of state' – and given rise to a neo-liberal 'business civilization' (Gill 1995, 1996: 210; see also Cox 1993; 1994).

Drawing upon Karl Polanyi, Cox and Gill see the social purposes of the state being subordinated to the market logics of capitalism, disembedding the economy from society, and producing a complex world order of increasing tension between principles of territoriality and interdependence (Cox 1993: 260–3; Gill 1996). Some of the consequences of this economic globalization are, as Cox (1999) and Gill (1996) note, the polarization of rich and poor, increasing anomie, a stunted civil society and, as a result, the rise of exclusionary populism (extreme right, xenophobic and racist movements).

The point of reflecting on changing world orders, as Cox (1999: 4) notes, is to 'serve as a guide to action designed to change the world so as to improve the lot of humanity in social equity'. After all, as both Cox (1989) and Maclean (1981) argue, an understanding of change should be a central feature of any theory of international relations. So it is with the express purpose of analysing the potential for structural transformations in world order that critical international theory identifies and examines 'emancipatory counter-hegemonic' forces. Counter-hegemonic forces could be states, such as a coalition of 'Third World' states which struggles to undo the dominance of 'core' countries, or the 'counterhegemonic alliance of forces on the world scale', such as trade unions, non-governmental organizations (NGOs) and new social movements, which grow from the 'bottom-up' in civil society (Cox 1999; Maiguaschca 2003; Eschle and Maiguaschca 2005).

The point of critical international theory's various sociological analyses is to illuminate how already existing social struggles might lead to decisive transformations in the normative bases of global political life. This has prompted Linklater (2002a) to undertake what he calls a 'sociology of states-systems'. More specifically, Linklater wishes to compare states-systems across time on the basis of how they deal with international and transnational harms. What kinds of harm are generated in particular states-systems, and to what extent are rules and norms against harm built into these states-systems? Linklater's initial research suggests that the modern states-system may be unique in its development of 'cosmopolitan harm conventions' (Linklater 2001). Drawing upon the work of sociologist Norbert Elias, Linklater has explored the impact of the 'civilizing process' on the modern states-system. Changing attitudes to violence and suffering have generated greater sensitivity towards emotions such as embarrassment, guilt, shame and disgust (Linklater 2007a: 10). This return to emotions is consistent with some early Frankfurt School writings, not least by Adorno, but it is a move away from the cold rationalism associated with Kant's Categorical Imperative. For Linklater, the larger point of returning to emotions is to place suffering and solidarity at the heart of the theoretical enterprise. It is an attempt to understand the way in which cosmopolitanism might be grounded in compassion, sympathy and other emotional attachments.

However, the civilizing gains made by the modern states-system may be under threat by developments since September 11. Though there are different responses to the terrorist attacks perpetrated by al-Qaeda, Linklater (2002b, 2007b) is concerned that the dominant White House rhetoric of a civilizational war against evil and relaxation of the global anti-torture norm threaten to unleash 'de-civilizing' potentials. The US-led 'war on terrorism', by privileging military means, putting more innocent lives at risk, suspending the rule of international law and employing 'constitutional torture', has raised the question of 'whether the vision of a world in which fewer human beings are burdened with preventable suffering has been dealt a blow from which it will not easily recover' (Linklater 2002b: 304). Implicit in Linklater, and explicit in the writings of others, is the argument that the greatest threat to world order may not be the terrorists who perpetrated such inexcusable harm, but the reaction by the United States. By placing itself outside the rules, norms and institutions of international society in its prosecution of its war on terrorism, the United States is not only diminishing the prospects of a peaceful and just world order, but undermining the very 'civilizing' principles and practices on which it was founded (Habermas 2003, 2006; Devetak 2005).

The praxeological dimension: cosmopolitanism and discourse ethics

One of the main intentions behind a sociology of the states-system is to assess the possibility of dismantling the modern state's totalizing project and moving towards more open, inclusive forms of community. This reflects critical international theory's belief that while totalizing projects have been tremendously successful, they have not been complete in colonizing modern political life. They have not been able to 'erode the sense of moral anxiety when duties to fellow-citizens clash with duties to the rest of humankind' (Linklater 1998: 150–1). In this section, I outline critical international theory's attempt to rethink the meaning of community in the light of this residual moral anxiety and an accumulating 'moral capital' which deepens and extends cosmopolitan citizenship. This involves not simply identifying the forces working to dismantle practices of social exclusion, but also identifying those working to supplant or at least supplement the system of sovereign states with cosmopolitan structures of global governance. For Thomas Diez and Jill Steans (2005: 132) this means facilitating institutional developments that concretize the dialogic ideal.

Linklater's work forms the most sustained and extensive interrogation of political community in international relations. In *Transformation of Political Community* (1998), Linklater elaborates his argument in terms of a 'triple transformation' affecting political community. The three transformational tendencies Linklater identifies are: a progressive recognition that moral, political and legal principles ought to be universalized, an insistence that material inequality ought to be reduced and greater demands for deeper respect for cultural, ethnic and gender differences. The triple transformation identifies processes that open the possibility of dismantling the nexus between sovereignty, territory, citizenship and nationalism and moving towards more cosmopolitan forms of governance. In this respect, the praxeological dimension closes the circle with the normative dimension by furthering the critique of the modern state's particularism. However, we should note a slight revision of this critique. Modern states are not just too particularistic for Linklater's liking, they are also too universalistic (Linklater 1998: 27). He here finesses his earlier critique of particularism by acknowledging the feminist and postmodern arguments that universalism runs the risk of ignoring or repressing certain marginalized or vulnerable groups unless it respects legitimate differences. Nonetheless, it remains consistent with the Enlightenment critique of the system of sovereign states, and the project to universalize the sphere in which human beings treat each other as free and equal.

If critical international theory's overall objective is to promote the reconfiguration of political community, not just by expanding political community beyond the frontiers of the sovereign state, but also by deepening it within those frontiers, then it must offer a more complex, multi-tiered structure of governance. Ultimately, it depends on reconstituting the state within alternative frameworks of political action that reduce the impact of social exclusion and enlarge democratic participation.

The key to realizing this vision is to sever the link between sovereignty and political association which is integral to the Westphalian system (Devetak 1995a: 43). A post-exclusionary form of political community would, according to Linklater, be post-sovereign or post-Westphalian. It would abandon the idea that power, authority, territory and loyalty must be focused around a single community or monopolized by a single site of governance. The state can no longer mediate effectively or exclusively among the many loyalties, identities and interests that exist in a globalizing world (see Devetak 2003). Fairer and more complex mediations can be developed, argues Linklater (1998: 60, 74), only by transcending the 'destructive fusion' achieved by the modern state and promoting wider communities of dialogue. The overall effect would thus be to 'de-centre' the state in the context of a more cosmopolitan form of political organization.

This requires states to establish and locate themselves in overlapping forms of international society. Linklater (1998: 166–7) lists three forms. First, a pluralist society of states in which the principles of coexistence work 'to preserve respect for the freedom and equality of independent political communities'. Second, a 'solidarist' society of states that have agreed to substantive moral purposes. Third, a post-Westphalian framework where states relinquish some of their sovereign powers so as to institutionalize shared political and moral norms (see Habermas 2006). These alternative frameworks of international society would widen the boundaries of political community by increasing the impact which duties to 'outsiders' have on decision making processes and contribute to what Linklater (1998) and Shapcott (2001) call 'dialogical cosmopolitanism'.

Linklater and Shapcott make the case for what they refer to as 'thin cosmopolitanism'. A 'thin cosmopolitanism' would need to promote universal claims yet do justice to difference (Shapcott 2000b, 2001). Within such a setup, loyalties to the sovereign state or any other political association cannot be absolute (Linklater 1998: 56; Devetak 2003). In recognizing the diversity of social bonds and moral ties, a 'thin cosmopolitan' ethos seeks to multiply the types and levels of political community. It should be noted, however, that this does not mean that duties to humanity override all others. There is no fixed 'moral hierarchy' within a 'thin cosmopolitan' framework (Linklater 1998: 161–8, 193–8). This version of 'thin cosmopolitanism' places the ideals of dialogue and consent at the centre of its project, and, to use Habermas' (2006) language, seeks to *juridify*, rather than moralize, international relations. That is, Habermas' cosmopolitan critical international theory wants to extend the progressive 'constitutionalization of international law' so as to realize a 'global domestic politics without a world government' (Habermas 2006: 135–7). The purpose of this multilevel global framework would be limited to securing international peace and protecting human rights (Habermas 2006: Chapter 8).

Another version of cosmopolitanism has been advanced, individually and collectively, by David Held and Daniele Archibugi (Archibugi and

Held 1995; Archibugi 2002, 2004a). Their work stems from an appreciation of the dangers and opportunities globalization presents to democracy. It seeks to globalize democracy even as it democratizes globalization (Archibugi 2004a: 438). The thrust of *cosmopolitan* democracy is captured by the question Archibugi asks (2002: 28): 'why must the principles and rules of democracy stop at the borders of a political community?' As he explains, it is not simply a matter of 'replicating, *sic et simpliciter*, the model we are acquainted with across a broader sphere' (2002: 29). It is a matter of strengthening the rule of law and citizens' participation in political life through differentiated forms of democratic engagement. Archibugi (2004b) has gone so far as to outline cosmopolitan principles governing humanitarian intervention. This controversial proposal stems from post-Cold War developments and a growing willingness on the part of international society to suspend sovereignty when extreme, large-scale cases of human suffering occur. Though difficult practical questions remain about 'who is authorized to decide when a humanitarian intervention is needed', Archibugi (2004b) strongly rejects the idea that states can unilaterally intervene under the humanitarian cause (see also Devetak 2002, 2007).

In this final section I outline briefly how the emphasis on dialogue is utilized in critical international theory. Linklater employs Habermas' notion of discourse ethics as a model for his dialogical approach. Discourse ethics is essentially a deliberative, consent oriented approach to resolving political issues within a moral framework. As elaborated by Habermas (1984b: 99), discourse ethics builds upon the need for communicating subjects to account for their beliefs and actions in terms which are intelligible to others and which they can then accept or contest. It is committed to the Kantian principle that political decisions or norms must be generalizable and consistent with the normative demands of public scrutiny if they are to attain legitimacy. At such moments when an international principle, social norm, or institution loses legitimacy, or when consensus breaks down, then discourse ethics enters the fray as a means of consensually deciding upon new principles or institutional arrangements. According to discourse ethics newly arrived at political principles, norms, or institutional arrangements can be said to be valid only if they can meet with the approval of all those who would be affected by them (Habermas 1993: 151).

There are three features worthy of note for our purposes. First, discourse ethics are *inclusionary*. It is oriented to the establishment and maintenance of the conditions necessary for open and non-exclusionary dialogue. No individual or group which will be affected by the principle, norm, or institution under deliberation should be excluded from participation in dialogue. Second, discourse ethics are *democratic*. It builds on a model of the public sphere which is bound to democratic deliberation and consent, where participants employ an 'argumentative rationality' for the purpose of 'reaching a mutual understanding based on a reasoned consensus, challenging the validity claims involved in any communication' (Risse 2000: 1–2). Combining the inclusionary and democratic impulses, discourse ethics provide a method that can test which principles, norms, or institutional arrangements would be 'equally good for all' (Habermas 1993: 151). Third, discourse ethics are a form of *moral-practical reasoning*. As such, it is not simply guided by utilitarian calculations or expediency, nor is it guided by an imposed concept of the 'good life'; rather, it is guided by *procedural fairness*. It is more concerned with the method of justifying moral principles than with the substantive content of those principles.

It is possible to identify three general implications of discourse ethics for the reconstruction of world politics which can only be briefly outlined here. First, by virtue of its consent oriented, deliberative approach, discourse ethics offers procedural guidance for democratic decision making processes. In light of social and material changes brought about by the globalization of production and finance, the movement of peoples, the rise of indigenous peoples and sub-national groups, environmental degradation and so on, the 'viability and accountability of national decision-making entities' is being brought into question (Held 1993: 26). Held (1993: 26–7) highlights the democratically deficient nature of the sovereign state when he asks: 'Whose consent is necessary and whose participation is justified in decisions concerning, for instance, AIDS, or acid rain, or the use of non-renewable resources? What is the relevant constituency: national, regional or international?' Under globalizing conditions it is apt that discourse ethics raise questions not only about 'who' is to be involved in decision making processes, but also 'how' and 'where' these decisions are to be made. The key here is 'to develop institutional arrangements that concretize the dialogic ideal' at all levels of social and political life (Linklater 1999). Apart from the constitutionalization of international law, this directs attention to an emerging global or international public sphere where 'social movements, non-state actors and "global citizens" join with states and international organizations in a dialogue over the exercise of power and authority across the globe' (Devetak and Higgott 1999: 491). As Marc Lynch (1999, 2000) has shown, this network of overlapping, transnational publics not only seeks to influence the foreign policy of individual states, it seeks to change international relations by modifying the structural context of strategic interaction. The existence of a global public sphere ensures that, as Risse (2000: 21) points out, 'actors have to regularly and routinely explain and justify their behaviour'. More than that, according

to Risse (2004), arguing and communicative action enable global governance institutions to attain greater legitimacy by providing 'voice opportunities to various stakeholders' and improved 'problem-solving
capacity' through deliberation. The growing interest in Axel Honneth's
work on 'struggles for recognition' is salient here. Jürgen Haacke (2005)
and Martin Weber (2007) have argued convincingly that Honneth's
account of the sources of social conflict, social identity and solidarity
may be fruitfully explored for the study of international relations. His
approach offers one way of thinking about how experiences of denigra-
tion, domination and exclusion may spur struggles for recognition which
carry inherent moral claims.

Second, discourse ethics offer a procedure for regulating violent
conflict and arriving at resolutions which are acceptable to all affected
parties. The cosmopolitan democratic procedures are geared towards
removing harm from international relations as far as possible. The invasion of Iraq by the United States and United Kingdom in March 2003 led
Habermas (2003: 369) to pronounce that 'multilateral will-formation in
interstate relations is not simply one option among others'. By giving up
its role as guarantor of international rights, violating international law
and disregarding the United Nations, Habermas (2003: 365) says, 'the
normative authority of the United States of America lies in ruins'. Even
though the fall of a brutal regime is a great political good, Habermas
condemned the war and rejected comparisons with the Kosovo war to
which he and other critical theorists lent their qualified support as a
humanitarian intervention. Habermas' reasons for condemning the Iraq
War are that it failed to satisfy any of the criteria of discourse ethics. Not
only did the United States and United Kingdom base their arguments on
questionable intelligence, they also contravened established norms of
dispute resolution and showed a less than convincing commitment to
'truth-seeking' aimed at mutual understanding and reasoned consensus.

Third, discourse ethics offer a means of criticizing and justifying the
principles by which humanity organizes itself politically. By reflecting on
the principles of inclusion and exclusion, discourse ethics can reflect on
the normative foundations of political life. From the moral point of view
contained within discourse ethics, the sovereign state as a form of community is unjust because the principles of inclusion and exclusion are not
the outcome of open dialogue and deliberation where all who stand to be
affected by the arrangement have been able to participate in discussion.
Against the exclusionary nature of the social bond underlying the sovereign state, discourse ethics have the inclusionary aim 'to secure the social
bond of all with all' (Habermas 1987: 346). In a sense, it is an attempt to
put into practice Kant's ideal of a community of co-legislators embracing
the whole of humanity (Linklater 1998: 84–9). As Linklater (1998: 10)

argues, 'all humans have *a prima facie* equal right to take part in universal communities of discourse which decide the legitimacy of global arrangements'. In sum, discourse ethics promotes a cosmopolitan ideal where the political organization of humanity is decided by a process of unconstrained and unrestricted dialogue.

Conclusion

There can be little doubt that critical theory has made a major contribution to international relations theory. One of these contributions has been to heighten awareness of the link between knowledge and politics. Critical international theory rejects the idea of the theorist as objective observer or detached bystander. Instead, the theorist is enmeshed in social and political life, and theories of international relations, like all theories, are informed by prior interests and convictions, whether they are acknowledged or not. A second contribution critical international theory makes is to rethink accounts of the modern state and political community. Traditional theories tend to take the state for granted, but critical international theory analyses the changing ways in which the boundaries of community are formed, maintained and transformed. It not only provides a sociological account, it provides a sustained normative analysis of the practices of inclusion and exclusion. Critical theory's aim of achieving an alternative theory and practice of international relations rests on the possibility of overcoming the exclusionary dynamics associated with the modern system of sovereign states and establishing a cosmopolitan set of arrangements that will better promote peace, freedom, justice, equality and security across the globe. It is thus an attempt radically to rethink the normative foundations of global politics.

8 | Post-structuralism

RICHARD DEVETAK

Previous versions of this chapter were entitled 'postmodernism'. These versions were always haunted by the presence of another label, 'post-structuralism'. Postmodernism and post-structuralism are labels with complicated and contested histories. The histories are complicated by the fact that no agreement exists as to the precise meaning of either term, let alone the relationship between them. Do the two labels refer to the same set of theoretical concepts and strategies, or do they refer to distinct and divergent theoretical approaches? This has induced some anxiety, not least in international relations, among those who prefer one label rather than another. In the end, the anxiety is probably unwarranted because the label we give to the theory is far less important than the conceptual tools and strategies we ascribe to it. But it is worth pausing to set out very briefly the relationship between the terms post-modernism and post-structuralism, and why this chapter has now adopted the term post-structuralism.

One of the difficulties that plagues any attempt to disentangle these two labels is the fact that some of the thinkers most closely associated with post-structuralism today have in the past been comfortable with the label post-modernism. For example, the first collection of 'post-modern readings of world politics' was published in James Der Derian and Michael J. Shapiro's *International/Intertextual Relations* (1989), containing chapters by leading exponents of post-structuralism, Richard K. Ashley, R. B. J. Walker and of course the editors themselves. No clear distinction is made between post-modernism and post-structuralism in this collection. Some authors self-identify with postmodernism, others with post-structuralism, often with no discernible differences in approach. On some occasions reference is made to 'postmodern and poststructural theories' (Der Derian and Shapiro 1989: xi) without clarifying what, if any, difference exists between the two terms. On other occasions post-structuralism is discussed as a critical theoretical practice, distinguishing it from post-modernism which is construed as a 'moment' or 'condition'. Postmodernism and post-structuralism are thus difficult

to disentangle. Because it has become the preferred label for most scholars working with the conceptual tools and strategies discussed below (see
Campbell 2007; Edkins 2007), this chapter shall use the term 'post-structuralism'. Theorists who are referred to, or who regard their own writing
as post-structuralist, deconstructive, genealogical and even postmodern
will be considered here.

The chapter is divided into four main sections. The first deals with the
relationship between power and knowledge in the study of international
relations. The second outlines the textual strategies employed by post-
structuralist approaches. The third is concerned with how post-structuralism deals with the state. The final part of the chapter outlines
post-structuralism's attempt to rethink the concept of the political.

Power and knowledge in international relations

Within orthodox social scientific accounts, knowledge ought to be
immune from the influence of power. The study of international relations, or any scholarly study for that matter, is thought to require the
suspension of values, interests and power relations in the pursuit of
objective knowledge – knowledge uncontaminated by external influences
and based on pure reason. Kant's (1970: 115) caution that 'the posses-
sion of power inevitably corrupts the free judgement of reason', stands as
a classic example of this view. It is this view that Michel Foucault, and
post-structuralism generally, have begun to problematize.

Rather than treat the production of knowledge as simply a cognitive
matter, post-structuralism treats it as a normative and political matter
(Shapiro 1999: 1). Foucault wanted to see if there was a common matrix
that hooked together the fields of knowledge and power. According to
Foucault, there is a general consistency, which cannot be reduced to an
identity, between modes of interpretation and operations of power.
Power and knowledge are mutually supportive; they directly imply one
another (Foucault 1977: 27). The task therefore is to see how operations
of power fit with the wider social and political matrices of the modern
world. For example, in *Discipline and Punish* (1977), Foucault investigates the possibility that the evolution of the penal system is intimately
connected to the human sciences. His argument is that a 'single process
of "epistemologico-juridical" formation' underlies the history of the
prison on the one hand, and the human sciences on the other (1977: 23).
In other words, the prison is consistent with modern society and modern
modes of apprehending 'man's' world.

This type of analysis has been attempted in international relations by
various thinkers. Richard Ashley has exposed one dimension of the

power-knowledge nexus by highlighting what Foucault calls the 'rule of immanence' between knowledge of the state and knowledge of 'man'. Ashley's (1989a) argument, stated simply, is that, '[m]odern statecraft is modern mancraft'. He seeks to demonstrate how the 'paradigm of sovereignty' simultaneously gives rise to a certain epistemological disposition and a certain account of modern political life. On the one hand, knowledge is thought to depend on the sovereignty of 'the heroic figure of reasoning man who knows that the order of the world is not God-given, that man is the origin of all knowledge, that responsibility for supplying meaning to history resides with man himself, and that, through reason, man may achieve total knowledge, total autonomy, and total power' (1989a: 264–5). On the other hand, modern political life finds in sovereignty its constitutive principle. The state is conceived by analogy with sovereign man as a pre-given, bounded entity which enters into relations with other sovereign presences. Sovereignty acts as the 'master signifier' as Jenny Edkins and Véronique Pin-Fat (1999: 6) put it. Both 'Man' and the state are marked by the presence of sovereignty, which contrasts with international relations which is marked, and violently so, by the absence of sovereignty (or alternatively stated, the presence of multiple sovereignties). In short, both the theory and practice of international relations are conditioned by the constitutive principle of sovereignty.

Genealogy

It is important to grasp the notion of genealogy, as it has become crucial to many post-structuralist perspectives in international relations. Genealogy is, put simply, a style of historical thought which exposes and registers the significance of power-knowledge relations. It is perhaps best known through Nietzsche's radical assault on the concept of origins. As Roland Bleiker (2000: 25) explains, genealogies 'focus on the process by which we have constructed origins and given meaning to particular representations of the past, representations that continuously guide our daily lives and set clear limits to political and social options'. It is a form of history which historicizes those things which are thought to be beyond history, including those things or thoughts which have been buried, covered, or excluded from view in the writing and making of history.

In a sense genealogy is concerned with writing counter-histories which expose the processes of exclusion and covering which make possible the teleological idea of history as a unified story unfolding with a clear beginning, middle and end. History, from a genealogical perspective, does not evidence a gradual disclosure of truth and meaning. Rather, it stages 'the endlessly repeated play of dominations' (Foucault 1987: 228). History proceeds as a series of dominations and impositions in knowledge and power, and the task of the genealogist is to unravel history to reveal the multifarious trajectories that have been fostered or closed off in the constitution of subjects, objects, fields of action and domains of knowledge. Moreover, from a genealogical perspective there is not one single, grand history, but many interwoven histories varied in their rhythm, tempo, and power-knowledge effects.

Genealogy affirms a perspectivism which denies the capacity to identify origins and meanings in history objectively. A genealogical approach is anti-essentialist in orientation, affirming the idea that all knowledge is situated in a particular time and place and issues from a particular perspective. The subject of knowledge is situated in, and conditioned by, a political and historical context, and constrained to function with particular concepts and categories of knowledge. Knowledge is never unconditioned. As a consequence of the heterogeneity of possible contexts and positions, there can be no single, Archimedean perspective which trumps all others. There is no 'truth', only competing perspectives. David Campbell's analysis of the Bosnian War in *National Deconstruction* (1998a) affirms this perspectivism. As he rightly reminds us, 'the same events can be represented in markedly different ways with significantly different effects' (1998a: 33). Indeed, the upshot of his analysis is that the Bosnian War can be known only through perspective.

In the absence of a universal frame of reference or overarching perspective, we are left with a plurality of perspectives. As Nietzsche (1969: III, 12) put it: 'There is *only* a perspective seeing, *only* a perspective "knowing".' The modern idea, or ideal, of an objective or all-encompassing perspective is displaced in post-structuralism by the Nietzschean recognition that there is always more than one perspective and that each perspective embodies a particular set of values. Moreover, these perspectives do not simply offer different views of the same 'real world'. The very *idea* of the 'real world' has been 'abolished' in Nietzsche's thought (1990: 50–1), leaving *only* perspectives, *only* interpretations of interpretations, or in Derrida's (1974: 158) terms, *only* 'textuality'.

Perspectives are thus not to be thought of as simply optical devices for apprehending the 'real world', such as a telescope or microscope, but also as the very fabric of that 'real world'. For post-structuralism, following Nietzsche, perspectives are integral to the constitution of the 'real world', not just because they are our only access to it, but because they are basic and essential elements of it. The warp and woof of the 'real world' is woven out of perspectives and interpretations, none of which can claim to correspond to reality-in-itself, to be a 'view from nowhere', or to be exhaustive. Perspectives are thus component objects and events that go towards making up the 'real world'. In fact, we should say that there is no object or event outside or prior to perspective or narrative. As

Campbell explains, after Hayden White, narrative is central, not just to understanding an event, but in constituting that event. This is what Campbell (1998a: 34) means by the 'narrativizing of reality'. According to such a conception events acquire the status of 'real' not because they occurred but because they are remembered and because they assume a place in a narrative (1998a: 36). Narrative is thus not simply a re-presentation of some prior event, it is the means by which the status of reality is conferred on events. But historical narratives also perform vital political functions in the present; they can be used as resources in contemporary political struggles (1998a: 84, 1999: 31).

The event designated by the name 'September 11' is a case in point. Is it best conceived as an act of terrorism, a criminal act, an act of evil, an act of war, or an act of revenge? Perhaps it is best thought of as an instance of 'Islamo-fascism' or the clash of civilization? Or perhaps as 'blowback'? Furthermore, which specific acts of commission and omission constitute this event? Did 'September 11' begin at 8.45 a.m. when American Airlines flight 11 crashed into the north tower of the World Trade Centre? Or at 7.59a.m. when the plane departed from Boston? Did it commence when the perpetrators began planning and training for the attack? Or did it begin even earlier, as a reaction (however unjustified) to US Middle East policy? These questions show that the event of 'September 11' is only constituted in a narrative that integrates it into a sequence of other events and thereby confers significance upon it.

It may be that, as Jenny Edkins (2002: 245–6) says, events like 'September 11' cannot be experienced in any normal sense. Rather, they exceed experience and our normal social and linguistic frameworks. Nevertheless, there will be, as Campbell (2002a: 1) notes, struggles over the meaning of 'September 11'. He, like Edkins, cautions against a hasty attempt to fix the meaning of 'September 11'. In particular he shows that, despite the White House asserting the unprecedented nature of the September 11 attacks, the 'war on terrorism' has returned to past foreign policy practices; in his words, it has morphed into the Cold War (1999: 17). 'This return of the past means that we have different objects of enmity, different allies, but the same structure for relating to the world through foreign policy' (2002a: 18). Cynthia Weber (2002) makes a similar argument, suggesting instead that the Pearl Harbor attacks of 7 December 1941 provide an interpretive framework for the US military response today. 'September 11' is thus read as if it had the same meaning as 'December 7'. For post-structuralism, the representation of any political event will always be susceptible to competing interpretations.

Genealogy is a reminder of the essential agonism in the historical constitution of identities, unities, disciplines, subjects and objects. From this perspective, 'all history, including the production of order, [is comprehended] in terms of the endless power political clash of multiple wills' (Ashley 1987: 409). Metaphors of war and battle are central to genealogy. In a series of lectures given at the Collège de France in 1975–76 under the title 'Society Must be Defended', Foucault employs genealogy to analyze power relations in the state. He explores a historico-political discourse dating from the end of the civil and religious wars of the sixteenth century that understood war to be 'a permanent social relationship, the ineradicable basis of all relations and institutions of power' (Foucault 2003: 49). This discourse, found in Sir Edward Coke, John Lilburne and Henri Comte de Boulainvilliers among others, challenged the prevailing assumption of the day that society is at peace. Instead, beneath the calm, peaceful order of law-governed society posited by philosophico-juridical discourses, this discourse perceives 'a sort of primitive and permanent war', according to Foucault (2003: 47).

Foucault (2003: 15) characterizes this discourse through an inversion of Clausewitz's famous proposition: 'politics is the continuation of war by other means'. Foucault means to analyse how war became viewed as an apt way of describing politics. He wants to know when political thought began to imagine, perhaps counter-intuitively, that war serves as a principle for the analysis of power relations within political order. This conflictual understanding of society is equally at odds with Kantian liberalism and Hobbesian realism. If anything, it seems to pre-empt Nietzsche's emphasis on struggle. Political power, instituted and legitimized in the sovereign state, does not bring war to an end; rather, 'In the smallest of its cogs, peace is waging a secret war' (2003: 50). This 'war discourse' posits a binary structure that pervades civil society, wherein one group is pitted against another in continuing struggle.

Foucault (1987: 236) claims as one of genealogy's express purposes the 'systematic dissociation of identity'. There are two dimensions to this purpose. First, it has a purpose at the ontological level: to avoid substituting causes for effects (metalepsis). It does not take identity or agency as given but seeks to account for the forces which underwrite this apparent agency. Identity or agency is an *effect* to be explained, not assumed. This means resisting the temptation to attribute essences to agents, things or events in history, and requires a transformation of the question 'what is?' into 'how is?' For Nietzsche, Foucault and thus post-structuralism, it is more important to determine the forces that give shape to an event or a thing than to attempt to identify its hidden, fixed essence. Second, it has an ethico-political purpose in problematizing prevailing identity formations which appear normal or natural. It refuses to use history for the purpose of affirming present identities, preferring to use it instead to disturb identities that have become dogmatized, conventionalized or normalized.

A good example of this genealogical method is to be found in Maja Zehfuss's (2003) analysis of 'September 11' and the war on terrorism. She challenges assumptions about unified agency and about the relationship between causes and effects. As she points out, to imply that the events of 'September 11' were an attack on 'the West', as the US and UK governments do, is to ignore the ambiguous character of Western identity. At a minimum, it is to ignore the fact that Western nations are complicit with the technologies and perpetrators, but it also ignores political dissent from those who do not wish the memory of the dead to be used to perpetuate further violence (2003: 524–5). Following Nietzsche, Zehfuss (2003: 522) also questions cause-and-effect thinking; 'cause and effect are . . . never as easily separated' as they appear to be. For example, governments leading the so-called war on terrorism imply that 'September 11' *caused* the war on terrorism. It is as if 'September 11' were 'an "uncaused" cause' (Zehfuss 2003: 521), or as if, in Judith Butler's (2004: 6) words, 'There is no relevant prehistory to the events of September 11'. But this ignores a good deal of prior political history which is essential to any adequate understanding.

It would be a mistake, however, to think that genealogy focuses only on what is forgotten. Zehfuss draws our attention to the politics of memory also. She points out that both Osama bin Laden and President George W. Bush want the world to remember the events of September 11. Bin Laden wants the world to remember the humbling of a hyperpower, Bush wants the world to remember the loss of innocent life. Both, says Zehfuss (2003: 514), 'have an interest in our memory of the events'. Zehfuss's (2003: 525) argument is that a 'certain way of using memory has become politically powerful', especially in the United States, where the White House has exploited the memory of 'September 11' to justify the curtailment of civil liberties at home, and an aggressive military response abroad. Her point is that we need to forget the dominant narratives before we can understand what makes 'September 11' a distinctive event.

It is in view of such genealogical analyses as these that we can understand Foucault's (1977: 31) attempt at 'writing the history of the present'. A history of the present asks: How have we made the present seem like a normal or natural condition? What has been forgotten and what has been remembered in history in order to legitimize the present and present courses of action?

One of the important insights of post-structuralism, with its focus on the power-knowledge nexus and its genealogical approach, is that many of the problems and issues studied in international relations are not just matters of epistemology and ontology, but of *power* and *authority*; they are struggles to impose authoritative interpretations of international relations. As Derrida (2003: 105) himself says in an interview conducted after September 11: 'We must also recognize here the strategies and relations of power. The dominant power is the one that manages to impose and, thus, to legitimate, indeed to legalize . . . on a national or world stage, the terminology and thus the interpretation that best suits it in a given situation.' The following section outlines a strategy which is concerned with destabilizing dominant interpretations by showing how every interpretation systematically depends on that for which it cannot account.

Textual strategies of post-structuralism

Der Derian (1989: 6) contends that post-structuralism is concerned with exposing the 'textual interplay behind power politics'. It might be better to say it is concerned with exposing the textual interplay *within* power politics, for the effects of textuality do not remain behind politics, but are intrinsic to them. The 'reality' of power politics (like any social reality) is always already constituted through textuality and inscribed modes of representation. It is in this sense that David Campbell (1992) refers to 'writing' security, Gearóid Ó Tuathail (1996) refers to 'writing' global space, and Cynthia Weber (1995) refers to 'writing' the state. Two questions arise: (1) What is meant by textual interplay? (2) How, by using which methods and strategies, does post-structuralism seek to disclose this textual interplay?

Textuality is a common post-structuralist theme. It stems mainly from Derrida's redefinition of 'text' in *Of Grammatology* (1974). It is important to clarify what Derrida means by 'text'. He is not restricting its meaning to literature and the realm of ideas, as some have mistakenly thought, rather, he is implying that the world is *also* a text, or better, the 'real' world is constituted like a text, and 'one cannot refer to this "real" except in an interpretive experience' (Derrida 1988: 148). Post-structuralism firmly regards interpretation as necessary and fundamental to the constitution of the social world. But as Roland Bleiker (2001, Bleiker and Leet 2006) and Michael J. Shapiro (2005, 2007) have shown extensively, matters of interpretation are also aesthetic matters.

Recognition of the relationship between interpretation and aesthetics, what Bleiker (2001) calls the 'aesthetic turn', does not mean reducing politics and international relations to works of art that can be measured against an ideal of beauty. Rather, it means analysing the relationship between forms of representation and the things represented, and the irreducible interpretive choices that are required. Not unlike artists, international relations students will have to make choices in how they represent or depict an event. Painters, for example, will need to choose the time of day, the angle of view, the level of detail, the type of paint, the palette of colours, the brush sizes, and so on. International relation students have similar choices to make: the time frame, the perspective, the selection of relevant data or facts, the key concepts, and so on. All of these decisions are necessary, but the individual choices are not self-evident; they will vary from one student to the next. And this is why political events are susceptible to different interpretations. There is nothing inherent to events or objects in the world which determines how they must be represented in either words or paintings. Instead, it is the structures of human consciousness and the various interpretive choices we make that shape how we perceive and depict the world around us (Bleiker 2001: 513; Shapiro 2005: 233–4). This post-positivist epistemology is a legacy of Kant's philosophical critique of empiricism. The important point for us, as Bleiker (2001: 510) shows, is that aesthetic insight compels us to recognize the politics involved in representation itself; that it is not a natural or neutral reflection of reality. This is but another way of making Campbell's point about the narrativization of reality.

But in order to tease out the textual interplay mentioned above, let us review two strategies employed by post-structuralism: *deconstruction* and *double reading*. These will show how 'textual interplay' is a mutually constitutive relationship between different interpretations in the representation and constitution of the world.

Deconstruction

Deconstruction is a general mode of radically unsettling what are taken to be stable concepts and conceptual oppositions. Its main point is to demonstrate the effects and costs produced by the settled concepts and oppositions, to disclose the parasitical relationship between opposed terms and to attempt a displacement of them. According to Derrida conceptual oppositions are never simply neutral but are inevitably hierarchical. One of the two terms in the opposition is privileged over the other. This privileged term supposedly connotes a presence, propriety, fullness, purity, or identity which the other lacks (for example, sovereignty as opposed to anarchy). Deconstruction attempts to show that such oppositions are untenable, as each term *always already* depends on the other. Indeed, the prized term gains its privilege only by disavowing its dependence on the subordinate term.

From a post-structuralist perspective, the apparently clear opposition between two terms is neither clear nor oppositional. Derrida often speaks of this relationship in terms of a structural parasitism and contamination, as each term is structurally related to, and already harbours, the other. Difference *between* the two opposed concepts or terms is always accompanied by a veiled difference *within* each term. Neither term is pure, self-same, complete in itself, or completely closed off from the other, though as much is feigned. This implies that totalities, whether conceptual or social, are never fully present and properly established. Moreover, there is no pure stability, only more or less successful stabilizations as there is a certain amount of 'play', or 'give', in the structure of the opposition.

As a general mode of unsettling, deconstruction is particularly concerned with locating those elements of instability or 'give' which ineradicably threaten any totality. Nevertheless, it must still account for stabilizations (or stability-effects). It is this equal concern with undoing or deconstitution (or at least their ever-present possibility) which marks off deconstruction from other more familiar modes of interpretation. To summarize, deconstruction is concerned with both the constitution and deconstitution of any totality, whether a text, theory, discourse, structure, edifice, assemblage, or institution.

Double reading

Derrida seeks to expose this relationship between stability-effects and destabilizations by passing through two readings in any analysis. As expressed by Derrida (1981: 6), double reading is essentially a duplicitous strategy which is 'simultaneously faithful and violent'. The first reading is a commentary or repetition of the dominant interpretation – that is, a reading which demonstrates how a text, discourse or institution achieves the stability-effect. It faithfully recounts the dominant story by building on the same foundational assumptions, and repeating conventional steps in the argument. The point here is to demonstrate how the text, discourse, or institution appears coherent and consistent with itself. It is concerned, in short, to elaborate how the identity of a text, discourse, or institution is put together or constituted. Rather than yield to the monologic first reading, the second, counter-memorializing reading unsettles it by applying pressure to those points of instability within a text, discourse, or institution. It exposes the internal tensions and how they are (incompletely) covered over or expelled. The text, discourse, or institution is never completely at one with itself, but always carries within it elements of tension and crisis which render the whole thing less than stable.

The task of double reading as a mode of deconstruction is to understand how a discourse or social institution is assembled or put together, but at the same time to show how it is always already threatened with its undoing. It is important to note that there is no attempt in deconstruction to arrive at a single, conclusive reading. The two mutually inconsistent readings, which are in a performative (rather than logical) contradiction, remain permanently in tension. The point is not to demonstrate the truthfulness or otherwise of a story, but to expose how any story depends on the repression of internal tensions in order to produce a stable effect of homogeneity and continuity.

Ashley's double reading of the anarchy problématique

Richard Ashley's double reading of the *anarchy problématique* is one of the earliest and most important deconstructions in the study of international relations. His main target is the conception of anarchy and the theoretical and practical effects. The *anarchy problématique* is the name Ashley gives to the defining moment of most inquiries in international relations. It is exemplified by Oye's (1985: 1) assertion that: 'Nations dwell in perpetual anarchy, for no central authority imposes limits on the pursuit of sovereign interests'. Most importantly, the *anarchy problématique* deduces from the absence of central, global authority, not just an empty concept of anarchy, but a description of international relations as power politics, characterized by self-interest, *raison d'état,* the routine resort to force, and so on.

The main brunt of Ashley's analysis is to problematize this deduction of power politics from the lack of central rule. Ashley's many analyses of the *anarchy problématique* can be understood in terms of double reading. The first reading assembles the constitutive features, or 'hard core' of the *anarchy problématique*, while the second reading disassembles the constitutive elements of the *anarchy problématique*, showing how it rests on a series of questionable theoretical suppositions or exclusions.

In the first reading, Ashley outlines the *anarchy problématique* in conventional terms. He describes not just the absence of any overarching authority, but the presence of a multiplicity of states in the international system, none of which can lay down the law to the individual states. Further, the states which comprise this system have their own identifiable interests, capabilities, resources and territory. The second reading questions the self-evidence of international relations as an anarchical realm of power politics. The initial target in this double reading is the opposition between sovereignty and anarchy, where sovereignty is valorized as a regulative ideal, and anarchy is regarded as the absence or negation of sovereignty. Anarchy takes on meaning only as the antithesis of sovereignty. Moreover, sovereignty and anarchy are taken to be mutually exclusive and mutually exhaustive. Ashley demonstrates, however, that the *anarchy problématique* works only by making certain assumptions regarding sovereign states. If the dichotomy between sovereignty and anarchy is to be tenable at all, then inside the sovereign state must be found a domestic realm of identity, homogeneity, order and progress guaranteed by legitimate force; and outside must lie an anarchical realm of difference, heterogeneity, disorder and threat, recurrence and repetition. But to represent sovereignty and anarchy in this way (that is, as mutually exclusive and exhaustive), depends on converting differences *within* sovereign states into differences *between* sovereign states (Ashley 1988: 257). Sovereign states must expunge any traces of anarchy that reside within them in order to make good the distinction between sovereignty and anarchy. Internal dissent and what Ashley (1987, 1989b) calls 'transversal struggles' which cast doubt over the idea of a clearly identifiable and demarcated sovereign identity must be repressed or denied to make the *anarchy problématique* meaningful. In particular, the opposition between sovereignty and anarchy rests on the possibility of determining a 'well-bounded sovereign entity possessing its own "internal" hegemonic centre of decision-making capable of reconciling "internal" conflicts and capable, therefore, of projecting a singular presence' (Ashley 1988: 245).

The general effect of the *anarchy problématique* is to confirm the opposition between sovereignty and anarchy as mutually exclusive and exhaustive. This has two particular effects: (1) to represent a domestic domain of sovereignty as a stable, legitimate foundation of modern political community, and (2) to represent the domain beyond sovereignty as dangerous and anarchical. These effects depend on what Ashley (1988: 256) calls a 'double exclusion'. They are possible only if, on the one hand, a single representation of sovereign identity can be imposed and, on the other hand, if this representation can be made to appear natural and indisputable. The double reading problematizes the *anarchy problématique* by posing two questions: first, what happens to the *anarchy problématique* if it is not so clear that fully present and completed sovereign states are ontologically primary or unitary? And, second, what happens to the *anarchy problématique* if the lack of central global rule is not overwritten with assumptions about power politics?

Problematizing sovereign states

States, sovereignty and violence are long-standing themes in the established traditions of international relations that have gained renewed importance after the September 11 terrorist attacks. They are also central themes in post-structuralist approaches to international relations. However, rather than adopt them uncritically from traditional approaches, post-structuralism revises them in view of insights gained from genealogy and deconstruction.

Post-structuralism seeks to address a crucial issue regarding interpretations and explanations of the sovereign state that state-centric approaches have obscured – namely, its historical constitution and reconstitution as the primary mode of subjectivity in world politics. This returns us to the type of question posed by Foucault's genealogy: how, by virtue of what political practices and representations, is the sovereign state instituted as the normal mode of international subjectivity? Posing the question in this manner directs attention, in Nietzschean fashion, less to what is the essence of the sovereign state than to how the sovereign state is made possible, how it is naturalized and how it is made to appear as if it had an essence.

To the extent that post-structuralism seeks to account for the conditions which make possible the phenomenon of the state as something which concretely affects the experience of everyday life, it is phenomenological. Yet this is no ordinary phenomenology. It might best be called a 'quasi-phenomenology' for, as already noted, it is equally concerned with accounting for those conditions which destabilize the phenomenon or defer its complete actualization. In this section, post-structuralism's quasi-phenomenology of the state will be explained. This comprises four main elements: (1) a genealogical analysis of the modern state's 'origins' in violence, (2) an account of boundary inscription, (3) a deconstruction of identity as it is defined in security and foreign policy discourses and (4) a revised interpretation of statecraft. The overall result is to rethink the ontological structure of the sovereign state in order to respond properly to the question of how the sovereign state is (re)constituted as the normal mode of subjectivity in international relations.

Violence

Modern political thought has attempted to transcend illegitimate forms of rule (such as tyranny and despotism) where power is unconstrained, unchecked, arbitrary and violent, by founding legitimate, democratic forms of government where authority is subject to law. In modern politics, it is *reason* rather than power or violence which has become the measure of legitimacy. However, as Campbell and Dillon (1993: 161) point out, the relationship between politics and violence in modernity is deeply ambivalent for, on the one hand, violence 'constructs the refuge of the sovereign community' and, on the other hand, it is 'the condition from which the citizens of that community must be protected'. The paradox here is that violence is both poison and cure.

The link between violence and the state is revealed in Bradley Klein's genealogy of the state as strategic subject. Klein's (1994: 139) broad purpose in *Strategic Studies and World Order* is to analyse 'the violent making and remaking of the modern world'. His more particular purpose is to explain the historical emergence of war making states. Rather than assume their existence, as realists and neo-realists tend to, Klein examines how political units emerge in history which are capable of relying upon force to distinguish a domestic political space from an exterior one. Consistent with other post-structuralists, he argues that 'states rely upon violence to constitute themselves as states', and in the process, 'impose differentiations between the internal and external' (1994: 38). Strategic violence is constitutive of states; it does not merely 'patrol the frontiers' of the state, it 'helps constitute them as well' (1994: 3).

The point made by post-structuralism regarding violence in modern politics needs to be clearly differentiated from traditional approaches. In general, traditional accounts take violent confrontation to be a normal and regular occurrence in international relations. The condition of anarchy is thought to incline states to war as there is nothing to stop wars from occurring. Violence is not constitutive in such accounts as these, but is 'configurative', or 'positional' (Ruggie 1993: 162–3). The ontological structure of the states is taken to be set up already before violence is undertaken. The violence merely modifies the territorial configuration, or is an instrument for power-political, strategic manoeuvres in the distribution or hierarchy of power. Post-structuralism, however; exposes the constitutive role of violence in modern political life. Violence is fundamental to the ontological structuring of states, and is not merely something to which fully formed states resort for power-political reasons. Violence is, according to post-structuralism, inaugural as well as augmentative.

This argument about the intimate and paradoxical relationship between violence and political order is taken even further by Jenny Edkins, who places the Nazis, concentration camps, NATO and refugee camps on the same continuum. All, she claims, are determined by a sovereign power that seeks to extend control over life. She argues that even humanitarianism can be placed on the spectrum of violence since it, too, is complicit with the modern state's order of sovereign power and violence, notwithstanding claims to the contrary. Indeed, she says that famine-relief camps are like concentration camps since they are both sites of 'arbitrary decisions between life and death, where aid workers are forced to choose which of the starving they are unable to help' (Edkins 2000: 13). Famine victims appear only as 'bare life' to be 'saved'; stripped of their social and cultural being, they are depoliticized, their political voices ignored (2000: 13–14). In different language, Campbell (1998b: 506) affirms this view by arguing that prevailing forms of humanitarianism construct people as victims, 'incapable of acting without intervention'. This insufficiently political or humane form of humanitarianism, therefore, 'is deeply implicated in the production of a sovereign political power that claims the monopoly of the legitimate use of violence' (Edkins 2000: 18). Mick Dillon and Julian Reid offer a similar reading of humanitarian responses to 'complex emergencies', but rather than assume an equivalence between humanitarianism and sovereign power, they see a susceptibility of the former to the operations of the latter. Global governance, they say, 'quite literally threatens nongovernmental and humanitarian agencies with recruitment into the very structures and practices of power against which they previously defined themselves' (Dillon and Reid 2000: 121).

Edkins and Dillon and Reid draw upon an influential and richly textured argument advanced by the Italian philosopher Giorgio Agamben in *Homo Sacer: Sovereign Power and Bare Life* (1998). Following Carl Schmitt, Agamben posits sovereignty as the essence of the political. The sovereign claims the right to decide the exception. This leads, among other things, to the sovereign's right to decide who is in and who is out of a political community. If one of the main concerns of critical theory (as outlined in Chapter 7) is examination of possibilities for more inclusive forms of community, Agamben focuses on exclusion as a condition of possibility of political community. He argues that 'In Western politics, bare life has the peculiar privilege of being that whose exclusion founds the city of men' (Agamben 1998: 7). 'Bare life', most basically, is the simple biological fact of not being dead. But Agamben assigns a further meaning to bare life, a meaning captured in the term *homo sacer* (sacred man), which refers to a life that can be taken but not sacrificed, a holy but damned life. Banished from society, *homo sacer* acts as the 'constitutive outside' to political life. But, in truth, *homo sacer* is neither inside nor outside political community in any straightforward sense. Instead, he occupies a 'zone of indistinction' or 'no-man's land'. Indeed, as Agamben (1998: 74, 80) points out, the Roman concept of *homo sacer* precedes the distinction between sacred and profane, which is why, paradoxically, a so-called '*sacred* man' can be killed. The clearest expression of this was the system of camps established under the Nazis before and during World War II. But similar systems were established during the Bosnian War. As David Campbell (2002b: 157) spells out, the Bosnian Serb camps at Omarska and Trnopolje were 'extra-legal spaces' integrated into an 'ethnic-cleansing strategy based on an exclusive and homogeneous' political community.

Judith Butler, in a brilliant essay titled 'Indefinite Detention' (in Butler 2004), applies Agamben's arguments in her reflections on America's 'war on terrorism'. Drawing from Agamben's writing on sovereign power, she notes how states suspend the rule of law by invoking a 'state of emergency'. There can be no more significant act demonstrating the state's sovereignty than withdrawing or suspending the law. Referring to the controversial detainment of terrorism suspects at Guantánamo Bay, Butler says: 'It is not just that constitutional protections are indefinitely suspended, but that the state (in its augmented executive function) arrogates to itself the right to suspend the Constitution or to manipulate the geography of detentions and trials so that constitutional and international rights are effectively suspended' (Butler 2004: 63–4). The detainees are thus reduced to bare life in a no-man's land beyond the law. Butler (2004: 68) observes that 'to be detained indefinitely . . . is precisely to have no definitive prospect for a reentry into the political fabric of life, even as one's situation is highly, if not fatally, politicized'. By employing Agamben, these post-structuralist works seek to show how sovereign states, even liberal democratic ones, constitute themselves through exclusion and violence.

Boundaries

To inquire into the state's (re)constitution, as post-structuralism does, is partly to inquire into the ways in which global political space is partitioned. The world is not naturally divided into differentiated political spaces, and nor is there a single authority to carve up the world. This necessarily leads to a focus on the 'boundary question', as Dillon and Everard (1992: 282) call it, because any political subject is constituted by the marking of physical, symbolic and ideological boundaries.

Post-structuralism is less concerned with *what* sovereignty is, than *how* it is spatially and temporally produced and how it is circulated. How is a certain configuration of space and power instituted? And with what consequences? The obvious implication of these questions is that the prevailing mode of political subjectivity in international relations (the sovereign state) is neither natural nor necessary. There is no necessary reason why global political space has to be divided as it is, and with the same bearing. Of crucial importance in this differentiation of political space is the inscription of *boundaries*. Marking boundaries is not an innocent, pre-political act. It is a political act with profound political implications as it is fundamental to the production and delimitation of political space. As Gearóid Ó Tuathail (1996: 1) affirms, '[g]eography is about power. Although often assumed to be innocent, the geography of the world is not a product of nature but a product of histories of struggle between competing authorities over the power to organize, occupy, and administer space'.

There is no political space in advance of boundary inscription. Boundaries function in the modern world to divide an interior, sovereign space from an exterior, pluralistic, anarchical space. The opposition between sovereignty and anarchy rests on the possibility of clearly dividing a domesticated political space from an undomesticated outside. It is in this sense that boundary inscription is a defining moment of the sovereign state. Indeed, neither sovereignty nor anarchy would be possible without the inscription of a boundary to divide political space. This 'social inscription of global space', to use Tuathail's (1996: 61) phrase, produces the effect of completed, bounded states, usually built around what Campbell (1998a: 11) calls the 'nationalist imaginary'.

However, as Connolly (1994: 19) points out, boundaries are highly ambiguous since they 'form an indispensable protection against violation and violence; but divisions they sustain in doing so also carry cruelty and violence'. At stake here is a series of questions regarding boundaries: how boundaries are constituted, what moral and political status they are accorded, how they operate simultaneously to include and exclude and how they simultaneously produce order and violence. Clearly, these questions are not just concerned with the location of cartographic boundaries, but with how these cartographic boundaries serve to represent, limit, and legitimate a political identity. But how, through which political practices and representations, are boundaries inscribed? And what implications does this hold for the mode of subjectivity produced?

Identity

There is, as Rob Walker (1995a: 35–6) notes, a privileging of spatiality in modern political thought and practice. By differentiating political spaces, boundaries are fundamental to the modern world's preference for the 'entrapment of politics' within discrete state boundaries (Magnusson 1996: 36). Post-structuralism asks: How has political identity been imposed by spatial practices and representations of domestication and distancing? And how has the concept of a territorially-defined self been constructed in opposition to a threatening other?

Of utmost importance here are issues of how security is conceived in spatial terms and how threats and dangers are defined and articulated, giving rise to particular conceptions of the state as a secure political subject. Debbie Lisle (2000) has shown how even modern tourism participates in the reproduction of this spatialized conception of security. By continuously reaffirming the distinction between 'safety here and now' and 'danger there and then' tourist practices help sustain the geo-political security discourse. Her reading suggests that war and tourism, rather than being two distinct and opposed social practices, are actually intimately connected by virtue of being governed by the same global security discourse.

A detailed account of the relationship between the state, violence and identity is to be found in David Campbell's post-structuralist account of the Bosnian war, in *National Deconstruction* (1998a). His central argument there is that a particular norm of community has governed the intense violence of the war. This norm, which he calls 'ontopology', borrowing from Derrida, refers to the assumption that political community requires the perfect alignment of territory and identity, state and nation (Derrida 1994a: 82; Campbell 1998a: 80). It functions to disseminate and reinforce the supposition that political community must be understood and organized as a single identity perfectly aligned with and possessing its allocated territory. The logic of this norm, suggests Campbell (1998a: 168–9), leads to a desire for a coherent, bounded, monocultural community. These 'ontopological' assumptions form 'the governing codes of subjectivity in international relations' (1998a: 170). What is interesting about Campbell's (1999a: 23) argument is the implication that the outpouring of violence in Bosnia was not simply an aberration or racist distortion of the ontopological norm, but was in fact an exacerbation of this same norm. The violence of 'ethnic cleansing' in pursuit of a pure, homogeneous political identity is simply a continuation, albeit extreme, of the same political project inherent in any modern nation-state. The upshot is that all forms of political community, insofar as they require boundaries, will be given to some degree of violence (Campbell 1998a: 13).

Post-structuralism focuses on the discourses and practices which substitute threat for difference in the constitution of political identity. Simon Dalby, for instance (1993), explains how cold wars result from the application of a geo-political reasoning which defines security in terms of spatial exclusion and the specification of a threatening other. 'Geopolitical discourse constructs worlds in terms of Self and Others, in terms of cartographically specifiable sections of political space, and in terms of military threats' (1993: 29). The geo-political creation of the external other is integral to the constitution of a political identity (self) which is to be made secure. But to constitute a coherent, singular political identity often demands the silencing of internal dissent. There can be internal others that endanger a certain conception of the self, and must be necessarily expelled, disciplined, or contained. Identity, it can be surmized, is an effect forged, on the one hand, by disciplinary practices which attempt to normalize a population, giving it a sense of unity and, on the other, by exclusionary practices which attempt to secure the domestic identity through processes of spatial differentiation, and various diplomatic, military and defence practices. There is a supplementary relationship between containment of domestic and foreign others, which helps to constitute political identity by expelling 'from the resultant "domestic" space . . . all that comes to be regarded as alien, foreign and dangerous' (Campbell 1992: Chapters 5,6, 1998a: 13).

If it is plain that identity is defined through difference, and that a self requires an other, it is not so plain that difference or otherness necessarily equates with threat or danger. Nevertheless, as Campbell (1992) points out the sovereign state is predicated on discourses of danger. The constant articulation of danger through foreign policy is thus not a threat to a state's identity or existence', says Campbell (1992: 12), 'it is its condition of possibility'. The possibility of identifying the United States as a political subject, for example, rested, during the Cold War, on the ability to impose an interpretation of the Soviet Union as an external threat, and the capacity of the US government to contain internal threats (1992: Chapter 6). Indeed, the pivotal concept of containment takes on a Janus-faced quality as it is simultaneously turned inwards and outwards to deal with threatening others, as Campbell (1992: 175) suggests. The end result of the strategies of containment was to ground identity in a territorial state.

It is important to recognize that political identities do not exist prior to the differentiation of self and other. The main issue is how something which is different becomes conceptualized as a threat or danger to be contained, disciplined, negated, or excluded. There may be an irreducible possibility that difference will slide into opposition, danger, or threat, but there is no necessity. Political identity need not be constituted against, and at the expense of, others, but the prevailing discourses and practices of security and foreign policy tend to reproduce this reasoning. Moreover, this relation to others must be recognized as a morally and politically loaded relation. The effect is to allocate the other to an inferior moral space, and to arrogate the self to a superior one. As Campbell (1992: 85) puts it, 'the social space of inside/outside is both made possible by and helps constitute a moral space of superior/inferior'. By coding the spatial exclusion in moral terms it becomes easier to legitimize certain politico-military practices and interventions which advance national security interests at the same time that they reconstitute political identities. As Shapiro (1988a: 102) puts it, 'to the extent that the Other is regarded as something not occupying the same moral space as the self, conduct toward the Other becomes more exploitive'. This is especially so in an international system where political identity is so frequently defined in terms of territorial exclusion.

Statecraft

The above section has sketched how violence, boundaries and identity function to make possible the sovereign state. This only partly deals with the main genealogical issue of how the sovereign state is (re)constituted as a normal mode of subjectivity. Two questions remain if the genealogical approach is to be pursued: how is the sovereign state naturalized and disseminated? And how is it made to appear as if it had an essence?

Post-structuralism is interested in how prevailing modes of subjectivity neutralize or conceal their arbitrariness by projecting an image of normalcy, naturalness, or necessity. Ashley has explored the very difficult question of how the dominant mode of subjectivity is normalized by utilizing the concept of hegemony. By 'hegemony' Ashley (1989b: 269) means not an 'overarching ideology or cultural matrix', but 'an ensemble of normalized knowledgeable practices, identified with a particular state and domestic society . . . that is regarded as a practical paradigm of sovereign political subjectivity and conduct'. 'Hegemony' refers to the projection and circulation of an 'exemplary' model, which functions as a regulative ideal. Of course the distinguishing characteristics of the exemplary model are not fixed but are historically and politically conditioned. The sovereign state, as the currently dominant mode of subjectivity, is by no means natural. As Ashley (1989b: 267) remarks, sovereignty is fused to certain 'historically normalized interpretations of the state, its competencies, and the conditions and limits of its recognition and empowerment'. The fusion of the state to sovereignty is, therefore, conditioned by changing historical and cultural representations and practices which serve to produce a particular form of political subjectivity. This is an idea explored by Derrida in one of his last books, *Rogues* (2005). He there explores the way that state sovereignty presupposes a particular form of self-hood that is the function of a distinctively modern kind of self-positing or self-positioning (Derrida 2005: 11–12). Derrida's recent ruminations on the self-referentiality of subjectivity include analysis of how the state's subjectivity or autonomy is inseparable from its auto-immune or suicidal tendencies (Derrida 2003: 94–109; 2005: 45). That is, states carry the potential to threaten the very things that can help sustain or secure their subjectivity.

A primary function of the exemplary model is to negate alternative conceptions of subjectivity or to devalue them as underdeveloped, incomplete or deviant. Anomalies are contrasted with the 'proper', 'normal', or 'exemplary' model. For instance, 'failed states', 'rogue states' and 'terrorist states' represent empirical cases of 'pathological' states which deviate from the norm by failing to display the recognizable or preferred signs of sovereign statehood (Constantinou 2004: 17; Bleiker 2005). In this failure, they help to reinforce hegemonic modes of subjectivity, and to reconfirm not just the sovereignty/anarchy opposition, but the presumed superiority of the North (Devetak 2008).

In order for the model of sovereign subjectivity to have any power at all, though, it must be replicable; it must be seen as a universally effective mode of subjectivity which can be invoked and instituted at any site. The pressures applied on states to conform to normalized modes of subjectivity are complex and various, and emanate both internally and externally. Some pressures are quite explicit, such as military intervention, others less so, such as conditions attached to foreign aid, diplomatic recognition and general processes of socialization. The point is that modes of subjectivity achieve dominance in space and time through the projection and imposition of power.

How has the state been made to appear as if it had an essence? The short answer to this question is that the state is made to appear as if it had an essence by performative enactment of various domestic and foreign policies, or what might more simply be called 'statecraft', with the emphasis on 'craft'. Traditionally, 'statecraft' refers to the various policies and practices undertaken by states to pursue their objectives in the international arena. The assumption underlying this definition is that the state is already a fully formed, or bounded, entity before it negotiates its way in this arena. The revised notion of statecraft advanced by post-structuralism stresses the ongoing political practices which found and maintain the state, having the effect of keeping the state in perpetual motion.

As Richard Ashley (1987: 410) stressed in his path-breaking article, subjects have no existence prior to political practice. Sovereign states emerge on the plane of historical and political practices. This suggests it is better to understand the state as performatively constituted, having no identity apart from the ceaseless enactment of the ensemble of foreign and domestic policies, security and defence strategies, protocols of treaty making and representational practices at the United Nations, among other things. The state's 'being' is thus an effect of performativity. By 'performativity' we must understand the continued iteration of a norm or set of norms, not simply a singular act, which produces the very thing it names. As Weber (1998: 90) explains, 'the identity of the state is performatively constituted by the very expressions that are said to be its result'.

It is in this sense that David Campbell (1998a: ix–x), in his account of the war in Bosnia, focuses on what he calls 'metaBosnia', by which he means 'the array of practices through which Bosnia . . . comes to be'. To help come to terms with the ceaseless production of Bosnia as a state or subject Campbell recommends that we recognize that we are never dealing with a given, *a priori* state of Bosnia, but with metaBosnia-that is, the performative constitution of 'Bosnia' through a range of enframing and differentiating practices. 'Bosnia', like any other state, is always under a process of construction.

To summarize then, the sovereign state, as Weber (1998: 78) says, is the 'ontological effect of practices which are performatively enacted'. As she explains, 'sovereign nation-states are not pre-given subjects but subjects in process' (1998), where the phrase 'subjects in process' should also be understood to mean 'subjects on trial' (as the French *'en procès'* implies). This leads to an interpretation of the state (as subject) as always in the process of being constituted, but never quite achieving that final moment of completion (Edkins and Pin-Fat 1999: 1). The state thus should not be understood as if it were a prior presence, but instead should be seen as the simulated presence produced by the processes of statecraft. It is never fully complete but is in a constant process of 'becoming-state'. Though 'never fully realized, [the state] is in a continual process of concretization' (Doty 1999: 593). The upshot is that, for post-structuralism, there is statecraft, but there is no completed state (Devetak 1995a).

Lest it be thought that post-structuralist theories of international relations mark a return to realist state-centrism, some clarification will be needed to explain its concern with the sovereign state. Post-structuralism does not seek to explain world politics by focusing on the state alone, nor does it take the state as given. Instead, as Ashley's double reading of the *anarchy problématique* testifies, it seeks to explain the conditions which make possible such an explanation and the costs consequent on such an approach. What is lost by taking a state-centric perspective? And most importantly, to what aspects of world politics does state-centrism remain blind?

Beyond the paradigm of sovereignty: rethinking the political

One of the central implications of post-structuralism is that the paradigm of sovereignty has impoverished our political imagination and restricted our comprehension of the dynamics of world politics. In this section, we review post-structural attempts to develop a new conceptual language to represent world politics beyond the terms of state-centrism in order to rethink the concept of the political.

Campbell (1996: 19) asks the question: 'can we represent world politics in a manner less indebted to the sovereignty problematic?' The challenge is to create a conceptual language that can better convey the novel processes and actors in modern (or post-modern) world politics. Campbell (1996: 20) recommends 'thinking in terms of a *political prosaics* that understands the *transversal* nature' of world politics. To conceptualize world politics in terms of 'political prosaics' is to draw attention to the multitude of flows and interactions produced by globalization that cut across nation-state boundaries. It is to focus on the many political, economic and cultural activities that produce a 'deterritorialization' of modern political life; activities that destabilize the paradigm of sovereignty.

The argument here draws heavily upon the philosophical work of Gilles Deleuze and Felix Guattari (1977, 1987). They have developed a novel conceptual language which has been deployed by post-structural theorists of international relations to make sense of the operation and impact of various non-state actors, flows and movements on the political institution of state sovereignty. The central terms here are reterritorialization and deterritorialization (see Patton 2000; Reid 2003). The former is associated with the totalizing logic of the paradigm of sovereignty, or 'State-form' as Deleuze and Guattari say, whose function is defined by processes of capture and boundary-marking. The latter, deterritorialization, is associated with the highly mobile logic of nomadism whose function is defined by its ability to transgress boundaries and avoid capture by the State-form. The one finds expression in the desire for identity, order and unity, the other in the desire for difference, flows and lines of flight.

The 'political prosaics' advocated by Campbell and others utilize this Deleuzian language to shed light on the new political dynamics and demands created by refugees, immigrants, and new social movements as they encounter and outflank the State-form. These 'transversal' groups and movements not only transgress national boundaries, they call into question the territorial organization of modern political life. As Roland Bleiker (2000: 2) notes, they 'question the spatial logic through which these boundaries have come to constitute and frame the conduct of international relations'. In his study of popular dissent in international relations, Bleiker argues that globalization is subjecting social life to changing political dynamics. In an age of mass media and telecommunications, images of local acts of resistance can be flashed across the world in an instant, turning them into events of global significance. Globalization, Bleiker suggests, has transformed the nature of dissent, making possible global and transversal practices of popular dissent (2000: 31). No longer taking place in a purely local context, acts of resistance 'have taken on increasingly transversal dimensions. They ooze into often unrecognized, but nevertheless significant grey zones between domestic and international spheres', blurring the boundaries between inside and outside, local and global (2000: 185). By outflanking sovereign controls and crossing state boundaries, the actions of transversal dissident groups can be read as 'hidden transcripts' that occur 'off-stage', as it were, behind and alongside the 'public transcript' of the sovereign state. The 'hidden transcripts' of transversal movements are therefore

deterritorializing in their function, escaping the spatial codes and practices of the dominant actors and making possible a critique of the sovereign state's modes of reterritorialization and exclusion (2000: Chapter
7).

This is also the case with refugees and migrants. They hold a different
relationship to space than citizens. Being nomadic rather than sedentary,
they are defined by movement across and between political spaces. They
problematize and defy the 'territorial imperative' of the sovereign state
(Soguk and Whitehall 1999: 682). Indeed, their wandering movement
dislocates the ontopological norm which seeks to fix people's identities
within the spatial boundaries of the nation-state (1999: 697). As a consequence they disrupt our state-centric conceptualizations, problematizing
received understandings of the character and location of the political.

Similar arguments are advanced by Peter Nyers and Mick Dillon
regarding the figure of the refugee. As Nyers (1999) argues, the figure of
the refugee, as one who cannot claim to be a member of a 'proper' political community, acts as a 'limit-concept', occupying the ambiguous zone
between citizen and human. Dillon (1999) argues that the refugee/
stranger remains outside conventional modes of political subjectivity
which are tied to the sovereign state. The very existence of the
refugee/stranger calls into question the settled, sovereign life of the political community by disclosing the estrangement that is shared by both citizens and refugees. As Soguk and Whitehall (1999: 675) point out,
refugees and migrants, by moving across state boundaries and avoiding
capture, have the effect of rupturing traditional constitutive narratives of
international relations.

Sovereignty and the ethics of exclusion

Post-structuralism's ethical critique of state sovereignty needs to be
understood in relation to the deconstructive critique of totalization and
the deterritorializing effect of transversal struggles. Deconstruction has
already been explained as a strategy of interpretation and criticism that
targets theoretical concepts and social institutions which attempt totalization or total stability. It is important to note that the post-structural
critique of state sovereignty focuses on *sovereignty*.

The sovereign state may well be the dominant mode of subjectivity in
international relations today, but it is questionable whether its claim to
be the primary and exclusive political subject is justified. The most thor-
oughgoing account of state sovereignty's ethico-political costs is offered
by Rob Walker in *Inside/Outside* (1993). Walker sets out there the
context in which state sovereignty has been mobilized as an analytical
category with which to understand international relations, and as the

primary expression of moral and political community. Walker's critique suggests that state sovereignty is best understood as a constitutive political practice which emerged historically to resolve three ontological contradictions. The relationship between time and space was resolved by containing time within domesticated territorial space. The relationship between universal and particular was resolved through the system of sovereign states which gave expression to the plurality and particularity of states on the one hand, and the universality of one system on the other. This resolution also allowed for the pursuit of universal values to be pursued within particular states. Finally, the relationship between self and other is also resolved in terms of 'insiders' and 'outsiders', friends and enemies (Walker 1995a: 320–1, 1995b: 28). In deconstructive fashion, Walker's (1993: 23) concern is to 'destabilise [these] seemingly opposed categories by showing how they are at once mutually constitutive and yet always in the process of dissolving into each other'. The overall effect of Walker's inquiry into state sovereignty, consistent with the 'political prosaics' outlined above, is to question whether it is any longer a useful descriptive category and an effective response to the problems that confront humanity in modern political life.

The analysis offered by Walker suggests that it is becoming increasingly difficult to organize modern political life in terms of sovereign states and sovereign boundaries. He argues that there are 'spatiotemporal processes that are radically at odds with the resolution expressed by the principle of state sovereignty' (1993: 155). For both material and normative reasons, Walker refuses to accept state sovereignty as the only, or best, possible means of organizing modern political life. Modern political life need not be caught between mutually exclusive and exhaustive oppositions such as inside and outside. Identity need not be exclusionary, difference need not be interpreted as antithetical to identity (1993: 123), and the trade-off between men and citizens built into the modern state need not always privilege claims of citizens above claims of humanity (Walker 2000: 231–2).

To rethink questions of political identity and community without succumbing to binary oppositions is to contemplate a political life beyond the paradigm of sovereign states. It is to take seriously the possibility that new forms of political identity and community can emerge which are not predicated on absolute exclusion and spatial distinctions between here and there, self and other (Walker 1995a: 307).

Connolly delivers a post-structuralist critique which brings the question of democracy to bear directly on sovereignty. His argument is that the notion of state sovereignty is incompatible with democracy, especially in a globalized late modernity. The point of his critique is to challenge the sovereign state's 'monopoly over the allegiances, identifications and energies of its members' (Connolly 1991: 479). The multiple modes of belonging and interdependence, and the multiplication of global risks that exist in late modernity, complicate the neat simplicity of binary divisions between inside and outside. His point is that obligations and duties constantly overrun the boundaries of sovereign states. Sovereignty, Connolly says, 'poses too stringent a limitation to identifications and loyalties extending beyond it', and so it is necessary to promote an ethos of democracy which exceeds territorialization by cutting across the state at all levels (1991: 480). He calls this a 'disaggregation of democracy', or what might better be called a 'deterritorialization of democracy'. 'What is needed politically', he says, 'is a series of cross-national, nonstatist movements organized across state lines, mobilized around specific issues of global significance, pressing states from inside and outside simultaneously to reconfigure established convictions, priorities, and policies' (Connolly 1995: 23).

A similar argument is advanced by Campbell. According to Campbell (1998a: 208), the norm of ontopology produces a 'moral cartography' that territorializes democracy and responsibility, confining it to the limits of the sovereign state. But Campbell, like Connolly, is interested in fostering an ethos of democratic pluralization that would promote tolerance and multiculturalism within and across state boundaries. By promoting an active affirmation of alterity it would resist the sovereign state's logics of territorialization and capture.

Post-structuralist ethics

Post-structuralism asks, what might ethics come to mean outside a paradigm of sovereign subjectivity? There are two strands of ethics which develop out of post-structuralism's reflections on international relations. One strand challenges the ontological description on which traditional ethical arguments are grounded. It advances a notion of ethics which is not predicated on a rigid, fixed boundary between inside and outside. The other strand focuses on the relation between ontological grounds and ethical arguments. It questions whether ontology must precede ethics.

The first strand is put forward most fully by Ashley and Walker (1990) and Connolly (1995). Fundamental to their writing is a critique of the faith invested in boundaries. Again, the main target of post-structuralism here is the sovereign state's defence of rigid boundaries. Territorial boundaries, which are thought to mark the limits of political identity or community, are taken by post-structuralism to be historically contingent and highly ambiguous products (Ashley and Walker 1990). As such, they hold no transcendental status. As a challenge to the ethical delimitations imposed by state sovereignty, post-structuralist ethics, or the 'diplomatic ethos', as Ashley and Walker call it, is not confined by any spatial or territorial limits. It seeks to 'enable the rigorous practice of this ethics in the widest possible compass' (1990: 395). No demarcatory boundaries should obstruct the universalization of this ethic which flows across boundaries (both imagined and territorial):

> Where such an ethics is rigorously practised, no voice can effectively claim to stand heroically upon some exclusionary ground, offering this ground as a source of a necessary truth that human beings must violently project in the name of a citizenry, people, nation, class, gender, race, golden age, or historical cause of any sort. Where this ethics is rigorously practised, no totalitarian order could ever be. (Ashley and Walker 1990: 395)

In breaking with the ethics of sovereign exclusion, post-structuralism offers an understanding of ethics which is detached from territorial limitations. The diplomatic ethos is a 'deterritorialized' ethics which unfolds by transgressing sovereign limits. This transgressive ethics complements the deterritorialized notion of democracy advanced by Connolly. Underlying both ideas is a critique of state sovereignty as a basis for conducting, organizing and limiting political life.

The other ethical strand is advanced by Campbell. He follows Derrida and Levinas by questioning traditional approaches which deduce ethics from ontology, specifically an ontology or metaphysics of presence (Campbell 1998a: 171–92; and see Levinas 1969: Section 1A). It does not begin with an empirical account of the world as a necessary prelude to ethical consideration. Rather, it gives primacy to ethics as, in a sense, 'first philosophy'. The key thinker in this ethical approach is Emmanuel Levinas who has been more influenced by Jewish theology than Greek philosophy. Indeed, the differences between these two styles of thought are constantly worked through in Levinas' thought as a difference between a philosophy of alterity and a philosophy of identity or totality.

Levinas overturns the hierarchy between ontology and ethics, giving primacy to ethics as the starting point. Ethics seems to function as a condition which makes possible the world of beings. Levinas offers a redescription of ontology such that it is inextricably tied up with, and indebted to, ethics, and is free of totalizing impulses. His thought is antagonistic to all forms of ontological and political imperialism or totalitarianism (Levinas 1969: 44; Campbell 1998a: 192). In Levinas' schema, subjectivity is constituted through, and as, an ethical relation. The effect of the Levinasian approach is to recast notions of subjectivity and responsibility in light of an ethics of otherness or alterity (see Campbell 1994: 463, 1998a: 176). This gives rise to a notion of ethics which diverges from the Kantian principle of generalizability and symmetry that we find in critical theory. Rather than begin with the Self and then generalize the imperative universally to a community of equals, Levinas begins with the Other. The Other places certain demands on the Self, hence there is an asymmetrical relationship between Self and Other. The end result is to advance a 'different figuration of politics, one in which its purpose is the struggle *for* – or *on behalf of* – alterity, and not a struggle to efface, erase, or eradicate alterity' (Campbell 1994: 477, 1998a: 191). But, as Michael Shapiro (1998b: 698–9) has shown, this ethos may not be so different from a Kantian ethic of hospitality that encourages universal tolerance of difference as a means of diminishing global violence.

Campbell (2005: 224) believes that post-structuralism adopts an 'ethos of political criticism' that seeks to disturb settled practices and expose the contingently constructed character of political structures and practices. In this respect, post-structuralism is not so far removed from the Kantian-inspired tradition of critical theory. As Richard Beardsworth (2005: 224) has rightly noted, post-structuralism, as a 'critical philosophy', should not underestimate 'how much good work reason can do, how much reason can shape contingencies of history, and how much reason can release difference'. This is in part what Derrida (2005) explores in his book *Rogues*, which is subtitled *Two Essays on Reason*.

The consequence of taking post-structuralism's critique of totality and sovereignty seriously is that central political concepts such as community, identity, ethics and democracy are rethought to avoid being persistently reterritorialized by the sovereign state. Indeed, de-linking these concepts from territory and sovereignty underlies the practical task of a post-structuralist politics or ethics. As Anthony Burke (2004: 353) explains in a forceful critique of Just War theory after September 11, post-structuralism's conception of an 'ethical peace' would refuse 'to channel its ethical obligations solely through the state, or rely on it to protect us violently'. It should be noted, however, that post-structuralism, as a critique of totalization, opposes concepts of identity and community only to the extent that they are tied dogmatically to notions of territoriality, boundedness and exclusion. The thrust of post-structuralism has always been to challenge both epistemological and political claims to totality and sovereignty and thereby open up questions about the location and character of the political.

Conclusion

Post-structuralism makes several contributions to the study of international relations. First, through its genealogical method it seeks to expose the intimate connection between claims to knowledge and claims to political power and authority. Second, through aesthetic insight and the textual strategy of deconstruction it seeks to problematize all claims to epistemological and political totalization by revealing the inherently political choices behind competing interpretations. This holds especially significant implications for how we conceptualize the sovereign state; not least because dominant understandings are predicated on practices of capture and exclusion. A more comprehensive account of contemporary world politics must therefore include an analysis of those transversal actors and movements that operate outside and across state boundaries. Third, post-structuralism seeks to rethink the concept of the political without invoking assumptions of sovereignty and reterritorialization. By challenging the idea that the character and location of the political must be determined by the sovereign state, post-structuralism seeks to broaden the political imagination and the range of political possibilities for transforming international relations. These contributions seem more important than ever after the events of September 11 and the War on Terror.

9 | Constructivism

CHRISTIAN REUS-SMIT

During the 1980s two debates structured International Relations scholarship, particularly within the American mainstream. The first was between neo-realists and neo-liberals, both of which sought to apply the logic of rationalist economic theory to international relations, but reached radically different conclusions about the potential for international cooperation. The second was between rationalists and critical theorists, the latter challenging the epistemological, methodological, ontological and normative assumptions of neo-realism and neo-liberalism, and the former accusing critical theorists of having little of any substance to say about 'real-world' international relations. Since the end of the Cold War, these axes of debate have been displaced by two new debates: between rationalists and constructivists, and between constructivists and critical theorists. The catalyst for this shift was the rise of a new constructivist approach to international theory, an approach that challenged the rationalism and positivism of neo-realism and neo-liberalism while simultaneously pushing critical theorists away from metatheoretical critique to the empirical analysis of world politics.

This chapter explains the nature and rise of constructivism in international theory, situating it in relation to both rationalist and critical theories. Constructivism is characterized by an emphasis on the importance of normative as well as material structures, on the role of identity in shaping political action and on the mutually constitutive relationship between agents and structures. When using the terms rationalism or rationalist theory, I refer not to the 'Grotian' or 'English' School of international theory, discussed by Andrew Linklater in Chapter 4 in this volume, but to theories that are explicitly informed by the assumptions of rational choice theory, principally neo-realism and neo-liberalism. I use the term 'critical theory' broadly to include all post-positivist theory of the Third Debate and after, encompassing both the narrowly defined critical theory of the Frankfurt School and post-modern international theory, discussed by Richard Devetak in Chapters 7 and 8, respectively. After revisiting the rationalist premises of neo-realism and neo-liberalism, and reviewing the broad-based critique of those premises mounted by critical theorists during the 1980s, I examine the origins of constructivism and its principal theoretical premises. I then distinguish between three different forms of constructivist scholarship in International Relations: systemic, unit-level and holistic. This is followed by some reflections on the emergent discontents that characterize constructivism as a theoretical approach, by a discussion of the contribution of constructivism to international relations theory, and by a brief consideration of recent developments in constructivism.

Rationalist theory

After World War II, realism became the dominant theory of international relations. Yet this dominance did not go unchallenged, with new theoretical perspectives emerging, forcing revisions in realist theory. In the 1970s, the classical realism of Claude, Carr, Morgenthau, Niebuhr and others was challenged by liberals, such as Robert Keohane and Joseph Nye, who emphasized interdependence between states, transnational relations and non-state actors, particularly multinational corporations (MNCs). International relations was not to be conceived as a system of 'colliding billiard balls', but as a cobweb of political, economic and social relations binding sub-national, national, transnational, international and supranational actors (Keohane and Nye 1972). This view was subsequently modified to pay greater attention to the role and importance of sovereign states, with Keohane and Nye reconceiving state power in the light of 'complex interdependence' (Keohane and Nye 1977). States were acknowledged to be the principal actors in world politics, but pervasive interdependence was thought to alter the nature and effectiveness of state power, with the balance of military power, so long emphasized by realists, no longer determining political outcomes, as sensitivity and vulnerability to interdependence produced new relations of power between states.

This challenge to realism did not go unanswered. As Jack Donnelly explains, in Chapter 2 of this volume, in 1979 Kenneth Waltz published the *Theory of International Politics* (1979), in which he advanced a radically revised realist theory, subsequently labelled 'neo-realism' or 'structural realism'. Waltz drew on two sources of intellectual inspiration: the philosopher of science Imre Lakatos' model of theory construction, and macroeconomic theory. The first led him to devise a theory with minimal assumptions, a parsimonious set of heuristically powerful propositions that could generate empirically verifiable hypotheses about international relations; the second encouraged him to emphasize the structural determinants of state behaviour. The resulting neo-realist theory built on two assumptions: that the international system is anarchical, in the sense that it lacks a central authority to impose order; and that in such a system states are primarily interested in their own survival. Waltz went on to argue that to ensure their survival states must maximize their power, particularly their military power. Because such power is zero-sum – with an increase in the military power of one state necessarily producing a decrease in the relative power of another – Waltz argued that states are 'defensive positionalists'. They are conscious of their position within the power hierarchy of states, and at a minimum seek to maintain that position, at a maximum to increase it to the point of domination. For this reason, Waltz claimed that the struggle for power is an enduring characteristic of international relations and conflict is endemic. In such a world, he argued, cooperation between states is at best precarious, at worst non-existent.

Theory of International Politics reinvigorated realism, giving realists a new identity – as neo- or structural realists – and a new confidence to the point of arrogance. Not all were convinced, though, and criticisms mounted on several fronts. The most moderate of these came from a new school of neo-liberal institutionalists, led by the repositioned Robert Keohane. Moving away from his previous concern with transnational relations and interdependence, Keohane took up the task of explaining cooperation under anarchy. Realists had long argued that if international cooperation was possible at all, it was only under conditions of hegemony, when a dominant state was able to use its power to create and enforce the institutional rules necessary to sustain cooperation between states. By the end of the 1970s, however, America's relative power was clearly on the wane, yet the framework of institutions it had sponsored after World War II to facilitate international economic cooperation was not collapsing. How could this be explained? In his 1984 book, *After Hegemony*, Keohane proposed a neo-liberal theory of international cooperation, a theory that embraced three elements of neo-realism: the importance of international anarchy in shaping state behaviour, the state as the most important actor in world politics and the assumption of states as essentially self-interested. He also endorsed the Lakatosian model of theory construction that informed neo-realism (Keohane 1984, 1989a).

Despite this common ground with neo-realism, neo-liberalism draws very different conclusions about the potential for sustained international cooperation. As noted above, neo-liberals accept that states have to pursue their interests under conditions of anarchy. In Axelrod and Keohane's words, anarchy 'remains a constant' (1993: 86). Nevertheless, anarchy alone does not determine the extent or nature of international cooperation. Neo-realists are closest to the mark, neo-liberals argue, when there is low interdependence between states. When economic and political interactions between states are minimal, there are few common interests to spur international cooperation. When interdependence is high, however, as since World War II, states come to share a wide range of interests, from the management of international trade to global environmental protection. The existence of mutual interests is a prerequisite for international cooperation, but neo-liberals insist that the existence of such interests does not itself explain the extent and nature of cooperative relations between states – international cooperation remains difficult to achieve. Even when states have interests in common, the lack of a central world authority often deters them from incurring the reciprocal obligations that cooperation demands. Without a central authority, states fear that others will cheat on agreements; they can see cooperation as too costly, given the effort they would have to expend; and often they lack sufficient information to know that they even have common interests with other states. This not only explains why states fail to cooperate even when they have common interests, it explains how they cooperate when they do. According to neo-liberals, states construct international institutions, or regimes, to overcome these obstacles to cooperation. Defined as 'sets of implicit or explicit principles, norms, rules and decision-making procedures around which actors' expectations converge in a given area of international relations', international regimes are said to raise the cost of cheating, lower transaction costs and increase information, thus facilitating cooperation under anarchy (Keohane 1984: 57, 85–109).

The debate between neo-realists and neo-liberals is often characterized as a debate between those who think that states are preoccupied with *relative* gains versus those who think that states are more interested in *absolute* gains. Because anarchy makes states fear for their survival, and because power is the ultimate guarantor of survival, neo-realists believe that states constantly measure their power against that of other states. They constantly monitor whether their position in the international power hierarchy is stable, declining, or on the rise, fearing decline above all else. This is why neo-realists are sceptical about international cooperation: if states are worried about relative gains, they will forgo cooperation if they fear that their gains will be less than those that accrue to others. Even if a trading agreement promises to net State A $100 million in profit, if that same agreement will net State B $200 million, State A may refuse to cooperate. In other words, the promise of absolute gains may not be sufficient to encourage states to cooperate, as they are primarily interested in relative gains. Neo-liberals deny that relative gains calculations pose such an obstacle to international cooperation. The world imagined by neo-realists is too simplistic, they argue. States that are confident in their survival, which amounts to a significant proportion of states, are not as preoccupied with relative gains as neo-realists think; states tend to evaluate the intentions of other states as well as their relative capabilities; and when states have multiple relationships with multiple states the constant calculation of relative gains is simply impractical. Neo-liberals thus characterize states not as defensive positionalists, as neo-realists do, but as utility-maximizers, as actors that will entertain cooperation so long as it promises absolute gains in their interests.

In spite of these differences, neo-realism and neo-liberalism are both rationalist theories; they are both constructed upon the choice-theoretic assumptions of microeconomic theory. Three such assumptions stand out. First, political actors – be they individuals or states – are assumed to be atomistic, self-interested and rational. Actors are treated as *pre-social*, in the sense that their identities and interests are autogenous. In the language of classical liberalism, individuals are the source of their own conceptions of the good. Actors are also *self-interested*, concerned primarily with the pursuit of their own interests. And they are *rational*, capable of establishing the most effective and efficient way to realize their interests within the environmental constraints they encounter. Second, and following from the above, actors' interests are assumed to be exogenous to social interaction. Individuals and states are thought to enter social relations with their interests already formed. Social interaction is not considered an important determinant of interests. Third, and following yet again from the above, society is understood as a strategic realm, a realm in which individuals or states come together to pursue their predefined interests. Actors are not, therefore, inherently social; they are not products of their social environment, merely atomistic rational beings that form social relations to maximize their interests.

These assumptions are most starkly expressed in neo-realism. As we have seen, states are defined as 'defensive positionalists', jealous guardians of their positions in the international power hierarchy. The formation of state interests is of no interest to neo-realists. Beyond maintaining that international anarchy gives states a survival motive, and that over time the incentives and constraints of the international system socialize states into certain forms of behaviour, they have no theory of interest formation, nor do they think they should have (Waltz 1979: 91–2, 127–8). Furthermore, international relations are considered so thoroughly strategic that neo-realists deny the existence of a society of states altogether, speaking of an 'international system' not an international society. How does neo-liberalism compare? The assumption of self-interest is expressed in the neo-liberal idea of states as rational egoists: actors who are concerned primarily with their own narrowly defined interests, and who pursue those interests in the most efficacious manner possible. Like neo-realists, neo-liberals treat state interests as exogenous to inter-state interaction, and see no need for a theory of interest formation. In fact, explaining the origins of state interests is explicitly excluded from the province of neo-liberal theory. Finally, neo-liberals move beyond the stark systemic imagery of neo-realism to acknowledge the existence of an international society, but their conception of that society remains strategic. States certainly come together in the cooperative construction and maintenance of functional institutions, but their identities and interests are not shaped or constituted in any way by their social interactions.

The challenge of critical theory

While neo-realists and neo-liberals engaged in a rationalist family feud, critical theorists challenged the very foundations of the rationalist project. Ontologically, they criticized the image of social actors as atomistic egoists, whose interests are formed prior to social interaction, and who enter social relations solely for strategic purposes. They argued, in contrast, that actors are inherently *social*, that their identities and interests are socially constructed, the products of inter-subjective social structures. Epistemologically and methodologically, they questioned the neo-positivism of Lakatosian forms of social science, calling for interpretive modes of understanding, attuned to the unquantifiable nature of many social phenomena and the inherent subjectivity of all observation. And normatively, they condemned the notion of value-neutral theorizing, arguing that all knowledge is wedded to interests, and that theories should be explicitly committed to exposing and dismantling structures of domination and oppression (Hoffman 1987; George and Campbell 1990).

Beneath the umbrella of this broad critique, modern and post-modern critical theorists stood united against the dominant rationalist theories. Just as the rationalists were internally divided, though, so too were the critics. The post-modernists, drawing on the French social theorists, particularly Jacques Derrida and Michel Foucault, adopted a stance of 'radical interpretivism'. They opposed all attempts to assess empirical and ethical claims by any single criterion of validity, claiming that such moves always marginalize alternative viewpoints and moral positions, creating hierarchies of power and domination. The modernists, inspired by the writings of Frankfurt School theorists such as Jürgen Habermas, assumed a position of 'critical interpretivism'. They recognized the contingent nature of all knowledge – the inherent subjectivity of all claims and the connection between knowledge and power – but they insisted that some criteria were needed to distinguish plausible from implausible knowledge claims, and that without minimal, consensually grounded ethical principles, emancipatory political action would be impossible. Mark Hoffman has characterized this difference between modernists and post-modernists in terms of a distinction between 'anti-foundationalism' and 'minimal foundationalism' (1991: 169–85).

Despite these important differences, the first wave of critical theory had a distinctive meta-theoretical or quasi-philosophical character. Critical international theorists roamed broadly over epistemological, normative, ontological and methodological concerns, and their energies were devoted primarily to demolishing the philosophical foundations of the rationalist project. Noteworthy empirical studies of world politics were certainly published by critical theorists, but the general tenor of critical writings was more abstractly theoretical, and their principal impact lay in the critique of prevailing assumptions about legitimate knowledge, about the nature of the social world, and about the purpose of theory (Cox 1987; Der Derian 1987). This general orientation was encouraged by a widely shared assumption among critical theorists about the relationship between theory and practice. This assumption was evident in the common refrain that realism constituted a 'hegemonic discourse', by which they meant two things. First, that realist assumptions, particularly dressed up in the garb of rationalism and neo-positivism, as was neo-realism, defined what counts as legitimate knowledge in the field of International Relations. And, second, that the influence of these assumptions extended far beyond the academy to structure policy making, particularly in the United States. Rationalist theories were thus doubly insidious. Not only did they dominate the discourse of International Relations, to the exclusion of alternative perspectives and forms of knowledge, they informed Washington's Cold War politics, with all the excesses of power these engendered. From this standpoint, theory was seen as having a symbiotic relationship with practice, and critiquing the discourse of International Relations was considered the essence of substantive analysis (Price and Reus-Smit 1998).

Constructivism

The end of the Cold War produced a major reconfiguration of debates within the dominant American discourse of international relations theory, prompted by the rise of a new 'constructivist' school of thought. While constructivism owes much to intellectual developments in sociology – particularly sociological institutionalism (see Finnemore 1996) – Richard Price and Chris Reus-Smit have argued that constructivism should be seen primarily as an outgrowth of critical international theory, as many of its pioneers explicitly sought to employ the insights of that theory to illuminate diverse aspects of world politics. Constructivism differs from first-wave critical theory, however, in its emphasis on *empirical analysis*. Some constructivists have continued to work at the meta-theoretical level (Onuf 1989; Wendt 1999), but most have sought conceptual and theoretical illumination through the systematic analysis of empirical puzzles in world politics. The balance of critical scholarship has thus shifted away from the previous mode of abstract philosophical argument toward the study of human discourse and practice beyond the narrow confines of international relations theory. Where first-wave critical theorists had rejected the rationalist depiction of humans as atomistic egoists and society as a strategic domain – proffering an alternative image of humans as socially embedded, communicatively constituted and culturally empowered – constructivists have used this alternative ontology to explain and interpret aspects of world politics that were anomalous to neo-realism and neo-liberalism. And where earlier theorists had condemned the neo-positivist methodology of those perspectives, calling for more interpretive, discursive and historical modes of analysis, constructivists have employed these latter techniques to further their empirical explorations.

The rise of constructivism was prompted by four factors. First, motivated by an attempt to reassert the pre-eminence of their own conceptions of theory and world politics, leading rationalists challenged critical theorists to move beyond theoretical critique to the substantive analysis of international relations. While prominent critical theorists condemned the motives behind this challenge, constructivists saw it as an opportunity to demonstrate the heuristic power of non-rationalist perspectives (Walker 1989). Second, the end of the Cold War undermined the explanatory pretensions of neo-realists and neo-liberals, neither of which had predicted, nor could adequately comprehend, the systemic transformations reshaping the global order. It also undermined the critical theorists' assumption that theory drove practice in any narrow or direct fashion, as global politics increasingly demonstrated dynamics that contradicted realist expectations and prescriptions. The end of the Cold War thus opened a space for alternative explanatory perspectives and prompted critically inclined scholars to move away from a narrowly defined meta-theoretical critique. Third, by the beginning of the 1990s a new generation of young scholars had emerged who embraced many of the propositions of critical international theory, but who saw potential for innovation in conceptual elaboration and empirically informed theoretical development (Klotz 1995: 20; Kier 1997; Price 1997; Hall 1999; Lynch 1999; Reus-Smit 1999; Tannenwald 1999; Rae 2002). Not only had the end of the Cold War thrown up new and interesting questions about world politics (such as the dynamics of international change, the nature of basic institutional practices, the role of non-state agency and the problem of human rights), the rationalist failure to explain recent systemic transformations encouraged this new generation of scholars to revisit old questions and issues so long viewed through neo-realist and neo-liberal lenses (including the control of WMD, the role and nature of strategic culture and the implications of anarchy). Finally, the advance of the new constructivist perspective was aided by the enthusiasm that mainstream scholars, frustrated by the analytical failings of the dominant rationalist theories, showed in embracing the new perspective, moving it from the margins to the mainstream of theoretical debate (Katzenstein 1996; Ruggie 1993).

Echoing the divisions within critical international theory, constructivists are divided between modernists and post-modernists. They have all, however, sought to articulate and explore three core ontological propositions about social life, propositions which they claim illuminate more about world politics than rival rationalist assumptions. First, to the extent that structures can be said to shape the behaviour of social and political actors, be they individuals or states, constructivists hold that *normative* or *ideational* structures are just as important as material structures. Where neo-realists emphasize the material structure of the balance of military power, and Marxists stress the material structure of the capitalist world economy, constructivists argue that systems of shared ideas, beliefs and values also have structural characteristics, and that they exert a powerful influence on social and political action. There are two reasons why they attach such importance to these structures. Constructivists argue that 'material resources only acquire meaning for human action through the structure of shared knowledge in which they are embedded' (Wendt 1995: 73). For example, Canada and Cuba both exist alongside the United States, yet the simple balance of military power cannot explain the fact that the former is a close American ally, the latter a sworn enemy. Ideas about identity, the logics of ideology and established structures of friendship and enmity lend the material balance of power between Canada and the United States and Cuba and the United States radically different meanings. Constructivists also stress the importance of normative and ideational structures because these are thought to shape the social identities of political actors. Just as the institutionalized norms of the academy shape the identity of a professor, the norms of the international system condition the social identity of the sovereign state. For instance, in the age of Absolutism (1555–1848) the norms of European international society held that Christian monarchies were the only legitimate form of sovereign state, and these norms, backed by the coercive practices of the community of states, conspired to undermine Muslim, liberal or nationalist polities.

Second, constructivists argue that understanding how non-material structures condition actors' identities is important because identities inform interests and, in turn, actions. As we saw above, rationalists believe that actors' interests are exogenously determined, meaning that actors, be they individuals or states, encounter one another with a pre-existing set of preferences. Neo-realists and neo-liberals are not interested in where such preferences come from, only in how actors pursue them strategically. Society – both domestic and international – is thus considered a *strategic domain*, a place in which previously constituted actors pursue their goals, a place that does not alter the nature or interests of those actors in any deep sense. Constructivists, in contrast, argue that understanding how actors develop their interests is crucial to explaining a wide range of international political phenomenon that rationalists ignore or misunderstand. To explain interest formation, constructivists focus on the social identities of individuals or states. In Alexander Wendt's words, 'Identities are the basis of interests' (Wendt 1992: 398). To return to the previous examples, being an 'academic' gives a person certain interests, such as research and publication, and being a Christian monarch in the age of Absolutism brought with it a range of interests, such as controlling religion within your territory pursuing rights of succession beyond that territory and crushing nationalist movements. Likewise, being a liberal democracy today encourages an intolerance of authoritarian regimes and a preference for free-market capitalism. Constructivists are not opposed to the idea that actors might be 'self-interested', but they argue that this tells us nothing unless we understand how actors define their 'selves' and how this informs their 'interests'.

Third, constructivists contend that agents and structures are *mutually constituted*. Normative and ideational structures may well condition the identities and interests of actors, but those structures would not exist if it were not for the knowledgeable practices of those actors. Wendt's emphasis on the 'supervening' power of structures, and the predilection of many constructivists to study how norms shape behaviour, suggest that constructivists are structuralists, just like their neo-realist and Marxist counterparts. On closer reflection, however, one sees that constructivists are better classed as structurationists, as emphasizing the impact of non-material structures on identities and interests but, just as importantly, the role of practices in maintaining and transforming those structures. Institutionalized norms and ideas 'define the meaning and identity of the individual actor and the patterns of appropriate economic, political, and cultural activity engaged in by those individuals' (Boli,

Meyer and Thomas 1989: 12), and it 'is through reciprocal interaction that we create and instantiate the relatively enduring social structures in terms of which we define our identities and interests' (Wendt 1992: 406). The norms of the academy give certain individuals an academic identity which brings with it an interest in research and publication, but it is only through the routinized practices of academics that such norms exist and are sustained. Similarly, the international norms that uphold liberal democracy as the dominant model of legitimate statehood, and which license intervention in the name of human rights and the promotion of free trade, exist and persist only because of the continued practices of liberal democratic states (and powerful non-state actors).

Normative and ideational structures are seen as shaping actors' identities and interests through three mechanisms: imagination, communication and constraint. With regard to the first of these, constructivists argue that non-material structures affect what actors see as the realm of possibility: how they think they should act, what the perceived limitations on their actions are and what strategies they can imagine, let alone entertain, to achieve their objectives. Institutionalized norms and ideas thus condition what actors consider necessary and possible, in both practical and ethical terms. A president or prime minister in an established liberal democracy will only imagine and seriously entertain certain strategies to enhance his or her power, and the norms of the liberal democratic polity will condition his or her expectations. Normative and ideational structures also work their influence through communication. When an individual or a state seeks to justify their behaviour, they will usually appeal to established norms of legitimate conduct. A president or prime minister may appeal to the conventions of executive government, and a state may justify its behaviour with reference to the norms of sovereignty – or, in the case of intervention in the affairs of another state, according to international human rights norms. As the latter case suggests, norms may conflict with one another in their prescriptions, which makes moral argument about the relative importance of international normative precepts a particularly salient aspect of world politics (Risse 2000). Finally, even if normative and ideational structures do not affect an actor's behaviour by framing their imagination or by providing a linguistic or moral court of appeal, constructivists argue that they can place significant constraints on that actor's conduct. Realists have long argued that ideas simply function as rationalizations, as ways of masking actions really motivated by the crude desire for power. Constructivists point out, though, that institutionalized norms and ideas work as rationalizations only because they already have moral force in a given social context. Furthermore, appealing to established norms and ideas to justify behaviour is a viable strategy only if the behaviour is in some measure consistent with the proclaimed principles. The very language of justification thus provides constraints on action, though the effectiveness of such constraints will vary with the actor and the context (Reus-Smit 1999: 35–6).

Given the preceding discussion, constructivism contrasts with rationalism in three important respects. First, where rationalists assume that actors are atomistic egoists, constructivists treat them as deeply *social*: not in the sense that they are 'party animals', but in the sense that their identities are constituted by the institutionalized norms, values and ideas of the social environment in which they act. Second, instead of treating actors' interests as exogenously determined, as given prior to social interaction, constructivists treat interests as *endogenous* to such interaction, as a consequence of identity acquisition, as learned through processes of communication, reflection on experience and role enactment. Third, while rationalists view society as a strategic realm, a place where actors rationally pursue their interests, constructivists see it as a *constitutive realm*, the site that generates actors as knowledgeable social and political agents, the realm that makes them who they are. From these ontological commitments, it is clear why constructivists are called 'constructivists', for they emphasize the social determinants of social and political agency and action.

In the 1990s, three different forms of constructivism evolved: systemic, unit-level and holistic constructivism. The first of these follows neo-realists in adopting a 'third-image' perspective, focusing solely on interactions between unitary state actors. Everything that exists or occurs within the domestic political realm is ignored, and an account of world politics is derived simply by theorizing how states relate to one another in the external, international domain. Wendt's influential writings provide the best example of systemic constructivism. In fact, one could reasonably argue that Wendt's writings represent the only true example of this rarefied form of constructivism (Wendt 1992, 1994, 1995, 1999). Like other constructivists, Wendt believes that the identity of the state informs its interests and, in turn, its actions. He draws a distinction, though, between the social and corporate identities of the state: the former referring to the status, role or personality that international society ascribes to a state; the latter referring to the internal human, material, ideological, or cultural factors that make a state what it is. Because of his commitment to systemic theorizing, Wendt brackets corporate sources of state identity, concentrating on how structural contexts, systemic processes, and strategic practices produce and reproduce different sorts of state identity. Though theoretically elegant, this form of constructivism suffers from one major deficiency: it confines the processes that shape international societies within an unnecessarily and unproductively narrow realm. The social identities of states are thought to be constituted by the normative and ideational structures of international society, and those structures are seen as the product of state practices. From this perspective, it is impossible to explain how fundamental changes occur, either in the nature of international society or in the nature of state identity. By bracketing everything domestic, Wendt excludes by theoretical fiat most of the normative and ideational forces that might prompt such change.

Unit-level constructivism is the inverse of systemic constructivism. Instead of focusing on the external, international domain, unit-level constructivists concentrate on the relationship between domestic social and legal norms and the identities and interests of states, the very factors bracketed by Wendt. Here Peter Katzenstein's writings on the national security policies of Germany and Japan (1996, 1999) are emblematic. Setting out to explain why two states, with common experiences of military defeat, foreign occupation, economic development, transition from authoritarianism to democracy and nascent great-power status, have adopted very different internal and external national security policies, Katzenstein stresses the importance of institutionalized regulatory and constitutive national social and legal norms. He concludes that:

> In Germany the strengthening of state power through changes in legal norms betrays a deep-seated fear that terrorism challenges the core of the state. In effect, eradicating terrorism and minimizing violent protest overcome the specter of a 'Hobbesian' state of nature . . . In Japan, on the other hand, the close interaction of social and legal norms reveals a state living symbiotically within its society and not easily shaken to its foundation. Eliminating terrorism and containing violent protest were the tasks of a 'Grotian' community . . . Conversely, Germany's active involvement in the evolution of international legal norms conveys a conception of belonging to an international 'Grotian' community. Japan's lack of concern for the consequences of pushing terrorists abroad and its generally passive international stance is based on a 'Hobbesian' view of the society of states. (Katzenstein 1996: 153–4)

While not entirely disregarding the role of international norms in conditioning the identities and interests of states, Katzenstein draws attention to the internal, domestic determinants of national policies. Unit-level constructivism of this sort has the virtue of enabling the explanation of variations of identity, interest and action across states, something that systemic constructivism obscures. It follows, though, that this form of constructivism has difficulty accounting for similarities between states, for patterns of convergence in state identity and interest.

Where systemic and unit-level constructivists reproduce the traditional dichotomy between the international and the domestic, holistic constructivists seek to bridge the two domains. To accommodate the entire range of factors conditioning the identities and interests of states, they bring the corporate and the social together into a unified analytical perspective that treats the domestic and the international as two faces of a single social and political order. Concerned primarily with the dynamics of global change – particularly the rise and possible demise of the sovereign state – holistic constructivists focus on the mutually constitutive relationship between this order and the state. This general perspective has spawned two distinctive, yet complementary, analyses of international change: one focusing on grand shifts between international systems, the other on recent changes within the modern system. The former is typified by John Ruggie's path-breaking work on the rise of sovereign states out of the wreck of European feudalism, work that emphasizes the importance of changing social epistemes, or frameworks of knowledge (1986, 1993). The latter is exemplified by Friedrich Kratochwil's writings on the end of the Cold War, which stress the role of changing ideas of international order and security (Kratochwil 1993; Koslowski and Kratochwil 1995). Though less parsimonious and elegant than systemic constructivism, holistic scholarship has the merit of being able to explain the development of the normative and ideational structures of the present international system, as well as the social identities they have engendered. The more concerned this form of constructivism becomes with grand tectonic transformations, however, the more structuralist it tends to become, and human agency tends to drop out of the story. Ideas change, norms evolve, and culture transforms, but these seem to move independently of human will, choice, or action.

Constructivism and its discontents

The articulation of a constructivist theoretical framework for the study of international relations has significantly altered the axes of debate within the field. The internecine debate between neo-realists and neo-liberals, which, until the middle of the 1990s was still being hailed as *the* contemporary debate, has been displaced as rationalists have haphazardly joined forces to confront a common constructivist foe. The rise of constructivism has also displaced the debate between rationalists and critical international theorists. The veracity of the epistemological, methodological and normative challenges that critical theorists levelled at rationalism has not diminished, but the rise of constructivism has focused debate on ontological and empirical issues, pushing the metatheoretical debate of the 1980s off centre stage. The core debate now animating the field revolves around the nature of social agency, the relative importance of normative versus material forces, the balance between continuity and transformation in world politics and a range of other empirical-theoretical questions. This does not mean, though, that rationalism and constructivism constitute unified, unproblematic or fully coherent theoretical positions, standing pristine in opposition to one another. We have already seen the significant differences within the rationalist fold, and I now turn to the discontents that characterize contemporary constructivism. Four of these warrant particular attention: the disagreements among constructivists over the nature of theory, the relationship with rationalism, the appropriate methodology and the contribution of constructivism to a critical theory of international relations.

It has long been the ambition of rationalists, especially neo-realists, to formulate a general theory of international relations, the core assumptions of which would be so robust that they could explain its fundamental characteristics, regardless of historical epoch or differences in the internal complexions of states. For most constructivists, such ambitions have little allure. The constitutive forces they emphasize, such as ideas, norms and culture, and the elements of human agency they stress, such as corporate and social identity, are all inherently variable. There is simply no such thing as a universal, transhistorical, disembedded, culturally autonomous idea or identity. Most constructivists thus find the pursuit of a general theory of international relations an absurdity, and confine their ambitions to providing compelling interpretations and explanations of discrete aspects of world politics, going no further than to offer heavily qualified 'contingent generalizations'. In fact, constructivists repeatedly insist that constructivism is not a theory, but rather an analytical framework. The one notable exception to this tendency is Wendt, who has embarked on the ambitious project of formulating a comprehensive social theory of international relations, placing himself in direct competition with Waltz. In pursuit of this goal, however, Wendt makes a number of moves that put him at odds with almost all other constructivists: namely, he focuses solely on the systemic level, he treats the state as a unitary actor and he embraces an epistemological position called 'scientific realism' (Wendt and Shapiro 1997). While these represent the theoretical proclivities of but one scholar, Wendt's prominence in the development of constructivism makes them important sources of division and disagreement within the new school. His *Social Theory of International Politics* (1999) is the most sustained elaboration of constructivist theory yet, and for many in the field it will define the very nature of constructivism. However, the vision of theory it presents has been vigorously contested by other constructivists, thus forming one of the principal axes of tension within constructivism over the coming years.

The second discontent within constructivism concerns the relationship with rationalism. Some constructivists believe that productive engagement is possible between the two approaches, engagement based on a scholarly division of labour. We have seen that constructivists emphasize how institutionalized norms shape the identities and interests of actors, and that rationalists, treating interests as unexplained givens, stress how actors go about pursuing their interests strategically. The first focuses on interest formation, the second on interest satisfaction. Seeking to build bridges instead of fences between the two approaches, some constructivists see in this difference a possible division of labour, with constructivists doing the work of explaining how actors gain their preferences and rationalists exploring how they realize those preferences. Constructivism is thus not a rival theoretical perspective to rationalism at all, but rather a complementary one. 'The result', Audie Klotz argues, 'is a reformulated, complementary research agenda that illuminates the independent role of norms in determining actors' identities and interests. Combined with theories of institutions and interest-based behaviour, this approach offers us a conceptually consistent and more complete understanding of international relations' (1995: 20). As attractive as this exercise in bridge-building appears, not all constructivists are convinced. Reus-Smit has demonstrated that the institutionalized norms that shape actors' identities help define not only their interests but also their strategic rationality (1999). Attempts to confine constructivist scholarship to the realm of interest-formation, and to concede rationalists the terrain of strategic interaction, have thus been criticized for propagating an unnecessarily 'thin form of constructivism' (Laffey and Weldes 1997).

Another discontent within constructivism involves the question of methodology. Critical theorists have long argued that the neo-positivist methodology championed by neo-realists and neo-liberals is poorly suited to the study of human action, as the individuals and groups under analysis attach meanings to their actions, these meanings are shaped by a pre-existing 'field' of shared meanings embedded in language and other symbols, and the effect of such meanings on human action cannot be understood by treating them as measurable variables that cause behaviour in any direct or quantifiable manner (Taylor 1997: 111). This led early constructivists to insist that the study of ideas, norms and other meanings requires an interpretive methodology, one that seeks to grasp 'the relationship between "intersubjective meanings" which derive from self-interpretation and self-definition, and the social practices in which they are embedded and which they constitute' (Kratochwil and Ruggie 1986; Kratochwil 1988/9; Neufeld 1993: 49). Curiously, these arguments have been forgotten by a number of constructivists, who defend a position of 'methodological conventionalism', claiming that their explanations 'do not depend exceptionally upon any specialized separate "interpretive methodology"' (Jepperson, Wendt and Katzenstein 1996: 67). They justify this position on the grounds that the field has been bogged down for too long in methodological disputes and, at any rate, the empirical work of more doctrinaire constructivists such as Kratochwil and Ruggie does not look all that different from that of conventional scholars. Neither of these grounds addresses the substance of the original constructivist argument about methodology, nor do the advocates of methodological conventionalism recognize that the similarity between mainstream empirical work and that of interpretive constructivists may have more to do with the failure of rationalists ever to meet their own neo-positivist standards. The gap between these rival methodological standpoints within constructivism is most clearly apparent in the contrast between those studies that employ quantitative methodological techniques and those that adopt genealogical approaches (Johnston 1995; Price 1997).

The final discontent concerns the relationship between constructivism and critical international theory. It is reasonable, we have seen, to view constructivism as an outgrowth of critical theory, and Price and Reus-Smit (1998) have argued that its development has great potential to further the critical project. Andrew Linklater (1992a) has identified three dimensions of that project: the normative task of critically assessing and revising how political organization, particularly the sovereign state, has been morally justified; the sociological task of understanding how moral community – locally, nationally and globally – expands and contracts; and the praxeological task of grasping the constraints and opportunities that bear on emancipatory political action (1992a: 92–4). Nowhere is the second of these tasks being undertaken with greater energy and rigour than within constructivism. Exploring the development and the impact of the normative and ideational foundations of international society is the constructivist stock in trade, and dialogue between constructivists and those engaged in the more philosophical project of normative critique and elaboration is the most likely path toward true praxeological knowledge. Constructivism is divided, however, between those who remain cognizant of the critical origins and potentiality of their sociological explorations, and those who have embraced constructivism simply as an explanatory or interpretive tool. Both standpoints are justifiable, and the work of scholars on both sides of this divide can be harnessed to the critical project, regardless of their individual commitments. It is imperative, though, that the former group of scholars work to bring constructivist research into dialogue with moral and philosophical argument, otherwise constructivism will lose its ethical veracity and critical international theory one of its potential pillars.

It is tempting to explain these discontents in terms of differences between modern and post-modern constructivists, differences outlined earlier. Yet disagreements over the nature of theory, the relationship to rationalism, the appropriate method and the contribution to critical international theory do not map neatly onto the divide between minimal and anti-foundationalism. While post-modern constructivists would never advocate the development of a general theory of international relations, task-sharing with rationalists, methodological conventionalism, or pure explanation, neither would many modern constructivists. Here Ted Hopf's (1998) distinction between 'conventional' and 'critical' constructivisms may be more fruitful: 'To the degree that constructivism creates theoretical and epistemological distance between itself and its origins in critical theory, it becomes "conventional" constructivism' (1998: 181). The discontents outlined above reflect the differences between those who have consciously or unconsciously created such distance and those who wish to stay in touch with constructivism's roots. Among the latter group, important differences remain between modernists and post-modernists. The most important of these differences concerns the questions they address, with the former focusing on *why* questions, the latter on *how* questions. For instance, Reus-Smit (1999) takes up the question of why different international societies have evolved different institutional practices to solve cooperation problems and facilitate coexistence among states, while Cynthia Weber asks 'How is the meaning of sovereignty fixed or stabilized historically via practices of international relations theorists and practices of political intervention?' (1995: 3).

The contribution of constructivism

In spite of these discontents, which are as much a sign of dynamism as division, the rise of constructivism has had several important impacts on the development of international relations theory and analysis. Thanks largely to the work of constructivists, the social, historical and normative have returned to the centre stage of debate, especially within the American core of the discipline.

Until the late 1980s, two factors conspired to marginalize societal analysis in International Relations scholarship. The first was the overwhelming materialism of the major theoretical perspectives. For neo-realists, the principal determinant of state behaviour is the underlying distribution of material capabilities across states in the international system, a determinant that gives states their animating survival motive, which in turn drives balance of power competition. To the extent that they discussed it, neo-liberals also saw state interests as essentially material, even if they did posit the importance of international institutions as intervening variables. The second factor was the prevailing rationalist conception of human action. As we have seen, both neo-realists and neo-liberals imagined humans – and, by extension, states – as atomistic, self-interested, strategic actors, thus positing a standard form of instrumental rationality across all political actors. When combined, the materialism and rationalism of the prevailing theories left little room for the social dimensions of international life, unless of course the social is reduced to power-motivated strategic competition. Materialism denied the causal significance of shared ideas, norms and values, and rationalism reduced the social to the strategic and ignored the particularities of community, identity and interest. By re-imagining the social as a constitutive realm of values and practices, and by situating individual identities and interests within such a field, constructivists have placed sociological inquiry back at the centre of the discipline. Because of the prominence of the 'international society' (or 'English') school, such inquiry had never disappeared from British International Relations scholarship. Constructivists, however, have brought a new level of conceptual clarity and theoretical sophistication to the analysis of both international and world society, thus complementing and augmenting the work of the English School.

By resuscitating societal analysis, the rise of constructivism has also sparked a renewed interest in international history. So long as International Relations theorists were wedded to the idea that states are driven by context-transcendent survival motives or universal modes of rationality, the lessons of history were reduced to the proposition that nothing of substance ever changes. Such assumptions denied the rich diversity of human experience and the possibilities of meaningful change and difference, thus flattening out international history into a monotone tale of 'recurrence and repetition'. Historical analysis became little more than the ritualistic recitation of lines from the celebrated works of Thucydides, Machiavelli and Hobbes, all with aim of 'proving' the unchanging nature of international relations, licensing the formulation of increasingly abstract theories. Such history had the paradoxical effect of largely suffocating the study of international history in the American core of the discipline. Aided by the momentous changes that attended the end of the Cold War, and also by the ongoing processes of globalization, the constructivist interest in the particularities of culture, identity, interest and experience created space for a renaissance in the study of history and world politics. If ideas, norms, and practices matter, and if they differ from one social context to another, then history in turn matters. Not surprisingly, in their efforts to demonstrate the contingency of such factors and their impact on the conduct of world politics, constructivists have sought to re-read the historical record, to re-think what has long been treated as given in the study of international relations. While a similar impulse came from International Relations scholars inspired by the re-birth of historical sociology, constructivists have dominated the new literature on international history (Ruggie 1986, 1993; Welch 1993; Thomson 1994; Kier 1997; Hall 1999; Reus-Smit 1999; Philpott 2001; Rae 2002).

Finally, constructivism may be credited with helping to re-invigorate normative theorizing in International Relations. Not because constructivists have been engaged in philosophical reflection about the nature of the good or the right, a project that has itself been re-energized by the multitude of ethical dilemmas thrown up by the end of the Cold War and the march of globalization, but because they have done much to demonstrate the power of ideas, norms and values in shaping world politics. While talk of the 'power of ideas' has at times carried considerable rhetorical force outside of academic International Relations, such talk within the field has long been dismissed as naive and even dangerous idealism. Material calculations, such as military power and wealth, have been upheld as the motive forces behind international political action, and ideational factors have been dismissed as mere rationalizations or instrumental guides to strategic action. Through sustained empirical research, constructivists have exposed the explanatory poverty of such materialist scepticism. They have shown how international norms evolve, how ideas and values come to shape political action, how argument and discourse condition outcomes and how identity constitutes agents and agency, all in ways that contradict the expectations of materialist and rationalist theories. While this 'empirical idealism' provides no answers to questions probed by international ethicists, it contributes to more philosophically oriented normative theorizing in two ways: it legitimizes such theorizing by demonstrating the possibility of ideas driven international change; and it assists by clarifying the dynamics and mechanisms of such change, thus furthering the development of E. H. Carr's proposed 'realistic utopianism'.

Recent developments in constructivism

Since the turn of the new millennium, debates within constructivism have continued apace, even if their general trajectory has remained largely the

same. As noted above, four discontents have characterized constructivism's evolution: differences over whether constructivists should aspire
to a general theory of international relations, over the relationship with
rationalism, over questions of method and over the relationship between
constructivism and critical theory. Since 2000, the first of these discontents has dissipated. Neo-realists and rationalists still call for constructivism's codification as a theoretical paradigm, capable of generating
testable hypotheses and law-like propositions. But among constructivists, the centre of gravity has moved away from Wendtian-style theorizing, even if Wendt himself has continued to produce innovative and
challenging theory (see Wendt 2003). The centre of gravity has moved
toward, on the one hand, a more eclectic, problem-driven kind of
research and, on the other, the critical strand of constructivism that has
been there from the outset. This has not, however, produced a strong
consensus among constructivists.

As the centre of gravity has moved away from general theorizing, the
other discontents concerning the relationship with rationalism, questions
of method and the critical nature of constructivism have become more
pronounced. The tendencies for constructivists in the American mainstream to advocate an analytical division of labour with rationalists, and
to deny that constructivism's focus on inter-subjective meanings
demands an interpretive methodology, have persisted. But they have also
transmuted into a new style of scholarship, one barely recognizable as
constructivism. Katzenstein has called for an 'eclectic' form of theorizing,
one that starts from concrete empirical puzzles and draws on diverse
theories to construct compelling explanations (Katzenstein and Okawara
2001/2; Suh, Katzenstein and Carlsen 2004). Constructivism thus
becomes one tool among many in the scholar's toolkit, and methodological conventionalism is taken as the norm. Parallel to these developments,
other scholars have sought to retain constructivism's critical edge, largely
by pushing its engagement with normative and ethical theory
(Kratochwil 2000; Reus-Smit 2000, 2002a; Shapcott 2000a).
Constructivism, in their view, should not only be about the politics of
ethics, but also the ethics of politics. The major statement of this position
is Price's *Moral Limit and Possibility in World Politics* (2008).

In the last edition of this chapter I commented on the relative autonomy of these debates and trends from the events of 11 September 2001
and their aftermath, arguing that 9/11 had not sparked any significant
shift in the nature of constructivism or in the general trajectory of international relations theorizing. This struck me as curious, especially since
many of the big and important questions facing the international
community play to constructivism's strengths. At the time I identified
three areas warranting particular attention by constructivists: the nature

of power, the relationship between international and world society, and the role of culture in world politics. In the last 5 years the paucity of constructivist scholarship in each of these areas has been replaced by a new wave of research.

Discussions of power in international relations have traditionally been seen as the preserve of realists. 'Absolute power', 'relative power', 'structural power' and 'the balance of power' are all realist conceptions, as are notions of 'the struggle for power' and 'hegemonic stability'. Yet, as Wendt argues persuasively, the 'proposition that the nature of international politics is shaped by power relations . . . cannot be a *uniquely* Realist claim' (1999: 96–7). What is uniquely realist is the 'hypothesis that the effects of power are constituted primarily by brute material forces' (1999: 97). Recent events, however, cast doubt over this hypothesis. The United States presently enjoys a greater degree of material preponderance than perhaps any other state in history, yet across a wide spectrum of issue areas it is struggling to translate that material advantage into sustained political influence or intended (as opposed to unintended) political outcomes. Power, it seems, is also constituted by non-material factors, most notably legitimacy and legitimacy is in turn conditioned by established or emergent norms of rightful agency and action. The debate in the Security Council over war with Iraq highlighted this complex interplay between institutional norms and processes, the politics of international legitimacy and the power of the United States. Washington commanded the material resources to oust Saddam Hussein from power, but without Security Council endorsement it has struggled to shake off an aura of illegitimacy and illegality, seriously undermining its capacity to socialize the costs of the occupation and reconstruction. The unilateralist turn in American foreign policy, the 'war against terrorism' and the advent of 'preventive' war against rogue states has prompted a number of constructivists to articulate a social conception of power that accommodates the complex relationship between norms, legitimacy and hegemonic power (Ikenberry 2000; Cronin 2001; Barnett and Duvall 2004; Reus-Smit 2004a). Along side this literature, constructivists have also probed the concept and politics of legitimacy (Bukovansky, 2002; Hurd, 2005, 2007; Clark and Reus-Smit 2007). Related to this work is the growing corpus of constructivist work on international law, an institution intimately related to the politics of norms, legitimacy and power (Brunnee and Toope 2000; Finnemore and Toope 2001; Reus-Smit 2004b).

It is common to distinguish conceptually between an 'international society' and a 'world society', the former being the 'club of states', with its norms and institutions of coexistence and cooperation, the latter being the broader web of social relations that enmesh states, NGOs, international organizations and other global social actors (Bull 1977). Without denying the continued relevance of the system of sovereign states, constructivists have done much to show how international society and its institutions have been shaped by actors within the wider world society. Margaret Keck and Kathryn Sikkink (1998) have demonstrated the ways in which NGOs operating within states, in association with international NGOs, have mobilized human rights norms to constrain the domestic exercise of state power. More recently, Michael Barnett and Martha Finnemore (2004) have shown how international organizations – created by states for state purposes – can gain degrees of autonomy that enable them to condition the terrain of international state action. Important as these insights are, constructivists have yet to see their relevance for understanding the normative politics of transnational terrorism. Like many humanitarian NGOs, transnational terrorist organizations operate in the social space transcending state borders and, like these NGOs, groups such as Al-Qaeda use forms of moral suasion and symbolic politics to redefine the terms of political discourse affecting state interests and actions. The novelty and magnitude of the violence they unleash often blinds us to the fact that they are ultimately seeking to transform ideas and values, both those of the 'West' and those of politically disaffected and economically alienated Moslems. Constructivists have taken two steps in the right direction by considering the way in which world society forces constitute the political fabric of international society, and by highlighting the politics of values that attends this process of constitution. Their task now is to confront three questions: What is the relationship between the exercise of violence and the erosion and propagation of social and political values, both by states and non-state actors? How has this constituted international society historically? And what are the implications of this nexus between violence and normative changes for international and global order? Recent work by Phillips takes up these questions, pushing constructivists into new terrain (Phillips, forthcoming).

The study of culture and international relations is closely identified with constructivism, an association reinforced by book titles such as *Cultural Realism* (by Alastair Iain Johnston) and *The Culture of National Security* (by Peter J. Katzenstein). By 'culture', however, constructivists generally mean social and legal norms and the ways in which these are deployed, though argument and communication, to constitute actors' identities and interests. Methodologically, this generally involves the identification of a particular norm, or set of norms, and the tracing of its effect on political action. Culture, understood more holistically as the broader framework of inter-subjective meanings and practices that give a society a distinctive character, has been largely neglected. The events of September 11 have, however, thrust culture, in this more expansive sense, on to the international agenda, creating an opening and an obligation for constructivists. Samuel Huntington's 'clash of civilizations' thesis has gained a new lease of life, with commentators, from diverse quarters, no longer inhibited in attributing essentialist characteristics to 'The West' and 'Islam'. Few now deny that culture is important in world politics, but the overwhelming tendency is to naturalize and reify culture, carving ethically and racially defined lines across the globe. The need for a constructivist voice here is crucial, as constructivists think culture matters but that it is inherently socially constructed, not rooted in blood and soil. Research is needed into how ideas of 'The West' and 'Islam', as radically different transnational communities, have been constituted, on how these ideas are related to the constitution, or erosion, of state power and on how these ideas can be mobilized to sustain system-transforming political projects, either on the part of liberal democracies, seeking to redefine the norms of sovereignty and global governance, or terrorist organizations seeking an end to the liberal capitalist world order. Outstanding constructivist work in this area is now appearing, with Elizabeth Shakman Hurd's writings on religion and secularism being emblematic (2004; 2007).

Conclusion

The rise of constructivism has heralded a return to a more sociological, historical and practice oriented form of International Relations scholarship. Where rationalists had reduced the social to strategic interaction, denied the historical by positing disembedded, universal forms of rationality and reduced the practical art of politics to utility maximizing calculation, constructivists have re-imagined the social as a constitutive domain, reintroduced history as realm of empirical inquiry and emphasized the variability of political practice. In many respects, constructivism embodies characteristics normally associated with the 'English School', discussed by Linklater in Chapter 4 in this volume. Constructivists have taken up the idea that states form more than a system – that they form a society – and they have pushed this idea to new levels of theoretical and conceptual sophistication. Their interest in international history also represents an important point of convergence with the English School, as does their stress on the cultural distinctiveness of different societies of states. Finally, their initial emphasis on interpretive methods of analysis echoes Hedley Bull's call for a classical approach, 'characterized above all by explicit reliance upon the exercise of judgement' rather than neo-positivist standards of 'verification and proof' (1969/1995: 20–38).

These similarities, as well as constructivism's roots in critical international theory, appeared to pose a challenge to conventional understandings of the field. An 'Atlantic divide' has long structured understandings of the sociology of International Relations as a discipline, with the field seen as divided between North American 'scientists' and European (mainly British) 'classicists'. Two of the defining 'great debates' of the discipline – between realists and idealists and positivists and traditionalists – have been mapped onto this divide, lending intellectual divisions a cultural overtone. At first glance, constructivism appears to confuse this way of ordering the discipline. Despite having taken up many of the intellectual commitments normally associated with the English School, constructivism has its origins in the United States. Its principal exponents were either educated in or currently teach in the leading American universities, and their pioneering work has been published in the premier journals and by the leading university presses. The United States also spawned much of the earlier wave of critical international theory, especially of a post-modern variety, but that work never achieved the same centrality within the American sector of the discipline. One of the reasons for constructivism's success in the United States has been its emphasis on empirically informed theorizing over meta-theoretical critique, an orientation much less confronting to the mainstream. With success, however, has come normalization, and this has seen the neglectful forgetting, or active jettisoning, of theoretical commitments that were central to constructivism in the early years. Disappearing, in the American discipline, are the foundational ideas that constructivism rests on a social ontology radically different from rationalism's, that studying norms, as social facts, demands an interpretive methodology, and that constructivism was linked, in important ways, to the emancipatory project of critical theory. The continued importance of these commitments to non-American constructivism suggests that a new manifestation of the 'Atlantic divide' may now be emerging.

10 | **Feminism**

JACQUI TRUE

Breaking with the powerful bond among manly men, states and war, feminist theories of international relations have flourished since the mid 1980s. These theories have introduced *gender* as a relevant empirical category and analytical tool for understanding global power relations as well as a normative position from which to consider alternative world orders. Like other constitutive theories such as constructivism, critical theory, postmodernism, and green theories, feminism shifts the study of international relations away from a singular focus on inter-state relations toward a comprehensive analysis of transnational actors and structures and their transformations. But with their focus on non-state actors, marginalized peoples and alternative conceptualizations of power and relationships, feminist perspectives bring fresh thinking and action to world politics.

In the new millennium there has been a proliferation of research on gender and international security, including feminist analysis of the gendered impacts of war and peace and quantitative analysis using gender as a variable to explain aspects of state behaviour and international conflict (Carpenter 2005; Nayak and Suchland 2006; Shepherd 2007). With this growth and range of feminist International Relations scholarship, feminists have recently given explicit accounts of their alternative methodological approaches to research on global politics (Ackerly, Stern and True 2006; Ackerly and True 2009). The axiological dimension of feminist International Relations is still relatively underdeveloped. But increasingly scholars are bringing the insights of feminist praxis to bear on discussions of universal human rights, social justice and economic globalization, democratization and peace processes. Within feminist practices there are resources for developing normative guidelines about the possibility for global dialogue across ethnic, cultural, national, racial, sexual and gender differences.

Until the 1980s, the field of International Relations studied the causes of war and conflict and the global expansion of trade and commerce with no particular reference to people. Indeed the use of abstract categories such as 'the state', 'the system', strategic security discourses such as nuclear deterrence and positivist research approaches effectively removed people as agents embedded in social and historical contexts from theories of international relations. This is ironic since the scholarly field emerged, following the end of World War I, to democratize foreign policy making and empower people as citizen-subjects rather than mere objects of elite statecraft (Hill 1999). So where does the study of people called 'women' and 'men' or the social construction of masculine and feminine genders fit within International Relations? How are the international system and the study of International Relations gendered? To what extent do feminist perspectives help us to explain, understand and improve global politics? This chapter explores these questions as they have been addressed by a diverse range of feminist scholars in and outside the International Relations field.

The chapter starts with a brief overview of the development of feminist International Relations. It differentiates three overlapping forms of feminist scholarship that represent a useful heuristic for discussing the varied contributions to International Relations. These are: (1) *empirical feminism*, that focuses on women and/or explores gender as an empirical dimension of international relations; (2) *analytical feminism*, that uses gender as a theoretical category to reveal the gender bias of International Relations concepts and explain constitutive aspects of international relations; and (3) *normative feminism*, that reflects on the process of theorizing as part of a normative agenda for global social and political change. These forms do not prefigure or suggest any particular feminist epistemology. For example, Jacqueline Berman's (2003) analysis of the way in which European states secure their borders through anti-sex trafficking policies is an example of an empirical feminist approach informed by post-structuralist attention to the politics of domination involved in all efforts to categorize and 'protect' human subjects. Empirical, analytical and normative feminist approaches that challenge the assumptions of explanatory theories of International Relations and help to construct new constitutive theories of global politics are discussed in the second, third and fourth sections of the chapter.

Changing international relations have greatly altered patterns of gender relations just as gender dynamics have influenced global processes of militarization and economic globalization (see Gray, Kittleson and Sandholtz 2006). Following on the second wave of the worldwide feminist movement, Cynthia Enloe dared to suggest that 'the personal which is political' is also 'international'. In *Bananas, Beaches, and Bases* (1989), she exposed how international politics frequently involves intimate relationships, personal identities and private lives. These informal politics are altogether less transparent than the stuff of official politics and they are typically ignored by International Relations scholars. Taking the view from below, feminists have sought to demonstrate that gender relations are an integral part of international relations. Diplomatic spouses smooth over the workings of power among states and statesmen (sic); opaque but trustworthy marital contracts facilitate transnational money laundering and sex trafficking; global icons such as *Cosmopolitan* conquer foreign cultures and prepare them for the onslaught of Western capitalism; and women and men organize in kitchens, churches and kin-communities to overthrow authoritarian regimes and make peace in the face of brutal conflict (Cockburn 1998; True 2003; Domett 2004).

Focusing on politics at the margins dispels the assumption that power is what comes out of the barrel of a gun or ensues from the declarations of world leaders. Indeed, feminist efforts to reinterpret power suggest that International Relations scholars have underestimated the pervasiveness of power and precisely what it takes, at every level and every day, to reproduce a grossly uneven and hierarchical world order (Enloe 1997). Feminist reconceptualizations of power and attention to the margins of global politics have allowed International Relations scholars to recognize and comprehend new political phenomena.

A first generation of feminist International Relations in the late 1980s challenged the conventional focus of the field, engaging in the 'third debate' about the impossibility of objectivity in International Relations and the embeddedness of scholarship in global power relations discussed in the introduction, Chapter 9 (constructivism) and Chapter 8 (poststructuralism). In this debate, feminist scholars contested the exclusionary, state-centric and positivist nature of the discipline primarily at a meta-theoretical level. Many of these feminist contributions sought to deconstruct and subvert *realism*, the dominant 'power politics' explanation of post-war International Relations. Often implicit in their concern with gender relations was the assumption of a feminist standpoint epistemology. Such a standpoint maintains that women's lives on the margins of world politics afford us a more critical and comprehensive understanding of international relations than the objectivist view of the realist theorist or foreign policy lens of the statesman since they are less biased by existing institutions and elite power (Keohane 1989a: 245; Sylvester 1994a: 13; see also Harding 1986; Runyan and Peterson 1991; Tickner 1992; Zalewski 1993).

These first-generation feminist challenges opened the space for critical International Relations scholarship but they begged the question of what a feminist perspective on world politics would look like substantively, and how distinctive it would be (Zalewski 1995). Two decades after the first journal in the field devoted a special issue to 'women and international relations' (Millennium 1988) much has also been accomplished by feminist International Relations scholars. Most courses on International Relations theory worldwide now consider gender issues or feminist perspectives due to the publication of a growing number of texts and monographs by feminist International Relations scholars, including this chapter (Tickner 1992, 2001; Pettman 1996; Peterson and Runyan 1999; Sylvester 2000; Peterson 2003; Steans 2005). Several key disciplinary journals have published whole issues on the subjects of women, gender and feminism in international relations, and in 1999 the *International Feminist Journal of Politics* was established to promote dialogue among scholars of feminism, politics and international relations.

A second generation of feminist research has further developed feminist International Relations by making gender a central analytic category in studies of foreign policy, security and global political economy that explore particular historical and geographical contexts (Moon 1997; Chin 1998; Hooper 2000; Prugl 2000; True 2003; Whitworth 2004; Stern 2005). Often analysing the intersection of gender, class, race, ethnicity, sexuality and nationality, second generation feminist scholarship is closely tied to developments in feminist methodologies, critical international theory, constructivist social science, and post-Marxist political economy. The newest feminist scholarship provides empirical support for first-generation theoretical challenges, while also generating new insight on the gendering of global politics, as the rest of the chapter illustrates.

Empirical feminism

Empirical feminism turns our attention to women and gender relations as empirical aspects of international relations. Feminist challenges to International Relations contend that women's lives and experiences have been, and still are, often excluded from the study of international relations. This 'sexist' exclusion has resulted in research which presents only a partial, masculine view in a field in which the dominant theories claim to explain the reality of world politics (Halliday 1988b). Empirical feminism corrects the denial or misrepresentation of women in world politics due to false assumptions that male experiences can count for both men and women, and that women are either absent from international political activities or not relevant to global processes. It is not that women have not been present or their experiences relevant to international relations. Rather, as Cynthia Enloe's (1989, 1994, 2000) scholarship demonstrates, women are and have always been part of international relations – if we choose to see them there. Moreover, it is in part because women's lives and experiences have not been empirically researched in the context of world politics, as Grant and Newland (1991: 5) argue, that International Relations has been 'excessively focused on conflict and anarchy and a way of practising statecraft and formulating strategy that is excessively focused on competition and fear'. Studies of the norms and ideas that make the reproduction of the state-system possible and of the structural violence (poverty, environmental injustice, socio-political inequality) that underpins direct state-sanctioned violence are seen as secondary to the manly study of war and conflict in international relations due to their association with domestic 'soft' (read: feminine) politics. As a result, neo-realist and neo-liberal International Relations scholars theorize politics and the international realm 'in a way that guarantees that women will be absent from their inquiry, and that their research agendas remain unaltered' (Steurnagel 1990: 79–80).

Feminist research is not a form of empiricism since feminist scholars need conceptual clarity, thus to engage in theoretical debates about the ontology of gender and international relations, in order to conduct empirical research. For instance, to make abstract concepts and relationships amenable to empirical exploration the feminist researcher must identify those which can be seen to exist and are the most important for closer study, while also developing a research methodology for translating and analysing them empirically (see Caprioli 2004; Ackerly, Stern and True 2006).

Empirical feminist International Relations addresses different questions and employs a variety of methodologies. Studies under the rubric of 'women in international development' (WID), and more recently gender and development (GAD), have documented how male bias in the development process has led to poor implementation of projects and unsatisfactory policy outcomes in terms of eradicating global poverty and empowering local communities (Newland 1988; Goetz 1991; Kardam 1991; Kabeer 1994; Rathergeber 1995). This scholarship makes visible the central role of women as subsistence producers and providers of basic needs in developing countries (Beneria 1982; Charlton, Everett and Staudt 1989). Empirical studies reveal that the most efficient allocation of overseas development assistance is often to provide women with appropriate agricultural technology, credit financing, education and health resources. For example, the United Nations (2000) estimates that while women's farming accounts for one-half of the food production in the developing world, it provides three-quarters of domestic food supply for family households. Gender sensitive researchers have found that investing in girls' education is one of the most cost-effective development policies, resulting in positive gains for a whole community by raising incomes and lowering population rates (see Sen 2001).

Economic globalization has intensified social and economic polarization, both within and across states. Feminist scholars document how globalization processes have increased the world-wide inequality between men and women. Their research has revealed 'the feminization of poverty', that is, the disproportionate numbers of women compared with men in poverty – due to Third World debt and financial crises, structural adjustment policies (SAPs) in the South and state restructuring in the North (Afshar and Dennis 1992; Sparr 1994; Porter and Judd 2000). As economic policy has become increasingly governed by the global imperatives of export earnings, financial markets and comparative labour costs, states have struggled to meet their commitments to full employment and citizen well-being. Empirical feminist research shows how this shift from a largely domestic state to global market provision of services has imposed a disproportionate burden on women to pick up the slack of the state (United Nations Development Programme 1999; Marchand and Runyan 2000; Hoskyns and Rai 2007).

In the global context also, a gendered international division of labour has emerged as migrant Third World women become a cheap and flexible source of labour for MNCs in free trade zones (Mitter 1986; Standing 1992; Ong 1997). Saskia Sassen's (1991, 1998a,b) research shows how global cities, the nodal points for global financial markets and economic transactions, are dependent on a class of women workers. Like 'intimate others' of economic globalization, domestic workers, typically immigrant women of colour, service the masculinized corporate elite in these urban centres (Boris and Prugl 1996; Stasilius and Bakan 1997; Chin 1998; Chang and Ling 2000). Feminist research reveals an even darker 'underside' of globalization, however, in the phenomenal growth of sex-tourism, 'male-order' brides and transnational trafficking of women and girls for prostitution (Pettman 1996; Prugl and Meyer 1999; Berman 2003). For subordinate states in the world system, these economic activities are key sources of foreign exchange and national income (Jeffrey 2002; Hanochi 2003). For example, Chin (1998) shows how Malaysian political elites maintained the legitimacy of their export oriented development strategy in the 1980s and 1990s by importing female domestic servants from the Philippines and Indonesia.

But women are not only victimized by global processes of structural change; in many cases, they are empowered by it. Feminist researchers explore how global trade and financial liberalization reshapes women's subjectivities and local gender relations as it transforms material conditions. These researchers highlight how new credit and employment opportunities have brought cultural changes in the lives of poor women in rural, developing areas (Gibson, Law and McKay 2001). Naila Kabeer (1994), for example, has investigated how changing material incentives provided by the re-siting of TNCs' garment production, opened up possibilities for young Bangladeshi women to make a better living and at the same time to challenge patriarchal gender arrangements. Jacqui True (2003) shows how the spread of global consumption, culture and information after the end of communism has enabled Czech women to create new gender and even feminist identities.

Feminist studies reveal the gendered construction of international organizations, which to an even greater extent than national institutions, are dominated by elite men (Prugl and Meyer 1999; Rai and Waylen 2008). Gender mainstreaming initiatives have allowed more women to join their policy making ranks (True and Mintrom 2001; True 2008a). For instance, women now head many of the United Nations' agencies, including the World Health Organisation (WHO), the United Nations Children's Fund (UNICEF), the Office of the High Commissioner for Refugees (UNHCR), the World Food Programme and the World Population Fund. The Deputy Secretary General and the High Commissioner for Human Rights are also both women. Yet, as these feminist studies point out, in institutions like the United Nations, women continue to be ghettoized in less powerful agencies and as secretarial helpmates, and are only gradually coming to have influence over the global security and development agenda (Pietila and Vickers 1996; Reanda 1999; Whitworth 2004). Indeed, the small UN agency devoted to addressing gender inequalities and the advancement of women (UNIFEM) has far less resources than the agency dedicated to children (UNICEF), even though the plight of children in the world is very much dependent on the relative status of their mothers.

International Organizations also institutionalize gender-based policies and priorities. In her study of the International Labour Organization (ILO) Sandra Whitworth (1994) shows how assumptions about gender relations shaped ILO policies that have had discriminatory effects in national and international labour markets, reinforcing women's inequality. Elisabeth Prugl (2000) employing a feminist constructivist approach in her study of home-workers, shows how the gendered rules and regimes of the ILO and the global solidarity networks that emerged to change them have been powerful forces in determining the plight of these mainly women workers around the world. At the regional level, Catherine Hoskyns (1996) shows how women's movements in member states have successfully used the European Union's supranational body of equal opportunities law and policy to address gender disparities at the national level. Hoskyns' gender-sensitive analysis shows how the process of European integration has had the effect of extending women's social citizenship rights in member states, although the European Union is only beginning to play a global role in advocating gender equality beyond its borders (Prügl 2007).

In the realm of foreign policy, feminist analyses have revealed the dominant masculine gender of policy makers and the gendered assumption that these policy makers are strategically rational actors who make life and death decisions in the name of an abstract conception of the 'national interest'. As Nancy McGlen and Meredith Sarkees (1993) have assessed in their study of the foreign policy and defence establishment, women are rarely 'insiders' of the actual institutions that make and implement foreign policy and conduct war. In 2008, the fact that 28 women were foreign ministers suggests that this male dominance of global diplomacy is undergoing some change; as do the establishment of the Council of Women World Leaders (currently headed by former Irish President and UN Human Rights Commissioner Mary Robinson) and the Nobel Women's Initiative (led by women winners of the Nobel Peace prize) that seek to leverage women leaders' collective strengths to bring about global peace and security (Stiehm 2006). Feminist scholars analyse the persistent 'gender gap' in the foreign policy beliefs of men and women foreign policy making elites and citizens; women leaders and citizens in Western states are consistently more likely to oppose the use of force in international actions and are typically more supportive of humanitarian interventions (Rosenau and Holsti 1982; Tessler, Nachtwey and Grant 1999). Attitudes toward gender equality and sexual liberty affect attitudes toward tolerance, human rights and democracy and are good predictors of more pacific attitudes to international conflict (Tessler and Warriner 1997).

Feminist research shows that those states with greater gender inequality are also more likely to go to war or to engage in state-sanctioned violence (Goldstein 2001). Domestic gender equality also reduces the likelihood that a state will use force first in inter-state disputes, limits the escalation of violence and decreases the severity of violence during international crises (Caprioli 2000; Caprioli and Boyer 2001). By the same token, those states that come closest to gender parity tend also to be more pacific in their relations, more generous aid donors and generally good citizens in the international realm (Regan and Paskeviciute 2003). However, our preoccupation with states can prevent us from seeing the multiple non-state actors who also play significant roles in foreign-policy making. Feminist researchers such as Enloe (1989, 2000) make visible the women who provide support services for military activities (domestic, psychological, medical and sexual). If we see militarization as a social process consisting of many gendered assignments that make possible those ultimate acts of state violence then, she argues, the official provision of sexual services on military bases for instance can be seen as a central factor in a foreign intervention. In *Sex Among Allies*, Katherine Moon (1997) argues that the exploitative sexual alliances between Korean prostitutes (*kijich'on* women) and US soldiers defined and supported the similarly unequal military alliance between the United States and South Korea in the post-war era. Among other things, under the Nixon Doctrine *kijich'on* women as personal ambassadors became the main indicator of Seoul's willingness to accommodate US military interests.

Women are more likely to be among the group of non-state actors in global politics. Feminist researchers highlight the activism of women, who are often marginalized, poor and vulnerable: whether in networks of sex-workers, home-workers, mothers or civil activists, in counter-cultural campaigns and performances. As well as highlighting local activism, however, feminist researchers have observed new forms of cross-border solidarity and identity formation. In recent years, women have played key roles in the global movement to ban landmines, the Campaign for Nuclear Disarmament (CND), and the feminist network protesting gender-based violence globally (Stienstra 1994; Friedman 1995; Rupp 1997; Clark, Friedman and Hochstetler, 1998; Williams and Goose 1998). For example, in two troubled conflict zones of the world, Israel/Palestine and the former Yugoslavia, groups known as 'Women in Black' have protested against the escalation of militarism, weaponry and war, and men's violence against women and children (Sharoni 1993; Cockburn 1998; Korac 1998; Jacoby 1999). Feminist researchers high-light peace activists and mothers protesting against their sons being conscripted in international conflicts but also female suicide bombers who transgress gendered social norms to take their own lives and others with them as a global political statement (Alison 2004; Gentry and Sjoberg 2008).

Noting how new female subjectivities create the momentum for new forms of collective action, feminist researchers trace the growth of transnational women's networks, the alliances forged between women's organizations, governments and inter-governmental actors, and the development of international legal and policy mechanisms promoting gender justice. For example, due to these alliances human rights instru-ments and global declarations increasingly acknowledge the gender-specificity of human rights (Peters and Wolper 1995; Philapose 1996; Ackerly and Okin 1999; Ackerly 2000). In 1990, Amnesty International, the global human rights NGO, recognized women's human rights by adding gender persecution to its list of forms of political persecution. Governments and international organizations have followed suit. For example, until the 1990s Yugoslav conflict, states and international agencies interpreted the persecution of women as a matter of personal privacy and cultural tradition (Rao 1995). However, as a result of the lobbying by transnational feminist networks and the widespread media coverage of rape as a specific war strategy in Yugoslavia, rape has now been prosecuted as a war crime under the Geneva Convention Against War Crimes (1949) by the International Criminal Court (Niarchos 1995; Philapose 1996; Chappell 2008).

Bringing women's lives and gender relations into view through empirical research has policy-relevant and material effects. Indeed, feminists argue that only when women are recognized as fundamental players in economic and political processes will they share an equal role in societal decision making. By redressing the empirical neglect of women and gender relations, feminist scholars both improve our understanding of global politics and help to put women's voices and concerns on the global agenda. But in order to make gender an important dimension of the study of international relations, it is necessary to challenge the conceptual framework which has excluded women from this study in the first place. Empirical feminism is thus complemented by analytical feminism that reveals the theoretical exclusions of the International Relations field and seeks to revision International Relations from a gender-sensitive perspective.

Analytical feminism

Analytical feminism deconstructs the theoretical framework of International Relations, revealing the gender bias that pervades key concepts and inhibits an accurate and comprehensive understanding of international relations. The feminist concept of gender refers to the asymmetrical social constructs of masculinity and femininity as opposed to ostensibly 'biological' male–female differences (although feminist post-modernists contend that both sex and gender are socially constructed categories, see Butler 1990; Gatens 1991). The hegemonic Western brand of masculinity is associated with autonomy, sovereignty, the capacity for reason and objectivity and universalism, whereas the dominant notion of femininity is associated with the absence or lack of these characteristics. For example, the routine practices of militaries replicate these hegemonic gender identities by training soldiers both to protect 'womenchildren' through killing and to suppress (feminine) emotions associated with bodily pain and caring (Goldstein 2001). Military training, in Barbara Roberts' (1984) words is 'socialization into masculinity carried to the extremes'. A common assumption is that gender identities are natural or 'human nature' and not subject to social constitution or human agency. When this assumption about gender is applied to other social and political phenomena, however, it has political effects in terms of reproducing the status quo or existing power relations. As Joan Scott (1988: 48) has stated, 'the binary opposition and the social process of gender relationships [have] both become part of the meaning of power itself' and, 'to question or alter any aspect of it, threatens the entire system'.

International Relations' key concepts are neither natural nor gender-neutral: they are derived from a social and political context where masculine hegemony has been institutionalized. Feminist scholars argue that notions of power, sovereignty, autonomy, anarchy, security and the levels of analysis typology in International Relations are inseparable from the gender division of public and private spheres institutionalized within and across states. These concepts are identified specifically with masculinity and men's experiences and knowledge derived from an exclusive, male-dominated public sphere. Theorizing, as Burchill and Linklater state in the Introduction to this volume (Chapter 1), is 'the process by which we give meaning to an allegedly objectified world "out there"'. A feminist analysis reveals that the International Relations conceptual framework is but one, partial, attempt to make sense of world politics.

The discursive separation of domestic and international politics, together with the neo-realist aversion to domestic explanations for inter-state relations, obscures the prior gendered public–private division within states and masculine aversion to the latter's association with emotion, subjectivity, reproduction, the body, femininity and women. Both explanatory and constitutive theories of world politics overlook this private sphere because it is submerged within domestic politics and state forms (Walker 1992; Sylvester 1994a). The ontology of realist International Relations theory conceives the private sphere like the international sphere as a natural realm of disorder. The lower being, represented by women, the body and the anarchical system, must be subordinated to the higher being, represented by men, the rational mind and state authority. Jean Elshtain (1992) insists that the realist narrative of International Relations, in particular, pivots on this public–private division and its essentialist construction of femininity and masculinity as the respective cause of disorder and bringer of order.

For feminist analysts, the independence of domestic politics from international politics and the separation of public from private spheres cannot be the basis for a disciplinary boundary, since anarchy outside and gender hierarchy at home may be mutually-reinforcing. Throughout modern history, for example, women have been told that they will receive equality with men, after the war, after liberation, after the national economy has been rebuilt and so on: but after all of these 'outside' forces have been conquered, the commonplace demand is for things to go back to normal, and women to a subordinate place. As Cynthia Enloe (1989: 131) has observed 'states depend upon particular constructions of the domestic and private spheres in order to foster smooth[er] relationships at the public/international level'.

Feminists seek to theorize the relationships between gender relations, domestic and international politics despite International Relations' conventional levels of analysis that treats the individual, the state and the international system as distinct analytic units. This theoretical schema has become 'the most influential way of classifying explanations of war, and indeed of organising our understanding of inter-state relations in general' (Walker 1987: 67). Gender analysis undermines the divisions between the individual, state and international system by showing how each level is preconditioned by an image of rational man that excludes women and femininity (Tickner 1992; Sylvester 1994a; True 2008b).

Kenneth Waltz (1959: 188) applies the analogy between man and the state as proof of the hostile reality that he observes in the anarchical system as a whole: '[a]mong men as among states there is no automatic adjustment of interests. In the absence of a supreme authority there is then the constant possibility that conflicts will be solved by force'. Reductionist arguments explaining international conflict through conceptions of 'evil' human nature are frequently used in realist International Relations. Hans Morgenthau argued that the objective 'national interest' is rooted deeply in human nature and thus, in the actions of statesmen (Tickner 1988). Even the neo-realist Waltz (1959: 238), who prefers systemic explanations, embraces Alexander Hamilton's polemic set forth in the 1788 *Federalist Papers*: 'to presume a lack of hostile motives among states is to forget that men are ambitious, vindictive and rapacious'. From a feminist perspective, the implication of this man/state analogy is that rationality is equated with men's behaviour and the state as a rational actor bears a male-masculine identity (Sylvester 1990).

Feminists theorize the state as the centralized, main organizer of gendered power, working in part through the construction of public–private, production–reproduction boundaries (Connell 1990). It is not a 'coherent identity subordinate to the gaze of a single interpretative centre' as in neo-realist theories (Ashley 1988: 230). This notion reflects, rather, an idealized model of hegemonic masculinity and the patriarchal foundations of the state form. International Relations feminists argue that the state manipulates gender identities for its own internal unity and external legitimacy. Men are socialized to identify with constructions of masculinity which emphasize autonomy, male superiority, fraternity, strength, public protector roles and ultimately the bearing of arms. Women, on the other hand, are taught to defer, as wives and daughters, to the protection and stronger will of men, while providing the private emotional, economic and social support systems for masculine war activities. Moreover, feminist analysts view states as implicated in a range of forms of violence against women. For instance, the liberal state supports inter-personal gender-based and state-sanctioned violence through its stance of non-intervention in the private sphere, and its legal definition of rape from a male standpoint, which assumes that the absence of overt coercion implies female consent despite prevailing gender hierarchies (Pateman 1989; Peterson 1992b: 46–7).

In conventional International Relations theories, the rational, self-interested actor is a metaphor for state behaviour in an anarchical international system. Abstracted from a place in time and space, from particular prejudices, interests and needs, feminist theorists claim that the model of rational man cannot be generalized: he is a masculine agent derived from a context of unequal gender relations, where women's primary care work supports the development of autonomous male selves, making cooperation for them a daily reality and relieving men of these necessities. Consequently, the vast majority of people, social relationships, and institutions that cannot be interpreted as coherent rational selves are thus denied agency in international politics. Feminist analysts Grant and Newland (1991: 1) argue that the study of International Relations is 'constructed overwhelmingly by men working with mental models of human activity seen through a[n elite] male eye and apprehended through a[n elite] male sensibility'.

Some feminists posit an alternative *female* model of agency as connected, interdependent and interrelated (Gilligan 1982; Tronto 1989). However, most feminist International Relations scholars are sceptical of positing a nurturing account of feminine nature to correct the gender bias of Waltzian man/state (cf. Elshtain 1985: 41). International Relations feminists search for richer, alternative models of agency that take account of both production and reproduction, redefine rationality to be less exclusive and instrumental and respect human relationships (across all levels) as well as the interdependence of human beings with nature (Tickner 1991: 204–6). For example, some scholars posit a feminist ethic of care as an ontological claim about 'the central role of care and other relational moral practices in the everyday lives of people in all settings' rather than an epistemological stance (Robinson 2006: 225). Other feminist scholars look for emancipatory models of agency at the margins – among Third World women and human rights activists (Ackerly 2000). Feminist alternatives to International Relations' levels of analysis reject universal abstractions. They demand greater historical and cultural contextualization in order to reflect more adequately the complexity and indeterminacy of human agency and social structure.

Feminist scholars use gender analysis to uncover the bias of core International Relations concepts such as power and security. Such bias not only limits their theoretical application, it has detrimental consequences for the practice of international relations. *Power* in International Relations theory has been almost exclusively conceived of as 'power-over': the power to force or influence someone to do something that they otherwise would not (Jaquette 1984). An individual's power rests on his or her autonomy from the power of others. In this view, power cannot be shared nor can power be readily increased by relationships with others in the context of interdependent or common interests. The accumulation of power capabilities and resources, according to Morgenthau, is both an end and a means to security. In the context of an anarchical state system which is interpreted as necessarily hostile and self-helping, states that act 'rationally' instinctively deduce their national interests as their maximization of power-over other states. The Waltzian notion of power is only mildly different. Waltz conceptualizes power as a means for the survival of a state but not as an end-goal in itself, to the extent that a stable, bipolar, balance of power configuration exists between states. Consequently, in the Waltzian world-view, the only power that really matters is the power-capability of 'Great Powers', whose bipolar or multipolar arrangement brings limited order to an anarchic international realm.

Tickner (1988) shows how the realist concept of power is based on masculine norms through her analysis of Hans Morgenthau's six principles of power politics. It reflects male self-development and objectivist ways of knowing in patriarchal societies where men's citizenship and personal authority has traditionally relied on their head-of-household power-over women's sexuality and labour. This concept of power also rests on a particularly gender-specific notion of autonomous agency that makes human relationships and affective connections invisible. If the human world is exhaustively defined by such gendered constructions of 'power-over', as in realist accounts, feminists ask, how do children get reared, collective movements mobilize and everyday life reproduced? Sylvester (1992: 32–8) argues that it is incoherent to posit self-help as the essential feature of world politics when many 'relations international' go on within households and other institutions. These relations include diplomatic negotiations, trade regimes and the socialization of future citizens, which are not based on self-help alone, but which take interdependent relations between self and other as the norm. The neo-realist International Relations' assumption that men and states are 'like units' presents power politics as a self-fulfilling prophecy.

Power politics, however, is a gendered and, therefore, biased account of world politics because its conceptualization of power depends upon the particular not the universal agency of rational man.

For feminists, power is a complex phenomenon of creative social forces which shape our personal gendered identities as men, women and national citizens rather than just the deployment of brute force. As such, Enloe (1997) argues that paying attention to women can expose how much 'power' it takes to maintain the international political system in its present form. To understand the nature of power at the international or global levels, feminists together with other constitutive theorists urge that we study the domestic and transnational social relations, which not only support the foreign policies of states but actually constitute the state as the territorial authority with a monopoly over the use of legitimate force.

Security as conventionally conceived in International Relations is also a gender-biased concept when seen from a feminist perspective. Rather than bringing security to individual women, men and children, it is equated with a situation of stability provided by militaristic states whose nuclear proliferation, ironically, is seen to prevent total war (if not the many 'small wars'). Security is examined only in the context of the presence and absence of war, because the threat of war is considered endemic to the sovereign state-system. This reactive notion of security is zero-sum and by definition 'national'. It presupposes what Peterson (1992a: 47–8) terms a 'sovereignty contract' established between states. According to this imaginary contract the use of military force is a necessary evil to prevent the outside – difference, irrationality, anarchy and potential conflict – from conquering the inside of homogeneous, rational and orderly states. States, in this feminist analysis, are a kind of 'protection racket' that by their very existence as bully 'protectors' create threats outside and charge for the insecurity that they bring to their 'protected' population 'inside'. In the name of protection, states demand the sacrifice of gendered citizens, including that of soldiers – in most cases men – through military conscription and mothers or families who devote their lives to socializing these dutiful citizens for the state/nation (Elshtain 1992; Goldstein 2001).

Feminists use gender analysis to critique gendered identities and security discourses (see Shepherd 2008). Employing a feminist approach, Helen Kinsella (2005) explores how the ostensibly gender-neutral distinction between civilians and combatants in the international laws of war is produced upon gender discourses that naturalize sex and gender difference. This categorical distinction moreover, has gendered implications: It treats male civilians in war as always already combatants, and women civilians in war as always already victims (2005: 253). She argues that neither women nor men are protected by the gendered immunity principle that extends from the laws of war. Moreover, the gender stereotypes on which the just war tradition is based 'affect the meaning of gender and the subordination of women outside wartime' re-inscribing gender hegemonies within domestic (familial) and international (civilized) orders (Barnett and Duvall 2005: 31).

In the post-9/11 global 'war on terror' feminist scholars have deconstructed American discourses of security that looked for 'manly men' to protect 'us' from 'them' and blamed feminism and homosexuality for weakening the resolve of the West to stamp out Islamic fundamentalism and other 'threats' (Bar On 2003: 456; Agathangelou and Ling 2004). Feminists also scrutinized the gendered discourses in the Islamic fundamentalist groups behind the terrorist acts of violence against the West and among the US occupation forces in Iraq (Kaufman-Osborn 2005). Differences in attitudes about gender and sexuality divide Western from the non-Western world (Norris and Ingelhart 2003), and are deployed to incite and to justify violence. The statements of Osama Bin Laden and the diary account left behind by the 9/11 terrorists suggest that their actions were directed not merely against the West but against the Western gender identities perceived to be so threatening to their vision of an Islamic and/or pan Arabic culture (Tickner 2002). When Islamic fundamentalists deride the depraved morals of the West, referring to sexual equality and women's rights norms, they heighten the potential for conflict between non-Western and Western states (True 2004).

Gender analysis reveals masculine identities and states, domestic and international violence, to be inextricably related. The limited security they provide allows them to consolidate their authority over other men and states, but importantly also over women and territory, on which they depend for a source of exploitable resources, and for the socio-cultural and biological reproduction of power relations. Paying attention to women's as well as men's experiences in peace and war, feminist analysts urge that security must be redefined. In particular, what is called 'national security' is profoundly endangering to human survival and sustainable communities (Tickner 1992). State military apparatuses create their own security dilemmas by purporting androcentric control and power-over to be the name of the game; a game we are persuaded to play in order to achieve the absolute and relative gains of state security.

Concepts such as 'rationality', 'security' and 'power' could be building blocks of explanation for a feminist theory of international politics (Tickner 1991). There is nothing inherent in the terms which suggests that they must be discarded, rather it is their narrow, gendered meanings in mainstream International Relations theory and practice which is problematic for feminist analysts. Runyan and Peterson (1991: 70) claim that dichotomous thinking – inside–outside, sovereignty–anarchy, domestic–international – prevents International Relations theory from being able to 'conceptualise, explain, or deliver the very things it says it is all about – security, power and sovereignty'. For International Relations feminists, these conceptual opposites reproduce the self-fulfilling security dilemma and reinforce masculine power politics, thus limiting the possibility for creating a more just and equal world order.

Normative feminism

Normative feminism reflects on the process of International Relations theorizing as part of a normative agenda for global change. 'All forms of feminist theorising are normative, in the sense that they help us to question certain meanings and interpretations in IR theory' (Sylvester 2002: 248). Feminists are self-consciously explicit about the position from which they are theorizing, how they enter the International Relations field and go about their research (Ackerly and True 2009). They view their social and political context and subjectivity as part of theoretical explanation. Gender is a *transformative* category from a normative perspective not because we can deconstruct or do away with it, but because once we understand it as a social construction we can transform how it works at all levels of social and political life.

Feminist empirical research and gender analysis are important contributions, but they are only starting points for feminist goals of transforming global social hierarchies (Persram 1994; Ship 1994; Hutchings 2000; Robinson 2006). Normative feminist theorists bring the experiences of women's activism to bear on debates about international ethics, humanitarian aid and intervention and human rights instruments (Cochran 1999; Robinson 1999; Ackerly 2000; Hutchings 2004). Care ethics is one example of how feminist theory can inform ethical guidelines for humanitarian intervention, multilateral peacekeeping, development aid, foreign security policy, and human rights protection among other practical global issues and dilemmas (see Hutchings 2000: 122–3). Joan Tronto (2006), for example, analyses the normative framework supporting multilateral peacekeeping from a feminist perspective. She stresses that the shift from the right to intervene in a sovereign state to a responsibility to protect citizens not protected by their own state, as a shift from liberal to care ethics, from the masculine assumption of an autonomous self – sovereign man or state – to the assumption of a relational self with responsibilities to others.

Linklater (Chapter 4) argues that the prospects for moral and political universals and for respect for difference are central to the debate among normative international theorists. Seen in this context, the different feminist epistemologies most commonly identified in International Relations' writings as feminist empiricism, feminist standpoint and feminist post-modernism are not discreet or contradictory approaches to gender-sensitive knowledge in International Relations (see Keohane 1989b; Weber 1994). On the contrary, these epistemologies are inter-related feminist challenges to the masculine universalism of science that suggest feminist alternatives for including or embracing different forms of knowledge (McClure 1992: 359). Feminist empiricism, standpoint and post-modernism share a *normative* struggle to sustain connections to practical feminist politics and the concrete workings of gendered power.

Feminist scholars problematize the defining dichotomies of the International Relations field that are reinforced through their association with the masculine-feminine gender dichotomy: for example, the association of women and femininity with peace, cooperation, subjectivism and 'soft' domestic politics and men and masculinity with war, competition, objectivity and 'hard' international politics (Elshtain 1987; Sylvester 1987, 1994a, 2002). They question how these gender hierarchies are reproduced in International Relations theories and how they serve to naturalize other forms of power and domination in world politics. From a normative feminist perspective attentive to the politics of knowledge, gender difference is not merely about the relations between masculine and feminine identities, it is about how and from what position in the hierarchy we can know.

Cynthia Enloe's research radically subverts conventional ways of knowing and doing International Relations. To make sense of international politics, she analyses the (extra)ordinary lives of women from below – which the history of the discipline would tell us is the least likely place for 'high politics'. Enloe reveals constructions of masculinity and femininity at the heart of international processes. She considers the withdrawal of Russian mothers' support for the Soviet army, due to the gross and unaccountable sacrifice of their sons in the USSR-Afghanistan war, as one of many personal expressions of gendered power that led to the delegitimization of the Soviet regime and the end of the Cold War (Enloe 1994). Her standpoint epistemology encourages us to broaden our ways of knowing 'the truth' of international politics, and to consider from whose perspective inter-state 'legitimate' force is the most significant expression of violence and potent explanation for war.

However, if asking questions about women's location in world politics, addressed by empirical feminist International Relations, is dependent upon bringing gender in as an analytical construct in order to account for the patterns of women's marginalization at every level of state and global politics then, normative feminism questions the binary concept of gender. The mutually exclusive opposition of masculinity and femininity is not 'the essence from which social organization can be explained' (Scott 1988: 2); rather, it is a social construction that must itself be explained before it can be transformed. While analytical feminist theories created the category of gender to reveal the social construction of women's oppression, normative feminist theories contextualize gender as an analytical device that harbours its own exclusions and, like International Relations theories, must also be critically interrogated (Sylvester 2002).

Since the 1990s there has been some controversy over the application of gender in International Relations, and across feminist studies. In International Relations, two main criticisms of gender as a concept have arisen. The first criticism is that the analytic use of gender masks other forms of oppression prevalent in global politics. Speaking to a Western women's studies' audience in the 1980s from a Third World feminist standpoint, Chandra Mohanty (1991) criticized Western feminism for constructing the victimized 'Third World woman' based on universal, Western assumptions of gender, emptied of all historical, cultural and geographical specificity, including realities of race and class oppression. As in the adage, 'the master's tools won't bring down the master's house', Mohanty made the point that Western categories cannot be used to challenge the imposition of Western categories and imperialist structures in non-Western societies.

The implication of the Third World feminist challenge for feminist International Relations is that a universal concept of gender cannot be applied globally. Indeed, if, as feminist scholars argue, gender relations are culturally and historically constructed, then it also follows that they cannot be the same everywhere. International Relations feminists seek to understand gender constructions at the global level and how they shape myriad local gender discourses and norms that have impacts on women and men's lives (Miller 1998; Baines 1999: 251; Prugl 2000).

Recognizing the potential for western imperialism when universal categories of 'woman' or 'man' are deployed, feminist scholarship explores a dynamic intersectional relationship between the global political economy, the state and culturally, geographically race- and class-specific gender relations (Chan-Tierberghien 2004; Agathangelou and Ling 2004). Feminist researchers analysing the global sex trade, for example, address this complexity of global power relations (Mackie 2001; Whitworth 2001; Berman 2003; Agathangelou 2004). They explore the specific constructions of gender and sexuality in the sending and receiving countries, which in turn depend upon particular constructions of class, ethnicity, nationality, and race. Feminist scholars begin their analysis of the sex trade with the observation that women are the core labourers in this multibillion dollar global business. However, as they engage in further research, drawing on non-elite knowledge and practice (such as that of the sex workers themselves) they are led to an understanding of the multiple and interlocking nature of oppressions, and of women's agency even in situations of physical coercion and other, more structural, forms of violence.

Normative feminism recognizes that there is no feminist 'high ground' from which to theorize about international relations. Sylvester (1994a: 12) argues that 'all places to speak and act as women are problematic', because they are socially and historically constructed and exclude other identities. She destabilizes the feminist standpoint position that women's experience can constitute the ground(s) for a more critical and universal theory of international relations, in favour of multiple feminist standpoints that question the discipline's hegemonic knowledge. Feminism, 'is the research posture of standing in many locations, illuminating important relations and practices darkened by the long shadows of official IR, of painting International Relations differently . . . Feminism has many types and shifting forms. It is non-uniform and non-consensual; it is a complex matter with many internal debates' (Sylvester 2002: 269). International Relations feminism demonstrates that it is possible to do research and make normative claims, despite there being no given and many different ontological starting points for theories of international relations.

Feminist identity and solidarity are problematic insofar as achieving feminism's normative goal of ungendering social and political relations depends on politically organizing on the basis of gender 'as women'. Contrary to the tenets of 1970s radical feminisms, there is no easily realized, readily mobilized, global sisterhood. Rather, feminist cooperation, as Christina Gabriel and Laura Macdonald (1994) show in their analysis of women's transnational organizing in the context of NAFTA, and Laurel Weldon (2006) reveals in her analysis of the global movement to eradicate violence against women, must be created by acknowledging and confronting, not ignoring, the differences among women. The very tension between positivist and post-positivist epistemologies that has divided contemporary theorists, including International Relations theorists, is the source of feminisms' theoretical dynamism and political relevancy. International Relations feminism acknowledges the lack of a foundational collective subject 'woman', and a relatively bounded realm of the international or the political, as well as the need to make a difference to women's daily lives, with the realization that gendered categories have historically served to marginalize many women and men.

Empirical and analytical feminist approaches challenge given ways of thinking about and doing International Relations, especially dominant rationalist approaches. But feminism does more than this. Feminist questions about why agents – statesmen and soldiers – typically discussed in International Relations theories tend to be men leads us to consider the normative status of International Relations, including the gendered identity of the knowers and the intersection of these identities with particular, so-called 'objective' ways of knowing that have been institutionalized in the International Relations field (see Ackerly and True 2008). Introducing the world-views of women who are differently situated in the present world order exemplifies the normative feminist perspective that there are multiple standpoints from which to view global politics, and that each may reveal diverse realities and relationships.

Conclusion

The three forms of feminism discussed in this chapter – empirical feminism, analytical feminism and normative feminism – all suggest that the theory and practice of international relations has suffered from its neglect of feminist perspectives. Feminists argue that conventional International Relations theories distort our knowledge of both 'relations' and the ongoing transformations of the 'international'. These International Relations theories overlook the political significance of gendered divisions of public and private institutionalized within and by the state and state-system and, as a result, ignore the political activities and activism of women: whether they are mobilizing for war, protesting state abrogation of their rights or organizing for the international recognition of women's human rights. Moreover, the objectivist approach of much International Relations theory produces relatively superficial knowledge and tends to reproduce the dichotomies which have come to demarcate the field. These dichotomies are gendered: they define power as power-over 'others', autonomy as reaction rather than relational, international politics as the negation of domestic, 'soft' politics and the absence of women, and objectivity as the lack of (feminine or feminized) subjectivity. In sum, approaches to international relations that fail to take gender seriously overlook critical aspects of world order and abandon a crucial opening for effecting change.

Feminist International Relations contributes to expanding and strengthening existing theories and analyses including liberal, critical theory, post-modern, constructivist and green theories of international relations. As well as introducing new questions and political phenomena to the traditionally narrowly-defined study of International Relations, feminist research has re-conceptualized non-feminist research questions on state behaviour, international norms and law, and global civil society, and adapted non-feminist methodologies such as quantitative analysis, frame analysis and institutional analysis for feminist purposes. Engaging with other International Relations theories has allowed feminism to contest existing criteria for what counts as good scholarship and to alert proponents of non-feminist theories to the illuminating effects that can come from viewing global social and political processes from a gender perspective.

This chapter began by asking, how do feminist perspectives help us understand and improve international relations? Addressing that question it explored the empirical, analytical and normative contributions of feminism. Feminists in and outside the field of International Relations are continually adding to our empirical and normative knowledge, while advancing the tools of gender analysis. But it is the feminist commitment to self-reflexivity, to attending to the power of epistemology, of boundaries and relationships in the very practice of theorizing and research that contributes most to the study of International Relations (Ackerly, Stern and True 2006). This critical feminist methodology rather than any single empirical approach or theory makes feminist International Relations distinctive among International Relations theories. Efforts to forge a unitary neo-feminist approach (Caprioli 2004) or non-feminist gender standpoint (Carpenter 2002) seek to mainstream gender analysis without this self-reflexive methodology. Such attempts to use gender to empirically and analytically examine aspects of international relations without being 'tainted' by normative content may be fruitful from neo-realist or neo-liberal perspectives, but they hinder efforts to advance feminist perspectives on international relations.

International Relations theories have been shown to have major blindspots with respect to global social and political change. This conceptual blindness frequently leads to empirical blindness. It is not surprising then that International Relations analysts are often caught off-guard by events in world politics. Clearly, a re-thinking of the basic assumptions of this discipline remains urgent if scholars want to understand global politics in the twenty-first century. Feminist scholarship of the sort reviewed in this chapter offers a way out of the darkness. If scholars want to gain fresh insights into the dynamics of world order, they need to take into account gendered social processes and marginalized subjects. Feminist perspectives reveal that, in many instances, the sites of global power and transformation are not just the domain of political and economic elites; such sites also exist in the invisible, underappreciated nooks and crannies of societies. Traditional expectations about the nature of states and international relations are both disrupted when a gender perspective is brought to bear. Feminism helps us to recognize power shifts within nation-states that have ramifications for world order. Surely, observing and interpreting such power shifts as they arise in a variety of global and local venues constitute core functions of International Relations scholarship.

11 | **Green Theory**

MATTHEW PATERSON

The past 40 years of global politics have been punctuated by cycles of concern about the basic sustainability of the trajectory on which human societies are headed, cycles which have been provoked by particular environmental scares but which have frequently been articulated as presaging a more systemic crisis. We moved thus from concerns about pesticides in the early 1960s, to those about 'limits to growth' and the 'population bomb' by the early 1970s. In a later cycle in the 1980s we moved from regional concerns about acid rain or nuclear fallout to 'global' concerns like ozone depletion, deforestation, biodiversity loss, or climate change. In the present cycle, climate change has again loomed large and is increasingly understood through a lens of its potential to cause industrial civilization to 'collapse'. As a cycle of concern returns, the systemic character of the crisis becomes more apparent, and the implications for the way that global politics is organized become more evident. Just as the most recent example, the rapid emergence of crises over food prices and scarcity provoked by the pursuit of biofuels, themselves ostensibly promoted as a response to climate change, suggest the complex and systemic character of the global socio-ecological crisis. While often this calls attention to the contradictions between the organization of global politics and the ecological predicament societies face (however such contradictions are conceptualized), there are also glimmers of changes in political practice and perhaps even structure, which may prefigure some more substantial transformations.

Theorists have approached the political character of the ecological crisis in a variety of ways. Not all accept that such a crisis may produce profound systemic change; indeed not all accept that an overall 'crisis', understood as a set of interlocking problems that require a 'holistic' response, even exists. But the *raison d'être* of this chapter is that such radical accounts – which I will group under the heading 'Green theory' – deserve to be taken seriously, and thus the potential for ecological crises to reshape global politics should be thought through. Indeed, as one strand of ecological IR theory now suggests (Eckersley 2004), as much as engaging in normative theory as to how global politics *ought* to be reshaped to meet the goal of sustainability, the challenge is to understand political transformations that are *already* under way. It should also be understood that for such accounts, the ambition of Green theory goes way beyond the narrow understanding of 'environmental issues'. The classic questions of International Relations – the search for peace, the operations of power politics, the question of global governance, normative questions such as global justice – all undergo a thorough rethinking in the light of the ecological challenge.

Jennifer Clapp and Peter Dauvergne (2005) provide us with a useful way to understand the range of theoretical approaches to global ecological politics. They distinguish between four principal variants of thought: free-market environmentalism, institutionalism, bioenvironmentalism, and social ecology. (I should say at the outset that while I think their categories are very useful, I apply them here with a number of differences to their accounts of each approach. I will also use the term Greens (with a capital G) to refer to proponents of both bioenvironmentalist and social green arguments, since these two types of arguments frequently coexist among activists in Green movements.) Anyway, these extend distinctions frequently made (e.g. Dobson 1990) between environmentalism and ecologism, and provide considerably more nuance about the variants of environmental ideology. I will however say little about free-market environmentalism, not because it is not important in the field of environmental ideology (indeed its practitioners dominate much of global environmental political practice), but rather because its proponents have nothing to say specifically about international relations. The key debate then is between institutionalists, who tend to eschew discussion of any broad 'environmental crisis', and focus on how international institutions deal with specific issue areas, and bioenvironmentalists and social greens, who insist on such a crisis and the need for political transformation to deal effectively with it. The former provide the bulk of the literature within IR on environmental questions – if you read articles on the environment in journals such as *International Organization*, or even the main journal in the field *Global Environmental Politics*, a good majority will be written from an institutionalist perspective. This chapter starts with a discussion of institutionalist approaches to global environmental politics, before moving on to what I argue are two variants of a properly Green approach to global politics.

Theorizing environment within international relations

From the earliest accounts of the global political character of environmental problems, they have been understood on the one hand as problems of collective action, and on the other through lenses of 'security'. Perhaps the founding metaphor for both of these is that of Garrett Hardin's 'Tragedy of the Commons' (1968). This suggests that the structural incentives of actors (states) operating in relation to open access resources (Hardin's misnamed commons) both lead to the over-use and abuse of those resources, and impede collective efforts to mitigate such abuse. Hardin's argument can also be seen as a basis for the notion of 'environmental security', which I leave largely aside here for reasons of space. The actors themselves in the situation he describes (and by extension, in relation to a whole range of 'real world' environmental problems) come to view both the environmental problem itself (land degradation) and the actions of the other actors as a threat to the security of their livelihood. Out of this observation, as well as out of more obviously problematic accounts of a 'population bomb' (Ehrlich 1968, for an updated version; Kaplan 1994), a whole industry has emerged focusing on 'environmental security', specifically examining various sorts of environmental change, notably resource shortages (water, oil) but also climate change, soil erosion, as sources either of interstate conflict or of social instability which then generates international instability. Much of this literature is clearly realist in inspiration; thus there are no specific ecological-theoretical insights to be developed about global politics. Some (notably Dalby 2002) do develop specific claims from a notion of ecological (as opposed to environmental) security that contribute to a rethinking of global politics from an ecological point of view, points I will elaborate below (for a broad selection of writings on this topic, see Myers 1993; Homer-Dixon 1999; Deudney and Matthew 1999; Barnett 2000; Klare 2001; Dalby 2002).

Hardin's argument proceeds from an ideal-type of a village commons, where herders from the village have the right to graze cows. The land can only support a fixed number of cows, but each herder has an incentive to graze more than their share on the land. They gain the income from the extra cow, while the damages are shared across all the herders. Hardin's initial motivation is to show that there is no technological solution to this problem (indeed, new technologies may simply accelerate the rate of destruction), but that the problem is rather structural – in the authority structure over the land which permits open access to all, and in the incentives herders face which lead to them over-using resources.

Hardin's conclusion, and that of some following his logic, is that the tragedy is insurmountable without an overarching change in the authority structure. William Ophuls (1977) elaborated this logic most fully, arguing explicitly for a world state with sufficient power to impose ecological restraint on actors across the world. His reasoning was precisely that the logic of collective action elaborated by Hardin would lead to ruin.

Institutionalist accounts of environmental politics

Hardin's claim is actually significantly milder. Having argued that 'freedom in a commons brings ruin to all' (Hardin 1968: 1244), his other catchphrase in the article is his call for 'mutual coercion, mutually agreed upon' (Hardin 1968: 1247). While much has been made of his term 'coercion', leading to him being called (along with Ophuls and others) 'eco-authoritarian', the logic of his claim is also shared by the liberal institutionalist school in IR and the way it analyses international environmental politics. (Note that this is a branch of liberal IR theory that differs from those emphasised in Scott Burchill's chapter (Chapter 3) on that approach. I use institutionalist to refer to approaches across the social sciences which emphasize the role that social and political institutions play in shaping the behaviour of actors and in mediation the outcomes such behaviour produces (for a general overview, see Hall and Taylor 1996). In IR, this translates to the liberal institutionalist perspective most closely associated with Robert Keohane (1989a). I leave out the 'liberal' qualifier in what follows, but when I use the term institutionalist I use it to refer to this perspective in IR.)

Hardin's logic mirrors much analysis of what are more often called 'collective action problems' across the social sciences. These refer to situations where actors recognize the necessity of acting in concert with others in the pursuit of specific goals, but where such collaboration may not be easy to achieve, for many of the reasons Hardin identifies. Collective action problems are usually understood through the lens of rational choice theory – that actors pursue their individual preferences in a systematic fashion.

In rational choice terms, Hardin's tragedy of the commons is similar to a game of Prisoner's Dilemma (PD). In that game, where (classically) two prisoners are held by the police and offered more lenient sentences in return for information which will lead to the conviction of their colleague for a more serious crime, the best outcome is that both keep quiet (cooperate) but in fact each is likely to spill the beans (defect). Similarly the best outcome in Hardin's commons is that all limit themselves to 10 cows (cooperate) but the dominant dynamic is that each puts an extra cow on the land (defects), thus undermining the interests of each.

Institutionalists argue that a number of features of 'real world' situations mean that such catastrophic outcomes are less likely than Hardin would anticipate. Specifically, the PD metaphor suggests that there are only two actors, they only play the game once, and cannot communicate with each other. It is not hard to understand how if these conditions are relaxed, cooperation might in general become more feasible. If the game is played over and over, actors can generate strategies to elicit cooperation from the others (a process outlined classically by Taylor 1976, or Axelrod 1984). If the actors can communicate with each other directly, they may then also be able to build the trust and confidence that each will cooperate. The numbers question is more ambiguous – while some increases in the number of actors may help cooperation, as actors may be able to use a third party to get round a stalemate between just two, once you get to large numbers of actors, the transaction costs of simply negotiating become high, while the possibilities of miscommunication and lack of confidence also increase.

On the basis of these arguments, institutionalists suggest that (a) the possibilities of cooperation are significantly greater than that allowed by Hardin (or in IR, by realists) and (b) international organizations and institutions may therefore play a significant role in fostering cooperation (see Young 1994). The concept of an international regime (Krasner 1983) is the central concept here elucidating research on the consequences of this – the development of a set of interlocking norms, rules, principles, which govern how states interact.

Not all institutionalists proceed from rational choice assumptions about state behaviour. Others, notably Oran Young (1989b, 1994, 1999a) or Peter Haas (1989, 2000) are more 'constructivist' in orientation (see Chapter 9). For Young, international institutions are constitutive of international politics, not simply the outcomes of state strategic interaction, and they build on each other – earlier institutions provide general norms which guide practice and thus create new norms, and so on. (The argument is also rather like the English School here (Chapter 4). For an account of international regimes that draws on environmental politics for its material and which explicitly compares institutionalist and English school approaches see Hurrell (1993, and for the same author's elaboration of environmental politics in English School terms, see Hurrell (2007: ch. 9).) At a most basic level, institutions construct not only how states interact, but also what states are. In addition, as Young shows (1989a) in the environmental field in particular, states face contradictory motivations and considerable ambiguity about outcomes, meaning that even if states could in other situations act according to the premises of rational choice theory, in this instance it is simply impossible. Finally, non-rationalist institutionalists also suggest that environmental regimes involve novel actors and processes, specifically concerning the role of scientists and scientific discourse in regime formation; the origin of 'cognitivist' accounts of international regimes is in analysis of environmental politics (Haas 1990, 1992).

To simplify things somewhat, institutionalists tend to ask one of two types of question. First, they ask what affects how regimes are established, to explain why regimes form in some circumstances and not others. Some of this literature is pitched at a broad theoretical level, typically outlining a three-fold account of theories based on power (realist explanations), interests (liberal, rational choice explanations) or knowledge ('cognitive', or constructivist explanations) of regime formation (e.g. Young 1994: 84–98; Vogler 1992; Hansenclever, Mayer and Rittberger 1996), for an application to the ozone and climate cases, see Rowlands 1994). Others (e.g. Hahn and Richards 1989, Young 1989a) focus rather on a series of more discrete factors, such as the number of actors, the problem structure of the issue at hand, the question of uncertainty, or notions of fairness.

Second, institutionalists attempt to explain the effectiveness of regimes (e.g. Bernauer 1995; Victor, Raustiala and Skolnikoff 1998; Young 1999b; Mitchell 2006). Under what conditions do they contribute to successful responses to the problem at hand? Haas (1990, 1992), Haas, Keohane and Levy (1993) outline three sorts of key elements, what they call the three Cs – concern, the contractual environment and capacity. That is, international institutions can contribute to the articulation of concern about particular problems and an understanding of their implications, they can reduce transaction costs and help identify possible sites of interstate agreement, and they can help states build their capacity to respond to environmental challenges, for example through the building of monitoring capacity. Most studies agree with these claims, but nevertheless a further link is necessary in order to deal with the normative question of effectiveness.

For our purposes here, two aspects of the institutionalist literature are worth emphasizing. First, when discussing the effectiveness of environmental regimes, analysts often withdraw to a more limited account of effectiveness – for example, along the lines of 'does the institution affect state behaviour?' or 'are emissions lower than they would have been without the institution?'. Asking the question 'have they contributed to a reversal of unsustainable trends?', would lead to a rather pessimistic assessment. Only in the ozone depletion case is a clear reversal of trends identifiable, with some more modest claims that could be made in the case of sulphur emissions and perhaps one or two other cases. More generally, as Princen eloquently establishes (2003, 2005), we have witnessed over the last 30 years an extraordinary process of cooperation and institution building, and *at the same time* a significant increase in the throughput of resources and pollution, and in corresponding environmental degradation. Returning to the starting metaphor, one could use this to suggest that Hardin's original logic was correct, that this is indeed a tragedy (in the sense, as he suggests, of a remorseless logic unfolding with its negative consequences). Alternatively, one could conclude that the problem has been mis-specified – that in fact the political origins of environmental problems are less to do with the problem of open-access resources, but rather have their origins in other causes. The bioenvironmentalists and social greens outlined below start with different analyses of the origins of environmental problems.

We could, however, take institutionalist conclusions in a different direction. Institutionalists start with the premise, shared with many perspectives in IR that international politics is to be characterized as a number of sovereign states interacting in an anarchic environment. But to the extent that environmental institution building becomes ever more complex, shaping more and more deeply state behaviour, increasingly involving a wide range of actors other than states, the utility of the international anarchy metaphor in explaining what happens declines. Institutionalists occasionally acknowledge this problem, and usually reject it, insisting that the world is still first and foremost an inter-state world (e.g. Young 1997). But at least the potential for what has become known as 'global environmental governance' to create possible post-sovereign politics exists (Paterson 2000: Chapter 7).

Beyond IR: Green politics and the challenge to world order

There are a number of limits to institutional analyses of global environmental politics. (For a fuller elaboration of these points, see Paterson 2002: Chapter 2.) The problem of establishing the ecological effectiveness of regimes is one, already alluded to. The limitation of focusing only on the interstate aspect of global politics, to the neglect of various phenomena (MNCs, global civil society, globalization, private governance, for example), is another. Most important perhaps is the lack of a sustained account of why environmental degradation occurs in the first place. Sometimes they deploy the metaphor of Hardin's tragedy of the commons (e.g. Vogler 1992: 118; Young 1994). But whereas these analyses tend to treat the metaphor in terms of obstacles to cooperation, Hardin developed it to explain the origins of environmental degradation. At other times, institutionalists offer a discussion of discrete, secular trends – in population, consumption, technology, individual behaviour (e.g. Choucri 1993; Homer-Dixon 1993). These however are treated as ad hoc explanations, and the phenomena are not considered as part of a broad structural whole – a set of imperatives for economic growth for example. The two perspectives elaborated below specifically start from a basis of insisting on this structural character of environmental degradation.

Perhaps most obviously however, if all there was to the study of global environmental politics was the institutionalist approach or the notion of environmental security, there would be little novel theoretically to say. All of the theoretical propositions entailed in the above discussion come from one or another variant of mainstream IR theory – realism, liberalism or constructivism in particular. However, a much more radical tradition exists in Green ideology, out of which a more distinctive Green theory of global politics can be fashioned. Clapp and Dauvergne (2005: 9–15) usefully distinguish between two broad types of radical approach to environmental politics – radical both in the sense that they properly try to 'get to the root of' the political origins of environmental degradation as suggested above, and in the more common sense usage of proposing far-reaching political changes in response to such degradation. They label proponents of these two approaches 'bioenvironmentalists' and 'social greens' respectively.

Bioenvironmentalism – authority, scale, and eco-centrism

Bioenvironmentalists tend to focus on the aggregate impact of human activity on the 'natural' environment. They couch their arguments in terms of a humanity-nature dualism, and that the objective is to reorganize human societies in order that they live 'in harmony' with nature. The approach is often developed in highly quantitative terms – in terms of increases in resource use, emissions levels, ecosystem tolerance, and so on. Key terms such as 'carrying capacity' and 'limits to growth' have been articulated principally within this framework. Both refer to an idea that the earth has definite biophysical limits in terms of the numbers of people and the level of economic activity that can be supported without undermining the life-support systems (water, air, etc) that the planet provides. Bioenvironmentalists suggest that two key trends in human societies – population growth and economic growth, both which are growing exponentially – are in the process of moving rapidly towards, or even going beyond those limits.

The classic study *The Limits to Growth* (Meadows, Randers and Behrens 1972) argued that the exponential economic and population growth of human societies was producing an interrelated series of crises. Exponential growth was producing a situation where the world was rapidly running out of resources to feed people or to provide raw material for continued industrial growth (exceeding *carrying capacity* and *productive capacity*), and simultaneously exceeding the *absorptive capacity* of the environment to assimilate the waste products of industrial production (Meadows, Randers and Behrens 1972; Dobson 1990: 15). Meadows, Randers and Behrens (1972) produced their arguments based on computer simulations of the trajectory of industrial societies. They predicted that, at current rates of growth, many raw materials would rapidly run out, pollution would quickly exceed the absorptive capacity of the environment, and human societies would experience 'overshoot and collapse' some time before 2100.

The details of their predictions have been fairly easily refuted. But it does not follow that their basic logic, that infinite growth in a finite system is impossible, is faulty. Most Greens have taken this principle to be a central plank of their position (e.g. Spretnak and Capra 1984; Trainer 1985; Porritt 1986). Dobson (1990: 74–80) suggests there are three arguments that are important here. First, technological solutions will not work – they may postpone the crisis but cannot prevent it occurring at some point. Second, the exponential nature of growth means that 'dangers stored up over a relatively long period of time can very suddenly have a catastrophic effect' (Dobson 1990: 74). Finally, the problems associated with growth are all inter-related. Simply dealing with them issue by issue will mean that there are important knock-on effects from issue to issue; solving one pollution problem alone may simply change the medium through which pollution is carried, or the scale over which it extends, not reduce pollution overall.

The idea of 'ecological footprints' (Wackernagel and Rees 1996) is a more recent version of this type of argument. Many analysts argue on this basis that human societies have already gone beyond the limits of the planet to absorb the impacts of human activity without irreversible damage. For example the WWF's *Living Planet Report* (Loh and Wackernagel 2004) argues that we are already in a situation of 'ecological debt', using more of the planet's resources than can be replenished. (For elaborations of the data in these reports, updated periodically, see the WWF's website at http://www.panda.org/news_facts/publications/living_planet_report/index.cfm, accessed 6 February 2008.)

Politically speaking, the bioenvironmentalist approach tends to go in one of three directions. One possibility is that the logic requires highly authoritarian solutions to environmental problems. As noted above, Hardin's logic has an authoritarian reading, and his metaphor was used to generate an argument that centralized global political structures would be needed to force changes in behaviour to reach sustainability (e.g. Hardin 1974; Ophuls 1977). In some versions, this involved the adoption of what were called 'lifeboat ethics' (Hardin 1974), where ecological scarcity meant that rich countries would have to practice triage on a global scale – to 'pull up the ladder behind them'. This argument, largely an ecological version of the world government proposals of 'Idealist' versions of liberal internationalism (see Chapter 3) has, however, been for the most part rejected by Greens.

Others suggest that authoritarianism may be required, but reject the idea that this can be on a global scale. The vision here is for small-scale, tightly knit communities run on hierarchical, conservative lines with self-sufficiency in their use of resources (*The Ecologist* 1972; Heilbroner 1974). It shares with the above position the idea that it is freedom and egoism which has caused the environmental crisis, and that these tendencies need to be curbed to produce sustainable societies.

A second type of political response to environmental degradation from this perspective is one focusing on the question of scale. There is a spatial dimension to the world-government proposals, but the spatial character of environmental problems does not necessarily lead to proposals for world government or authoritarianism. Some bioenvironmentalists tend to argue for a position known as bioregionalism (e.g. Sale 1980). Here, the argument for 'living within nature's limits' takes the form of suggesting that the spatial character of ecosystems should determine the spatial scale of social, political and economic activity. Particularly important is water, such that watersheds become the key spatial category.

But the most common spatial argument by bioenvironmentalists is to argue for radical decentralization of power. This is the position O'Riordan long ago termed the 'anarchist solution' (1981: 303–7). Most Greens argue that this is the best interpretation of the implications of limits to growth. For many, it is also regarded as a principle of Green politics in its own right (for example, as one of the four principles of Green politics in the widely cited *Programme of the German Green Party* 1983). The term 'anarchist' is used loosely in this typology. It means that Greens envisage global networks of small-scale self-reliant communities. This position would for example be associated with people like E. F. Schumacher (1976). It shares the focus on small-scale communities with the previous position, but has two crucial differences. First, relations within communities would be libertarian, egalitarian and participatory. This reflects a very different set of assumptions about the origins of the environmental crisis; rather than being about the 'tragedy of the commons', it is seen to be about the emergence of hierarchical social relations and the channelling of human energies into productivism and consumerism (Bookchin 1982). Participatory societies should provide means for human fulfilment that do not depend on high levels of material consumption. Second, these communities, while self-reliant, are seen to be internationalist in orientation. They are not cut off from other communities, but in many ways conceived of as embedded in networks of relations of obligations, cultural exchanges and so on.

However, whether or not one shares such anarchist leanings, the decentralist impulse is nevertheless the most important theme coming out of Green politics for IR. One of the best-known Green political slogans is 'think globally, act locally'. While obviously fulfilling rhetorical purposes, it is often seen to follow from the two above principles. It stems

from a sense that while global environmental and social/economic problems operate on a global scale, they can be successfully responded to only
by breaking down the global power structures which generate them
through local action and the construction of smaller-scale political
communities and self-reliant economies.

One of the best-developed arguments for decentralization within
Green theory is given in John Dryzek's *Rational Ecology* (1987).
Dryzek summarizes the advantages of decentralization thus; small-
scale communities are more reliant on the environmental support
services in their immediate locality and therefore more responsive to
disruptions in that environment (Dryzek 1987: Chapter 16). Self-
reliance and smallness shortens feedback channels, so it is easier to
respond quickly before disruptions become severe. Dryzek also
suggests that they are more likely to develop a social ontology which
undermines pure instrumental ways of dealing with the rest of nature,
commonly identified as a cause of environmental problems (Dryzek
1987: 219; see also *The Ecologist* 1993 for extended discussions of
similar arguments).

The advocacy of radical decentralization has been widely criticized
both within academic debates and by some within green movements.
On the one hand, it is seen as politically 'unrealistic', and Green parties
have certainly scaled back their commitments to decentralization in
response to electoral success and the corresponding need for 'realism'
(Doherty and de Geus 1996: 4). Beyond this pragmatic concern, the
principal criticisms of proposals are threefold (see earlier editions of
this chapter; and Carter 1999). First, some claim that small-scale anar-
chistic communities would be too parochial and potentially self-
interested to provide atmospheres conducive to cross-community
cooperation. Part of this argument is therefore that it would be stulti-
fying or oppressive for those within the community, but it also suggests
that they would be unconcerned with effects across their borders (e.g.
Dobson 1990: 101, 124). Second, decentralized small-scale communities, it is claimed, will have little chance of developing effective mechanisms for resolving global environmental problems (see in particular
Goodin 1992). While small-scale communities might be able to deal
better with local environmental problems, for the reasons Dryzek
(1987) outlines, the coordination problems would escalate beyond
control with a massive increase in the number of actors at the international level. A third critique is rather different. Rather than arguing
that Greens' attempts to abandon sovereignty and decentralize power
means that there is insufficient coordinating capacity, many in fact
suggest that Green politics remains committed to a sovereign model of
politics (e.g. Kuehls 1996, Wapner 1996, Lipschutz 1997 or Dalby

1998). Part of this argument takes us back to the spatial character of ecological problems, which some of these authors (in particular Dalby 1998, 2002) suggest should be understood as about flows and networks, not closed spaces. Part also starts from the observation that contemporary global politics is also now organized through flows and networks, thus creating possibilities for political engagement without relying on the metaphor of territorial sovereignty (see in particular Spaargaren, Mol and Buttel 2006 for an attempt to think through environmental governance in terms of flows).

The third bioenvironmentalist account of politics is that the environmental crisis requires a new ethical sensibility to guide political practice. Most refer to this through the notion of *eco-centrism*; Greens reject anthropocentric ethics (with humans at the centre of the moral world) in favour of an eco-centric approach. For Eckersley (1992), eco-centrism has a number of central features. Empirically, it involves a view of the world as ontologically composed of *inter-relations* rather than individual entities (1992: 49). All beings are fundamentally 'embedded in ecological relationships' (1992: 53). Consequently, there are no convincing criteria that can be used to make a hard and fast distinction between humans and non-humans (1992: 49–51). Ethically, therefore, since there is no good reason to make rigid distinctions between humans and the rest of nature, a broad emancipatory project, to which Eckersley allies herself, ought to be extended to non-human nature. Eco-centrism is about 'emancipation writ large' (1992: 53). All entities are endowed with a relative autonomy, within the ecological relationships in which they are embedded, and therefore humans are not ethically free to dominate the rest of nature.

Politically, Eckersley (1992) argues against the decentralist emphasis in much Green thought. On the basis of her reading of the implications of eco-centrism, she develops a political argument from this that is statist in orientation. Although she does not adopt the position of the 'eco-authoritarians' mentioned above, she suggests, in direct contradiction to the eco-anarchism that is widespread in Green political thought, that the modern state is a necessary political institution from a Green point of view. She suggests that eco-centrism requires that we both decentralize power down within the state, but also centralize power up to the regional and global levels. She argues that a 'multitiered' political system, with dispersal of power both down to local communities and up to the regional and global levels is the approach that is most consistent with eco-centrism (Eckersley 1992: 144, 175, 178).

This position could be developed within a conventional perspective in International Relations (such as liberal institutionalism) to look at the character of a wide variety of inter-state treaties and practices. The most obvious would be those regarding biodiversity, acid rain, or climate change. But it could also be developed for global economic institutions such as the World Bank, or the military practices of states.

Eckersley's account could also be developed in the context of the literature on 'global environmental governance', which implies forms of governance emerging which do not rely solely on sovereign states (Paterson 1999a; Humphreys, Paterson and Pettiford 2003). One view of this is that we are currently witnessing a simultaneous shift of authority up to international/transnational institutions, and down to local organizations (Rosenau 1992; Hempel 1996). Rosenau makes this claim concerning patterns of authority in global politics in general, but also specifically in relation to global environmental politics (Rosenau 1993). For Hempel, such forms of global environmental governance are emerging because the spatial scale of the state is inadequate for dealing with the scales of environmental change. The state is simultaneously too small and too big to deal effectively with such change, and thus practices of governance move towards regional and global levels and at the same time towards local levels, in response. Eckersley's position in her (1992) book is a normative claim justifying such shifts in authority.

A core problem with this argument is that the interpretation of eco-centrism, which underpins Eckersley's (1992) book, is challengeable. Eco-centrism is in itself politically indeterminate. It can have many variants, ranging from anarchist to authoritarian, with Eckersley's version in the middle of the continuum. The predominant alternative interpretation within Green thought suggests that it is the emergence of modern modes of thought which is the problem from an eco-centric point of view. The rationality inherent in modern Western science is an instrumental one, where the domination of the rest of nature (and of women by men) and its use for human instrumental purposes have historically at least been integral to the scientific project on which industrial capitalism is built (e.g. Merchant 1980; Plumwood 1993). In other words, environmental ethics are given a historical specificity and material base – the emergence of modern forms of anthropocentrism is located in the emergence of modernity in all its aspects.

This interpretation argues therefore that since modern science is inextricably bound up with other modern institutions such as capitalism, the nation-state and modern forms of patriarchy, it is inappropriate to respond by developing those institutions further, centralizing power through the development of global and regional institutions. Such a response will further entrench instrumental rationality that will undermine the possibility for developing an eco-centric ethic. An eco-centric position therefore leads to arguments for scaling down human communities, and in particular for challenging trends towards globalization and homogenization, since it is only by celebrating diversity that it will be possible to create spaces for eco-centric ethics to emerge. More importantly, thinking through this logic suggests that talking about environmental politics as if the character of human societies is more or less irrelevant has severe limits. It is this gap which social greens fill.

Social greens – limits to growth and political economy

Clapp and Dauvergne's (2005) final category is that of social greens. These tend to agree with bioenvironmentalists about the existence of physical limits to growth, particularly economic growth (they at least downplay, and often reject, arguments about population, as patriarchal and/or imperialist). But they insist that such an observation must be understood in terms of the social systems which generate such growth, and thus of the complex interactions between social and ecological problems. At a general level, social greens are united in a claim that the power structures – capitalist, statist, patriarchal – of contemporary societies, are at the same time highly exploitative, unjust or oppressive, and systematically generate environmental degradation.

In terms specifically of global politics, these arguments can be most clearly seen in those writers who identify global inequalities as key to understanding global (environmental) politics, and also who often suggest that dominant political forces deploy environmental concerns to extend their global control, a process exemplified by Vandana Shiva's phrase (1993) 'the greening of global reach'. We can best understand their arguments on the one hand through their critique of the discourse of sustainable development (which shows their distinct take on limits to growth), and on the other through their reinterpretation of the notion of the commons (which gives Greens a distinct political economy).

Social limits to growth

As the notion of sustainable development became fashionable in the 1980s, and as the specific predictions of Meadows *et al.* concerning resource exhaustion proved inaccurate, belief in limits subsided. But in the 1990s a politics rejecting economic growth as the primary purpose of governments and societies re-emerged. It came, however, less out of the computer-modelling methods of Meadows *et al.* (although her team did produce a twenty-year-on book, *Beyond the Limits*, Meadows and Randers 1992) than out of emerging critiques of development in the

South from the 1980s onwards. Such 'post-development' perspectives draw heavily on post-modernism and feminism (e.g. Escobar 1995; Shiva 1988), and have been used by Greens in the North to develop what might be called a 'global ecology' perspective. Through the critique of 'development', economic growth again became the subject of critique, although in this vein critics made much closer connections between its ecological and its social consequences (Douthwaite 1992; Wackernagel and Rees 1996; Booth 1998).

One reason why the 'global ecology' writers object to development is because of limits to growth arguments, abandoned by much of the environmental movement during the 1980s. Implicit throughout their work is a need to accept the limits imposed by a finite planet, an acceptance ignored by the planet's managers and mainstream environmentalists (e.g. Sachs 1993). They are also sceptical of the idea that it is possible to decouple the concept of development from that of growth. While many environmentalists try to distinguish the two by stating that 'growth is quantitative increase in physical scale while development is qualitative improvement or unfolding of potentialities' (Daly 1990; Ekins 1993), others would suggest that in practice it is impossible to make such neat distinctions. For the practitioners of sustainable development, 'sustainable growth' and 'sustainable development' are in practice usually conflated, and certainly the Brundtland Commission regarded the pursuit of economic growth as essential for sustainable development (WCED 1987).

However, their arguments are more subtle than simply re-asserting limits to growth arguments. They focus on a number of *anti-ecological* elements of development. One of the central features of development is the enclosure of commons in order to expand the realm of commodity production and thus of material throughput (*The Ecologist* 1993). A second is the way such enclosure redistributes and concentrates resources, which has direct ecological consequences and creates a growth-supporting dynamic as growth mitigates the effects of enhanced inequality. A third is the concentrations of power that are involved in enclosure, as smaller numbers of people are able to control the way that land is used (and often able to insulate themselves from the ecological effects of the way land is used, for example by reserving for themselves privileged access to uncontaminated water sources). A fourth is the way such enclosure and the concentrations of power and wealth it effects produce shifts in knowledge relations and systems, typically involving the marginalization of 'indigenous knowledges' and the empowerment of 'experts' (*The Ecologist* 1993: 67–70; Appfel-Marglin and Marglin 1990). Finally, such a set of shifts in property systems, distribution of resources and power-knowledge relations entrenches the world-view which regards the non-human world in purely instrumental terms, thus legitimizing the destructive use of non-human nature.

The global ecology writers present a powerful set of arguments as to how development is inherently anti-ecological. This is not only because of abstract limits to growth-type arguments, but because they show in a subtler fashion how development in practice undermines sustainable practices. It takes control over resources away from those living sustainably in order to organize commodity production, it empowers experts with knowledge based on instrumental reason, it increases inequality which produces social conflicts and so on.

Back to the commons

While adding in a socio-ecological critique of growth to the bioenvironmentalists techno-scientific one, social greens do something similar for arguments about decentralization of power. On the one hand, for many Greens, much of the decentralist impulse has its origins in a rejection of the state similar to that of anarchists. For example, Spretnak and Capra (1984) suggest that it is the features identified by Weber as central to statehood that are the problem from an ecological point of view (1984: 177). Bookchin (1980) gives similar arguments, suggesting that the state is the ultimate hierarchical institution that consolidates all other hierarchical institutions. Carter (1993) suggests that the state is part of the dynamic of modern society that has caused the present environmental crisis. He outlines a 'environmentally hazardous dynamic', where '[a] centralized, pseudo-representative, quasi-democratic state stabilizes competitive, inegalitarian economic relations that develop "non-convivial", environmentally damaging "hard" technologies whose productivity supports the (nationalistic and militaristic) coercive forces that empower the state' (Carter 1993: 45). Thus the state is not only unnecessary from a Green point of view, it is positively undesirable.

The decentralist impulse is also expressed in the re-appropriation of the notion of the commons. The 'global ecology' writers reinforce a political-theoretic argument for decentralization by giving it a political economy. By this I mean they make it so that it is not only a question of the scale of political organization and the authoritarian character of the state, but also a reorganization of the structural form of political institutions, and in particular a re-conceptualization of how economic production, distribution and exchange – the direct way in which human societies transform 'nature' – is integrated into political life. Their positive argument is that the most plausibly Green form of political economy is the 'commons'. This argument is most fully developed by the editors of

The Ecologist magazine in their book *Whose Common Future? Reclaiming the Commons* (1993).

The argument is essentially that common spaces are sites where the most sustainable practices currently operate. They are under threat from development that continuously tries to enclose them in order to turn them into commodities. Therefore a central part of Green politics is resistance to this enclosure. But it is also a (re)constructive project – creating commons where they do not exist.

What are commons? First, they are not that identified by Hardin as such, which is rather an 'open access' resource (*The Ecologist* 1993: 13). They are not 'public' in the modern sense, which connotes open access under control by the state, while commons are often not open to all, and the rules governing them do not depend on the hierarchy and formality of state institutions. Nor are they 'private' – no-one person owns and controls the resource. They are rather resources held in common, where the relevant community collectively develops rules governing the use of the resources. This has been a widespread form of resource governance throughout human history, and as *The Ecologist* (1993) show, still persists in many places today.

Commons, therefore, are not 'anarchic' in the sense of having no rules governing them. They are spaces whose use is closely governed, often by informally defined rules, and by the communities that depend on them. They depend for their successful operation on a rough equality between the members of the community, as imbalances in power would make some able to ignore the rules of the community. They also depend on particular social and cultural norms prevailing – for example, the priority of common safety over accumulation, or distinctions between members and non-members (although not necessarily in a hostile sense, or one which is rigid and unchanging over time) (*The Ecologist* 1993: 9).

They key point is that they are typically organized for the production of use values rather than exchange values – that is, they are not geared to commodity production and are not susceptible to the pressures for accumulation or growth inherent in capitalist market systems. Commons are therefore held to produce sustainable practices, for a number of reasons. First, the rough equality in income and power means that none can usurp or dominate the system (*The Ecologist* 1993: 5). Second, the local scale at which they work means that the patterns of mutual dependence make cooperation easier to achieve. Third, this also means that the culture of recognizing one's dependence on others, and therefore having obligations, is easily entrenched. Finally, commons make practices based on accumulation difficult to adopt, usufruct being more likely.

The idea of the commons is clearly very consistent with the arguments about the necessity of decentralization of power, and grassroots democracy. It should be obvious that from this perspective the term 'global commons', in widespread use in mainstream environmental discussions or in institutionalist literature to refer to problems such as global warming or ozone depletion (e.g. Vogler 1995; Buck 1998), is literally nonsensical. However it supplements the decentralist argument by showing how small-scale democratic communities, working with particular sorts of property systems, are the most likely to produce sustainable practices within the limits set by a finite planet.

Both bioenvironmentalists and social greens propose concrete analyses of the origins of environmental degradation and unsustainability, and make far reaching normative claims about the political changes responding to such a crisis entails. They differ in their analysis broadly between a dualistic account of 'humanity' versus 'nature', as opposed to a social analysis of the origins of unsustainability in particular social systems and the intertwining of social and ecological crises. But they share a sense of the radical nature of the changes required.

Greening global politics

How then might global politics be 'Greened'? One of the things that the proponents of all of Clapp and Dauvergne's (2005) positions tend to share, is a rather static account of the relationship between political systems and environmental degradation. For example, for bioenvironmentalists there is an ahistoric 'naturalizing' account of population and economic growth, or in Ophuls (1997) a reification of the states system as having a 'timeless' logic that never changes. For some social greens (Bookchin (1980), for example) there is equally an identification of 'the state' as the problem, as if 'the state' is not itself undergoing constant change. Given that political systems are in constant flux, this may create possibilities as well as obstacles to the pursuit of sustainability. We might want to ask what an *immanent* Green critique of global politics might look like, as opposed to a *transcendental* Green critique of the (reified) states system.

It is in this light that Eckersley's *The Green State* (2004) comes to the fore. (I use Eckersley's book as the point of departure for this discussion as it remains the fullest expression of what can now be termed an emerging literature on 'the greening of the state' (see also Dryzek *et al.* 2003, Barry and Eckersley 2005) or Spaargaren, Mol and Buttel 2006; for an exchange on Eckersley's book, see the forum published in *Politics and Ethics Review* 2006).) In this book, Eckersley ends up with similar conclusions to the political conclusions she draws from eco-centrism in her earlier book. But the argument is developed in much greater detail,

and is based not on the transcendental claims of eco-centric ethics but on
the importance of an immanent critique of contemporary global politics.
That is, she starts from an analysis both of the contemporary anti-ecological tendencies and structures within global politics (for her, these are inter-state anarchy, global capitalism, the limits of liberal democracy) *and* the contemporary trends that create the possibility of countering these tendencies (environmental multilateralism, ecological modernization, deliberative/discursive democracy).

Collectively, Eckersley argues that these three elements create the possibility of an ecological world order which works from existing practices, rather than having to develop a world order anew. Thus she draws heavily on constructivist accounts of international politics (see also Reus-Smit, Chapter 9 in this volume), particularly on the notion of 'cultures of anarchy' (Wendt 1999) to argue that sovereignty need not simply mean relentless hostility and competition between states (as assumed in both eco-authoritarian arguments for world government and in eco-anarchist arguments against the state), but can entail the development of mutual obligations and extensive cooperation, and suggests that the development of environmental multilateralism to date is evidence for the possibilities here. Eckersley draws on accounts of ecological modernization (e.g. Hajer 1995; Christoff 1996; Mol 1996) to suggest that the growth and globalization dynamic of global capitalism is only one possible future for the world economy, while remaining highly critical of the 'weak' nature of most actually existing ecological modernization. Finally, she draws on work on deliberative and transnational democracy (Held 1995; Dryzek 1990, 1992, 1999; Linklater 1998) and implicitly at least on ecological citizenship (Dobson 2003) both to suggest that the former would enable the move to 'strong' ecological modernization which would properly ecologize economic processes, and the latter could embed properly the transformations of sovereignty away from the Hobbesian image.

Once Green critiques of international politics are understood this way, the door is open for a critical but constructive re-engagement with other International Relations traditions thinking similarly about the way that the states-system is undergoing transformation and how such transformations might be pushed in a radical direction. In the environmental sphere, work such as that by Hurrell on challenges to sovereignty and the states-system (1994), Shue on global justice and global environmental politics (1992), or Dobson on ecological citizenship (2003) all suggest, in differing ways, how Green conceptions of necessary global political reforms could fruitfully engage with specific existing elements of global politics in the manner indicated at a more general level by Eckersley. Outside the environmental sphere,

Linklater's account of critical theory (Linklater 1998; Chapter 6 in this volume) in terms of the possible transformations of forms of political community, or related debates about cosmopolitan or transnational democracy (Held 1995; Dryzek 1999) would be obvious sites of potential engagement.

An objection to this argument would be to question the focus on democratic deliberation in Eckersley's arguments. Fundamentally, she assumes that it is the character of *democratic deliberation* that underpins (un)sustainable polities. That is, while in *Environmentalism and Political Theory* (1992), it was eco-centric ethics which underpinned political claims about sustainability, in *The Green State* (2004) what sustainability requires politically is that 'all those potentially affected by ecological risks ought to have some meaningful opportunity to participate, or be represented, in the determination of policies or decisions that may generate risks' (2004: 243). This assumption generates the focus both on the weak nature of deliberative processes in liberal democracy, and the need to enable deliberative processes that do not exclude those beyond the borders of individual states. The main Green criticism here could come from the lines of argument developed by the 'global ecology' writers. Eckersley's account of democratic deliberation rightly questions the uncritical nature of 'individual preferences' as invoked by liberal democratic rhetoric – or, if you like, the separation of public and private, but fails to question also its (related) separation of politics and economics. Thus in the 'reclaiming the commons' literature, what is evident is that it is the embeddedness of political institutions in concrete socio-economic forms which engenders sustainable practices, whereas in Eckersley's account of ecological democracy it is clear that the practices of democratic deliberation and the practices of the production of daily life are much more clearly removed from each other, disembodied if you will. (This line of argument could be extended to a broader discussion of the relationship between capitalism and the state, and thus the implications for the character of political transformations implied by 'greening the state' (for discussions of this question, see for example Paterson 2007; Paterson *et al.* 2006, Meadowcroft 2006).) However, what is at the same time clear is that Eckersley's arguments concerning ecological democracy, if given a 'decentralist' twist – that is, if her insistence on the national state as the starting point for thinking about the site of political activity is dropped – then become significantly more attractive for most Greens, and an enormously sophisticated and valuable addition to Green arguments.

What is perhaps also at stake is Eckersley's account of contemporary global political developments that inform therefore the 'limits of the possible' out of which her immanent critique can then be developed. To

repeat, this is for her the emergent potential of environmental multilateralism, ecological modernization and deliberative democracy arising out
of inter-state anarchy, global capitalism and liberal democracy. What is
interesting in this context is perhaps the lack of a discussion of 'anti-globalization' movements, in which Greens have played prominent roles, as
well as an acknowledgement that the commons as a form of political
economy that Greens want to promote *already exists* in many areas
around the world. If one adds this dimension of contemporary global
developments to those Eckersley discusses, then this transforms what one
thinks of the potential by decentralism as argued by Greens. These movements can, of course, be analysed as pressures that support more
reformist movements developing environmental multilateralism, ecological modernization and discursive democracy. But they can also be
analysed as movements generating political change in their own right,
embedded in a broader pattern of Green social and political change
which challenge the power of global capital, the centralization of power
and so on, and act as the agents that help to forge and sustain ecological
democracy and citizenship.

Conclusions

My main aim in this chapter has been to show that between the two
approaches that Clapp and Dauvergne (2005) label 'bioenvironmentalist' and 'social green', there is a set of theories which can properly be
called a Green approach to global politics. While these theories certainly
arise out of the *problématique* of the environmental crisis, it would be a
mistake to limit their import to that 'issue area'. Rather, their character
as theories entails claims about the whole range of 'issues' that make up
the global political agenda, as well as calling into question the basic character of global politics.

Greens make claims about peace and war (both that environmental
problems result from militarism but more broadly that war-like practices
result from the same worldview based on accumulation, domination,
exploitation, which lead to unsustainability), about development (not
only about its environmental unsustainability but its dominating character) and about global governance (in various, at times contradictory,
ways as we have seen in the chapter). These claims are not add-on extras
to a Green approach, but logical extensions of the character of the claims
Greens make.

In the introduction to the book (Chapter 1) some of the central questions and distinctions concerning theoretical traditions in International
Relations were outlined. Green politics should clearly be regarded as a

critical rather than problem-solving theory. It is one, however, which aims to be both explanatory and normative – it tries both to explain a certain range of phenomena and problems in global politics and provide a set of normative claims about the sorts of global political changes necessary to respond to such problems. Writers within this tradition have to date spent less time engaging in constitutive-theoretical activity – reflecting on the nature of their theorizing *per se*, although there is attention, in particular among the writers in what I have called the 'global ecology' school to power/knowledge questions (but cf. Doran 1995).

For Greens, the central object of analysis and scope of enquiry is the way in which contemporary human societies are *ecologically unsustainable*. Such a destructive mode of existence is deplored both because of the independent ethical value held to reside in organisms and ecosystems, and because human society ultimately depends on the successful function of the biosphere as a whole for its own survival. Regarding International Relations specifically, Greens focus on the way in which prevailing political structures and processes contribute to this destruction. This is the root of their rejection of institutionalist accounts that suggest institutions can be built to 'tame' international anarchy or global capitalism. The purpose of enquiry is thus explicitly normative – to understand how global political structures can be reformed to prevent such destruction and provide for a sustainable human relationship to the planet and the rest of its inhabitants. Like Idealism, the normative imperative is the original impulse in Green politics – the explanation of environmental destruction comes later. Methodologically, while Greens are hostile to positivism, not least because of its historical connection to the treating of 'nature' (including humans) as objects, purely instrumentally, there is no clearly identifiable 'Green' methodology. Eckersley (2004: 8–10) proposes 'critical political ecology' as a method for Green politics. But this turns out to be the method of immanent critique of Frankfurt School critical theory, with an ecological focus. Finally, Greens share with many other perspectives a rejection of any claimed separation of International Relations from other disciplines. As Chapter 1 suggests, the possibility of the emergence of a distinct Green perspective in International Relations has seen the breaking down of disciplinary boundaries.

Regarding other International Relations traditions, Green politics has a number of features in common with many other critical approaches. First, it shares the rejection of a hard and fast fact/value distinction with feminism, critical theory and post-structuralism, by making clear attempts to integrate normative and explanatory concerns. Its conception of theory is clearly incompatible with positivist conceptions that have such a clear distinction. Second, it shares an interest in resisting the concentration of power, the homogenizing forces in contemporary world

politics and the preservation of difference and diversity with post-structuralism and feminism. Third, it shares a critique of the states-system
with critical theory and others, although it adopts a position that rejects
the idea of global power structures emerging in correspondence with
some idea of a 'global community' in favour of decentralizing power
away from nation-states to more local levels. (For an account with many
similarities to that of Linklater in relation to environmental politics, see
Low and Gleeson 1998: Chapter 7. For a critique of such universalist
thinking along the lines of the 'global ecology' writers discussed above,
see Esteva and Prakash 1997). While for critical theorists such as
Linklater (1998), the idea of community at the global level is about
balancing unity and diversity rather than one which wishes to create a
homogeneous global identity, there is a much stronger sense in Green
politics that community only makes sense at the very local level – the idea
of a 'global community' is for Greens nonsensical, if not potentially total-
itarian (Esteva and Prakash 1997). Nevertheless, there is a shared sense
that the purpose of theory is to promote emancipation (Laferrière 1996;
Laferrière and Stoett 1999; 2006). Allied to this normative rejection of
the states-system is a rejection of a clear empirical split between domestic and international politics shared in particular with pluralists such as
John Burton, but also with Marxists, critical theorists and feminists.
Greens would not believe it useful therefore to think in terms of 'levels of
analysis', a form of thinking still prevalent in realism, as it arbitrarily
divides up arenas of political action which should be seen as fundamentally interconnected. Finally, there is a clear focus on political economy,
and the structural inequality inherent in modern capitalist economies
also focused on by Marxists and dependency theorists.

However, in contrast to post-structuralism, it shares to an extent an
element of modernist theorizing, in the sense that Greens are clearly
trying to understand the world in order to make it possible to improve
it. For Hovden (1999), this makes it more compatible with Frankfurt
School-type critical theory and feminism than with post-structuralism,
as these both have a clear emancipatory normative goal, and in particular a clearer sense that their explanations or interpretations of the world
are connected to a clear political project. This is linked to post-structuralism's rejection of foundationalism, which marks a clear difference
from Green politics that necessarily relies on fairly strong foundational
claims, of both the epistemological and ethical variety. However, this
argument should not be pushed too far, as there are also tensions with
the way in which critical theory tries to reconstruct Enlightenment rationality. Eckersley, for example (1992: Chapter 5), makes much of
attempts by Habermas in particular (she contrasts Habermas to
Marcuse) to reclaim science for radical political purposes, suggesting

that it necessarily ends up justifying human domination of nature. I would ultimately concur with Mantle (1999), who argues that the closest connections that Green theory has to other approaches in International Relations are to feminism.

Green theory therefore clearly has its own distinctive perspective. The focus on humanity-nature relations and the adoption of an eco-centric ethic with regard to those relations, the focus on limits to growth, the particular perspective on the destructive side of development and the focus on decentralization away from the nation-state are all unique to Green politics. This chapter has illustrated how the purpose of Green theory within International Relations is to provide an explanation of the ecological crisis facing humanity, to focus on that crisis as possibly the most important issue for human societies to deal with, and to provide a normative basis for dealing with it.

12 | International Political Theory

TERRY NARDIN

This chapter examines some ideas that compose the domain of international political theory, with the aim, as in other chapters in this book, of presenting an overview and guide to further study. I give particular attention to ideas about international and global justice because they are central to that domain. And because that domain includes past as well as present ideas, I discuss some ideas about the history of international thought.

Theorizing international politics

Readers of this book might be puzzled by the title of Wight's famous essay, 'Why is There No International Theory?' Published on the eve of a vast expansion of academic theorizing on international relations, the essay is often used as a starting point for discussing the field. The present book is no exception. As Scott Burchill and Andrew Linklater suggest in their introduction, we may no longer assume – or as Wight did, even provocatively assert – that there is no international relations theory. The theorizing of the past 50 years, which is covered in this book and to which Wight himself contributed, invites us to re-examine his verdict that 'international theory is marked, not only by paucity but also by intellectual and moral poverty' (Wight 1966a: 20). No one who has read the preceding chapters will complain that there is too little of it! But what of Wight's charge of intellectual and moral poverty?

I can imagine readers voicing a complaint often brought against theory in any field: that international relations theory is arcane, obscure, and irrelevant to practical concerns. But the complaint says more about misplaced expectations than about theory itself. Theorizing, by digging beneath the surface to question presuppositions, demands new ways of thinking and yields unfamiliar conclusions. Thinking about an activity is not the same as engaging in it. Because the aims of theorizing are different from the practical aims of making decisions and taking actions, the theories that are most relevant to practice may be the least genuinely theoretical. Much of what is called political theory is no more than ordinary opinion turned into a doctrine or ideology, which is in turn applied to conduct. If theorizing criticizes ordinary ways of thinking, it cannot be the criterion of success that its conclusions are validated by common sense.

Wight looked for international theory in the writings of statesmen and diplomats, international lawyers, peace advocates, theorists of reason of state, philosophers and historians. If we survey the half century that has passed since his essay was published, we can find examples of theorizing in each of these categories, but it is the writings of those he calls 'philosophers and historians' that have altered the theoretical landscape most. Moral and political philosophers have written extensively on international affairs during this period, as have historians of political thought, and their work has been critical, systematic and cumulative. We must also consider a body of writing that Wight does not mention, in what appears to be a deliberate snub: the writing of academic international relations specialists. Wight found little to admire in the emerging discipline of International Relations, which seemed to him to combine a misguided scientism with mere journalism (Hall 2006: 88–97). Although that charge would be harder to sustain today, the work of the philosophers and historians whose efforts have shaped what is now called 'international political theory' comes closest to refuting the charge of intellectual and moral poverty.

The philosophers who wrote on international affairs in the 1960s addressed practical questions arising from nuclear deterrence, the Vietnam War, and famines in Africa. Attention to such questions marked a turn away from the moral philosophy of the 1950s, which had focused on the definition and foundation of moral judgement. Whatever its origins, the turn to 'applied ethics' soon became self-perpetuating as philosophers responded to each other's arguments and as issues like nationalism and terrorism were added to the agenda. Today, it is hard even for specialists to keep up with the flood of writing on human rights, humanitarian intervention, economic inequality, and other ethically significant topics. Philosophers writing on these topics see themselves as contributing to 'ethics and international affairs' or 'international ethics', though many would acknowledge that the subject has a distinctly *political* character that is sometimes overlooked when the focus is on *ethics*. We neglect the political when we assume that principles of interpersonal ethics can be applied without change to relations between states (Graham 2008: 35–8). 'The domestic analogy', which treats international relations as analogous to relations between persons, can result in arguments that ignore its institutional aspects. Rescuing a community from poverty is not the same as pulling a child from a pond. 'International ethics' is therefore a misleading name for inquiry into the rights and wrongs of international affairs, which requires that we distinguish between moral and institutional duties and recognize, with philosophers from Aristotle onwards, that politics is a distinct sphere of activity whose principles are not necessarily those of individual conduct (Kant 1999: 22–7). Institutions create special obligations that can modify, even if they do not erase, general or non-institutional ('natural') duties, which means that justice in civil or international society cannot be reduced to natural justice but must include duties imposed by civil and international law.

Because it acknowledges the political, the expression 'international political theory' seems preferable to 'international ethics' as a way of identifying the subject. The former also implies a bit more distance between theory and practice: whereas international ethics is often understood to be normative or applied ethics – the practical activity of guiding and judging action – international political theory puts the emphasis on *theorizing* as distinct from judging and acting. Instead of using moral principles, whose validity is presupposed, to reach a practical conclusion (a decision or a prescription), the theorist questions those principles to uncover their presuppositions. Theorizing aims not at approving or disapproving choices, or recommending or dissuading action, but at understanding the grounds on which choices are made, defended and judged.

Some would reject both expressions, however, arguing that politics is increasingly global as transnational networks and other modes of 'global governance' replace traditional inter-state diplomacy. For them, globalization means changes that will eventually erase the subject of this book by transforming the international system into a global one. But even if states retain their identity and independence, one can question conventional understandings of sovereignty or the moral significance of national boundaries. International political theory must be understood to include 'cosmopolitan' theorizing that challenges state-centric assumptions. We need, then, to consider the implications of globalization for international political theory, paying particular attention to the emergence of 'global justice' as a focus of debate.

Historians as well as philosophers have contributed to international political theory in recent decades by bringing professional standards to the study of past ideas. Scholars in the field of international relations have been interested in history mainly as a source of ideas for present use – Kenneth Waltz's *Man, the State, and War* (1959) is an example of that enterprise. Or they have sought to claim legitimacy for their own views by linking them to an adopted canonical ancestor. Political realists appeal to Thucydides and Hobbes, internationalists and cosmopolitans to Grotius and Kant. But attention to the past can be strikingly unhistorical when a discipline looks for founders or seeks to recruit past thinkers to current causes. Although efforts to find a useable past continue (Lebow 2003; Deudney 2007), there is emerging within the discipline a genuinely historical concern with its own ideas as well as with the ideas of those who thought about international affairs before there was a discipline. Historical scholarship is revising our understanding of just war theory, the realism-idealism debate, the origins of international relations as an academic discipline, and many other topics. That scholarship challenges the assumptions about sovereignty and the belief in progress that Wight thought were characteristic of international theorizing and that have distorted many previous efforts to write the history of international thought. Historians today do not write progressive or other meta-narratives, despite the persistence of such narratives in the more popular literature under titles like 'the end of history' or 'the clash of civilizations'. A more sophisticated approach to intellectual history has led to the recovery of forgotten texts and greater attention to particular ideas, thinkers and discourses in place of comprehensive histories of international thought.

The approaches that I have distinguished are not entirely separate from one another. There is no sharp line between the ethical and the political, the international and the global, or the philosophical and the historical. Nor are these approaches entirely separate from those treated in preceding chapters. As Burchill and Linklater suggest, theories can be critical as well as explanatory. Realism and liberalism are concerned to prescribe as well as to describe foreign policy. Marxists and feminists criticize as well as explain class and gender systems. Green theory has both ethical and explanatory concerns. Wight and other members of the English School emphasized the moral and historical aspects of international relations at a time when American scholars were reinventing the discipline in scientific terms. In seeing the subject in humanistic rather than scientific terms, they have received support from constructivism, which pays attention to norms. But constructivists have on the whole been more concerned with how norms shape choices than with the ethical content of those norms, and some have been unable to avoid sliding back into scientism. And though ethical concerns appear in the writings of critical theorists and post-structuralists, both claim to reject common moral ideas. In short, the character of international political theory remains contested, as do the boundaries that divide it from other approaches to international relations.

Although international political theory has emerged in recent years as an approach, it is only slowly coming into focus as a domain of inquiry distinct from international *relations* theory. One way of distinguishing the two is to say that the concerns of international political theory are 'normative' and those of international relations theory 'empirical'. But this way of making the distinction equivocates between whether it is the *object of inquiry* or the *inquiry itself* that is 'normative'. If the former, political theory is the disengaged *study* of norms; if the latter, it is an engagement to *use* norms to judge and guide conduct. The word 'empirical' is equally problematic, echoing a discredited view of science as resting on the accumulation of theory-independent facts that is in tension with the idea of empirical *theory*. International relations theory is identified in mainstream (in fact, largely American) thought with scientific theorizing. But this identification is misleading because much of the discourse that goes on under that label – in this book, for example – has abandoned the scientific paradigm. It is interpretative rather than quantitative and epistemologically plural rather than wedded to the idea of a single, unshakeable foundation for knowledge. The distinction between international relations theory and international political theory is eroding along with the normative versus empirical distinction formerly accepted by theorists on both sides of the divide. Also eroding is the assumption that the study of international relations can ignore past theorizing, which sought to explain as well as to prescribe and generated explanations that are not necessarily inferior to our own. Nor can it ignore ideas from civilizations beyond the West. International political theory connects mainstream international relations theorizing with moral questions, with the political issues posed by globalization, and with the history of international thought, including that of non-Western peoples. Its concerns – ethical, institutional and historical – are central to the activity of theorizing about international relations.

In my view, international political theory comes into its own when it distinguishes itself from the activity of making practical judgements by questioning the assumptions on which those judgements rest. Political theorists do many sorts of things, but the vocation of the theorist is not that of a citizen or politician in academic dress but of one who stands back from politics to understand it better. The political theorist, *qua* theorist, is an observer, not a participant in the activities he observes. This is not a prescriptive claim but rather an effort to capture what distinguishes theoretical from other kinds of investigation and, especially, theorizing from moral advocacy. But such detachment is hard to achieve, and one must always be willing to acknowledge one's own commitments and biases or risk hypocrisy and self-deception.

Justice in war

Theories are the outcome of theorizing, and theorizing often starts with ordinary experience, which may raise questions about received beliefs or invite efforts to give those beliefs a more solid foundation. Plato captures this aspect of theorizing well in his parable of the cave, in which through an effort of 'turning around' its prisoners learn that what they had assumed were real figures are only shadows projected on the wall in front of them. When, unchained, they rise and walk through the cave and then out into the sunlight, they see things from new angles and with increasing clarity. It is the same for the theorist of international relations, who by questioning the idea of sovereignty or the distinction between foreign and domestic affairs gains a fresh view of the subject. Whether we start by examining naïve experience or sophisticated interpretation, our aim in theorizing is to question the ideas that are the subject of our inquiry so that we can better understand and possibly transcend them.

What has come to be called just war theory illustrates this activity of theorizing. We might begin with a simple judgement ('our cause is just, they are the aggressor') or a complex proposition like the so-called principle of double effect ('one may harm civilians provided the harm done is not one's end, nor a means to that end, and does not unfairly distribute costs between those inflicting and those suffering the harm'). Examining such arguments, we can affirm or revise them or try to understand how they are related to other arguments by uncovering the assumptions on which they rest. A theoretical inquiry seldom ends by simply affirming the original judgement.

I discuss justice in war before turning to international or global justice, for several reasons. First, war is pre-international, by which I mean that it antedates the modern states system and occurs within as well as between states (Keegan 1993; Keeley 1996). Second, the principles of just war theory are clear, consistent, and relatively stable, unlike the distributive principles that have figured prominently in debates over international and global justice. And third, thinking about war allows us to begin not with a theory but with the actual or vicarious experience of fighting. The reader of military history or war memoirs, or even someone who watches war movies or plays video games, acquires some knowledge of war and its *mores*, and that knowledge, however selective or distorted, can invite critical reflection – even if it often doesn't. There is a phenomenology of war, moving from the experience of combat to reflections on cruelty, loyalty, friendship and guilt, unmediated by the abstractions of just war ethics that can provide a useful corrective to those abstractions (Gray 1959). Thinking about who fights, who reads about war, or who plays war games suggests that war is a highly gendered experience. And if war is central to international relations, one might wonder how far gender categories pervade the latter as well.

Let's start with an intuitive judgement and work up to the principles that explain and justify it. The word 'atrocity' comes pre-packaged with the judgement that any act so described is morally wrong. The 1940 Katyn Forest massacre, in which the Soviets killed 8,000 Polish officers together with twice that number of civilians, would have been hard to justify – the murders were, in fact, covered up. Efforts have been made to *excuse* those who killed at least 400 civilians, including many children, at My Lai in Vietnam in 1968, but it is not seriously argued that the killings were morally *justified*. In every war women are the victims of rape, but the rationalizations that are occasionally offered merely highlight the atrocity. Implicit in the idea of atrocity is the principle that innocent people should not be deliberately killed or abused. But this principle can be examined instead of being used as the basis for a judgement. What, for example, is meant by the words 'innocent' and 'deliberately'? One answer is that 'innocent', in this context, means 'not engaged in harming'. 'Deliberately' means that the deaths were not inadvertent but were planned and carried out as a matter of policy. The idea that innocents should not be deliberately harmed – that doing so is always wrong – is basic to morality (Nagel 1985). It is also part of the laws of war, as they were understood long before 1940 or 1968. Those laws forbid deliberately killing unarmed and unresisting soldiers and civilians, thereby formalizing a basic moral idea as the principle of 'noncombatant immunity' (Primoratz 2007). By clarifying the grounds for identifying an event as an atrocity, we come to understand some important principles of just war theory.

All principles are provisional, however. They can be questioned and revised. If we acknowledge that it is wrong to kill civilians and non-combatant soldiers (such as prisoners of war), does this mean that killing soldiers in combat is *not* an atrocity? Because they are fighting, soldiers are not 'innocent' (as that word is defined by the laws of war), and for that reason we do not usually regard their deaths in combat as murder. But some philosophers have questioned that judgement along with the definition of innocence on which it rests, arguing (for example) that conscripted soldiers are forced labourers unjustly pushed into battle by their superiors. Such soldiers become 'innocent attackers' whose deaths in battle are as atrocious as the deaths of non-combatants. Others defend the conventional view that soldiers lose their immunity to harm, arguing, for example, that their actions pose a material threat to those they are attacking which the latter are entitled to resist in self-defence, and that killing them in the course of that resistance is therefore not murder. Still others argue that the deaths of soldiers are a foreseeable even if not wished-for effect of resisting an enemy state whose unwilling agents they sometimes happen to be. On this view, if the principle of double effect can justify the deaths of bystanders it can also justify the deaths of combatants. In the course of the philosophical debate, which in recent years has grown increasingly abstruse, it has become evident that principles of individual self-defence may not be applied directly to national defence (Rodin 2002). Whatever its outcome, the debate illustrates the theorist's characteristic behaviour of *not* taking conventional distinctions for granted.

Instead of non-combatant immunity we might focus on the issue of culpability. People are sometimes excused from responsibility for wrongs they commit if they acted in ignorance or under duress. Questions about responsibility and culpability are distinct from questions of justification. Arguing that a soldier who deliberately kills civilians on the orders of a superior is not guilty of murder might excuse the killer from responsibility but it cannot justify the killing. There is a difference between justifying an action as right and excusing the perpetrator of an action admitted to be wrong.

We call the kind of thinking through which just and unjust uses of military force are sorted out 'the just war tradition'. It is often contrasted with two others, pacifism and political realism, that de-emphasize the distinction between just and unjust wars. We can think of these three traditions – pacifism, just war, and political realism – as comprising a continuum of progressively more permissive attitudes toward the use of force.

For many pacifists, war means killing and killing is inherently wrong. All wars are unjust. But not all versions of pacifism reach this conclusion. The one that comes closest we might call 'moral pacifism': it is morally wrong for *me* to kill, which means I cannot serve in war. This, however, is an individual ethic, not a policy. It is the view of early pre-Constantine Christians and in modern times of Mennonites and Quakers (Koontz 1996). It should be distinguished from a commitment to abolish the institution of war. Abolitionism is based not only on moral revulsion against war but also on doubts about its utility. But unlike moral pacifists, abolitionists don't refuse on principle to fight. Instead they focus on transformation by emphasizing the moral duty to establish arrangements that will make war less likely (Bok 1989). Finally, there is a kind of pacifism, sometimes called 'non-violence', that urges passive resistance to aggression as an alternative to armed force. Non-violent power is regarded as being morally superior to using military force and sometimes as being more effective as well (Sharp 1973).

Political realism is at the other end of the continuum, and it, too, comes in several flavours. One is moral scepticism, the view that war is essentially outside the realm of moral judgement. Another is reason of state, the view that war is an instrument of national policy, which implies confidence in the utility of armed force, properly used. The decision to make war should be dictated by prudence, not morality. And prudence suggests that force should be both necessary and proportionate. But no method of violence is absolutely forbidden if it meets these prudential criteria. Realism should not be confused with militarism, which glorifies war or defends it on religious or ideological grounds without appealing to necessity or national defence. Still, the line between realism and militarism can be hard to discern. 'Glory' for the ancient Romans and for Renaissance humanists like Machiavelli could be a means of defence as well as an end in itself: the glorious victor, like the breast-pounding gorilla, ensures his dominance by overawing potential rivals.

As I've sketched it here, just war thinking falls between pacifism and realism. Unlike pacifism, it does not reject the use of force in principle or deny its efficacy. Unlike realism, it does not exclude war from the jurisdiction of morality and law. Decisions to use force must respond to moral as well as prudential considerations. National interests alone cannot dictate when and how a state makes war. There are justified and unjustified uses of force, just and unjust wars. And just as there are different versions of pacifism and realism, there are also different just war traditions, each a historically distinguishable discourse of war.

One strand of just war thinking descends from the scholastic tradition of medieval Christianity, sometimes called Thomistic natural law theory because of its reliance on the teachings of St Thomas Aquinas. Aquinas distilled a complex medieval debate down to three principles: just cause, proper authority and right intention (Russell 1975; Barnes 1982). The just cause requirement is that a war must aim at righting a wrong – for example, defending a community against aggression – or punishing that wrong. But the tradition has moved away from the idea that one state can lawfully punish another, for that would make the punishing state both a party to the dispute and its judge (Finnis 1996: 20–4; Boyle 2006: 38–41). As this implies, having a just cause is not enough; one must also be authorized to fight. A government can ask its citizens to defend the community, but the government of one state has no authority to punish the government or people of another. And because Thomistic just war theory is a moral theory, not merely a theory of external law, it adds a third criterion, right intention, which refers to the internal motive or spirit in which one fights. It is implicit in this principle that the innocent must not be intentionally harmed.

A second strand of just war theory is a modern legal and political tradition that binds just war theory to ideas about the modern state. For as long as international law was thought to be a part of natural law, legal and political arguments were not clearly distinguished. But since the beginning of the nineteenth century international law has had its own sources and modes of argument that distinguish legal arguments from those of just war moralists. Both international lawyers and political theorists start, however, from the premise that self-defence by states against foreign aggression is the basis of just war ethics. They agree in condemning preventive war but disagree on the question of humanitarian intervention. Lawyers typically argue that international law, and especially the UN Charter, forbids humanitarian intervention because intervention violates the principle of state sovereignty (Byers 2005: 89–111). The political theorist Michael Walzer, in contrast, defends humanitarian intervention because he sees sovereignty as justified only to the degree that it protects the rights of citizens (Walzer 1977: 108). This principle of responsible sovereignty also undergirds his account of self-defence: he argues that a state may defend itself against aggression (but not against justified humanitarian intervention) because it provides the order under which its citizens enjoy their rights and make a common life. But this is not the only way to see things. There are Jews who do not recognize the state of Israel because it was founded by human force before the coming of the Messiah. Medieval Muslim theory, embraced by some Islamists today, has no room for territorial states on the European model. Instead, it distinguishes the realm of faith from the realm of worldly affairs, which is one of discord and war (Hashmi 2002; Kelsay 2007). In focusing on the territorial state, Walzer, like the international lawyers, privileges a way of ordering human affairs that is at odds with other views of how the world might be ordered (Sorabji and Rodin 2006; Brekke 2006).

Because both doctrines privilege the state, just war and reason of state are not entirely at odds. But it is worth noting some differences. For the political realist, every state is entitled to preserve itself, which means that a war can be just on both sides because even an aggressor might fight to preserve its independence. This 'relativism of patriotism', as it has been called (Tuck 1999: 31–4), is not the claim that each side thinks its cause is just. It is the more radical claim that a war can actually *be* just on both sides. It is in denying this claim that even statist versions of just war theory are distinguished from political realism. In just war theory, one side is an aggressor, the other a defender. The aggressor is a criminal whom the defender resists justly. But the aggressor does not always strike first, for aggression can occur without force having been used. A state should be able to defend itself against the threat of imminent attack but it may not wage preventive war against a powerful but not (yet) violent neighbour. The distinction between preemption and prevention is a relative one – the line between them shifts its position depending on contingencies – but there is still some distance between a limited doctrine of preemption and the claim that a government can do whatever it thinks is necessary to deal with security threats (Shue and Rodin 2007). The tilt of 'political' just war theory towards political realism is most evident in arguments for overriding just war limits in situations of supreme emergency or where nuclear deterrence, which rests on the threat to kill innocent people, is concerned. Here the theory comes close to, or collapses into, reason of state (Walzer 2004: 33–50; Finnis, Boyle, and Grisez 1987).

The argument that moral limits must give way in emergencies is often advanced to justify injustice in response to terrorism. Consequentialist arguments about the necessity to choose 'the lesser evil' (Ignatieff 2004) in what has been construed after 9/11 as 'the war on terrorism', including arguments for legalizing torture in 'ticking bomb' situations, have been revived and challenged (Brecher 2007; Ramraj 2008). Such debates, by focusing on the relationship between justice and prudence, reveal distinct understandings of the character of justice itself.

International justice

As just war theory illustrates, a common way of conceiving justice in the international system is through an analogy with the idea of the state as an association of citizens. On this view, citizens have equal liberty and may not interfere forcibly in one another's affairs except if necessary to thwart unjustified interference. By analogy, states have equal liberty. They are politically independent or 'sovereign' and must avoid interfering in one another's affairs. International law forbids 'aggression' (the wrongful use of force against another state) and 'intervention' (the wrongful use of force within the territory of another state). But there is also a significant disanalogy: unlike civil society, international society is without a superior to define and enforce the rights of its members. The society of states is, in the words of Hedley Bull, an 'anarchical society' – anarchical in lacking a central authority but still a society ordered to some extent by common interests and common rules (Bull 1977).

This idea of international society continues to be a point of departure for theorists, generating a debate between 'pluralists', who argue that international society presupposes only common rules that states agree to respect, and 'solidarists', who argue that international society rests on shared goals that states cooperate to promote. The standard charge of pluralism against solidarism is that it improperly suppresses cultural differences and limits the liberty of states by imposing common goals (Nardin 1983: 309–24). The standard charge of solidarism against pluralism is that it arbitrarily privileges sovereignty and offers an unacceptably thin concept of global justice. Solidarists argue that the pluralist idea of international coexistence on the basis of common rules might have been acceptable in the past but 'cannot be applied satisfactorily to the conditions of global political life in the twenty-first century, which require the identification of substantive collective goals and the creation of institutionalized structures of governance to implement them' (Hurrell 2007: 298).

A much-discussed defence of the pluralist conception of international justice is that advanced by John Rawls in *The Law of Peoples* (1999). Rawls thinks political, economic and cultural differences among nations are tolerable, provided such differences are consistent with principles that all can accept as a reasonable basis for public order. These principles, which are incorporated in contemporary international law, require states to respect one another's political sovereignty and territorial integrity, observe treaty obligations and limits on the conduct of war, and cooperate to assist states to become more just internally by alleviating poverty and other problems. States may use force only in self-defence or for generally acknowledged humanitarian ends. This principle reflects the moral imperative to suppress external and internal violence: states should not tolerate aggression or genocide if they can deter or suppress it. The pluralism that remains when such violence has been thwarted is the pluralism of a just international order. Global justice does not require that states disappear. Nor, Rawls argues, does it require that every state be ordered internally according to the principles of liberal democracy. What it does require is that states with different political traditions coexist on the basis of principles (roughly those of international law) that respect such differences within reasonable limits.

Against this pluralism, Rawls's critics argue that a morally legitimate international order is one whose members are morally legitimate states (Buchanan 2004). If liberal principles are valid internally, they should apply internationally as well (Beitz 1979; Barry 1998). A morally legitimate international society cannot tolerate morally illegitimate states as members. A legitimate state violates its own principles if it accepts illegitimate ones as equal members of international society (Tan 2000). The critics differ, however, on what they mean by liberal principles. Some think a morally legitimate state is one that protects basic human rights, others that only liberal democratic states are morally legitimate. For Rawls and other pluralists, such arguments rest on an indefensibly narrow definition of legitimacy. The principles that provide the basis of public order in one society are not necessarily appropriate for other societies. For Rawls, liberal democratic principles constitute a 'comprehensive doctrine' suitable for ordering liberal democracies. But the liberalism that is appropriate to international society, 'political liberalism', respects the right of people in different societies to live according to their own comprehensive doctrines. Just as liberal democracy prescribes respect for non-liberal persons and groups internally, provided they obey the law, so political liberalism at the international level prescribes respect for non-liberal societies, provided those societies are reasonably just internally and obey international law. The principles of political liberalism rest on the idea of 'public reason', which prescribes that when arguing across doctrinal lines liberal democrats must frame their arguments in such a way as to find the common ground. In this, Rawls is not far from Habermas and others who connect justice with principles that might emerge within a free public realm (Linklater 1998). To insist that all peoples should govern themselves solely according to liberal democratic principles is parochial and even barbaric.

Framing the dispute between pluralists and solidarists as a debate over the definition of moral legitimacy helps us to see that a central issue is the limits of international toleration. Both sides draw a line beyond which a state loses its immunity to forcible resistance or intervention, but they draw it in different places. The pluralist would rule out aggression or crimes against humanity but thinks it permissible to tolerate less serious moral breaches. The solidarist thinks that violating a wider range of human rights or democratic principles puts a regime beyond the pale.

Some theorists have sought to accommodate both pluralism and solidarism by means of an ascending scale of legal orders. Kant, for example, distinguishes between two kinds of international association. The first is composed of states that recognize the principle of national self-determination, are willing to renounce aggression, intervention, and atrocities in war, and are committed to reducing the influence of what would later be called 'the military-industrial complex' by avoiding standing armies and a huge military debt. The second – a subset of the first, composed of states that meet a higher standard – is an international association whose members are committed to the rule of law internally and cooperation to secure the rule of law internationally (Kant 1991: 93–108). Kant's distinction is reflected in the contrast between the European Union, which is a confederation of rule-of-law states, and the United Nations, a looser association whose members are not necessarily rule-of-law states, though all are committed (or pretend to be committed) to coexistence. Rawls offers a similar typology, in which what he calls 'well-ordered peoples' are capable of achieving a level of justice in their relations with one another that cannot be achieved in their relations with societies that are not well-ordered. The well-ordered category includes, besides liberal democracies, societies with consultative hierarchical regimes that respect religious freedom and other basic human rights and give people some input into governing. Societies that are not well-ordered are absolutist, corrupt, ineffective or violent. Like Kant, who sees minimal coexistence being replaced by cooperation among states committed to the rule of law (Kant 1991: 108–114), Rawls envisions an expanding 'democratic peace' (Rawls 1999: 44–54) that might gradually replace less just forms of international association.

Rawls's theory of international justice has renewed the debate on the limits of pluralism (Martin and Reidy 2006), but has not significantly altered it. What Rawls has done is provide a new vocabulary to augment the existing discourse of human rights, which is also concerned with the moral legitimacy of states and the limits of sovereignty. That discourse is based not on the domestic analogy but on a more nuanced view of justice that distinguishes between governments and citizens and holds governments accountable for how they treat citizens. The idea of humanitarian intervention illustrates that international justice can be understood without employing the domestic analogy. Some dismiss humanitarian intervention as irrelevant in a world ordered by realist self-interest. But this dismissal overlooks its moral and theoretical significance.

Humanitarian intervention can be defined as the use of force by one state within the territory of another without the latter's consent, to protect people who are not nationals of the intervening state from violence committed or permitted by the government of the target state. One question about humanitarian intervention is whether it is permissible under international law. Those who rely on the UN Charter say 'no'; others, who look to customary international law, are less certain (Holzgrefe and Keohane 2003). Another question is whether, leaving international law aside, humanitarian intervention is morally permissible. When does one state have the moral right to use military force inside the territory of another? The question challenges both the non-intervention principle and the domestic analogy on which it rests. According to that analogy, if citizens must respect one another's autonomy and bodily integrity, states must respect one another's political sovereignty and territorial integrity. If one state has the right to manage its own affairs free of interference by other states, other states have no right to exercise their authority, which includes using force, inside its territory. On this view, intervention, for any purpose, is an act of aggression. But this blanket ban on intervention forgets the justification of political sovereignty and territorial integrity: that states exist to protect the rights of human beings. If a state violates those rights, or allows them to be violated, this justification ceases and the state forfeits its immunity to intervention. It cannot invoke its sovereignty to justify its violence or incompetence.

When a government fails to protect those it governs from violence, their rights do not disappear. The duty to defend those rights falls on others, and intervention can be a way to perform it. This duty rests on the principle of beneficence or humanity, which prescribes assisting others when one can do so without disproportionate inconvenience, and especially when the need is great – as would be the case in situations of collective violence. It also rests on the duty to resist injustice when one can. We cannot simply transplant these principles from the interpersonal to the international level, but neither can we plausibly deny that they ground a general duty to protect others from violence, and that this duty might sometimes include international action. One of the puzzles of humanitarian intervention is to decide whose duty it is to intervene. Does that duty fall on certain states, on every state, or on organizations representing the international community? How can an abstract general duty become the special duty of a particular agent? Some argue that the duty to protect people from violence can be performed only by agencies that have been authorized and equipped to perform it. In that case, a general duty to resist violence becomes the specific duty of that agency to intervene militarily (Tan 2006).

The debate over humanitarian intervention illustrates how the ideas of sovereignty and non-intervention are altered when one dissects the domestic analogy. Looking beneath the surface of state sovereignty to discover its moral rationale, we qualify the non-intervention principle to make it consistent with that rationale. The amended principle makes room for human rights by imposing a duty to respect those rights and a duty to prevent others from violating them. International justice therefore requires not only that states treat other states justly, as the domestic analogy would imply, but also that they concern themselves with the rights and well-being of people everywhere. This formula goes beyond the domestic analogy by making explicit the 'cosmopolitan' basis of 'international' justice. A morally legitimate state is one that can claim immunity from intervention because it does not grossly abuse those it governs.

Both pluralists and solidarists, then, are concerned with the moral legitimacy of states, which they do not dismiss as irrelevant (as a moral sceptic would) or assume as given (as would a defender of reason of state). Those who take either position are labelled political realists, but the positions are distinct and indeed incompatible. Political realism as an ethical doctrine challenges the view that one may not do evil for the sake of good. It is distinguished by the claim that defending a state justifies its government in violating moral limits. Realist ethics is consequentialist because it makes consequences the criterion of whether an action is right. But unlike utilitarianism, which focuses on the welfare of humanity as a whole, realism is concerned with the welfare of a particular state. It does not follow, however, that political realists must entirely repudiate morality. They may grant it provisional authority yet argue that moral considerations must yield to necessity. Most realists distinguish between situations in which morality applies and those in which moral principles should be set aside, but they differ over where the boundary lies. Some suggest that it divides private from public affairs, others domestic from foreign affairs – as Wight does in writing that 'international theory is the theory of survival' (Wight 1966a: 33). But some realists do allow a place for morality in foreign affairs: in the 'low politics' of economic policy in contrast to the 'high politics' of national defence, for example, or in the ordinary conduct of war as opposed to the conduct of war in situations of 'supreme emergency', which invite us to set aside moral considerations.

Realist arguments can be further distinguished according to whether they hold that consequential expediency for the sake of defending a people makes an action 'just' or, more coherently, that justice must simply yield to prudence. The bottom line might be the same, but the arguments are different, and for the theorist arguments matter. The kind of realism that appeals to prudence rather than to morality – that does not seek to justify injustice – respects the categories of prudence or utility, on the one hand, and morality or justice, on the other. Prudential arguments depend on calculating the relative worth of various outcomes, moral arguments on interpreting antecedently authoritative principles. Prudential realists like Machiavelli and Weber distinguish between justice and policy, that is, between acting on the basis of principle and acting expediently to establish or maintain a just civil or international order. A policy of pursuing the balance of power can be moralized by presenting it as a response to aggression, but statesmen from Pitt the Younger to Churchill have understood it more clearly and less sentimentally as a necessarily ruthless way to preserve the states system from imperial hegemony.

Global justice

The word 'global' seems to be displacing the word 'international' in many contexts, but there is little agreement on what it means. Global can be a synonym for universal or cosmopolitan but its spatial and temporal connotations, which evoke this earth in our epoch, undercut the claim to universality. These ambiguities carry over into the expression 'global justice', which has yet to acquire an agreed meaning. For some, it seems to identify a residual category that includes everything pertaining to justice in world affairs *except* justice in war (Jones 1999; Mandle 2006; Pogge and Moellendorf 2008). For others, it marks a debate about the limits of cultural difference or the moral significance of national boundaries (Tan 2000; De Grieff and Cronin 2002). In some contexts, global justice is distributive justice or, more broadly, a moral duty to relieve poverty (Pogge 2001). In others it is retributive justice administered though a regime of international criminal law under which people are held accountable for war crimes and other human rights abuses (Robertson 2006). Efforts have been made to link the themes of just war, humanitarian duty, economic inequality, cultural diversity, democracy, and legal order (Moellendorf 2002; Caney 2005), but in the absence of a precise definition of justice and a systematic theoretical framework the project must be regarded as unfinished. The obscurity of the words 'global' and 'justice' is not lessened simply by putting them together. The question, then, is whether 'global justice' is something other than a catchall.

Two ideas are necessary if the expression 'global justice' is to be made coherent. One is the idea of universal moral principles prescribing how people should treat one another as human beings, not as members of a particular community. These principles constitute what was once called natural law and is now called human rights. As these expressions imply, principles of global justice prescribe obligations for everyone regardless of whether everyone acknowledges their authority: it is not permissible to violate them, regardless of local norms. If this reasoning is roughly correct, a theory of global justice must be 'cosmopolitan' in the sense that it is based on universal moral principles.

The second idea we need is the idea of duty. To say that something is a matter of justice is to say that it involves a duty, which implies a body of law – moral or positive – on which the duty is based. This law also grounds the rights of those to whom the duty is owed. Justice is a virtue and implies a standard of conduct but it is not the only virtue or standard. We need to distinguish what is just from what is virtuous or desirable on other grounds. Not all moral principles, even universal ones, are properly enforceable and therefore a matter of 'justice' – some are principles of utility, humanity, generosity, compassion, courage, honour, or other values. An act may be desirable as a matter of personal virtue or public policy, yet fall outside the realm of justice. Principles of justice prescribe moral duties that could without moral impropriety be prescribed by positive law as well (Nardin 2005, 2006, 2008).

Principles of global justice, then, are universal moral principles that could properly be enforced as part of civil, international or supranational law. An old debate is whether global justice can be achieved through a combination of civil and international law or requires supranational institutions whose authority supersedes that of states. Some argue that global justice can only be secured by moving towards a global order. States are no longer able to respond effectively to problems that affect them because these problems are now global rather than local (Held 1995), or because justice can be realised only within a legal order (Nagel 2005). But these arguments depend in part on contingencies that fall outside the scope of a theory of justice. Others argue that achieving global justice will require new forms of order because states as we know them are morally illegitimate. Whether a legal order is morally legitimate is a question that *does* fall within the scope of a theory of justice. It is a familiar argument in the history of political thought that a state can be morally legitimate, provided it is reasonably just, because even though its laws are coercive, it is the product of choices to establish, join, or remain a member of an association of citizens. The requirement that the state be just arises from the coercive character of civil association, for to enforce unjust laws would be to violate the freedom of the associates. If this argument is sound, a theory of global justice cannot ignore the rights of states, for these rights are grounded on the moral rights of those who choose to live according to their laws. Nor can it ignore international law, whose authority derives from the rights of states. A society of states is no less legitimate than a single global society. To put it differently, if territorial states are illegitimate, it is hard to see how a global state could be legitimate.

The tension between state-centric and global frameworks for international justice is evident in the debate over economic inequality. A generation ago, that debate centred on the gap between rich and poor countries, the 'haves' and the 'have-nots', and on demands for a 'new international economic order' in which wealth would be redistributed. Developed states would acknowledge the sovereign right of less-developed states to own their natural resources, seize foreign owned assets and settle compensation claims under local law. They would agree to terms of trade more favourable to commodity-exporting countries, share their knowledge and technology, and increase their levels of foreign aid. Distributive justice in the context of this debate meant redistributing wealth and power from rich to poor countries, which is not the same as redistributing wealth within a country. Foreign aid can even increase inequality in poor countries if it is stolen by corrupt elites. The proposals for a new international economic order that were advanced by former colonies in the sixties and seventies did not challenge the state-centric premises of the existing international order.

Theorists of international distributive justice from the seventies onwards have argued that redistribution must be global, not international (O'Neill 1986; Singer 2002). Here once again, Rawls has been at the centre of the debate. As the leading theorist of justice after the publication of *A Theory of Justice*, he disappointed those, like Brian Barry and Charles Beitz, who wanted to see his principles applied internationally, by failing to articulate principles of distributive justice beyond the state. His original reason for ignoring the topic was that in a theory of justice as fairness, which is all that he claimed his theory was, distributive justice means the fair allocation of benefits and burdens in a society understood to be a 'cooperative venture for mutual advantage' (Rawls 1971: 4). But international society is not such a venture, Rawls argued. This claim provoked the rejoinder that economic interdependence was transforming the international system into a scheme of social cooperation by linking national economies in a single global economy. If principles of distributive justice apply within a national economy, it is inconsistent to hold that they do not apply in the world economy (Beitz 1979). But this argument had the perverse result of implying that principles of distributive justice apply most strongly between countries with tightly integrated economies, like those of Western Europe, and least between rich and poor countries with few economic ties. Instead of challenging the proposition that there is no injustice in ignoring those with whom we have minimal contact, it seemed to reinforce it. The idea that a society is a scheme of social cooperation for the production of collective benefits is in any case a highly contentious idea, one that is at odds with the liberal conception of the state as a framework for enabling the coexistence of individual wills: a civil order, not a collective enterprise. That the world might be a single society does not settle the question of what kind of society it is or ought to be.

Some argue that global distributive justice requires 'shared meanings' as the basis for an agreed 'scheme of global social cooperation' and a 'meaningful global justice community' (Walzer 1983: 29–30; Hurrell 2007: 317). For them, the ideal of global distributive justice is either a mirage or an invitation to construct the global community it requires. Others regard shared meanings as less relevant in determining duties of global justice than the consideration that human needs know no borders. If people are impoverished, those who are affluent have a duty to assist them that is independent of economic relationships or cultural affinities. The degree to which people share meanings or feel sympathy with one another may explain their willingness to help one another. It is not relevant, however, to whether they should treat each other justly (Van Parijs 2007: 644). The duty to relieve poverty is not a special obligation, like the obligation to care for our children or elderly parents; it is a general obligation premised on our common humanity. We have a duty to assist the 'distant needy' (Chatterjee 2004) as well as duties to assist those closer to home. This debate, sometimes cast as a debate between 'communitarians' and 'cosmopolitans' (Brown 1992a), has a long history and, probably, a long future.

Rawls's reply, in *The Law of Peoples*, seeks the middle ground. There is a duty to help economically burdened societies establish just and effective institutions. But principles of distributive justice that apply within a liberal state do not apply globally because they assume a comprehensive doctrine, liberal egalitarianism, that is accepted in some societies but not in others and that cannot be made a doctrine for all if legitimate cultural differences are to be respected (Rawls 1999: 105–20). As mentioned in the preceding section, the key idea for Rawls is public reason, which requires that the principles for evaluating and ameliorating global poverty should be principles acknowledged by all, not those particular to liberal egalitarians (Rawls 1999: 121–8). This amounts to saying that principles of economic distribution are, within wide limits, principles of choice, not justice. They may represent a desirable goal but unlike basic human rights and rules against violence they do not prescribe enforceable duties.

The argument that global poverty is a matter of distributive justice presupposes a relative standard. When theorists of global justice emphasize the gap between rich and poor, they imply that injustice arises from inequality rather than from the mere fact of poverty. If everyone in the world were equally poor, there would (on this theory) be much suffering but no injustice. This has led some to conclude that relieving poverty is better viewed as a matter of humanity or beneficence than of justice (Campbell 2007), a point also made by feminists who approach the topic from the standpoint of an ethics of care. The global poverty debate may be turning away from the idea of distributive justice to the ideas of freedom, capability, and human rights, which may be better suited to the topic. As a consequence of efforts to replace humanitarian intervention with a broader 'responsibility to protect' on the part of governments and international institutions, the suggestion that everyone has a duty to support policies that would reduce violence and suffering has gained acceptance (Barry and Pogge 2005; Kuper 2005; Young 2006). David Miller relies on the idea of responsibility to ground a theory of global justice, but although he distinguishes 'moral responsibility' (by which he means culpability) from causal responsibility, he does not consistently distinguish culpability from duty (Miller 2007). Arguably these are distinct. We judge the rightness of actions considered objectively in relation to rules that prescribe duties and support claims to rights. But we also judge the responsibility of agents for actions considered subjectively, with respect to motive and the extent to which the actions are voluntary. Agents cannot be blamed for actions, no matter how wrong, unless they are responsible in this sense. Using the word 'responsibility' to encompass judgements of duty and of culpability obscures the distinction between them.

Those who debate the duty to protect are puzzled by the so-called 'agency problem': if there is an international duty to protect people from harm, whose duty is it? Duties based on capacity to protect or on ties of community are obvious candidates (Miller 2007: 103–4) but they do not resolve the agency problem when there are many agents meeting the criterion (Tan 2006: 97–102), Conventional internationalism assigns to states the duties to maintain order, protect human rights, relieve poverty, settle international disputes and deal with common problems like climate change. Globalists apportion those duties among a wider range of participants, from individuals acting through international advocacy groups in an emerging global 'civil society' to public officials coordinating their activities in transnational networks to formal international organizations. Paralleling a concern with 'responsibility' in the discourse of global justice is a concern with 'institutions', though whether the institutions in question are legal ones is a matter for debate (Weinstock 2005). In the past, theorists of global order took a universal legal system as the ideal towards which the world should move, perhaps through a gradually expanding confederation of states committed to the rule of law (Kant 1991; Bohman and Lutz-Bachmann 1997). Theorists of global order now talk less about law and more about 'governance', by which they mean the management of global policies in the absence of a central government.

The idea of global governance is that both public and private decisions contribute to the 'norms' – not 'laws' – that regulate world affairs. The outcome is a system of horizontal interactions in which officials in different branches of government work with counterparts in other countries and with bankers, scientists, activists and others outside government (Sinclair 2003). Those who are optimistic about global governance think it can solve global problems more effectively than traditional diplomacy (Held 2004; Slaughter 2004). Pessimists worry that, under the conditions of complexity and speed that characterize globalization, the effect will be to weaken democracy and the rule of law (Scheuerman 2004; Cohen 2004). They argue that the idea of global governance blurs the distinction between law and non-law by relying on ideas like regulatory regimes, soft law and private authority, and that it treats law as an instrument of policy while overlooking its importance as a constraint on policy-making. The distinction between law and policy vanishes when public deliberation is replaced by administrative decision-making or when procedural constraints are ignored for the sake of executive efficiency. The rule of law is most starkly challenged when emergency powers are asserted, but it also suffers erosion when law is displaced by policy ('deformalization') or divided into functionally distinct regulatory regimes managed to advance particular interests ('fragmentation'). Both practices weaken the public realm and the legal order on which it depends (Koskenniemi 2007).

Advocates for global governance fail to grasp the importance of law for securing the democracy, justice and rationality they claim to value. Democracy presupposes deliberation within a legally constituted association. Public deliberation is discussion focused on the laws of a state or other political association. Because law involves obligations, public deliberation concerns the obligations that should be imposed by law. Theorists of global democracy overlook this point when they detach deliberation from making decisions about law (Dryzek 2006). One of the prerequisites of democratic politics is the existence of a public realm in which citizens can voice their opinions on public affairs. Mirroring the idea of the public realm in the internal politics of the modern state is the idea of a global public realm as a space for free discussion of the laws of an emergent global polity. That discussion needs to be theorized in a way that links the idea of global justice to ideas about democracy, the rule of law and civil society (understood, perhaps naïvely, as an arena for the activities of voluntary associations to advance conceptions of the common good).

The global justice debate seems to be moving beyond the claim that justice must be global *as opposed to* international. It is widely understood that universal obligations can be implemented locally, that states can have moral legitimacy, and that even if globalization is eroding sovereignty, states continue to engage the loyalty of their citizens and to do business with one another. For better or worse, international law provides a framework for ordering the globe whose rationale is both moral and pragmatic. And this means that a theory of global justice cannot ignore the rights and duties of states. Instead of choosing between the global and the international, the theorist of justice needs to consider both. And if law is to be kept in the picture, the proper focus of theorizing is not 'global governance' but global *government* through formal agreements, supranational institutions and perhaps (as theorists from Kant to Rawls have imagined) an expanding confederation of rule-of-law states, for which the European Union remains a model.

For the moment, global justice is the centre of attention in international political theory. One cannot help thinking, however, that from the standpoint of theory, there is less here than meets the eye. To the extent that one emphasizes the global over the international, the global justice debate simply becomes a debate about 'justice' without qualification. Too often, those who write on global justice advance familiar ideas about social justice without explaining how they are supposed to work at the global level. Or, focusing on injustice, they descend into distinctly untheoretical advocacy. Lacking historical perspective, they fail to see how their arguments are related to those of previous generations.

The history of international thought

Many questions prominent in the global justice debate – the relationship between universal principles and local practices, the problem of poverty, the responsibility to protect, and the emergence of a global public realm – invite inquiry into earlier debates over the Spanish conquest of America, international socialism, the civilizing mission of empire and the dependence of peace on enlightened public opinion. Historians of political thought have paid more attention to internal politics than to world affairs, for the most part touching on ideas about international relations only at the margins of their inquiries. But significant studies of international themes, thinkers and texts have appeared in recent years. International political thought is no longer a marginal concern.

Intellectual history in a given field depends on identifying relevant texts. Shortly before the First World War the Carnegie Institution began a project of editing and translating what it saw, not always correctly, as the foundational texts of international law, and though one can question their selection and scholarship these editions remain indispensable. The writings on international affairs of Vattel, Kant, Burke, Mill and many other thinkers were dusted off and anthologized on both sides of the Atlantic (Wolfers and Martin 1956; Forsyth, Keens-Soper and Savigear 1970), and by the end of the century new editions of the Carnegie classics had begun to appear. One sign that the history of international thought had become an accepted academic subject was the appearance of textbooks (Boucher 1998; Pangle and Ahrensdorf 1999; Keene 2005) and anthologies (Brown, Nardin and Rengger 2002; Reichberg, Syse and Begby 2006). But such books depend on primary historical scholarship, which includes the recovery and translation of non-canonical texts.

Theorists of international relations often draw inspiration from their predecessors, as Hobbes did from Thucydides or Rousseau from Saint-Pierre. But one cannot use a text without wondering whether one has understood it correctly, and to do that one must notice that words change their meaning over time and in translation. One must know not only the texts but their contexts as well. Yet the more one focuses on meaning and context, the less one is concerned with using a text and the more with simply understanding it. That effort encompasses investigating its author's intention, the conventions or shared meanings he or she could draw upon, how the text came to be written and rewritten, and other matters we would understand to be 'historical' rather than theoretical. These points, which have assumed the status of orthodoxy in the study of the history of political thought, are often ignored by international relations scholars. It is all too easy for those interested in current affairs to read old authors as if they were dealing with current questions rather than questions of their own. But to understand their meaning one must know the questions they were trying to answer, and this means understanding the discourses that are the context of their texts. Those discourses do not determine what can or cannot be said – an author can choose to challenge or ignore conventional meanings – but they provide evidence about what he or she might have been thinking. Similarly, to locate a text within a tradition or lineage one must know how the author's contemporaries and successors understood it, and this too requires historical evidence and judgement (Jahn 2006: 12–17).

Making sense of past thought about international relations in a genuinely historical manner requires that we avoid reading our own concerns back into the past. It is tempting to recruit luminaries like Thucydides or Grotius to one's cause, but there are dangers in doing so. The historian of international thought cultivates a detached and critical attitude towards the field's intellectual inheritance. Against claims that Thucydides was a political realist, for example, historical scholarship has given us studies of the relevant texts and contexts that support a more complex portrait (White 1984; Johnson 1993). Instead of honouring Grotius as the father of international law or making him stand for a constructed tradition of international theorizing, we can now read him in his own context as a theologian, humanist, and politician who was in some ways more medieval than modern and in others closer to Hobbes than is usually thought (Tierney 1997; Tuck 1993). It is anachronistic to treat Grotius as a theorist of 'international society' when there is scant evidence that he held any such idea (Jeffery 2006) and misleading to emphasize his remarks on sociability while ignoring those on self-preservation, especially when there is evidence that the former were politically motivated. Nor does it make sense to call Grotius an 'international lawyer' when the idea of international law (as we understand it) had not yet been invented and when he wrote his most famous book not as a lawyer, which he was not, but as a propagandist for the Dutch East India Company.

Received views of Thomas Hobbes as an archetypal political realist and theorist of international anarchy are also being reconsidered. The first view, Hobbes as realist, neglects the contradictory forms that realism can take, conflating moral scepticism with political realism and leaving the character of Hobbes's alleged realism unresolved. It also fails to acknowledge that Hobbes, like Thucydides, is a brilliant ironist and severe moralist. The second view, Hobbes as theorist of international anarchy, was undercut by Murray Forsyth 30 years ago in a perceptive article (Forsyth 1979); Noel Malcolm has now assembled additional evidence to refute it (Malcolm 2002). Hobbes was identified as a theorist of international anarchy only in the twentieth century with the invention of 'anarchy' as an organizing idea for the emerging discipline of international relations (Schmidt 1998; Armitage 2006).

Instead of using interpretative categories drawn from current concerns ('realism', 'anarchy'), the historian reads early modern thinkers who concerned themselves with war, diplomacy and trade in terms of categories appropriate to their time and place. In discussing the sixteenth and seventeenth centuries, a distinction between humanism and scholasticism (Tuck 1999) makes more sense than the distinction between realism and internationalism. In place of timeless 'traditions' of political and international thought like realism and idealism, historians have advanced the idea of contextually specific 'languages' of inquiry and debate, such as Spanish Thomism in the debate over the Indies, modern (or Protestant) natural law and the language of commerce in eighteenth-century Britain (Pagden 1987). This approach has proven productive because it enables the scholar to see that a language of ideas, like a natural language, can be used to say different things and to disagree as well as to agree. The word 'language' lends itself less easily than the word 'tradition' to the idea of doctrinal unity, though every tradition can be a tradition of debate (questions) rather than doctrine (answers): even those who agree about many things do not agree about everything. The traditions of just war and reason of state, for example, developed in dialogue with one another and might even be viewed as a single tradition of debate over the relationship in war between morality and prudence. Traditions or discursive languages can be defined more or less broadly according to purpose. But the categories that are most useful for historical inquiry are likely to be those rooted in a particular time and place, not theoretical or ideological abstractions.

The category of 'international relations' is itself historically specific. It best suits the period between the emergence of the European territorial state in the late seventeenth century and the emergence of global institutions in the mid-twentieth. The word 'international' (or a similar word in another language) was not available to Europeans living before the middle of the seventeenth-century, so to read Vitoria or Grotius as a theorist of international relations, as we understand it, is to risk anachronism. But if the word 'international' presumes a world organized on the basis of territorial states, some other word is needed for relations between pre-political tribes, ancient city-states, medieval realms, dynastic monarchies and other political communities that are not exactly 'states'. The word 'foreign' (or its equivalent) is probably as old as the idea of a distinct people, making an expression like 'foreign affairs' suitable for use across broad swaths of time and space. The same can be said for words like war, trade and diplomacy, which can be defined in ways independent of the institutional forms they have acquired in particular times and places.

Diplomatic representation does not depend on the institution of the resident ambassador, which was invented in the Renaissance and is therefore specifically modern (Mattingly 1956). The balance of power as a practice of resisting imperial conquest may have a long history, but 'the balance of power' as a self-conscious policy of combining to preserve the states system by preserving the independence of its members is, once again, a distinctly modern idea.

At the end of the modern period the category 'international' is being reconsidered in what many regard as a world being transformed by globalization. Whether the disappearance of international relations is real or illusory remains controversial and globalist arguments are part of that controversy. It would, however, be a mistake to overlook the globalist discourses of earlier periods. The claim that we live in 'one world' (Singer 2002) – that political, military, economic and physical events around the world are now so interconnected as to constitute 'a closed system' – was central to geo-politics a century ago (Mackinder 1919: 29–30). At the moral level, the idea that people everywhere can be imagined as citizens of a single world community goes back to the Stoics. This might not count as 'globalism' if we view that idea as distinctly modern, but it is certainly universalist or cosmopolitan in discounting the moral significance of the political boundaries. Pre-modern ideas of natural law (moral precepts binding on all rational beings) and the law of nations (rules found in the laws and customs of different peoples) live on in many of today's 'cosmopolitan' theories of human rights and global justice.

It has been argued that the category 'international' is misleading even for the modern period because in concentrating on an intra-European international order it neglects patterns of order that prevailed elsewhere in the world. The pluralist understanding of international society paints a picture of world order in which states coexist with one another on the basis of international law, but outside Europe the order has historically been one in which European states conquered and ruled non-European peoples in the name of 'civilization' (Keene 2002). In their preoccupation with the equality of states and balance of power within the European system, international relations theorists overlook the unequal and unbalanced relationship between Europe and the rest of the world. They assume that the anarchical pattern is normal and that the imperial pattern is an aberration; in fact, international society displays both. There was certainly an international element in the competition among European imperial powers for trade and territory, starting with the search for gold and spices in the Indies in the sixteenth century and ending with the 'scramble for Africa' at the end of the nineteenth. But the *idea* of empire is a denial of international relations, for each empire imagines itself the guardian of a potentially unitary world order governed not horizontally by international law but vertically through imperial administration. One might find this argument overstated or not especially novel but the politics of imperial imagination has nevertheless proven a fruitful area for historical inquiry (Muthu 2003; Pitts 2006; Bell 2007).

The solution to the categorical problem in writing the history of international thought is to resist broad generalizations by narrowing the focus of inquiry to topics that can be securely grounded on historical evidence. Sometimes that focus is achieved by examining a particular text, like Kant's *Perpetual Peace* (1795), or the writings of a particular thinker, like J. A. Hobson or Leonard Woolf (Long 1996; Wilson 2003). It can also be achieved by studying a tradition or attitude, like twentieth-century political realism (Smith 1986) or English idealism between the wars (Morefield 2005). With a well-defined thematic focus the historian can cover an extended historical period without anachronism: a history of world government or international law from the Greeks to the present is a non-starter, historically speaking, but a history of international legal theory from 1870 to 1960 or even a history of confederation in modern Europe can be successfully presented (Koskenniemi 2001; Forsyth 1981).

Theorizing international justice can be difficult for philosophers because in treating justice in a world assumed to be their own, defining it theoretically and being in favour of it practically are hard to keep separate. The danger is that the theorizing will be distorted by advocacy. This fate is more easily avoided by the historian, who contemplates a world that can never be other than it is – a past that can be understood but not improved. The danger of covert advocacy still exists, however, because the historian does not passively contemplate the past as given but is actively engaged in constructing it, and in doing so can succumb to partisanship. The historical profession has canons of inquiry that serve to limit partisanship, though they are not always observed. But the historian may have an easier time than the philosopher when the latter is reflecting on the politics of his own time. For that reason, if no other, the history of international thought has an important place in international political theory, and Martin Wight was right to insist on its importance.

Bibliography

Abrams, P. (1982) *Historical Sociology* (Shepton Mallet).

Ackerly, B.A. (2000) *Political Theory and Feminist Social Criticism* (Cambridge).

—— (2001a) *Political Theory and Feminist Social Criticism* (Cambridge).

—— (2001b) 'Women's Human Rights Activists as Cross-Cultural Theorists', *International Journal of Feminist Politics*, 3(3).

Ackerley, B.A.. and Okin, S. M. (1999) 'Feminist Social Criticism and the International Movement for Women's Rights as Human Rights', in I. Shapiro and C. Hacker-Cordon (eds), *Democracy's Edges* (Cambridge).

Ackerly, B.A., Stern, M. and True, J. (eds) (2006) *Feminist Methodologies for International Relations* (Cambridge).

Ackerly, B. and True, J. (2006) 'Studying the Struggles and Wishes of the Age: Feminist Theoretical Methodology and Feminist Theoretical Methods', in B. Ackerly, M. Stern and J. True (eds), *Feminist Methodologies for International Relations* (Cambridge).

—— (2008) 'An Intersectional Analysis of International Relations: Recasting the Discipline', *Politics and Gender*, 4(1).

—— (2009) *Doing Feminist Research in the Political and Social Sciences* (New York).

Adler, E. and Barnett, M. (1998) *Security Communities* (Cambridge).

Afshar, H. and Dennis, C. (1992) *Women and Adjustment in the Third World* (London).

Agamben, G. (1998) *Homo Sacer: Sovereign Power and Bare Life* (Stanford).

Agathangelou, A. (2004) *The Global Political Economy of Sex: Desire, Violence and Insecurity in Mediterranean Nation States* (New York).

Agathangelou, A. M. and Ling, L. H. M. (2004) 'Power, Borders, Security, Wealth: Lessons of Violence and Desire from September 11', *International Studies Quarterly*, 48(3).

Alison, M. (2004) 'Women as Agents of Political Violence: Gendering Security', *Security Dialogue*, 35.

Amnesty International (1990) *Women in the Front Lines: Human Rights Violations Against Women* (London).

Anderson, P. (1974) *Lineages of the Absolutist State* (London).

—— (1983) *In the Tracks of Historical Materialism* (London).

Anievas, A. (2005) 'Critical Dialogues: Habermasian Social Theory and International Relations', *Politics*, 25(3).

Apel, K.-O. (1980) *Towards a Transformation of Philosophy* (London).

Appfel-Marglin, F. and Marglin, S. (eds) (1990) *Dominating Knowledge: Development, Culture and Resistance* (Oxford).

Arblaster, A. (1984) *The Rise and Decline of Western Liberalism* (Oxford).

Archibugi, D. (ed.) (1998) *Re-Imagining Political Community: Studies in Cosmopolitan Democracy* (Cambridge).

—— (2002) 'Demos and Cosmopolis', *New Left Review*, 13.

—— (2004a) 'Cosmopolitan Democracy and its Critics: A Review', *European Journal of International Relations*, 10(3).

—— (2004b) 'Cosmopolitan Guidelines for Humanitarian Intervention', *Alternatives*, 29(1).

Archibugi, D. and Held, D. (eds) (1995) *Cosmopolitan Democracy: An Agenda for a New World Order* (Cambridge).

Armitage, D. (2006) 'Hobbes and the Foundations of Modern International Thought', in A. Brett and J. Tully, with H. Hamilton-Bleakley (eds), *Rethinking the Foundations of Modern Political Thought* (Cambridge).

Art, R. J. and Waltz, K. N. (1983) 'Technology, Strategy, and the Uses of Force', in R. J. Art and K. N. Waltz (eds), *The Use of Force* (Lanham).

Ashley, R. K. (1981) 'Political Realism and Human Interests', *International Studies Quarterly*, 25.

—— (1987) 'The Geopolitics of Geopolitical Space: Toward a Critical Social Theory of International Politics', *Alternatives*, 12(4).

—— (1988) 'Untying the Sovereign State: A Double Reading of the Anarchy Problematique', *Millennium*, 17(2).

—— (1989a) 'Living on Border Lines: Man, Poststructuralism and War', in J. Der Derian and M. J. Shapiro (eds), *International/Intertextual Relations: Postmodern Readings of World Politics* (Massachusetts).

—— (1989b) 'Imposing International Purpose: Notes on a Problematic of Governance', in E.-O. Czempiel and J. Rosenau (eds), *Global Changes and Theoretical Challenges: Approaches to World Politics for the 1990s* (Massachusetts).

Ashley, R. K. and. Walker, R. B. J. (1990) 'Speaking the Language of Exile: Dissidence in International Studies', *International Studies Quarterly*, 34(3).

Axelrod, R. (1984) *The Evolution of Cooperation* (New York).

Axelrod, R. and Keohane, R. O. (1986) 'Achieving Cooperation under Anarchy: Strategies and Institutions', in K. A. Oye (ed.), *Cooperation under Anarchy* (Princeton). Reprinted in D. Baldwin (ed.) (1993), *Neorealism and Neoliberalism: The Contemporary Debate* (New York).

Bain, W. (2003) *Between Anarchy and Society* (Oxford).

Baines, E. K. (1999) 'Gender Construction and the Protection Mandate of the UNHCR: Responses from Guatemalan Women', in E. Prugl and M. K. Meyer (eds), *Gender Politics and Global Governance* (Lanham).

Bairoch, P. (1993) *Economic and World History* (Chicago).

Bakker, I. (ed.) (1994) *The Strategic Silence: Gender and Economic Policy* (London).

Banks, M. (1985) 'The Inter-Paradigm Debate', in M. Light and A. J. R. Groom (eds), *International Relations: A Handbook of Current Theory* (London).

Barbalet, J. (ed.) (2002) *Emotions and Sociology* (Oxford).

Barnes, J. (1982) 'The Just War', in N. Kretzmann, A. Kenny and J. Pinborg (eds), *The Cambridge History of Late Medieval Philosophy* (Cambridge).

Barnett, J. (2000) 'Destabilizing the Environment-Conflict Thesis,' *Review of International Studies*, 26(2).

Barnett, M. and Duvall, R. D. (2004) 'Power in World Politics', *International Organization*, 59(1).

—— (eds) (2005) 'Power in Global Governance', in their own *Power in Global Governance* (Cambridge).

Barnett, M. and Finnemore, M. (2004) *Rules for the World: International Organizations in Global Politics* (Ithaca).

Bar On, B. (2003) 'Manly After-Effects of 11 September 2001: Reading William J. Bennett's Why We Fight: Moral Clarity and the War on Terrorism', *International Feminist Journal of Politics*, 5(3).

Barry, B. (1998) 'International Society from a Cosmopolitan Perspective', in D. R. Mapel and T. Nardin (eds), *International Society: Diverse Ethical Perspectives* (Princeton).

Barry, C. and Pogge, T. W. (eds) (2005) *Global Institutions and Responsibilities: Achieving Global Justice* (Malden).

Barry, J. (1995) 'Towards a Theory of the Green State', in S. Elworthy *et al.* (eds), *Perspectives on the Environment* 2 (Aldershot).

—— (1999) *Rethinking Green Politics: Nature, Virtue and Progress* (London).

Barry, J. and Eckersley, R. (eds) (2005) *The Global Ecological Crisis and the Nation-State* (Cambridge).

Baylis, J. and Smith, S. (eds) (2005) *The Globalisation of World Politics* (Oxford).

Beardsworth, R. (2005) 'The Future of Critical Philosophy and World Politics', *Millennium*, 34(1).

Beitz, C. (1979) *Political Theory and International Relations* (Princeton).

Bell, D. (ed.) (2007) *Victorian Visions of Global Order: Empire and International Relations in Nineteenth-Century Political Thought* (Cambridge).

Beneria, L. (ed.) (1982) *Women and Development: The Sexual Division of Labor in Rural Societies* (New York).

Benhabib, S. (1986) *Critique, Norm and Utopia: A Study of the Foundations of Critical Theory* (New York).

Benner, E. (1995) *Really Existing Nationalisms: A Post-Communist View from Marx and Engels* (Oxford).

Berman, J. (2003) '(Un)popular Strangers and Crises (Un)bounded: Discourses of Sex Trafficking, the European Political Community and the Panicked State of the Modern State', *European Journal of International Relations*, 9(1).

Bernauer, T. (1995) 'The Effectiveness of International Environmental Institutions: How We Might Learn More', *International Organization*, 49(2).

Bjola, C. (2005) 'Legitimating the Use of Force in International Politics: A Communicative Action Perspective', *European Journal of International Relations*, 11(2).

Bleiker, R. (2000) *Popular Dissent, Human Agency and Global Politics* (Cambridge).

—— (2001) 'The Aesthetic Turn in International Political Theory', *Millennium*, 30(3).

—— (2005) *Divided Korea: Toward a Culture of Reconciliation* (Minnesota).

Bleiker, R. and Hutchison, E. (2008) 'Fear no More: Emotions and World Politics', *Review of International Studies*, 34, special issue.

Bleiker, R. and Leet, M. (2005) 'From the Sublime to the Subliminal: Fear, Awe and Wonder in International Politics', *Millennium*, 34(3).

Block, F. (1980) 'Beyond State Autonomy: State Managers as Historical Subjects', *Socialist Register*.

Block, F. and Somers, M. (1984) 'Beyond the Economistic Fallacy: The Holistic Social Science of Karl Polanyi', in T. Skocpol (ed.), *Vision and Method in Historical Sociology* (Cambridge).

Bohman, J. (2002) 'How to Make a Social Science Practical: Pragmatism, Critical Social Science and Multiperspectival Theory', *Millennium*, 31(3).

Bohman, J. and Lutz-Bachmann, M. (eds) (1997) *Perpetual Peace: Essays on Kant's Cosmopolitanism* (Cambridge).

Bok, S. (1989) *A Strategy for Peace: Human Values and the Threat of War* (New York).

Boli, J., Meyer, J. and Thomas, G. (1989) 'Ontology and Rationalization in the Western Cultural Account', in G. Thomas *et al.* (eds), *Institutional Structure: Constituting State, Society, and the Individual* (London).

Bookchin, M. (1980) *Toward an Ecological Society* (Montreal).

—— (1982) *The Ecology of Freedom: The Emergence and Dissolution of Hierarchy* (Palo Alto).

—— (1992) 'Libertarian Municipalism: An Overview', *Society and Nature*, 1(1).

Booth, D. (1998) *The Environmental Consequences of Growth: Steady-State Economics as an Alternative to Ecological Decline* (London).

Booth, K. (1991a) 'Security and Emancipation', *Review of International Studies*, 17(4).

—— (1991b) 'Security in Anarchy: Utopian Realism in Theory and Practice', *International Affairs*, 67(3).

—— (1997) 'A Reply to Wallace', *Review of International Studies*, 22(3).

Booth, K. and Dunne T. (eds) (2002) *Worlds in Collision: Terror and the Future of Global Order* (London).

Booth, K. and Wheeler, N. J. (2007) *The Security Dilemma: Fear, Security and Distrust* (Basingstoke).

Boris, E. and Prugl, E. (eds) (1996) *Homeworkers in Global Perspective* (New York).

Bottomore, T. B. and Goode, P. (eds) (1978) *Austro-Marxism* (Oxford).

Boucher, D. (1998) *Political Theories of International Relations: From Thucydides to the Present* (Oxford).

Boyle, J. (2006) 'Traditional Just War Theory and Humanitarian Intervention' in T. Nardin and M. S. Williams (eds), *Humanitarian Intervention* (New York).

Brecher, B. (2007) *Torture and the Ticking Bomb* (Malden).

Brekke, T. (ed.) (2006) *The Ethics of War in Asian Civilizations: A Comparative Perspective* (London).

Brewer, A. (1990) *Marxist Theories of Imperialism: A Survey* (London).

Bromley, S. (1999) 'Marxism and Globalisation', in A. Gamble *et al.* (eds), *Marxism and Social Science* (London).

Brown, C. J. (1988) 'The Modern Requirement: Reflections on Normative International Theory in a Post-European World', *Millennium*, 17(2).

—— (1992a) *International Relations Theory: New Normative Approaches* (New York).

—— (1992b) 'Marxism and International Ethics', in T. Nardin and D. R. Napel (eds), *Traditions of International Ethics* (Cambridge).

—— (2002) *Understanding International Relations*, 2nd edn (Basingstoke).

Brown, C., Nardin, T. and Rengger, N. (eds) (2002) *International Relations in Political Thought: Texts from the Ancient Greeks to the First World War* (Cambridge).

Brunnee, J. and. Toope, S. J. (2000) 'International Law and Constructivism: Elements of an International Theory and of International Law', *Columbia Journal of Transnational Law*, 39(1).

Bryant, R. and Bailey, S. (eds) (1997) *Third World Political Ecology* (London).

Buchanan, A. (2004) *Justice, Legitimacy, and Self-Determination: Moral Foundations for International Law* (Oxford).

Buck, S. J. (1998) *The Global Commons: An Introduction* (London).

Bukharin, N. (1972) *Imperialism and World Economy* (London).

Bukovansky, M. (2002) *Legitimacy and Power Politics* (Princeton).

Bull, H. (1966a) 'The Grotian Conception of International Society', in H. Butterfield and M. Wight (eds), *Diplomatic Investigations: Essays in the Theory of International Relations* (London).

—— (1966b) 'International Theory: The Case for a Classical Approach', *World Politics*, 18. Reprinted in K. Knorr and J. N. Rosenau (eds) (1969), *Contending Approaches to International Relations* (Princeton).

—— (1969/1995) 'The Theory of International Politics, 1919–1969', in B. Porter (ed.), *The Aberystwyth Papers* (London). Reprinted in J. Der Derian (ed.) (1995), *International Theory: Critical Investigations* (Basingstoke).

—— (1973) 'Foreign Policy of Australia', *Proceedings of Australian Institute of Political Science*, (Sydney).

—— (1977) *The Anarchical Society: A Study of Order in World Politics* (London).

—— (1979a) 'Human Rights and World Politics', in R. Pettman (ed.), *Moral Claims in World Affairs* (London).

—— (1979b) 'The State's Positive Role in World Affairs', *Daedalus*, 108.

—— (1982) 'The West and South Africa', *Daedalus*, 111.

—— (1983) The International Anarchy in the 1980s', *Australian Outlook*, 37.

—— (ed.) (1984) *Intervention in World Politics* (Oxford).

—— (ed.) (1984a) 'Justice in International Relations', *The Hagey Lectures, The University of Waterloo* (Ontario).

—— (ed.) (1984b) 'The Revolt Against the West', in H. Bull and A. Watson (eds), *The Expansion of International Society* (Oxford).

Bull, H. and Watson, A. (eds) (1984) *The Expansion of International Society* (Oxford).

Bunyard, P. and Morgan-Grenville, F. (eds) (1987) *The Green Alternative* (London).

Burguiere, A. (1982) 'The Fate of the History of Mentalities in the Annales', *Comparative Studies in Society and History*, 24(4).

Burke, A. (2004) 'Just War or Ethical Peace? Moral Discourses of Strategic Violence After 9/11', *International Affairs*, 80(2).

—— (2005) 'Against the New Internationalism', *Ethics and International Affairs*, 9(2).

Burke, P. (ed.) (1973) *A New Kind of History: From the Writings of Lucien Febvre* (London).

—— (2003) 'The Annales, Braudel and Historical Sociology', in G. Delanty and E. Isin (eds), *Handbook of Historical Sociology* (London).

—— (2005) History and Social Theory (Cambridge).

Butler, J. (1990) *Gender Trouble: Feminist Subversions of Identity* (New York).

—— (2004) *Precarious Life: The Powers of Mourning and Violence* (London).

Butterfield, H. (1949) *Christianity and History* (London).

—— (1953) *Christianity, Diplomacy, and War* (London).

—— (1979) *Herbert Butterfield: Writings on Christianity and History* (New York).

Butterfield, H. and Wight, M. (eds) (1966) *Diplomatic Investigations* (London).

Buzan, B. (2001) 'The English School: An Exploited Resource in IR', *Review of International Studies*, 27.

—— (2003) 'Implications for the Study of International Relations', in M. Buckley and R. Fawn (eds), *Global Responses to Terrorism* (London).

—— (2004) *From International Society to World Society? English School Theory and the Social Structure of Globalisation* (Cambridge).

Buzan, B., Jones, C. A. and Little, R. (1993) *The Logic of Anarchy: Neorealism to Structural Realism* (New York).

Buzan, B. and Little, R. (2000) *International Systems in World History: Remaking the Study of International Relations* (Oxford).

—— (2001) 'Why International Relations Has Failed as a Project and What to Do About It', *Millennium*, 31(1).

—— (2002) 'International Systems in World History: Remaking the Study of International Relations', in S. Hobden and J. M. Hobson (eds), *Historical Sociology and International Relations* (Cambridge).

Buzan, B. and Waever, O. (2003) *Regions and Powers: The Structure of International Security* (Cambridge).

Byers, M. (2005) *War Law: Understanding International Law and Armed Conflict* (New York).

Calhoun, C. (2003) 'Afterword: Why Historical Sociology?', in G. Delanty and E. Isin (eds), *Handbook of Historical Sociology* (London).

Campbell, D. (1992) *Writing Security: United States Foreign Policy and the Politics of Identity* (Minneapolis).

—— (1994) 'The Deterritorializing of Responsibility: Levinas, Derrida and Ethics after the End of Philosophy', *Alternatives*, 19.

—— (1996) 'Political Prosaics, Transversal Politics, and the Anarchical World', in M. J. Shapiro and H. Alker (eds), *Challenging Boundaries: Global Flows, Territorial Identities* (Minneapolis).

—— (1998a) *National Deconstruction: Violence, Identity, and Justice in Bosnia* (Minneapolis).

—— (1998b) 'Why Fight? Humanitarianism, Principles, and Post-Structuralism', *Millennium*, 27(3).

—— (1999) 'Violence, Justice and Identity in the Bosnian Conflict', in J. Edkins, N. Persram and V. Pin-Fat (eds), *Sovereignty and Subjectivity* (Boulder).

—— (2002a) 'Time is Broken: The Return of the Past in the Response to September 11', *Theory and Event*, 5(4).

—— (2002b) 'Atrocity, Memory, Photography: Imaging the Concentration Camps of Bosnia – the Case of ITN versus Living Marxism, Part 1', *Journal of Human Rights*, 1(1).

—— (2005) 'Beyond Choice: The Onto-Politics of Critique', *International Relations*, 19(1).

—— (2007) 'Poststructuralism', in T. Dunne, M. Kurki and S. Smith (eds), *International Relations Theory: Discipline and Diversity* (Oxford).

Campbell, D. and Dillon, M. (1993) 'Introduction', in D. Campbell and M. Dillon (eds), *The Political Subject of Violence* (Manchester).

Campbell, T. (2007) 'Poverty as a Violation of Human Rights: Inhumanity or Injustice?' in T. Pogge (ed.), *Freedom from Poverty as a Human Right: Who Owes What to the Very Poor?* (Oxford).

Caney, S. (2005) *Justice Beyond Borders: A Global Political Theory* (Oxford).

Caprioli, M. (2000) 'Gendered Conflict', *Journal of Peace Research*, 37.

—— (2004) 'Feminist IR Theory and Quantitative Methodology', *International Studies Review*, 6(2).

Caprioli, M. and Boyer, M. (2001) 'Gender, Violence, and International Crisis', *Journal of Conflict Resolution*, 45.

Carpenter, R. C. (2002) 'Gender Theory in World Politics: Contributions of a Nonfeminist Standpoint?', *International Studies Review*, 4(3).

—— (2005) 'Women, Children and Other Vulnerable Groups: Gender, Strategic Frames and the Politics of Civilian Immunity', *International Studies Quarterly*, 49, 2.

—— (2006) *Innocent Women and Children: Gender, Norms and the Protection of Civilians* (London).

Carr, E. H. (1939/1945/1946) *The Twenty Years' Crisis: 1919–1939: An Introduction to the Study of International Relations* (London).

—— (1945) *Nationalism and After* (New York).

—— (1953) 'The Marxist Attitude to War', in E. H. Carr, *A History of Soviet Russia, 3, The Bolshevik Revolution, 1917–23* (London).

Carter, A. (1993) 'Towards a Green Political Theory', in A. Dobson and P. Lucardie (eds), *The Politics of Nature: Explorations in Green Political Theory* (London).

—— (1999) 'Game Theory and Decentralization', *Journal of Applied Philosophy*, 16(3).

Carver, T. (1998) *The PostModern Marx* (Manchester).

Chakrabarty, D. (2003) 'Subaltern Studies and Postcolonial Historiography', in G. Delanty and E. Isin (eds), *Handbook of Historical Sociology* (London).

Chan-Tiberghien, J. (2004) 'Gender Scepticism or Gender Boom? Poststructural Feminisms, Transnational Feminisms and the World Conference Against Racism', *International Feminist Journal of Politics*, 6(3).

Chang, K. and Ling, L. H. M. (2000) 'Globalization and its Intimate Other: Filipina Domestic Workers in Hong Kong', in M. Marchand and A. S.

Runyan (eds), *Gender and Global Restructuring: Sites, Sightings and Resistances* (New York).

Chappell, L. (2008) 'The International Criminal Court: A New Arena for Transforming Justice' in S. M. Rai and G. Waylen (eds), *Global Governance: Feminist Perspectives* (New York).

Charlton, S. E., Everett, J. and Staudt, K. (eds) (1989) *Women, the State, and Development* (Albany).

Chatterjee, D. K. (ed.) (2004) *The Ethics of Assistance: Morality and the Distant Needy* (Cambridge).

Chatterjee, P. and Finger, M. (1994) *The Earth Brokers: Power, Politics and World Development* (London).

Chayes, A. and Chayes, A. H. (1993) 'On Compliance', *International Organization*, 47(2).

Chin, C. B. (1998) *In Service and Servitude: Foreign Female Domestic Workers and the Malaysian Modernity Project* (New York).

Chomsky, N. (1969) *American Power and the New Mandarins* (Harmondsworth).

—— (1994) *World Orders, Old and New* (London).

—— (1999a) *The New Military Humanism: Lessons from Kosovo* (London).

—— (1999b) *Profit Over People: Neoliberalism and the Global Order* (New York).

Choucri, N. (1993) 'Introduction: Theoretical, Empirical, and Policy Perspectives', in N. Choucri (ed.), *Global Accord: Environmental Challenges and International Responses* (Cambridge).

Christensen, T. J. and Snyder, J. (1990) 'Chain Gangs and Passed Bucks: Predicting Alliance Patterns in Multipolarity', *International Organization*, 44.

Christoff, P. (1996) 'Ecological Modernisation, Ecological Modernities', *Environmental Politics*, 5(3).

Clairmont, F. F. (1996) *The Rise and Fall of Economic Liberalism* (Penang).

Clapp, J. and Dauvergne, P. (2005) *Paths to a Green World: The Political Economy of the Global Environment* (Cambridge).

Clark, A. M., Friedman, E. J. and Hochstetler, K. (1998) 'The Sovereign Limits of Global Civil Society: A Comparison of NGO Participation in UN World Conferences on the Environment, Human Rights, and Women', *World Politics*, 51.

Clark, I. (1989) *The Hierarchy of States* (Cambridge).

—— (2005) *Legitimacy and International Society* (Oxford).

—— (2007) *International Legitimacy and World Society* (Oxford).

Clark, I., and Reus-Smit, C. (eds) (2007) 'Resolving International Crises of Legitimacy', *International Relations*, 44(2/3).

Cochran, M. (1999) *Normative Theory in International Relations: A Pragmatic Approach* (Cambridge).

Cockburn, C. (1998) *The Space Between Us: Negotiating Gender and National Identity in Conflict Zones* (London).

Cohen, J. (1990) 'Discourse Ethics and Civil Society', in D. Rasmussen (ed.), *Universalism vs Communitarianism* (Massachusetts).

—— (2004) 'Whose Sovereignty? Empire versus International Law', *Ethics and International Affairs*, 18(3).

Connell, R. J. (1990) 'The State and Gender Politics', *Theory and Society*, 19.

Connolly, W. (1991) 'Democracy and Territoriality', *Millennium*, 20(3).

—— (1994) 'Tocqueville, Territory and Violence', *Theory, Culture and Society*, 11.

—— (1995) *The Ethos of Pluralization* (Minneapolis).

Constantinou, C. (2004) *States of Political Discourse: Words, Regimes, Seditions* (London).

Copeland, D. C. (1996) 'Neorealism and the Myth of Bipolar Stability: Toward a New Dynamic Realist Theory of Major War', *Security Studies*, 5.

Cox, R. W. (1981) 'Social Forces, States and World Orders: Beyond International Relations Theory', *Millennium*, 10(2).

—— (1983) 'Gramsci, Hegemony and International Relations', *Millennium*, 12(2).

—— (1986) 'Postscript 1985', in R. O. Keohane (ed.), *Neorealism and Its Critics* (New York).

—— (1987) *Production, Power and World Order: Social Forces in the Making of History* (New York).

—— (1989) 'Production, the State, and Change in World Order', in E.-O. Czempiel and J. Rosenau (eds), *Global Change and Theoretical Challenges* (Cambridge).

—— (1992a) 'Towards a Post-Hegemonic Conceptualization of World Order: Reflections on the Relevancy of Ibn Khaldun', in J. N. Rosenau and E.-O. Czempiel (eds), *Governance Without Government: Order and Change in World Politics* (Cambridge).

—— (1992b) 'Multilateralism and World Order', *Review of International Studies*, 18.

—— (1993) 'Structural Issues of Global Governance: Implications for Europe', in S. Gill (ed.), *Gramsci, Historical Materialism and International Relations* (Cambridge).

—— (1994) 'Global Restructuring: Making Sense of the Changing International Political Economy', in R. Stubbs and G. Underhill (eds), *Political Economy and the Changing Global Order* (London).

—— (1999) 'Civil Society at the Turn of the Millennium: Prospects for an Alternative World Order', *Review of International Studies*, 25(1).

Crawford, N. C. (2000) 'The Passions of World Politics: Propositions on Emotions and Emotional Relationships', *International Security*, 24(4).

—— (2002) *Argument and Change in World Politics: Ethics, Decolonization, and Humanitarian Intervention* (Cambridge).

Cronin, B. (1999) *Community under Anarchy: Transnational Identity and the Evolution of Cooperation* (New York).

—— (2001) 'The Paradox of Hegemony: America's Ambiguous Relationship with the United Nations', *European Journal of International Relations*, 7(1).

Cummins, I. (1980) *Marx, Engels and National Movements* (London).

Cusack, T. R. and Stoll, R. J. (1990) *Exploring Realpolitik: Probing International Relations Theory with Computer Simulation* (Boulder).

Dalby, S. (1993) *Creating the Second Cold War: The Discourse of Politics* (London).

—— (1998) 'Ecological Metaphors of Security: World Politics in the Biosphere', *Alternatives*, 23(3).

—— (2002) *Environmental Security* (Minneapolis).

—— (2004) 'Ecological Politics, Violence, and the Theme of Empire', *Global Environmental Politics*, 4(2).

Daly, H. E. (1990) 'Toward Some Operational Principles of Sustainable Development', *Ecological Economics*, 2(1).

Daly, H. E. and Cobb, J. B., Jr (1989) *For the Common Good* (Boston), 2nd edn (1994).

De Geus, M. (1995) 'The Ecological Restructuring of the State', in B. Doherty and M. de Geus (eds), *Democracy and Green Political Thought* (London).

De Grieff, P. and Cronin, C. (eds) (2002) *Global Justice and Transnational Politics* (Cambridge, MA).

De Swaan, A. (1995) 'Widening Circles of Identification: Emotional Concerns in Sociogenetic Perspective', *Theory, Culture and Society*, 12.

—— (1997) 'Widening Circles of Disidentification: On the Psycho- and Sociogenesis of the Hatred of Distant Strangers: Reflections on Rwanda', *Theory, Culture and Society*, 14.

Dean, M. (1994) *Critical and Effective Histories: Foucault's Method and Historical Sociology* (London).

Delanty, G., and Isin, E. (2003) 'Introduction: Reorienting Historical Sociology', in G. Delanty and E. Isin (eds) *Handbook of Historical Sociology* (London).

—— (eds) (2003) *Handbook of Historical Sociology* (London).

Deleuze, G. and Guattari, F. (1977) *Anti-Oedipus: Capitalism and Schizophrenia* (New York).

—— (1987) *A Thousand Plateaus: Capitalism and Schizophrenia* (Minneapolis).

Denemark, R., Friedman, J., Gills, B. K., and Modelski, G., (eds) (2000) *World System History: The Social Science of Long-Term Change* (London).

Der Derian, J. (1987) *On Diplomacy: A Genealogy of Western Estrangement* (Oxford).

—— (1989) 'The Boundaries of Knowledge and Power in International Relations', in J. Der Derian and M. J. Shapiro (eds), *International/Intertextual Relations: Postmodern Readings of World Politics* (Lexington).

—— (2002) 'The War of Networks', *Theory and Event*, 5(4).

Derrida, J. (1974) *Of Grammatology* (Baltimore).

—— (1978) *Writing and Difference* (Henley).

—— (1981) *Positions* (Chicago).

—— (1988) *Limited Inc.* (Evanston).

—— (1994a) 'Spectres of Marx', *New Left Review*, 205.

—— (1994b) *Spectres of Marx: The State of the Debt, the Work of Mourning and the New International* (London).

—— (2003) 'Autoimmunity: Real and Symbolic Suicides – A Dialogue with Jacques Derrida', in G. Borradori (ed.), *Philosophy in a Time of Terror: Dialogues with Jürgen Habermas and Jacques Derrida* (Chicago).

—— (2005) *Rogues: Two Essays on Reason* (Stanford).

Deudney, D. (2007) *Bounding Power: Republican Security Theory from the Polis to the Global Village* (Princeton).

Deudney, D. and Matthew, R. (eds) (1999) *Contested Grounds: Security and Conflict in the New Environmental Politics* (Albany).

Deutsch, K. W. and Singer, J. D. (1964) 'Multipolar Power Systems and International Stability', *World Politics*, 16.

Devetak, R. (1995a) 'Incomplete States: Theories and Practices of Statecraft', in J. MacMillan and A. Linklater (eds), *Boundaries in Question: New Directions in International Relations* (London).

—— (1995b) 'The Project of Modernity and International Relations Theory', *Millennium*, 24(1).

—— (2002) 'Signs of a New Enlightenment? Concepts of Community and Humanity after the Cold War', in S. Lawson (ed.), *The New Agenda for International Relations: From Polarization to Globalization in World Politics* (Cambridge).

—— (2003) 'Loyalty and Plurality: Images of the Nation in Australia', in M. Waller and A. Linklater (eds), *Political Loyalty and the Nation-State* (London).

—— (2005) 'Violence, Order and Terror', in A. Bellamy (ed.), *International Society and Its Critics* (Oxford).

—— (2007) 'Between Kant and Pufendorf: Humanitarian Intervention, Statist Anti-Cosmopolitanism and Critical International Theory', *Review of International Studies*, 33 (Special Issue).

—— (2008) 'Failures, Rogues and Terrorists: States of Exception and the North/South Divide', in A. Bellamy, R. Bleiker, S. Davies and R. Devetak (eds), *Security and the War on Terror* (London).

Devetak, R. and Higgott, R. (1999) 'Justice Unbound? Globalization, States and the Transformation of the Social Bond', *International Affairs*, 75(3).

Diamond, J. (1997) *Guns, Germs and Steel: A Short History of Everybody for the Last Thirteen Thousand Years* (London).

DiCicco, J. M. and Levy, J. S. (1999) 'Power Shifts and Problem Shifts: The Evolution of the Power Transition Research Program', *Journal of Conflict Resolution*, 43.

Diez, T. and Steans, J. (2005) 'A Useful Dialogue? Habermas and International Relations', *Review of International Studies*, 31(1).

Dillon, M. (1999) 'The Sovereign and the Stranger', in J. Edkins, N. Persram and V. Pin-Fat (eds), *Sovereignty and Subjectivity* (Boulder).

Dillon, M. and Everard, J. (1992) 'Stat(e)ing Australia: Squid Jigging and the Masque of State', *Alternatives*, 17(3).

Dillon, M. and Reid, J. (2000) 'Global Governance, Liberal Peace, and Complex Emergency', *Alternatives*, 25(1).

Dobson, A. (1990) *Green Political Thought* (London).

—— (2003) *Citizenship and the Environment* (Oxford).

Doherty, B. and de Geus, M. (1996) 'Introduction', in B. Doherty and M. de Geus (eds), *Democracy and Green Political Thought* (London).

Domett, T. (2005) 'Soft Power in Global Politics? Diplomatic Partners as Transversal Actors', *Australian Journal of Political Science*, 40(2).

Donnelly, J. (1992) 'Twentieth Century Realism', in T. Nardin and D. Mapel (eds), *Traditions of International Ethics* (Cambridge).

—— (1995) 'Realism and the Academic Study of International Relations', in J. Farr, J. S. Dryzek and S. T. Leonard (eds), *Political Science in History: Research Programs and Political Traditions* (Cambridge).

—— (2000) *Realism and International Relations* (Cambridge).

—— (2003) *Universal Human Rights in Theory and Practice* (2nd ed Cornell).

Doran, P. (1993) 'The Earth Summit (UNCED): Ecology as Spectacle', *Paradigms*, 7(1).

—— (1995) 'Earth, Power, Knowledge: Towards a Critical Global Environmental Politics', in J. MacMillan and A. Linklater (eds), *New Directions in International Relations* (London).

Doty, R. L. (1999) 'Racism, Desire, and the Politics of Immigration', *Millennium*, 28(3).

Douthwaite, R. (1992) *The Growth Illusion* (Dublin).

Doyle, M. (1983) 'Kant, Liberal Legacies and Foreign Affairs', *Philosophy and Public Affairs*, 12.

—— (1986) 'Liberalism and World Politics', *American Political Science Review*, 80.

—— (1995) 'Liberalism and World Politics Revisited', in C. W. Kegley Jr (ed.), *Controversies in International Relations Theory* (New York).

—— (1997) *Ways of War and Peace: Realism, Liberalism and Socialism* (New York).

Dryzek, J. (1987) *Rational Ecology: Environment and Political Economy* (Oxford).

—— (1990) *Discursive Democracy: Politics, Policy, and Political Science* (Cambridge).

—— (1992) 'Ecology and Discursive Democracy: Beyond Liberal Capitalism and the Administrative State', *Capitalism, Nature, Socialism*, 3(2).

—— (1999) 'Transnational Democracy', *Journal of Political Philosophy*, 7(1).

—— (2006) *Deliberative Global Politics: Discourse and Democracy in a Divided World* (Cambridge).

Dryzek, J., Downes, D., Hunold, C., Schlosberg, D. and Hernes, H.-K. (2003) *Green States and Social Movements: Environmentalism in the United States, United Kingdom, Germany, and Norway* (Oxford).

Dunne, T. (1998) *Inventing International Society: A History of the English School* (Basingstoke).

—— (2003) 'Society and Hierarchy in International Relations', *International Relations*, 17.

—— (2008) 'Good Citizen Europe', *International Affairs*, 84(1).

Dunne, T. and Wheeler, N. J. (eds) (1999) *Human Rights in Global Politics* (Cambridge).

Durkheim, É. (1993) *Ethics and the Sociology of Morals* (New York).

Eckersley, R. (1992) *Environmentalism and Political Theory: Towards an Ecocentric Approach* (London).

—— (2004) *The Green State: Rethinking Democracy and Sovereignty* (Massachusetts).

Edelman, N. (1990) 'Global Prohibition Regimes: The Evolution of Norms in International Society', *International Organisation*, 44(4).

Edkins, J. (1999) *Poststructuralism and International Relations: Bringing the Political Back In* (Boulder).

—— (2000) 'Sovereign Power, Zones of Indistinction, and the Camp', *Alternatives*, 25(1).

—— (2002) 'Forget Trauma? Responses to September 11', *International Relations*, 16(2).

—— (2007) 'Poststructuralism', in M. Griffiths (eds), *International Relations Theory for the Twenty-First Century: An Introduction* (London).

Edkins, J. and Pin-Fat, V. (1999) 'The Subject of the Political', in J. Edkins, N. Persram and V. Pin-Fat (eds), *Sovereignty and Subjectivity* (Boulder).

Ehrlich, P. (1968) *The Population Bomb* (New York).

Eisenstadt, S. N. (1963) *The Political Systems of Empires* (London).

Ekins, P. (1993) 'Making Development Sustainable', in W. Sachs (ed.), *Global Ecology* (London).

Elias, N. (1983) *The Court Society* (Oxford).

—— (1994) *Reflections on a Life* (Cambridge).

—— (1998a) 'An Interview in Amsterdam', in J. Goudsblom and S. Mennell (eds), *The Norbert Elias Reader* (Oxford).

—— (1998b) 'The Retreat of Sociologists into the Present', in J. Goudsblom and S. Mennell (eds), *The Norbert Elias Reader* (Oxford).

—— (2000) *The Civilizing Process: Sociogenetic and Psychogenetic* (Oxford).

—— (2007) *Involvement and Detachment* (Dublin).

Elshtain, J. B. (1985) 'Reflections on War and Political Discourse: Realism, Just War, and Feminism in a Nuclear Age', *Political Theory*, 13.

—— (1987) *Women and War* (New York).

—— (1992) 'Sovereignty, Identity, Sacrifice', in V. S. Peterson (ed.), in *Gendered States: Feminist (Re)visions of International Relations Theory* (Boulder).

Emmanuel, A. (1972) *Unequal Exchange: A Study of the Imperialism of Trade* (New York).

Emy, H. V. (1993) *Remaking Australia* (Melbourne).

Enloe, C. (1989) *Bananas, Beaches and Bases: Making Feminist Sense of International Politics* (London).

—— (1994) *The Morning After: Sexual Politics at the End of the Cold War* (Berkeley).

—— (1997) 'Margins, Silences, and Bottom-Rungs: How to Overcome the Underestimation of Power in the Study of International Relation', in S. Smith, K. Booth and M. Zalewski (eds), *International Theory: Positivism and Beyond* (Cambridge).

—— (2000) *Manoeuvers: The International Politics of Militarizing Women's Lives* (Berkeley).

Eschle, C. and Maiguaschca, B. (eds) (2005) *Critical Theories, World Politics, and the 'Anti-Globalization Movement'* (London).

Escobar, A. (1995) *Encountering Development: The Making and Unmaking of the Third World* (Princeton).

Escudé, C. (1997) *Foreign Policy Theory in Menem's Argentina* (Gainesville).

Esteva, G. and Prakash, M. S. (1997) 'From Global Thinking to Local Thinking', in M. Rahnema (ed.) with V. Bawtree, *The Post-Development Reader* (London), originally in *Interculture*, 29(2) (1996).

Falk, R. (1999) *Predatory Globalization: A Critique* (Cambridge).

Ferguson, Y. H., and Mansbach, R. W. (1996) *Polities: Authorities, Identities and Change* (South Carolina).

Fierke, K. M. (1998) *Changing Games, Changing Strategies: Critical Investigations in Security* (Manchester).

—— (2007) *Critical Approaches to International Security* (Cambridge).

Finger, M. (1993) 'Politics of the UNCED Process', in W. Sachs (ed.), *Global Ecology* (London).

Finnemore, M. (1996) 'Norms, Culture, and World Politics: Insights from Sociology's Institutionalism', *International Organization*, 50(2).

—— (2001) 'Exporting the English School?', *Review of International Studies*, 27(3).

Finnemore, M. and Toope, S. J. (2001) 'Alternatives to "Legalization": Richer Views of Law and Politics', *International Organization*, 55(3).

Finnis, J. (1996), 'The Ethics of War and Peace in the Catholic Natural Law Tradition', in T. Nardin (ed.), *The Ethics of War and Peace: Religious and Secular Perspectives* (Princeton).

Finnis, J., Boyle, J. M., and Grisez, G. (1987) *Nuclear Deterrence, Morality and Realism* (Oxford).

Fischer, M. (1992) 'Feudal Europe, 800–1300: Communal Discourse and Conflictual Practices', *International Organisation*, 46(2).

Forbes, I. and Hoffman, M. (eds) (1993) *Political Theory, International Relations and the Ethics of Intervention* (Basingstoke).

Forde, S. (1992) 'Classical Realism', in T. Nardin and D. Mapel (eds), *Traditions of International Ethics* (Cambridge).

Forsyth, M. (1979) 'Thomas Hobbes and the External Relations of States', *British Journal of International Studies*, 5.

—— (1981) *Unions of States: The Theory and Practice of Confederation* (New York).

Forsyth, M., Keens-Soper, H. M. A. and Savigear P. (eds) (1970) *The Theory of International Relations: Selected Texts from Gentili to Treitschke* (New York).

Forum on Chomsky, *Review of International Studies*, 29(4).

Foucault, M. (1977) *Discipline and Punish* (Harmondsworth).

—— (1987) 'Nietzsche, Genealogy, History', in M. T. Gibbons (ed.), *Interpreting Politics* (London).

—— (2003) 'Society Must be Defended': Lectures at the College de France, 1975–1976 (New York).

Frank, A. G. (1967) *Capitalism and Underdevelopment in Latin America* (New York).

Frank, A. G., and Gills, B.K., (eds) (1993) *The World System: Five Hundred Years or Five Thousand?* (London).

Friedman, E. (1995) Women's Human Rights: The Emergence of a Movement', in J. Peters and A. Wolper (eds), *Women's Rights/Human Rights: International Feminist Perspectives* (New York).

Friedman, G. (1981) *The Political Philosophy of the Frankfurt School* (New York).

Friedman, T. (2000) *The Lexus and the Olive Tree* (London).

Fukuyama, F. (1992) *The End of History and the Last Man* (London).

—— (2002) 'History and September 11', in K. Booth and T. Dunne (eds), *Worlds in Collision* (London).

Gabriel, C. and Macdonald, L. (1994) Women's Transnational Organizing in the Context of NAFTA: Forging Feminist Internationality', *Millennium*, 23(3).

Gaddis, J. (1992–3) 'International Relations Theory and the End of the Cold War', *International Security*, 15, 5–53.

Gallie, W. B. (1978) *Philosophers of Peace and War* (Cambridge).

Gamble, A. (1981) *An Introduction to Modern Social and Political Thought* (London).

—— (1999) 'Marxism after Communism: Beyond Realism and Historicism', *Review of International Studies*, 25.

Gardner, R. N. (1990) 'The Comeback of Liberal Internationalism', *The Washington Quarterly*, 13(3).

Garnett, J. C. (1984) *Commonsense and the Theory of International Politics* (London).

Gatens, M. (1991) *Feminism and Philosophy* (Bloomington).

Gellner, E. (1974) *Legitimation of Belief* (Cambridge).

Gentry, C. and Sjoberg, L. (2008) *Mothers, Monsters, Whores: Women's Violence in Global Politics* (London).

George, J. (1994) *Discourses of Global Politics: A Critical (Re)Introduction* (Boulder).

George, J. and Campbell, D. (1990) 'Patterns of Dissent and the Celebration of Difference: Critical Social Theory and International Relations', *International Studies Quarterly*, 34(3).

Gibson, K., Law, L. and McKay, D. (2001) 'Beyond Heroes and Victims: Filipina Contract Migrants, Economic Activism and Class Transformations', *International Feminist Journal of Politics*, 3(3).

Giddens, A. (1981) *A Contemporary Critique of Historical Materialism* (London).

—— (1985) *The Nation-State and Violence* (Cambridge).

Gill, S. (ed.) (1993a) *Gramsci, Historical Materialism and International Relations* (Cambridge).

—— (1993b) 'Gramsci and Global Politics: Towards a Post-Hegemonic Research Agenda', in S. Gill, *Gramsci, Historical Materialism and International Relations* (Cambridge).

—— (1995) 'Globalization, Market Civilisation and Disciplinary Neo-Liberalism', *Millennium*, 24(4).

—— (1996) 'Globalization, Democratization, and the Politics of Indifference', in J. Mittelman (ed.), *Globalization: Critical Reflections* (Boulder).

—— (2003) *Power and Resistance in the New Global Order* (London).

Gilligan, C. (1982) *In a Different Voice: Psychological Theory and Women's Development* (Cambridge).

Gills, B. K., and Thompson, W. R., (eds) (2006) *Globalization and Global History* (Abingdon).

Gilpin, R. (1981) *War and Change in World Politics* (Cambridge).

—— (1986) 'The Richness of the Tradition of Political Realism', in R. O. Keohane (ed.), *Neo-Realism and Its Critics* (New York).

—— (1996) 'No One Loves a Political Realist,' *Security Studies*, 5.

Glaser, C. L. (1997) 'The Security Dilemma Revisited,' *World Politics*, 50.

Glaser, C. L. and Kaufmann, C. (1998) 'What is the Offense-Defense Balance and Can We Measure It?', *International Security*, 22.

Goetz, A.-M. (1991) 'Feminism and the Claim to Know: Contradictions in Feminist Approaches to Women in Development', in R. Grant and K. Newland (eds), *Gender and International Relations* (London).

Goldstein, J. (2001) *War and Gender* (Cambridge).

Goldthorpe, J. (1991) 'The Uses of History in Sociology: Reflections on Some Recent Tendencies', *British Journal of Sociology*, 42(2).

Gong, G. (1984) *The Standard of Civilisation in International Society* (Oxford).

Goodin, R. (1992) *Green Political Theory* (Cambridge).

Gouldner, A. (1980) *The Two Marxisms: Contradictions and Anomalies in the Development of Theory* (New York).

Graham, G. (2008) *Ethics and International Relations*, 2nd edn (Malden).

Grant, R. and Newland, K. (eds) (1991) *Gender and International Relations* (London).

Gray, J. G. (1959) *The Warriors* (New York).

—— (2004) *Al Qaeda and What It Means To Be Modern* (London).

Gray, M. M., Kittleson, M. C., and Sandholtz, W. (2006) 'Women and Globalization: A Study of 180 Countries, 1975–2000', *International Organization*, 60(2).

Grieco, J. M. (1988) 'Anarchy and the Limits of Cooperation', *International Organization*, 42(3).

—— (1997) 'Realist International Theory and the Study of World Politics', in M. W. Doyle and G. J. Ikenberry (eds), *New Thinking in International Relations Theory* (Boulder).

Gulick, E. V. (1967) *Europe's Classical Balance of Power: A Case History of the Theory and Practice of One of the Great Concepts of European Statecraft* (New York).

Guzzini, S. (1998) *Realism in International Relations and International Political Economy: The Continuing Story of a Death Foretold* (London).

Haacke, J. (2005) 'The Frankfurt School and International Relations: On the Centrality of Recognition', *Review of International Studies*, 31(1).

Haas, P. (1989) 'Do Regimes Matter? Epistemic Communities and Mediterranean Pollution Control', *International Organization*, 43(3).

—— (1990) *Saving the Mediterranean: The Politics of International Environmental Cooperation* (New York).

—— (1992) 'Introduction: Epistemic Communities and International Policy Coordination', *International Organization*, 46(1).

—— (2000) 'Social Constructivism and the Evolution of Multilateral Environmental Governance', in A. Prakash and J. Hart (eds), *Globalization and Governance* (London).

Haas, P. M., Keohane, R. O. and Levy, M. A. (1993) *Institutions for the Earth: Sources of Effective Environmental Protection* (Massachusetts).

Habermas, J. (1979) *Communication and the Evolution of Society* (Boston).

—— (1984a) *Communication and the Evolution of Society* (London).

—— (1984b) *The Theory of Communicative Action, 1: Reason and the Rationalization of Society* (Cambridge).

—— (1987) *The Philosophical Discourse of Modernity: Twelve Lectures* (Cambridge).

—— (1990) *Moral Consciousness and Communicative Action* (Cambridge).

—— (1993) *Justification and Application: Remarks on Discourse Ethics* (Cambridge).

—— (1994) *The Past as Future* (Cambridge).

—— (1997) 'Kant's Idea of Perpetual Peace, with the Benefit of Two Hundred Years' Hindsight', in J. Bohman and M. Lutz-Bachmann (eds), *Perpetual Peace: Essays on Kant's Cosmopolitan Ideal* (London).

—— (1998) *The Inclusion of the Other: Studies in Political Theory* (Cambridge).

—— (1999) 'Bestiality and Humanity: A War on the Border between Legality and Morality', *Constellations*, 6(3).

—— (2003a) 'Interpreting the Fall of a Monument', *Constellations*, 10(3).

—— (2003b) 'Fundamentalism and Terror – A Dialogue with Jürgen Habermas', in Giovann Borradori (ed.), *Philosophy in a Time of Terror: Dialogues with Jürgen Habermas and Jacques Derrida* (Chicago).

—— (2006) *The Divided West* (Cambridge).

Habermas, J. and Derrida, J. (2003) 'February 15, or What Binds Europeans Together: A Plea for a Common Foreign Policy, Beginning in the Core of Europe', *Constellations*, 10(3).

Hahn, R.W. and Richards, K.R. (1989) 'The Internationalisation of Environmental Regulation', *Harvard International Law Journal*, 30(2).

Hajer, M. (1995) *The Politics of Environmental Discourse: Ecological Modernisation and the Policy Process* (Oxford).

Hall, I. (2006) *The International Political Thought of Martin Wight* (Basingstoke).

Hall, P.A. and Taylor, R.C.R. (1996) 'Political Science and the Three New Institutionalisms', *Political Studies*, 44(5).

Hall, R. B. (1999) *National Collective Identity: Social Constructs and International Systems* (New York).

Hall, R. B., and Kratochwil, F. (1993) 'Medieval Tales: Neorealist "Science" and the Abuse of History', *International Organisation*, 47(3).

Halliday, F. (1983) *The Making of the Second Cold War* (London).

—— (1988a) 'Three Concepts of Internationalism', *International Affairs*, 64.

—— (1988b) 'Hidden from International Relations: Women and the International Arena', *Millennium*, 17(3).

—— (1990) 'The Pertinence of International Relations', *Political Studies*, 38(1).

—— (1994) *Rethinking International Relations* (London).

—— (1999) *Revolution and World Politics: The Rise and Fall of the Fifth Great Power* (Basingstoke).

Hanochi, S. (2003) 'Constitutionalism in a Modern Patriarchal State: Japan, the Sex Sector and Social Reproduction', in I. Bakker and S. Gill (eds), *Power, Production and Social Reproduction* (Basingstoke).

Hansenclever, A., Mayer, P. and Rittberger, V. (1996) 'Interests, Power, Knowledge: The Study of International Regimes', *Mershon International Studies Review*, 40(2).

Hardin, G. (1968) 'The Tragedy of the Commons', *Science*, 162.

—— (1974) 'The Ethics of a Lifeboat', *BioScience*.

Harding, S. (1986) *The Science Question in Feminism* (Ithaca).

—— (1987) *Feminism and Methodology* (Bloomington).

Harvey, D. (2003) *The New Imperialism* (Oxford).

Hashmi, S. H. (ed.) (2002) *Islamic Political Ethics: Civil Society, Pluralism, and Conflict* (Princeton).

Haslam, J. (2002) *No Virtue Like Necessity: Realist Thought in International Relations since Machiavelli* (New Haven).

Havel, V. (1999) 'Speech on Kosovo', *The New York Review of Books*, June 10.

Hay, C. (1999) 'Marxism and the State', in A. Gamble *et al.* (eds), *Marxism and Social Science* (London).

Hayward, T. (1995) *Ecological Thought: An Introduction* (Cambridge).

—— (1998) *Political Theory and Ecological Values* (Cambridge).

Heilbroner, R. (1974) *An Inquiry into the Human Prospect* (New York).

Heins, V. (2008) *Non Governmental Organizations in International Society: Struggles over Recognition* (Basingstoke).

Held, D. (ed.) (1993) *Prospects for Democracy: North, South, East, West* (Cambridge).

—— (1995) *Democracy and the Global Order: From the Modern State to Cosmopolitan Democracy* (Cambridge).

—— (2004) *Global Covenant: The Social Democratic Alternative to the Washington Consensus* (Cambridge).

Held, D. and McGrew, A. (eds), *The Global Transformations Reader* (Cambridge).

Held, D., McGrew, A., Goldblatt, D. and Perraton, J. (1999) *Global Transformations* (Cambridge).

Helleiner, E. (1996) 'International Political Economy and the Greens', *New Political Economy*, 1(1).

—— (2000) 'New Voices in the Globalization Debate: Green Perspectives on the World Economy', in R. Stubbs and G. Underhill (eds), *Political Economy and the Changing Global Order*, 2nd edn (Oxford).

Helman, G. B. and Ratner, S. R. (1992–93) 'Saving Failed States', *Foreign Policy*, 89.

Hempel, L. (1996) *Environmental Governance: The Global Challenge* (Washington).

Herz, J. H. (1976) *The Nation-State and the Crisis of World Politics: Essays on International Politics in the Twentieth Century* (New York).

Hildyard, N. (1993) 'Foxes in Charge of the Chickens', in W. Sachs (ed.), *Global Ecology* (London).

Hill, C. J. (1999) 'Where are we Going? International Relations, the Voice from Below', *Review of International Studies*, 25(1).

—— (2003) *The Changing Politics of Foreign Policy* (Basingstoke).

Hintze, O. (1975) *The Historical Essays of Otto Hintze* (edited with an introduction by Felix Gilbert), (Oxford).

Hirst, P. and Thompson, G. (1996) *Globalization in Question: The International Economy and the Possibilities of Governance* (Cambridge).

Hobden, S. (1998) *International Relations and Historical Sociology: Breaking Down Boundaries* (London).

Hobden, S., and Hobson, J. M. (eds) (2002) *Historical Sociology and International Relations* (Cambridge).

Hobsbawm, E. (2000) *The New Century* (London).

—— (2002) The Observer, 22 September, http://www.observer.co.uk/comment/story/0,6903,796531,00.html

—— (2007) *Globalisation, Democracy and Terrorism* (Little, Brown).

Hobson, J. (2004) *The Eastern Origins of Western Civilisation* (Cambridge).

Hoffman, M. (1987) 'Critical Theory and the Inter-Paradigm Debate', *Millennium*, 16(2).

—— (1991) 'Restructuring, Reconstruction, Reinscription, Rearticulation: Four Voices in Critical International Theory', *Millennium*, 20(2).

—— (1992) 'Third-Party Mediation and Conflict-Resolution in the Post-Cold War World', in J. Baylis and N. Rengger (eds), *Dilemmas of World Politics* (Oxford).

—— (1993) 'Agency, Identity and Intervention', in I. Forbes and M. Hoffman (eds), *Political Theory, International Relations and the Ethics of Intervention* (London).

Hoffmann, S. (1990) 'International Society', in J. D. B. Miller and R. J. Vincent (eds), *Order and Violence: Hedley Bull and International Relations* (Oxford).

—— (1995) 'The Crisis of Liberal Internationalism', *Foreign Policy*, 98.

Hollis, M. and Smith S. (1990) *Explaining and Understanding International Relations* (Oxford).

Holsti, K. (1985) *The Dividing Discipline: Hegemony and Diversity in International Theory* (Boston).

Holzgrefe, J. L. and Keohane, R. O. (eds) (2003) *Humanitarian Intervention: Ethical, Legal, and Political Dilemmas* (Cambridge).

Homer-Dixon, T. (1993) 'Physical Dimensions of Global Change', in N. Choucri (ed.), *Global Accord: Environmental Challenges and International Responses* (Cambridge).

—— (1999) *Environment, Scarcity and Violence* (Princeton).

Hooper, C. (2000) *Manly States: Masculinities, International Relations, and Gender Politics* (New York).

Hopf, T. (1998) 'The Promise of Constructivism in International Relations Theory', *International Security*, 23(1).

Horkheimer, M. (1972) *Critical Theory* (New York).

Horkheimer, M. and Adorno, T. (1972) *Dialectic of Enlightenment* (New York).

Hoskyns, C. (1996) *Integrating Gender: Women, Law and Politics in the European Union* (London).

Hoskyns, C. and Rai, S. (2007) 'Recasting the Global Political Economy: Counting Women's Unpaid Work', *New Political Economy*, 12(3).

Hovden, E. (1999) 'As If Nature Doesn't Matter: Ecology, Regime Theory and International Relations', *Environmental Politics*, 8(2).

Howard, M. (1978) *War and the Liberal Conscience* (Oxford).

Hui, V. T.-B. (2005) *War and State Formation in Ancient China and Early Modern Europe* (Cambridge).

Humphreys, D., Paterson, M. and Pettiford, L. (eds) (2003) 'Global Environmental Governance for the 21st Century', *Global Environmental Politics,* Special Issue, 3(2).

Hunt, L. (2007) *Inventing Human Rights: A History* (Norton).

Huntington, S. (1993) 'The Clash of Civilisations', *Foreign Affairs*, 72.

—— (1996) *The Clash of Civilizations and the Remaking of World Order* (New York).

Hurd, I. (2005) 'The Strategic Use of Liberal Internationalism: Libya and Sanctions, 1992–2003', *International Organization*, 59.

—— (2007) *After Anarchy: Legitimacy and Power in the United Nations Security Council* (Princeton).

Hurrell, A. (1993) 'International Society and the Study of International Regimes: A Reflective Approach', in V. Rittberger (ed.), *Regime Theory and International Relations* (Oxford).

—— (1994) 'A Crisis of Ecological Viability – Global Environmental Change and the Nation-State', *Political Studies,* Special Issue, 42.

—— (2002) 'There Are No Rules (George W. Bush): International Order after September 11', *International Relations*, 16.

—— (2006) 'The State', in A. Dobson and R. Eckersley (eds), *Political Theory and the Ecological Challenge* (Cambridge).

—— (2007) *On Global Order: Power, Values and the Constitution of International Society* (Oxford).

Hurrell, A. and Kingsbury, B. (1992) *The International Politics of the Environment* (Oxford).

Hutchings, K. (1999) *International Political Theory: Rethinking Ethics in a Global Era* (London).

—— (2000) 'Towards a Feminist International Ethics', *Review of International Studies,* Special Issue, 26.

—— (2004) 'From morality to politics and back again: Feminist international ethics and the civil society argument', *Alternatives*, 24.

Ignatieff, M. (2004) *The Lesser Evil: Political Ethics in an Age of Evil* (Princeton).

Ikenberry, J. G. (2000) *After Victory* (Princeton).

IUCN (1980) *World Conservation Strategy* (Gland).

Jackson, R. (1990) *Quasi-States: Sovereignty, International Relations and the Third World* (Cambridge).

—— (2000) *The Global Covenant: Human Conduct in a World of States* (Oxford).

—— (2008) 'From Colonialism to Theology: Encounters with Martin Wight's International Thought', *International Affairs*, 84(2).

Jacoby, T. (1999) 'Feminism, Nationalism and Difference: Reflections on the Palestinian Women's Movement', *Women's Studies International Forum*, 22(5).

Jahn, B. (ed.) (2006) *Classical Theory in International Relations* (Cambridge).

Jaquette, J. (1984) 'Power as Ideology: A Feminist Analysis', in J. H. Stiehm (ed.), *Women's Views of the Political World of Men* (Dobbs Ferry).

Jay, M. (1973) *The Dialectical Imagination* (Boston).

Jeffery, L. A. (2002) *Sex and Borders: Gender, National Identity and Prostitution Policy in Thailand* (Basingstoke).

Jeffery, R. (2006) *Hugo Grotius in International Thought* (Basingstoke).

Jepperson, R., Wendt, A. and Katzenstein, P. J. (1996) 'Norms, Identity, and Culture in National Security', in Peter J. Katzenstein (ed.), *The Culture of National Security: Norms and Identity in World Politics* (New York).

Jervis, R. (1978) 'Cooperation Under the Security Dilemma,' *World Politics*, 30.

—— (1998) 'Realism in the Study of World Politics,' *International Organization*, 52.

Johnson, C. (2002) *Blowback*, 2nd edn (London).

Johnson, L. M. (1993) *Thucydides, Hobbes, and the Interpretation of Realism* (DeKalb).

Johnston, A. I. (1995) *Cultural Realism: Strategic Culture and Grand Strategy in Chinese History* (Princeton).

Jones, C. (1999) *Global Justice: Defending Cosmopolitanism* (Oxford).

Jones, D. (1999) *Cosmopolitan Mediation? Conflict Resolution and the Oslo Accords* (Manchester).

—— (2001) 'Creating Cosmopolitan Power: International Mediation as Communicative Action', in R. Wyn Jones (ed.), *Critical Theory and World Politics* (Boulder).

Jones, R. E. (1981) 'The English School of International Relations: A Case for Closure', *Review of International Studies*, 7(1).

Joseph, J. (2002) *Hegemony: A Realist Analysis* (London).

—— (2006) *Marxism and Social Theory* (London).

Kabeer, N. (1994) *Reversed Realities: Gender Hierarchies in Development Thought* (London).

Kahler, M. (1997) 'Inventing International Relations: International Relations Theory After 1945', in M. W. Doyle and G. J. Ikenberry (eds), *New Thinking in International Relations Theory* (Boulder).

Kant, I. (1970) *Kant's Political Writings,* ed. H. Reiss, trans H. Nisbet (Cambridge).

—— (1991) *Political Writings*, ed. H. Reiss, trans. H. B. Nisbet (Cambridge).

—— (1999) *Metaphysical Elements of Justice*, ed. J.Ladd, 2nd edn (London).

Kaplan, R. (1994) 'The Coming Anarchy', *Atlantic Monthly*, February.

Kapoor, I. (2004) 'Deliberative Democracy and the WTO', *Review of International Political Economy*, 11(3).

Kapstein, E. and Mastanduno, M. (eds) (1999) *Unipolar Politics: Realism and State Strategies after the Cold War* (New York).

Kardam, N. (1991) *Bringing Women in: Women's Issues in International Development Programs* (Boulder).

—— (2004) 'The Emerging Global Gender Equality Regime from Neoliberal and Constructivist Perspectives in International Relations', *International Feminist Journal of Politics*, 6(1).

Kassiola, J. J. (2003) 'Afterword: The Surprising Value of Despair and the Aftermath of September 11th', in J. J. Kassiola (ed.), *Explorations in Environmental Political Theory* (Armonk).

Katzenstein, P. J. (1996) *Cultural Norms and National Security: Police and Military in Postwar Japan* (Ithaca).

—— (1999) *Tamed Power: Germany in Europe* (Ithaca).

Katzenstein, P. J. and Okawara, N. (2001/2) 'Japan, Asian-Pacific Security, and the Case for Analytical Eclecticism', *International Security*, 26(3).

Kaufman, S. J., (1997) 'The Fragmentation and Consolidation of International Systems', *International Organization*, 51.

Kaufman, S., Little, R., and Wolhforth, W.C. (eds) (2007) *The Balance of Power in World History* (Basingstoke).

Kaufman-Osborn, T. (2005) 'Gender Trouble at Abu-Ghraib', *Politics and Gender*, 1(4).

Keal, P. (1983) *Unspoken Rules and Superpower Dominance* (London).

—— (2003) *European Conquest and the Rights of Indigenous Peoples: The Moral Backwardness of International Society* (Cambridge).

Keck, M. and Sikkink, K. (1998) *Activist Beyond Borders* (Ithaca).

Keegan, J. (1993) *A History of Warfare* (New York).

Keeley, L. H. (1996) *War before Civilization: The Myth of the Peaceful Savage* (Oxford).

Keene, E. (2002) *Beyond the Anarchical Society: Grotius, Colonialism and Order in World Politics* (Cambridge).

—— (2005) *International Political Thought: A Historical Introduction* (Cambridge).

Kelly, D. (2003) 'Karl Marx and Historical Sociology', in G. Delanty and E. Isin (eds) *Handbook of Historical Sociology* (London).

Kelsay, J. (2007) *Arguing the Just War in Islam* (Cambridge, MA).

Kennan, G. F. (1954) *Realities of American Foreign Policy* (Princeton).

—— (1985/6) 'Morality and Foreign Policy,' *Foreign Affairs*, 63.

Keohane, R. O. (1984) *After Hegemony: Cooperation and Discord in the World Political Economy* (Princeton).

—— (1986) 'Theory of World Politics: Structural Realism and Beyond', in R. O. Keohane (ed.), *Neo-Realism and Its Critics* (New York).

—— (1988) 'International Institutions: Two Approaches', *International Studies Quarterly*, 32(4).

—— (1989a) *International Institutions and State Power: Essays in International Relations Theory* (Boulder).

—— (1989b) 'International Relations Theory: Contributions of a Feminist Standpoint', *Millennium*, 18(2).

Keohane, R. O. and Nye, J. (eds) (1972) *Transnationalism and World Politics* (Massachusetts).

—— (1977) *Power and Interdependence: World Politics in Transition* (Boston).

Kier, E. (1997) *Imagining War: French and British Military Doctrine Between the Wars* (Princeton).

Kinsella, H. M. (2005) 'Securing the Civilian: Sex and Gender in the Laws of War' in M. Barnett and R. Duvall (eds), *Power in Global Governance* (Cambridge).

Kiser, E., and Hechter, M. (1991) 'The Role of General Theory in Comparative-Historical Sociology', *American Journal of Sociology*, 97(1).

—— (1998) 'The Debate on Historical Sociology: Rational Choice Theory and its Critics', *American Journal of Sociology*, 104(3).

Kissinger, H. A. (1957) A *World Restored: Metternich, Castlereagh and the Problems of Peace, 1812–22* (Boston).

—— (1977) *American Foreign Policy* (New York).

Klare, M. (2001) *Resource Wars: The New Landscape of Global Conflict* (New York).

Klein, B. (1994) *Strategic Studies and World Order: The Global Politics of Deterrence* (Cambridge).

Klotz, A. (1995) *Norms in International Relations: The Struggle Against Apartheid* (Ithaca).

Knei-Paz, B. (1978) *The Social and Political Thought of Leon Trotsky* (Oxford).

Koontz, T. J. (1996) 'Christian Nonviolence: An Interpretation', in T. Nardin (ed.), *The Ethics of War and Peace: Religious and Secular Perspectives* (Princeton).

Korac, M. (1998) 'Ethnic Nationalism, War and the Patterns of Social, Political and Sexual Violence against Women: The Case of Post-Yugoslav Countries', *Identities*, 5(2).

Koskenniemi, M. (2001) *The Gentle Civilizer of Nations: The Rise and Fall of International Law 1870–1960* (Cambridge).

—— (2007) 'The Fate of Public International Law: between Technique and Politics', *Modern Law Review*, 70(1).

Koslowski, R. and Kratochwil, F. (1995) 'Understanding Change in International Politics: The Soviet Empire's Demise and the International System', in R. N. Lebow and T. Risse-Kappen (eds), *International Relations Theory after the Cold War* (New York).

Kothari, A. (1992) 'The Politics of the Biodiversity Convention', *Economic and Political Weekly*, 27.

Krasner, S. (1983) 'Structural Causes and Regime Consequences: Regimes as Intervening Variables', in S. D. Krasner (ed.), *International Regimes* (Ithaca).

—— (1999) *Sovereignty: Organized Hypocrisy* (Princeton).

Kratochwil, F. (1988/9) 'Regimes, Interpretation and the "Science" of Politics: A Reappraisal', *Millennium*, 17(2).

—— (1993) 'The Embarrassment of Changes: Neo-realism as the Science of Realpolitik Without Politics', *Review of International Studies*, 19(1).

—— (2000) 'Constructing a New Orthodoxy? Wendt's' "Social Theory of International Politics and the Constructivionist Challenge"', *Millennium: Journal of International Studies*, 29(1).

Kratochwil, F and Ruggie, J. G. (1986) 'International Organization: A State of the Art on an Art of the State?', *International Organization*, 40(4).

Krieken, R. van (1998) *Norbert Elias* (London).

Krippendorf, E. (1982) *International Relations as a Social Science* (Brighton).

Kubalkova, V. and Cruickshank, A. (1980) *Marxism-Leninism and the Theory of International Relations* (London).

Kuehls, T. (1996) *Beyond Sovereign Territory: The Space of Ecopolitics* (Minneapolis).

Kuper, A. (2005) *Global Responsibilities: Who Must Deliver on Human Rights?* (London).

Kymlicka, W. (1989) *Liberalism, Community and Culture* (Oxford).

Labs, E. J. (1997) 'Beyond Victory: Offensive Realism and the Expansion of War Aims', *Security Studies*, 6.

Laferrière, E. (1996) 'Emancipating International Relations Theory: An Ecological Perspective', *Millennium*, 25(1).

Laferrière, E. and Stoett, P. (1999) *Ecological Thought and International Relations Theory* (London).

—— (2006) *International Ecopolitical Theory: Critical Approaches*, (Vancouver).

Laffey, M. and Weldes, J. (1997) 'Beyond Belief: Ideas and Symbolic Technologies in the Study of International Relations', *European Journal of International Relations*, 3(2).

Lawson, G. (2007) 'Historical Sociology in International Relations: Open Society, Research Programme and Vocation', *International Politics*, 44(4).

Layne, C. (1993) 'The Unipolar Illusion: Why New Great Powers Will Arise', *International Security*, 17.

Lebow, R. N. (2003) *The Tragic Vision of Politics: Ethics, Interests and Orders* (Cambridge).

Lee, K. (1993) 'To De-Industrialize – Is it so Irrational?', in A. Dobson and P. Lucardie (eds), *The Politics of Nature: Explorations in Green Political Theory* (London).

Lenin, V. (1964) *Collected Works*, 20 (Moscow).

—— (1968) *Imperialism: The Highest Stage of Capitalism* (Moscow).

Levinas, E. (1969) *Totality and Infinity: An Essay on Exteriority* (Pittsburgh).

Levy, J. S. (1989) 'The Causes of War: A Review of Theories and Evidence', in P. E. Tetlock (ed.), *Behaviour, Society and Nuclear War* (New York).

Ling, L. H. (2001) *Post-colonial IR: Conquest and Desire between Asia and the West* (London).

Linklater, A. (1990a) *Men and Citizens in the Theory of International Relations*, 2nd edn (London).

—— (1990b) *Beyond Realism and Marxism: Critical Theory and International Relations* (London).

—— (1992a) 'The Question of the Next Stage in International Relations Theory: A Critical Theoretical Point of View', *Millennium*, 21(1).

—— (1992b) 'What is a Good International Citizen?', in P. Keal (ed.), *Ethics and Foreign Policy* (Canberra).

—— (1993) 'Liberal Democracy, Constitutionalism and the New World Order', in R. Leaver and J. L. Richardson (eds), *Charting the Post-Cold War Order* (Colorado).

—— (1997) 'The Achievements of Critical Theory', in S. Smith, K. Booth and M. Zalewski (eds), *International Theory: Positivism and Beyond* (Cambridge).

—— (1998) *The Transformation of Political Community; Ethical Foundations of the Post-Westphalian Era* (Cambridge).

—— (1999) 'Transforming Political Community: A Response to the Critics', *Review of International Studies*, 25(1).

—— (2001) 'Citizenship, Humanity and Cosmopolitan Harm Conventions', *International Political Science Review*, 22(3).

—— (2002a) 'The Problem of Harm in World Politics: Implications for the Sociology of States-Systems', *International Affairs*, 78(8).

—— (2002b) 'Unnecessary Suffering', in K. Booth and T. Dunne (eds), *Worlds in Collision: Terror and the Future of Global Order* (London).

—— (2007a) *Critical Theory and World Politics: Citizenship, Sovereignty and Humanity* (London).

—— (2007b) 'Torture and Civilisation', *International Relations*, 21(1).

Linklater, A. and Suganami, H. (2006) *The English School of International Relations: A Contemporary Assessment* (Cambridge).

Lipschutz, R. D. (1997) 'From Place to Planet: Local Knowledge and Global Environmental Governance', *Global Governance*, 3(1).

Lisle, D. (2000) 'Consuming Danger: Reimagining the War/Tourism Divide', *Alternatives*, 25(1).

Litfin, K. (ed.) (1998) *The Greening of Sovereignty in World Politics* (Cambridge, MA).

Little, R. (2000) 'The English School's Contribution to the Study of International Relations', *European Journal of International Relations*, 6.

Locher, B. and Prugl, E. (2001) 'Feminism and Constructivism: Worlds Apart or Sharing the Middle Ground?', *International Studies Quarterly*, 45(1).

Loh, J. and Wackernagel, W. (eds) (2004) *The Living Planet Report 2004* (Gland).

Long, D. (1996) *Towards a New Liberal Internationalism: The International Theory of J. A. Hobson* (Cambridge).

Long, D. and Wilson, P. (eds) (1995) *Thinkers of the Twenty Years' Crisis* (Oxford).

Low, N. and Gleeson, B. (1998) *Justice, Nature and Society* (London).

Luke, T. L. (1997) *Ecocritique: Contesting the Politics of Nature, Economy, and Culture* (Minneapolis).

Lukes, S. (1985) *Marxism and Morality* (Oxford).

Lynch, C. (1999) *Beyond Appeasement: Reinterpreting Interwar Peace Movements in World Politics* (Ithaca).

Lynch, M. (1999) *State Interests and Public Spheres: The International Politics of Jordanian Identity* (New York).

—— (2000) 'The Dialogue of Civilisations and International Public Spheres', *Millennium*, 29(2).

Lynn-Jones, S. M. (1995) 'Offense-Defense Theory and Its Critics', *Security Studies*, 4.

Lynn-Jones, S. M. and Miller, S. E. (1995) 'Preface', in M. E. Brown, S. M. Lynn-Jones and S. E. Miller (eds), *The Perils of Anarchy: Contemporary Realism and International Security* (Cambridge).

Lyotard, J.-E. (1984) *The PostModern Condition: A Report on Knowledge* (Manchester).

—— (1993) 'The Other's Rights', in S. Shute and S. Hurley (eds), *On Human Rights: The Oxford Amnesty Lectures* (New York).

Machiavelli, N. (1970) *The Discourses* (Harmondsworth).

—— (1985) *The Prince* (Chicago).

Mackie, V. (2001) 'The Language of Globalization, Transnationality, and Feminism', *International Feminist Journal of Politics*, 3(2).

Mackinder, H. J. (1919) *Democratic Ideals and Reality: A Study in the Politics of Reconstruction* (New York).

Maclean, J. (1981) 'Marxist Epistemology, Explanations of "Change" and the Study of International Relations', in B. Buzan and R. B. Jones (eds), *Change in the Study of International Relations: The Evaded Dimension* (London).

MacMillan, J. (1995) 'A Kantian Protest Against the Peculiar Discourse of Inter-Liberal State Peace', *Millennium*, 24(4).

—— (1998) *On Liberal Peace: Democracy, War and International Order* (London).

MacPherson, C. B. (1973) *Democratic Theory* (Oxford).

—— (1977) *The Life and Times of Liberal Democracy* (Oxford).

Magnusson, W. (1996) *The Search for Political Space: Globalization, Social Movements and the Urban Political Experience* (Toronto).

Maiguaschca, B. (2003) 'Introduction: Governance and Resistance in World Politics', *Review of International Studies*, 29.

Malcolm, N. (2002) 'Hobbes's Theory of International Relations', in N. Malcolm, *Aspects of Hobbes* (Oxford).

Mandalios, J. (2003) 'Civilizational Complexes and Processes: Elias, Nelson and Eisenstadt', in G. Delanty and E. Isin (eds) *Handbook of Historical Sociology* (London).

Mandle, J. (2006) *Global Justice* (Cambridge).

Mann, M. (1986) *The Sources of Social Power, vol. 1: A History of Power from the Beginning to 1760AD* (Cambridge).

—— (1994) *The Sources of Social Power, vol. 2: The Rise of Classes and Nation States, 1760–1914* (Cambridge).

—— (1994) 'In Praise of Macro-Sociology: Reply to Goldthorpe', *British Journal of Sociology*, 45(1).

Manning, P. (2003) *Navigating World History: Historians Create Global Past* (Basingstoke).

Mantle, D. (1999) *Critical Green Political Theory and International Relations Theory – Compatibility or Conflict*, PhD thesis, Keele University.

Maoz, Z. and Russett, B. (1993) 'Normative and Structural Causes of Democratic Peace, 1946–1986', *American Political Science Review*, 87(3).

Marchand, M. and Runyan, A. S. (eds) (2000) *Gender and Global Restructuring: Sites, Sightings and Resistances* (New York).

Martin, R. and Reidy, D. A. (eds) (2006) *Rawls's Law of Peoples: A Realistic Utopia?* (Malden).

Marx, K. (1966) *The Poverty of Philosophy* (Moscow).

—— (1973) *Grundrisse* (Harmondsworth).

—— (1977a) 'Capital', 1, in D. McLellan (ed.), *Karl Marx: Selected Writings* (Oxford).

—— (1977b) 'Theses on Feuerbach', in D. McLellan (ed.), *Karl Marx: Selected Writings* (Oxford).

—— (1977c) 'Towards A Critique of Hegel's Philosophy of Right: Introduction', in D. McLellan (ed.), *Karl Marx: Selected Writings* (Oxford).

—— (1977d) 'Economic and Philosophical Manuscripts', in D. McLellan (ed.), *Karl Marx: Selected Writings* (Oxford).

—— (1977e) 'The Eighteenth Brumaire of Louis Bonaparte', in D. McLellan (ed.), *Karl Marx: Selected Writings* (Oxford).

Marx, K. and Engels, F. (1971) *Ireland and the Irish Question* (London).

—— (1977) 'The Communist Manifesto', in D. McLellan (ed.), *Karl Marx: Selected Writings* (Oxford).

Mastanduno, M. (1991) 'Do Relative Gains Matter? America's Response to Japanese Industrial Policy,' *International Security*, 16.

—— (1997) 'Preserving the Unipolar Moment: Realist Theories and US Grand Strategy after the Cold War,' *International Security*, 21.

Mattingly, G. (1956) *Renaissance Diplomacy* (Boston).

May, L. (2004) *Crimes against Humanity: A Normative Account* (Cambridge).

Mayall, J. (ed.) (1996) *The New Interventionism 1991–1994: United Nations Experience in Cambodia, Former Yugoslavia and Somalia* (Cambridge).

—— (2000) *World Politics: Progress and its Limits* (Cambridge).

Mazlish, B. (1989) *The New Science: The Breakdown of Connections and the Birth of Sociology* (Oxford).

—— (2006) *The New Global History* (Abingdon).

Mazlish, B., and Irigye, A. (eds) (2005) *The Global History Reader* (London).

McClure, K. (1992) 'The Issue of Foundations: Scientized Politics, Politicized Science and Feminist Critical Practice', in J. W. Scott and J. Butler (eds), *Feminists Theorize the Political* (New York).

McGlen, N. E. and Sarkees, M. R. (eds) (1993) *Women in Foreign Policy: The Insiders* (New York).

McIntire, C. T. (ed.) (1979) *Herbert Butterfield: Writings on Christianity and History* (New York).

McNeill, J. R., and McNeill, W. H. (2003) *The Human Web: A Bird Eye's View of World History* (New York).

McNeill, W. H. (1979) *A World History* (Oxford).

—— (1986) *Mythistory and other Essays* (London).

—— (1995) 'The Changing Shape of World History', *History and Theory*, 34(2).

Meadowcroft, J. (2006) 'Greening the State', *Politics and Ethics Review*, 2(2).

Meadows, D. and Randers, J. (1992) *Beyond the Limits* (London).

Meadows, D., Meadows, D., Randers, J. and Behrens, W. (1972) *The Limits to Growth* (London).

Mearsheimer, J. (1990) ' "Back to the Future": Instability in Europe After the Cold War', *International Security*, 15(1).

—— (1994/5) 'The False Promise of International Institutions', *International Security*, 19.

—— (1995) 'A Realist Reply', *International Security*, 20.

—— (2001) *The Tragedy of Great Power Politics* (New York).

Mearsheimer, J. and Walt, S. M. (2002) *Can Saddam Be Contained? History Says Yes*, Belfer Centre for Science and International Affairs, Harvard University (Massachusetts).

Mennell, S. (1990) 'The Globalization of Human Society as a Very Long-Term Social Process: Elias's Theory', *Theory, Culture and Society*, 7(3).

—— (1994) 'The Formation of We-Images: A Process Theory' in C. Calhoun (ed.), *Social Theory and the Politics of Identity* (Oxford).

—— (2007) *The American Civilizing Process* (Cambridge).

Merchant, C. (1980) *The Death of Nature: Women, Ecology and the Scientific Revolution* (San Francisco).

Micklewait, J. and Wooldridge, A. (2000) *A Future Perfect: The Challenge and Hidden Promise of Globalization* (New York).

Mievelle, C. (2005) *Between Equal Rights: A Marxist Theory of International Law* (Leiden).

Millennium: Journal of International Studies (1988), Special Issue: Women and International Relations, 17, 3.

Miller, D. (2007) *National Responsibility and Global Justice* (Cambridge).

Miller, F. (1998) 'Feminisms and Transnationalism', *Gender and History*, 10(3).

Miller, P. (2003) 'Gender and Patriarchy in Historical Sociology', in G. Delanty and E. Isin (eds), *Handbook of Historical Sociology* (London).

Mitchell, R. (2006) 'Problem Structure, Institutional Design, and the Relative Effectiveness of International Environmental Agreements', *Global Environmental Politics*, 6(3).

Mitrany, D. (1948) 'The Functional Approach to World Organisation', *International Affairs*, 24.

Mitter, S. (1986) *Common Fate, Common Bond: Women in the Global Economy* (London).

Modelski, G. (1978) 'The Long Cycle of Global Politics and the Nation-State', *Comparative Studies in Society and History*, 20(2).

Moellendorf, D. (2002) *Cosmopolitan Justice* (Cambridge, MA).

Mohanty, C. (1991) 'Under Western Eyes: Feminist Scholarship and Colonial Discourses', in C. Mohanty, T. A. Russo and L. Torres (eds), *Third World Women and the Politics of Feminism* (Bloomington).

Mol, A. (1996) 'Ecological Modernisation and Institutional Reflexivity: Environmental Reform in the Late Modern Age', *Environmental Politics*, 5(2).

Moon, K. (1997) *Sex Among Allies: Military Prostitution in US–Korea Relations* (New York).

Morefield, J. (2005) *Covenants without Swords: Idealist Liberalism and the Spirit of Empire* (Princeton).

Morgenthau, H. J. (1946) *Scientific Man Versus Power Politics* (Chicago).

—— (1948/54/73) *Politics Among Nations: The Struggle for Power and Peace* (New York).

—— (1951) *In Defense of the National Interest: A Critical Examination of American Foreign Policy* (New York).

—— (1962) *Politics in the Twentieth Century, I: The Decline of Democratic Politics* (Chicago).

—— (1970) *Truth and Power: Essays of a Decade, 1960–70* (New York).

Morton, A. (2007) *Unravelling Gramsci: Hegemony and Passive Revolution in the Global Political Economy* (London).

Mueller, J. (1989) *Retreat from Doomsday* (New York).

Muthu, S. (2003) *Enlightenment against Empire* (Princeton).

Myers, N. (1993) *Ultimate Security: The Environment as the Basis of Political Stability* (New York).

Nagel, T. (1985) 'War and Massacre', in C. R. Beitz, M. Cohen, T. Scanlon and A. J. Simmons (eds), *International Ethics* (Princeton).

—— (1986) *The View from Nowhere* (Oxford).

—— (2005) 'The Problem of Global Justice', *Philosophy and Public Affairs*, 33(2).

Nairn, T. (1981) *The Break-up of Britain* (London).

Nardin, T. (1983) *Law, Morality, and the Relations of States* (Princeton).

—— (2005) 'Justice and Coercion', in A. J. Bellamy (ed.), *International Society and Its Critics* (Oxford).

—— (2006) 'The Question of Justice', *International Affairs*, 82(3).

—— (2008) 'International Ethics', in C. Reuss-Smit and D. Snidal (eds), *The Oxford Handbook of International Relations* (Oxford).

Nayak, M. and Suchland, J. (2006) 'Gender Violence and Hegemonic Projects: Introduction', *International Feminist Journal of Politics*, 8(4).

Nederveen Pieterse, J. (2004) *Globalization or Empire?* (London).

Nelson, B. (1973) 'Civilizational Complexes and Intercivilizational Encounters', *Sociological Analysis*, 34(2).

Neufeld, M. (1993) 'Interpretation and the "Science" of International Relations', *Review of International Studies*, 19(1).

—— (1995) *The Restructuring of International Relations Theory* (Cambridge).

—— (2000) 'Thinking Ethically – Thinking Critically: International Ethics as Critique', in M. Lensu and J.-S. Fritz (eds), *Value Pluralism, Normative Theory and International Relations* (London).

Newland, K. (1988) 'From Transnational Relationships to International Relations: Women in Development and the International Decade for Women', *Millennium*, 17(3).

Niarchos, C. N. (1995) 'Women, War, and Rape: Challenges Facing the International Tribunal for the Former Yugoslavia', *Human Rights Quarterly*, 17.

Niebuhr, R. (1932) *Moral Man and Immoral Society: A Study in Ethics and Politics* (New York).

—— (1941) *The Nature and Destiny of Man: A Christian Interpretation, I: Human Nature* (New York).

—— (1943) *The Nature and Destiny of Man: A Christian Interpretation, II: Human Destiny* (New York).

Nietzsche, F. (1969) *On the Genealogy of Morals, and Ecce Homo* (New York).

—— (1990) *Twilight of the Idols/The Anti-Christ* (Harmondsworth).

Nisbet, R. A. (1966) *The Sociological Tradition* (London).

Norris, P. and Ingelhart, R. (2003) *Rising Tide: Gender Equality and Cultural Change Around the World* (Cambridge).

Nye, J. S. (1988) Neorealism and Neoliberalism', *World Politics*, 40.

Nyers, P. (1999) 'Emergency or Emerging Identities? Refugees and Transformations in World Order', *Millennium*, 28(1).

O'Neill, O. (1986) *Faces of Hunger: An Essay on Poverty, Justice and Development* (London).

Ohmae, K. (1995) *The End of the Nation State* (New York).

Ong, A. (1997) 'The Gender and Labor Politics of Postmodernity', in L. Lowe (ed.), *The Politics of Culture Under the Shadow of Capital* (Durham).

Onuf, N. (1989) *World of Our Making: Rules and Rule in Social Theory and International Relations* (Columbia).

Ophuls, W. (1977) *Ecology and the Politics of Scarcity* (San Francisco).

Organski, A. F. K. and Kugler, J. (1980) *The War Ledger* (Chicago).

O'Riordan, T. (1981) *Environmentalism*, 2nd edn (London).

Ostrom, E. (1990) *Governing the Commons: The Evolution of Institutions for Collective Action* (Cambridge).

Owen, J. M. (1994) 'How Liberalism Produces Democratic Peace', *International Security*, 19(2).

Oye, K. (1985) 'Explaining Cooperation Under Anarchy: Hypotheses and Strategies', *World Politics*, 38(1).

Pagden, A. (ed.) (1987) *The Languages of Political Theory in Early-Modern Europe* (Cambridge).

Pangle, T. L. and Ahrensdorf, P. J. (1999) *Justice among Nations: On the Moral Basis of Power and Peace* (Lawrence, KS).

Pateman, C. (1986) 'Introduction', in C. Pateman and E. Gross, *Feminist Challenges: Social and Political Thought* (Sydney).

—— (1989) *The Disorder of Women* (Stanford).

Paterson, M. (1999a) 'Overview: Interpreting Trends in Global Environmental Governance', *International Affairs*, 75(4).

—— (1999b) 'Globalisation, Ecology, and Resistance', *New Political Economy*, 4(1).

—— (2000) *Understanding Global Environmental Politics: Domination, Accumulation, Resistance* (Basingstoke).

—— (2007) 'Environmental Politics: Sustainability and the Politics of Transformation', *International Political Science Review*, 28(5)

Paterson, M., Doran, P. and Barry, J. (2006) 'Green Theory', in D. Marsh, C. Hay and M. Lister (eds), *State Theory: Theories and Issues* (London).

Patomaki, H. (2007) 'Back to the Kantian 'Idea for a Universal History'? Overcoming Eurocentric Accounts of the International Problematic', *Millennium*, 35(3).

Patton, P. (2000) *Deleuze and the Political* (London).

Persram, N. (1994) 'Politicizing the Feminine, Globalizing the Feminist', *Alternatives*, 19(3).

Peters, J. and Wolper, A. (eds) (1995) *Women's Rights/Human Rights: International Feminist Perspectives* (New York).

Peterson, V. S. (1992a) 'Transgressing Boundaries: Theories of Gender, Knowledge and International Relations', *Millennium*, 21(2).

—— (1992b) 'Security and Sovereign States: What is at Stake in Taking Feminism Seriously?', in V. S. Peterson (ed.), *Gendered States: Feminist (Re)visions of International Theory* (Boulder).

—— (2003) *A Critical Rewriting of Global Political Economy: Integrating Reproductive, Productive and Virtual Economies* (New York).

Peterson, V. S. and Runyan, A. S. (1999) *Global Gender Issues*, 2nd edn (Boulder).

Peterson, V. S. and True, J. (1998) 'New Times and New Conversations', in M. Zalewski and J. Parpart (eds), *The Man Question in International Relations* (Boulder).

Pettman, J. (1996) 'An International Political Economy of Sex', in J. Pettman (ed.), *Worlding Women: Towards a Feminist International Politics* (New York).

Philapose, E. (1996) 'The Laws of War and Women's Human Rights', *Hypatia*, 11(4).

Phillips, A. (forthcoming) 'The Protestant Ethic and the Spirit of Jihadism – Transnational Religious Insurgencies and the Transformation of International Orders', *Review of International Studies*.

Philpott, D. (2001) *Revolutions in Sovereignty: How Ideas Shaped Modern International Relations* (Princeton).

Pietila, H. and Vickers, J. (1996) *Making Women Matter: The Role of the United Nations*, 3rd edn (London).

Pijl, K. van der (1998) *Transnational Classes and International Relations* (London).

—— (2007) *Nomads, Empires, States: Modes of Foreign Relations and Political Economy, vol. 1* (London).

Pitts, J. (2006) *A Turn to Empire: The Rise of Imperial Liberalism in Britain and France* (Princeton).

Plumwood, V. (1993) *Feminism and the Mastery of Nature* (London).

Pogge, T. (ed.) (2001) *Global Justice* (Malden).

—— (2002) *World Poverty and Human Rights* (Cambridge).

Pogge, T. and Moellendorf, D. (2008) *Global Justice: Seminal Essays* (St Paul).

Polanyi, K. (1944) *The Great Transformation* (Boston).

—— (1968) 'Our Obsolete Market Mentality', in G. Dalton (ed.), *Primitive, Archaic and Modern Economies* (New York).

Politics and Ethics Review (2006) 'Symposium on Robyn Eckersley's *The Green State*', *Politics and Ethics Review*, 2(2).

Porritt, J. (1986) *Seeing Green* (Oxford).

Porter, G. and Brown, J. W. (1991) *Global Environmental Politics* (Boulder).

Porter, M. and Judd, E. (eds) (2000) *Feminists Doing Development: A Practical Critique* (London).

Powell, R. (1994) 'Anarchy in International Relations Theory: The Neorealist-Neoliberal Debate', *International Organization*, 48.

Price, R. (1997) *The Chemical Weapons Taboo* (Ithaca).

—— (ed.) (2008) *Moral Limit and Possibility in World Politics* (Cambridge).

Price, R. and Reus-Smit, C. (1998) 'Dangerous Liasions: Critical International Theory and Constructivism', *European Journal of International Relations*, 4(3).

Primoratz, I. (2007) *Civilian Immunity in War* (Oxford).

Princen, T. (2003) 'Principles for Sustainability: From Cooperation and Efficiency to Sufficiency', *Global Environmental Politics*, 3(1).

——— (2005) *The Logic of Sufficiency* (Cambridge).

Programme of the German Green Party (1983) (London).

Prugl, E. (2000) *The Global Construction of Gender* (New York).

——— (2007) 'Gender and EU Politics' in K. E. Jorgensen, M. A. Pollack and B. Rosamond (eds), *The Handbook of European Union Politics* (Oxford).

Prugl, E. and Meyer, M. K. (eds) (1999) *Gender Politics and Global Governance* (Lanham).

Rae, H. (2002) *State Identities and the Homogenization of Peoples* (Cambridge).

Rai, S. M. and Waylen, G. (eds) (2008), *Global Governance: Feminist Perspectives* (New York).

Ralph, J. (2007) *Defending the Society of States: Why America Opposes the International Criminal Court and its Vision of World Society* (Oxford).

Ramraj, V. V. (ed.) (2008) *Emergencies and the Limits of Legality* (Cambridge).

Rao, A. (1995) 'Gender and Culture', in J. Peters and A. Wolper (eds), *Women's Rights/Human Rights: International Feminist Perspectives* (New York).

Rathergeber, M. (1995) 'Gender and Development in Action', in M. H. Marchand and J. L. Parpart (eds), *Feminism/Postmodernism/Development* (London).

Rawls, J. (1971) *A Theory of Justice* (Cambridge, MA).

——— (1999) *The Law of Peoples* (Cambridge, MA).

Raymond, G. A. (1997) 'Problems and Prospects in the Study of International Norms', *Mershon International Studies Review*, 41.

Reanda, L. (1999) 'Engendering the United Nations: The Changing International Agenda', *European Journal of Women's Studies*, 6.

Regan, P. M. and Paskeviciute, A. (2003) Women's Access to Politics and Peaceful States', *Journal of Peace Research*, 40.

Reichberg, G. M., Syse, H., and Begby, E. (eds) (2006) *The Ethics of War: Classic and Contemporary Readings* (Malden).

Reid, J. (2003) Deleuze's War Machine: Nomadism against the State', *Millennium*, 32(1).

Rengger, N. and Thirkell-White, B. (2007) 'Editors' Introduction', Special Issue on Critical International Relations Theory After 25 Years, *Review of International Studies*, 33.

Reus-Smit, C. (1996) 'The Normative Structure of International Society', in F. Osler Hampson and J. Reppy (eds), *Earthly Goods: Environmental Change and Social Justice* (Ithaca).

——— (1999) *The Moral Purpose of the State: Culture, Social Identity and Institutional Rationality in International Relations* (Princeton).

——— (2000) 'In Dialogue on the Ethic of Consensus: A Reply to Shapcott', *Pacifica Review*, 12(3).

——— (2002a) 'Imagining Society: Constructivism and the English School', *British Journal of Politics and International Relations*, 4(3).

——— (2002b) 'The Idea of History and History with Ideas', in S. Hobden and J. M. Hobson (eds), *Historical Sociology and International Relations* (Cambridge).

——— (2004a) *American Power and World Order* (Cambridge).

——— (ed.) (2004b) *The Politics of International Law* (Cambridge).

Ricardo, D. (1911) *The Principles of Political Economy and Taxation* (London).

Richardson, J. L. (1997) 'Contending Liberalisms – Past and Present', *European Journal of International Relations*, 3(1).

Risse, T. (2000) ' "Let's Argue!": Communicative Action in World Politics', *International Organization*, 54(1).

—— (2004) 'Global Governance Communication Action', *Government and Opposition*, 39(2).

Roberts, A. (1993) 'Humanitarian War: Military Intervention and Human Rights', *International Affairs*, 69(3).

Roberts, B. (1984) 'The Death of Machothink: Feminist Research and the Transformation of Peace Studies', *Women's Studies International Forum*, 7.

Robertson, G. (2006) *Crimes against Humanity: The Struggle for Global Justice* (New York).

Robinson, F. (1999) *Globalizing Care: Ethics, Feminist Theory, and International Relations* (Boulder).

—— (2006) 'Methods of Feminist Normative Theory: A Political Ethic of Care for International Relations' in B. Ackerly, M. Stern and J. True (eds), *Feminist Methodologies for International Relations* (Cambridge).

Robinson, W. I. (2004) *A Theory of Global Capitalism: Production, Class and State in a Transnational World* (Baltimore).

Robinson, W. I., and Harris, J. (2000) 'Towards a Global Ruling Class? Globalization and the Transnational Capitalist Class', *Science and Society*, 64(1).

Roderick, R. (1986) *Habermas and the Foundations of Critical Theory* (London).

Rodin, D. (2002) *War and Self-Defense* (Oxford 2002).

Rose, G. (1998) 'Neoclassical Realism and Theories of Foreign Policy', *World Politics*, 51.

Rosecrance, R. N. (1966) 'Bipolarity, Multipolarity, and the Future', *Journal of Conflict Resolution*, 10.

—— (1986) *The Rise of the Trading State* (New York).

Rosenau, J. (1992) 'Governance, Order, and Change in World Politics', in J. N. Rosenau, and E.-O. Czempiel (eds), *Governance Without Government: Order and Change in World Politics* (Cambridge).

—— (1993) 'Environmental Challenges in a Turbulent World', in K. Conca and R. Lipschutz (eds), *The State and Social Power in Global Environmental Politics* (New York).

Rosenau, J. and Holsti, O. (1982) 'Women Leaders and Foreign Policy Opinions', in E. Boneparth and E. Stoper (eds), *Women, Power, and Politics* (New York).

Rosenberg, J. (1994) *The Empire of Civil Society: A Critique of the Realist Theory of International Relations* (London).

—— (2000) *The Follies of Globalization Theory: Polemical Essays* (London).

—— (2006) 'Why is there no International Historical Sociology?', *European Journal of International Relations*, 12(3).

—— (2007) 'International Relations – The Higher Bullshit: A Reply to the Globalization Theory Debate', *International Politics*, 44 (4).

Rosenthal, J. H. (1991) *Righteous Realists: Political Realism, Responsible Power, and American Culture in the Nuclear Age* (Baton Rouge).

Rowlands, I.H.. (1994) *The Politics of Global Atmosphere* (Manchester).

Ruggie, J. (1983) 'Continuity and Transformation in the World Polity: Toward a Neo-Realist Synthesis', *World Politics*, 35(2).

—— (1986) 'Continuity and Transformation in the World Polity: Toward a Neorealist Synthesis', in R. O. Keohane (ed.), *Neorealism and Its Critics* (New York).

—— (1993) 'Territoriality and Beyond: Problematizing Modernity in International Relations', *International Organization*, 47(1).

Runyan, A. S. and Peterson, V. S. (1991) 'The Radical Future of Realism: Feminist Subversions of IR Theory', *Alternatives*, 16(1).

Rupert, M. (1995) *Producing Hegemony: The Politics of Mass Production and American Global Power* (Cambridge).

—— (2000) *Ideologies of Globalization: Contending Visions of a New World Order* (London).

—— (2003) 'Globalising Common Sense: A Marxian–Gramscian (Re-vision) of the Politics of Governance/Resistance', *Review of International Studies*, 29.

Rupert, M., and Solomon, M. S. (2005) *Globalization and International Political Economy: The Politics of Alternative Futures* (Lanhan).

Rupp, L. (1997) *Worlds of Women: The Making of an International Women's Movement* (Princeton).

Russell, F. H. (1975) *The Just War in the Middle Ages* (Cambridge).

Russell, G. (1990) *Hans J. Morgenthau and the Ethics of American Statecraft* (Baton Rouge).

Russett, B. (1993) *Grasping the Democratic Peace* (Princeton).

Rustin, C. (1999) 'Habermas, Discourse Ethics, and International Justice', *Alternatives*, 24(2).

Sachs, W. (ed.) (1992) *The Development Dictionary: A Guide to Knowledge as Power* (London).

—— (1993) 'Global Ecology and the Shadow of "Development"', in W. Sachs (ed.), *Global Ecology* (London).

—— (ed.) (1993) *Global Ecology* (London).

Said, E. (1979) *Orientalism: Western Conceptions of the Orient* (London).

Sale, K. (1980) *Human Scale* (San Francisco).

Sassen, S. (1991) *The Global City: New York, London, Tokyo* (Princeton).

—— (1998a) 'Notes on the Incorporation of Third World Women into Wage Labor through Immigration and Offshore Production', in S. Sassen, *Globalization and its Discontents* (New York).

—— (1998b) 'Toward a Feminist Analysis of the Global Economy', in S. Sassen, *Globalization and its Discontents* (New York).

Scarre, C. (ed.) (2005) *The Human Past: World Prehistory and the Evolution of Human Societies* (London).

Scheuerman, W. E. (2004) *Liberal Democracy and the Social Acceleration of Time* (Baltimore).

Schmidt, B. C. (1998) *The Political Discourse of Anarchy: A Disciplinary History of International Relations* (Albany).

Scholte, J.-A. (2000) *Globalization: A Critical Introduction* (Basingstoke).

Schumacher, E. F. (1976) *Small is Beautiful* (London).

Schwarzenberger, G. (1951) *Power Politics: A Study of International Society* (London/New York).

Schweller, R. L. (1994) 'Bandwagoning for Profit: Bringing the Revisionist State Back In', *International Security*, 19.

—— (1997) 'New Realist Research on Alliances: Refining, Not Refuting, Waltz's Balancing Proposition', *American Political Science Review*, 91.

—— (1998) *Deadly Imbalances: Tripolarity and Hitler's Strategy of World Conquest* (New York).

—— (1999) 'Managing the Rise of Great Powers: History and Theory', in A. I. Jonston and R. S. Ross (eds), *Engaging China: The Management of an Emerging Power* (London).

—— (2003) 'The Progressivism of Neoclassical Realism', in C. Elman and M. F. Elman (eds), *Progress in International Relations Theory: Appraising the Field* (Cambridge).

—— (2006) *Unanswered Threats: Political Constraints on the Balance of Power* (Princeton).

Schweller, R. L. and Priess, D. (1997) 'A Tale of Two Realisms: Expanding the Institutions Debate', *Mershon International Studies Review*, 41.

Scott, J. W. (1988) *Gender and the Politics of History* (New York).

Sen, A. (2001) *Development as Freedom* (New York).

Shakman Hurd, E. (2004) 'The Political Authority of Secularism in International Relations', *European Journal of International Relations*, 10(2).

—— (2007) *The Politics of Secularism in World Politics* (Princeton).

Shapcott, R. (1994) 'Conversation and Co-existence: Gadamer and the Interpretation of International Society', *Millennium*, 23(1).

—— (2000a) 'Solidarism and After: Global Governance, International Society and the Normative "Turn"', *Pacifica Review*, 12(2).

—— (2000b) 'Beyond the Cosmopolitan/Communitarian Divide: Justice, Difference and Community in International Relations', in M. Lensu and J.-S. Fritz (eds), *Value Pluralism, Normative Theory and International Relations* (London).

—— (2001) *Justice, Community and Dialogue in International Relations* (Cambridge).

Shapiro, M. J. (1988a) *The Politics of Representation* (Madison).

—— (1998) 'The Events of Discourse and the Ethics of Global Hospitality', *Millennium*, 27(3).

—— (2005) 'The Fog of War', *Security Dialogue*, 36(2).

—— (2007) 'The New Violent Cartography', *Security Dialogue*, 38(3).

Sharoni, S. (1993) 'Middle-East Politics Through Feminist Lenses: Toward Theorizing International Relations from Women's Struggles', *Alternatives*, 18.

Sharp, G. (1973) *The Politics of Nonviolent Action* (Boston).

Shepherd, L. J. (2007) 'Victims, Perpetrators and Actors' Revisited: Exploring the Potential for a Feminist Reconceptualisation of (International) Security and (Gender) Violence', *British Journal of Politics and International Relations*, 9(1).

—— (2008) 'Power and Authority in the Production of United Nations Security Council Resolution 1325', *International Studies Quarterly*, 52(2).

Ship, S. J. (1994) 'And What About Gender? Feminism and International Relations Theory's Third Debate', in W. S. Cox and C. T. Sjolander (eds), *Beyond Positivism: Critical International Relations Theory* (Boulder).

Shiva, V. (1988) *Staying Alive: Women, Ecology and Development* (London).

—— (1993) 'The Greening of the Global Reach', in W. Sachs (ed.), *Global Ecology* (London).

Shue, H. (1992) 'The Unavoidability of Justice', in A. Hurrell and B. Kingsbury (eds), *The International Politics of the Environment* (Oxford).

—— (1995) 'Ethics, the Environment, and the Changing International Order', *International Affairs,* 71(3).

—— (1999) 'Global Environment and International Inequality', *International Affairs*, 75(3).

Shue, H. and Rodin, D. (eds) (2007) *Preemption: Military Action and Moral Justification* (Oxford).

Simpson, G. (2004) *Great Powers and Outlaw States: Unequal Sovereigns in the International Legal Order* (Cambridge).

Sinclair, T. J. (ed.) (2003) *Global Governance* (London).

Singer, J. D. (1961) 'The Level-of-Analysis Problem in International Relations', *World Politics*, 14(1).

Singer, P. (2002) *One World: The Ethics of Globalization* (New Haven).

Skocpol, T. (1979) *States and Social Revolutions: A Comparative Analysis of France, Russia and China* (Cambridge).

—— (1984) 'Sociology's Historical Imagination', in T. Skocpol (ed.), *Visions of Historical Sociology* (Cambridge).

Slaughter, A.-M. (2004) *A New World Order* (Princeton).

Smith, D. (1990) *The Rise of Historical Sociology* (Cambridge).

Smith, M. J. (1986) *Realist Thought from Weber to Kissinger* (Baton Rouge).

Smith, S. (1995) 'The Self-Image of a Discipline: A Genealogy of International Relations Theory', in K. Booth and S. Smith (eds), *International Relations Theory Today* (Cambridge).

—— (1996) 'Positivism and Beyond', in S. Smith, K. Booth and M. Zalewski (eds), *International Theory: Positivism and Beyond* (Cambridge).

—— (1997) 'Power and Truth: A Reply to Wallace', *Review of International Studies*, 22(4).

Smith, S., Booth, K. and Zalewski, M. (eds) (1996) *International Theory: Positivism and Beyond* (Cambridge).

Snyder, G. H. (1996) 'Process Variables in Neorealist Theory', *Security Studies*, 5.

—— (1997) *Alliance Politics* (Ithaca).

—— (2002) 'Mearsheimer's World: Offensive Realism and the Struggle for Security', *International Security*, 27.

Snyder, J. (1991) *Myths of Empire: Domestic Politics and International Ambition* (Ithaca).

Soguk, N. and Whitehall, G. (1999) 'Wandering Grounds: Transversality, Identity, Territoriality, and Movement', *Millennium*, 28(3).

Sorabji, R. and Rodin, D. (eds) (2006) *The Ethics of War: Shared Problems in Different Traditions* (Aldershot).

Spaargaren, G., Mol, A. and Buttel, F. (eds) (2006), *Governing Environmental Flows: Global Challenges to Social Theory* (Cambridge MA).

Sparr, P. (ed.) (1994) *Mortgaging Women's Lives: Feminist Critiques of Structural Adjustment* (London).

Spretnak, C. and Capra, F. (1984) *Green Politics: The Global Promise* (London).

Spykman, N. J. (1942) *America's Strategy in World Politics: The United States and the Balance of Power* (New York).

Stalin, J. (1953) 'Marxism and the National Question', *Collected Works* (Moscow).

Standing, G. (1992) 'Global Feminization Through Flexible Labor', in C. K. Wilber and K. P. Jameson (eds), *The Political Economy of Development and Underdevelopment*, 5th edn (New York).

StasiUlis, D. and Bakan, A. B. (1997) 'Negotiating Citizenship: The Case of Foreign Domestic Workers in Canada', *Feminist Review*, 57.

Steans, J. (1995) *Gender and International Relations*, 2nd edn (Cambridge).

Stearns, P. N., and Stearns, C. Z. (1985) 'Emotionology: Clarifying the History of Emotions and Emotional Standards', *American Historical Review*, 90(4).

Stern, M. (2005) *Naming Insecurity-Constructing Identity* (Manchester).

Steuernagel, G. A. (1990) 'Men do not do Housework! The Image of Women in Political Science', in M. Paludi and G. A. Steuernagel (eds), *Foundations for a Feminist Restructuring of the Academic Disciplines* (New York).

Stewart, C. (1997) 'Old Wine in Recycled Bottles: The Limitations of Green International Relations Theory', Paper presented to the BISA Annual Conference.

Stiehm, J. H. (2006) *Champions for Peace: Women Winners of the Nobel Peace Prize* (Lanham).

Stienstra, D. (1994) *Women's Movements and International Organizations* (Toronto).

Strange, S. (1985) 'Protectionism and World Politics', *International Organisation*, 39(2).

—— (1991) 'New World Order: Conflict and Co-operation', *Marxism Today*, January.

—— (1996) *The Retreat of the State* (Cambridge).

—— (1998) *Mad Money* (Michigan).

Suganami, H. (1989) *The Domestic Analogy and World Order Proposals* (Cambridge).

—— (1996) *On the Causes of War* (Oxford).

Suh, J. J., Katzenstein, P. J. and Carlson, A. (2004) *Rethinking Security in East Asia: Identity, Power, and Efficiency* (Palo Alto).

Sylvester, C. (1987) 'The Dangers of Merging Feminist and Peace Projects', *Alternatives*, 8(4).

—— (1990a) 'The Emperors' Theories and Transformations: Looking at the Field through Feminist Lens', in D. Pirages and C. Sylvester (eds), *Transformations in the Global Political Economy* (London).

—— (1990b) *Feminist International Relations: An Unfinished Journey* (Cambridge).

—— (1992) 'Feminist Theory and Gender Studies in International Relations', *International Studies Notes*, 16(1).

—— (1994a) *Feminist Theory and International Relations in a Postmodern Era* (Cambridge).

—— (1994b) 'Empathetic Co-Operation: A Feminist Method for IR', *Millennium*, 23(2).

—— (2002) *Feminist International Relations: An Unfinished Journey* (Cambridge).

Sznaider, N. (2001) *The Compassionate Society: Care and Cruelty in Modern Society* (Oxford).

Taliaferro, J. W. (2000/1) 'Security Seeking under Anarchy: Defensive Realism Revisited,' *International Security*, 25.

Tan, K.-C. (2000) *Toleration, Diversity, and Global Justice* (University Park).

—— (2004) *Justice without Borders: Cosmopolitanism, Nationalism and Patriotism* (Cambridge).

—— (2006) 'The Duty to Protect', in T. Nardin and M. S. Williams (eds), *Humanitarian Intervention* (New York).

Tannenwald, N. (1999) 'The Nuclear Taboo: The United States and the Normative Basis of Nuclear Non-Use', *International Organization*, 53(3).

Taylor, A. J. P. (1961) *The Origins of the Second World War* (Harmondsworth).

Taylor, B. (ed.) (1995) *Ecological Resistance Movements: The Global Emergence of Radical and Popular Environmentalism* (Albany).

Taylor, C. (1997) 'Interpretation and the Sciences of Man', in F. Dallmayr and T. McCarthy (eds), *Understanding and Social Inquiry* (Notre Dame).

Taylor, M. (1976) *Anarchy and Cooperation* (London).

—— (1987) *The Possibility of Co-operation* (Cambridge).

Tellis, A. (1995/6) 'Reconstructing Political Realism: The Long March to Scientific Theory', *Security Studies*, 5.

Teschke, B. (1998) 'Geopolitical Relations in the European Middle Ages', *International Organisation*, 52(2).

—— (2003) *The Myth of 1648: Class, Geopolitics and the Making of Modern International Relations* (London).

Tessler, M., Nachtwey, J. and Grant, A. (1999) 'Further Tests of the Women and Peace Hypothesis: Evidence from Cross-National Survey Research in the Middle East', *International Studies Quarterly*, 43(3).

Tessler, M. and Warriner, I. (1997) 'Gender, Feminism and Attitudes toward International Conflict: Exploring Relationships with Survey Data from the Middle East', *World Politics*, 49.

The Ecologist (1972) *Blueprint for Survival* (Harmondsworth).

—— (1993) *Whose Common Future? Reclaiming the* Commons (London).

Thomas, C. (1999) 'Where is the Third World Now?', *Review of International Studies*, Special Issue, 25.

Thomas, S. (2001) 'Faith History and Martin Wight: The Role of Religion in the Historical Sociology of the English School of International Relations', *International Affairs*, 77(4).

Thompson, K. W. (1985) *Moralism and Morality in Politics and Diplomacy* (Lanham).

Thompson, K. W. and Meyers, R. J. (eds) (1977) *Truth and Tragedy: A Tribute to Hans Morgenthau* (Washington).

Thomson J. E. (1994) *Mercenaries, Pirates and Sovereigns* (Princeton).

Thucydides (1982) *The Peloponnesian War* (New York).

Tickner, J. A. (1988) 'Hans Morgenthau's Political Principles of Political Realism: A Feminist Reformulation', *Millennium*, 17(3).

—— (1991) 'On the Fringes of the World Economy: A Feminist Perspective', in C. Murphy and R. Tooze (eds), *The New International Political Economy* (Boulder).

—— (1992) *Gender in International Relations* (New York).

—— (2001) *Gendering World Politics: Issues and Approaches in the Post-Cold War Era* (New York).

—— (2002) 'Feminist Perspectives on 9/11', *International Studies Perspectives*, 3(4).

Tierney, B. (1997) *The Idea of Natural Rights* (Atlanta).

Tilly, C. (1992) *Coercion, Capital and European States: AD 990–1992* (Oxford).

Trainer, F. E. (1985) *Abandon Affluence!* (London).

Treitschke, H. V. (1916) *Politics* (London).

Tronto, J. (1989) 'Woman, the State and War: What Difference Does Gender Make?', in V. S. Peterson (ed.), *Clarification and Contestation: A Conference Report* (Los Angeles).

—— (2006) 'Is Peacekeeping care Work?', paper presented at the Canadian Political Science Asociation, June.

True, J. (2003) *Gender, Globalization and Postsocialism: The Czech Republic After Communism* (New York).

—— (2004) 'Feminism', in A. Bellamy (ed.), *International Society and its Critics* (Oxford).

—— (2008a) 'Gender Mainstreaming and Regional Trade Governance in Asia Pacific Economic Cooperation (APEC)' in S. M. Rai and G. Waylen (eds), *Global Governance: Feminist Perspectives*, (New York).

—— (2008b) 'The Unlikely Coupling of Feminism and Realism in International Relations' in A. Freyberg-Inan, E. Harrison and P. James (eds), *Rethinking Realism in International Relations: Between Tradition and Innovation* (Baltimore).

True, J. and Mintrom, M. (2001) 'Transnational Networks and Policy Diffusion: The Case of Gender Mainstreaming', *International Studies Quarterly*, 45(1).

Tuathail, G. Ó. (1996) *Critical Geopolitics: The Politics of Writing Global Space* (Minneapolis).

Tuck, R. (1993) *Philosophy and Government 1572–1651* (Cambridge).

—— (1999) *The Rights of War and Peace: Political Thought and the International Order from Grotius to Kant* (Oxford).

Tucker, R. W. (1977) *The Inequality of Nations* (New York).

—— (1985) *Intervention and the Reagan Doctrine* (New York).

Turner, B. (2003) 'Historical Sociology of Religion: Politics and Modernity' in G. Delanty and E. Isin (eds), *Handbook of Historical Sociology* (London).

United Nations (1992) *Framework Convention on Climate Change* (New York).
United Nations (2000) *The World's Women's Progress* (New York).
United Nations Development Programme (UNDP) (1999) *Human Development Report 1999: Globalization with a Human Face* (Oxford).
Van Evera, S. (1998) 'Offense, Defense, and the Causes of War,' *International Security*, 22.
Van Parijs, P. (2007) 'International Distributive Justice', in R. E. Goodin, P. Pettit, and T. Pogge (eds), *A Companion to Contemporary Political Philosophy*, 2nd edn (Malden).
Vasquez, J. A. (1998) *The Power of Power Politics: From Classical Realism to Neotraditionalism* (Cambridge).
Victor, D., Raustiala, K. and Skolnikoff, E. (eds) (1998), *The Implementation and Effectiveness of International Environmental Commitments: Theory and Practice* (Cambridge).
Vincent, R. J. (1984a) 'Edmund Burke and the Theory of International Relations', *Review of International Studies*, 10.
—— (1984b) 'Racial Equality', in H. Bull and A. Watson (eds), *The Expansion of International Society* (Oxford).
—— (1986) *Human Rights and International Relations* (Cambridge).
—— (1994) *Non-Intervention and International Order* (Princeton).
Vincent, R. J. and Wilson, P. (1994) 'Beyond Non-Intervention', in I. Forbes and M. Hoffman (eds), *Political Theory, International Relations and the Ethics of Intervention* (London).
Vogel, U. (2003) 'Cosmopolitan Loyalties and Cosmopolitan Citizenship in the Enlightenment', in M. Waller and A. Linklater (eds), *Political Loyalty and the Nation-State* (London).
Vogler, J. (1992) 'Regimes and the Global Commons: Space, Atmosphere and Oceans' in A. McGrew and P. Lewis (eds), *Global Politics: Globalisation and the Nation-State* (Cambridge).
—— (1995) *The Global Commons: A Regime Analysis* (London).
Wackernagel, M. and Rees, W. (1996) *Our Ecological Footprint: Reducing Human Impact on the Earth* (Gabriola Island).
Walker, R. B. J. (1987) 'Realism, Change and International Political Theory', *International Studies Quarterly*, 31(1).
—— (1989) 'History and Structure in the Theory of International Relations', *Millennium*, 18(2).
—— (1992) 'Gender and Critique in the Theory of International Relations', in V. S. Peterson (ed.), *Gendered States: Feminist (Re)visions of International Relations Theory* (Boulder).
—— (1993) *Inside/Outside: International Relations as Political Theory* (Cambridge).
—— (1995a) 'From International Relations to World Politics', in Camilleri, A. Jarvis and A. Paolini (eds), *The State in Transition: Reimagining Political Space* (Boulder).
—— (1995b) 'International Relations and the Concept of the Political', in Booth and S. Smith (eds), *International Relations Theory Today* (Cambridge).

—— (2000) 'International Relations Theory and the Fate of the Political', in M. Ebata and B. Neufeld (eds), *Confronting the Political in International Relations* (London).

Wall, D. (1994) 'Towards a Green Political Theory – In Defence of the Commons?', in P. Dunleavy and J. Stanyer (eds), *Contemporary Political Studies: Proceedings of the Annual Conference* (Belfast).

Wallace, W. (1996) 'Truth and Power, Monks and Technocrats: Theory and Practice in International Relations', *Review of International Studies*, 22(3).

Waller, M. and Linklater, A. (eds) (2003) *Political Loyalty and the Nation-State* (London).

Wallerstein, I. (1974) *The Modern World-System: Capitalist Agriculture and the Origins of the European World-Economy in the Sixteenth Century* (London).

—— (1979) *The Capitalist World Economy* (Cambridge).

Walt, S. M. (1987) *The Origins of Alliances* (Ithaca).

Walter, A. (1996) 'Adam Smith and the Liberal Tradition in International Relations', in I. Clark and I. B. Neumann (eds), *Classical Theories of International Relations* (Oxford).

Waltz, K. N. (1959) *Man, the State and War* (New York).

—— (1964) 'The Stability of a Bipolar World', *Daedalus*, 93.

—— (1979) *Theory of International Politics* (Reading).

—— (1986) 'Reflections on Theory of International Politics: A Response to My Critics', in R. O. Keohane (ed.), *Neo-Realism and Its Critics* (New York).

—— (1990) 'Nuclear Myths and Political Realities', *American Political Science Review*, 84.

—— (1991a) 'America as a Model for the World?', *PS: Political Science and Politics*, 24(4).

—— (1991b) 'Realist Thought and Neo-Realist Theory', in R. L. Rothstein (ed.), *The Evolution of Theory in International Relations: Essays in Honor of William T. R. Fox* (Columbia).

—— (1993) 'The Emerging Structure of International Politics', *International Security*, 18.

—— (1996) 'International Politics Is Not Foreign Policy', *Security Studies*, 6.

—— (2002) 'The Continuity of International Politics', in K. Booth and T. Dunne (eds), *Worlds in Collision: Terror and the Future of Global Order* (Basingstoke).

Walzer, M. (1977) *Just and Unjust Wars: A Moral Argument with Historical Illustrations* (New York).

—— (1983) *Spheres of Justice: A Defense of Pluralism and Equality* (New York).

—— (2004) *Arguing about War* (New Haven).

Wapner, P. (1996) *Environmental Activism and World Civic Politics* (Albany).

Warren, B. (1980) *Imperialism: Pioneer of Capitalism* (London).

Watson, A. (1982) *Diplomacy: The Dialogue between States* (London).

—— (1987) 'Hedley Bull, States Systems and International Societies', *Review of International Studies*, 13.

—— (1993) *The Evolution of International Society* (London).

WCED (1987) *Our Common Future – Report of the World Commission on Environment and Development* (Oxford).

Weber, C. (1994) 'Good Girls, Little Girls, and Bad Girls: Male Paranoia in Robert Keohane's Critique of Feminist International Relations', *Millennium*, 23(2).

—— (1995) *Simulating Sovereignty: Intervention, the State, and Symbolic Exchange* (Cambridge).

—— (1998) 'Performative States', *Millennium*, 27(1).

—— (2002) 'Flying Planes Can be Dangerous', *Millennium*, 31(1).

Weber, M. (1948) 'Social Psychology of the World Religions', in H. H. Gerth and C. Wright Mills (eds), *From Max Weber: Essays in Sociology* (London).

—— (2002) 'Engaging Globalization: Critical Theory and Global Political Change', *Alternatives*, 27(3).

—— (2005) ''The Critical Social Theory of the Frankfurt School, and the "Social Turn" in IR', *Review of International Studies*, 31(1).

—— (2007) 'The Concept of Solidarity in the Study of World Politics: Towards a Critical Theoretic Understanding', *Review of International Studies*, 33(4).

Weinstock, D. (2005) *Global Justice, Global Institutions* (Calgary).

Weiss, L. (1998) *The Myth of the Powerless State: Governing the Economy in a Global Era* (Cambridge).

Welch, D. (1993) *Justice and the Genesis of War* (Cambridge).

Weldon, L. (2006) 'Inclusion, Solidarity and Social Movements: The Global Movement Against Gender Violence', *Perspectives on Politics*, 4(1).

Wendt, A. (1992) 'Anarchy is what States Make of it', *International Organization*, 46.

—— (1994) 'Collective Identity Formation and the International State', *American Political Science Review*, 88(2).

—— (1995) 'Constructing International Politics', *International Security*, 20(1).

—— (1999) *Social Theory of International Politics* (Cambridge).

—— (2003) 'Why a World State is Inevitable', *European Journal of International Relations*, 9(4).

Wendt, A. and Shapiro, I. (1997) 'The Misunderstood Promise of Realist Social Theory', in K. R. Monroe (ed.), *Contemporary Empirical Theory* (Berkeley).

Wheeler, N. J. (2000) *Saving Strangers: Humanitarian Intervention in International Society* (Oxford).

—— (2004) 'The Kosovo Bombing Campaign', in C. Reus-Smit (ed.), *The Politics of International Law* (Cambridge).

Wheeler, N. J. and Dunne, T. (1996) 'Hedley Bull's Pluralism of the Intellect and Solidarism of the Will', *International Affairs*, 72.

—— (1998) 'Good International Citizenship: A Third Way for British Foreign Policy', *International Affairs*, 74.

Wheen, F. (1999) *Karl Marx* (London).

White, J. B. (1984) *When Words Lose their Meaning: Constitutions and Reconstitutions of Language, Character, and Community* (Chicago).

Whitworth, S. (1994) *Feminism and International Relations: Towards a Political Economy of Gender in Interstate and Non-Governmental Institutions* (London).

—— (2001) 'The Practice, and Praxis, of Feminist Research in International Relations', in R. W. Jones (ed.), *Critical Theory and World Politics* (Boulder).

—— (2004) *Men, Militarism and UN Peacekeeping: A Gendered Analysis* (Boulder).

Wight, M. (1966a) 'Why is there no International Theory?', in H. Butterfield and M. Wight (eds), *Diplomatic Investigations, Essays in the Theory of International Relations* (London). Reprinted in J. Der Derian (ed.) (1995), *International Theory: Critical Investigations* (Basingstoke).

—— (1966b) 'Western Values in International Relations', in H. Butterfield and M. Wight (eds), *Diplomatic Investigations, Essays in the Theory of International Relations* (London).

—— (1977) *Systems of States* (Leicester).

—— (1991) *International Theory: The Three Traditions*, ed. G. Wight and B. Porter (Leicester).

—— (1992) *International Theory: The Three Traditions* (New York).

Williams, J. (2006) *The Ethics of Territorial Borders: Drawing Lines in the Shifting Sand* (Basingstoke).

Williams, J. and Goose, S. (1998) 'The International Campaign to Ban Land Mines' in A. Maxwell, R. Cameron, J. Lawson and B. W. Tomlin (eds), *To Walk Without Fear: The Global Movement to Ban Landmines* (Toronto).

Wilson, P. (1998) 'The Myth of the First Great Debate', *Review of International Studies*, Special Issue, 24.

—— (2003) *The International Theory of Leonard Woolf* (London).

Wohlforth, W. C. (1999) 'The Stability of a Unipolar World', *International Security*, 24.

—— (2008) 'Realism', in C. Reus-Smit and D. Sindal (eds), *Oxford Handbook of International Relations* (Oxford).

Wohlforth, W. C., Little, R., Kaufman, S. J., *et al.* (2007) 'Testing Balance-of-Power Theory in World History', *European Journal of International Relations*, 13.

Wolfers, A. and Martin, L. W. (eds) (1956) *The Anglo-American Tradition in Foreign Affairs: Readings from Thomas More to Woodrow Wilson* (New Haven).

Wyn Jones, R. (2001) 'Introduction: Locating Critical International Relations Theory', in R. W. Jones (ed.), *Critical Theory and World Politics* (Boulder).

Yergin, D. (1990) *Shattered Peace*, rev. edn (London).

Young, I. M. (2006) *Global Challenges: War, Self-Determination and Responsibility for Justice* (Cambridge).

Young, O. R. (1982) 'Regime Dynamics', *International Organization*, 36(2).

—— (1989a) 'The Politics of International Regime Formation: Managing Natural Resources and the Environment', *International Organization*, 43(3).

—— (1989b) *International Cooperation: Building Regimes for Natural Resources and the Environment* (Ithaca).

—— (1994) *International Governance: Protecting the Environment in a Stateless Society* (Ithaca).

—— (1997) 'Global Governance: Towards a Theory of Decentralized World Order', in O.R. Young (ed.), *Global Governance: Drawing Insights from the Environmental Experience*, (Ithaca).

—— (1999a) *Governance in World Affairs* (Ithaca).

—— (ed.) (1999b), *The Effectiveness of International Environmental Regimes: Causal Connections and Behavioral Mechanisms* (Cambridge).

Zacher, M. W. and Matthew, R. A. (1995) 'Liberal International Theory: Common Threads, Divergent Strands', in C. W. Kegley Jr (ed.), *Controversies in International Relations Theory* (New York).

Zakaria, F. (1998) *From Wealth to Power: The Unusual Origins of America's World Role* (Princeton).

Zalewski, M. (1993) 'Feminist Standpoint Theory Meets International Relations Theory', *The Fletcher Forum for World Affairs*, 75(1).

—— (1995) 'Well, What is the Feminist Perspective on Bosnia?', *International Affairs*, 71(2).

Zalewski, M. and Parpart, J. (eds) (1998) *The 'Man' Question in International Relations* (Boulder).

Zehfuss, M. (2003) 'Forget September 11', *Third World Quarterly*, 24(3).

Zolberg, A. (1981) 'Origins of the Modern World System: A Missing Link', *World Politics*, 33(2).

Index